THE FINAL KINGDOM

Horizons of the Fourth Political Theory
and Geopolitics of the Apocalypse

ORTHODOX LOGOS PUBLISHING

THE FINAL KINGDOM
HORIZONS OF THE FOURTH POLITICAL THEORY
AND GEOPOLITICS OF THE APOCALYPSE

by Pyotr Volkov

© 2021, Orthodox Logos Publishing,

The Netherlands

www.orthodoxlogos.com

ISBN: 978-1-914337-14-7

This book is in copyright. No part of this publication may be reproduced, stored in a retrieval system or transmitted in any form or by any means without the prior permission in writing of the publisher, nor be otherwise circulated in any form of binding or cover other than that in which it is published without a similar condition, including this condition, being imposed on the subsequent purchaser.

PYOTR VOLKOV

THE FINAL KINGDOM

Horizons of the Fourth Political Theory
and Geopolitics of the Apocalypse

ORTHODOX LOGOS PUBLISHING

CONTENTS

PROLOGUE TO THE ENGLISH LANGUAGE VERSION,
BY BORIS NAD 9

VOLUME I: HORIZONS OF THE FOURTH POLITICAL THEORY . . 13
   INTRODUCTION 14
   PART I: THE REASONS FOR AN ALTERNATIVE 21
      INTRODUCTION TO THE FOURTH POLITICAL THEORY . . . 22
         THE LANGUAGE OF THE FOURTH POLITICAL THEORY . . 22
         DOWNFALL AND REBIRTH IN RUSSIA 37
      THE PHILOSOPHY FOR A CHANGE
      OF POLITICAL PARADIGM 44
         SOCIETY AS AN ORGANIC WHOLE 44
         THE POLITICAL WILL OF HUMAN BEINGS 51
         HISTORICAL SITUATIONS AND THE DNA OF LIBERALISM . 57
      THE ORIGIN AND BASIS OF CAPITALISM 61
         THE DILEMMA OF A WORLD RUNNING OUT 61
         CONCEPTUALIZING THE CAPITALIST SYSTEM
         AS A WAY OF UNDERSTANDING ITS REALITIES 67
   PART II: THE NORMATIVE ECONOMIC SYSTEM 81
      THE NORMATIVE ALTERNATIVE 82
         STATE CONTROL OVER BUSINESS INVESTMENTS 82
         THE PATRIOTIC ECONOMIC POLICY 95
         THE FAILURE OF THE COMMUNIST MODEL
         DRIVEN INSIDE (AND OUTSIDE) THE U.S.S.R 110
         OTHER COMMUNIST MODELS 116

THE THIRD POLITICAL THEORY 126

PART III: THE STRUGGLE FOR WHAT IS SACRED 131

ROME'S UNIVERSALISM AGAINST
THE ORTHODOX CHURCH. 132

    FROM THE SCHISM OF 1054 TO THE FALL OF CZARISM . . 132

    FROM HITLER TO THE NEW SCHISM OF 2018. 137

THE ANCESTRAL ORIGIN OF ORTHODOX
THOUGHT IN RUSSIA. 143

    DOCTRINE OF THE TRINITY. 143

    A BRIEF SUMMARY OF ORTHODOX TEACHING 148

    THE NEED FOR A CALENDAR DIFFERENT
    FROM THE WESTERN CALENDAR. 151

    THE ANCIENT ORIGIN OF RUSSIAN CIVILIZATION . . . 157

THINKING IN SPIRITUAL RACES INSTEAD
OF BIOLOGICAL RACES. 163

    TWO SPIRITUAL RACES. 163

    PROTEST MOVEMENTS AND THE FALLEN RACE. . . . 172

    THE RIGHTEOUS SPIRITUAL RACE IS
    THE ONLY BEARER OF CIVILIZATION 184

GOD'S RULE AND THE IDEA OF THE THEOCRATIC STATE . . 200

    THE POLITICAL SYSTEM. 200

    MAKING AWAY WITH THE POISON OF LIBERALISM . . 205

EDUCATION FOR LIVING INSTEAD
OF EDUCATION FOR MISERY. 215

    EDUCATION IN THE THEOCRATIC STATE. 215

    APPROACHING AUTHENTIC WILL. 226

VOLUME II: GEOPOLITICS OF THE APOCALYPSE 235

INTRODUCTION. 236

PART I: BASIC CONSIDERATIONS 243

    A REAL CONSPIRACY 244

    THE US IS A COUNTRY SCHEDULED FOR DISSOLUTION. . 244

GEOPOLITICAL RELEVANCE:
SHAPING ALL WORLD ORDERS 252

A WORLD OF CHANGE. 260

FOUNDATIONS FOR A FUTURE FOREIGN POLICY 266

   AIMING TOWARDS COMPLETE SUCCESS 266

   THE FOLLY OF RESTORING
   THE RUSSIAN BORDERS AS A FINAL GOAL 271

EUROPEAN UNITY IS IMPOSSIBLE WITHOUT RUSSIA . . . 279

   EUROPEAN UNION AS DISUNION 279

   EUROPEAN PUBLIC OPINION 288

PART II: EURO-SIBERIAN VS EURASIAN ORIENTATION . . . 295

THE CHINESE JUGGERNAUT 296

   PROBLEMS WITH THE EURASIAN ORIENTATION . . . 296

   ALLIANCES ARE NOT JUST PARTNERSHIPS 305

   INNER CHINESE CONDITIONS 310

THE BATTLE OF CIVILIZATIONS 317

   FUTURE DISTRIBUTIONS OF POWER 317

   NATO AND CHINA ARE PART OF THE SAME PLAN . . . 322

   NATO'S THREAT 327

SPIRITUAL RACES AND GEOPOLITICS
OF THE APOCALYPSE 337

   A BASIC INSIGHT INTO GEOPOLITICS
   OF THE APOCALYPSE 337

   SPIRITUAL RACE AS A MEANS TO EXPAND
   POLITICAL AND CULTURAL INFLUENCE 346

   THE ELEMENTS OF WEAKNESS
   VERSUS THE BASIS FOR STRENGTH 352

PART III: EXECUTION OF AN EURO-SIBERIAN DOCTRINE . . 357

NAVAL STRATEGY AND ITS CONSEQUENCES 358

   RUSSIA'S NAVAL MUSCLE 358

   NAVAL AND DIPLOMATIC STRATEGY
   IN A FUTURE BIPOLAR WORLD 364

INDIA AND CENTRAL ASIA 372
    INDIA AS AN ALLY 372
    ASSESSMENT OF THE SITUATION IN CENTRAL ASIA . . . 382
TOWARDS THE FEDERATION 387
    THE REALITY OF EUROPEAN NATIONALISM 387
    A EURO-SIBERIAN FEDERATION WILL BE
    THE ONLY TRUE EURASIAN UNION 394
    EURO-SIBERIA'S LAST RELIGIOUS BATTLE 399

INDEX 405

PROLOGUE TO THE ENGLISH LANGUAGE VERSION, BY BORIS NAD.

Pyotr Volkov's book The Final Kingdom belongs to the books that open a much-needed and necessary discussion about the Fourth Political Theory, originally proposed by Aleksandr Dugin. It points out to us - among other things - the necessity of the emergence of the Fourth Political Theory itself: "Summarizing the various reactions provoked by the emergence of the Fourth Political Theory in the West (as well as in the East, where the book was also translated and published)," says its author Dugin, "I agree that ideas live their own lives, independent of the author. The idea belongs to the one who understands it. If you agree with the logic of the fourth political theory - that liberalism is a totalitarian and openly nihilistic ideology, if you reject it because of that and if you want to go further than communism and fascism - the fourth political theory is yours as much as mine."

The fourth theory is an open intellectual project. "If you accept its basic principles, you can propose or make your own version of the fourth political theory." Pyotr Volkov belongs to those authors who seek to develop it further. It is a necessity. "The fourth political theory is neither left, nor right, nor center," Volkov himself says, "since people are extremely complex, we are more than a sector in the political spectrum." And also: "To a greater or lesser extent, we mix parts of different thoughts when situations require it, and moral pragmatism must displace labels that are useless, and which only cause divisions." I believe with complete certainty that a good ideology should be based on seeing such a comprehensive and transferable reality as thinkers achieve, because improving knowledge about things opens the door to improving the power of creation. " Volkov's book, in fact, has the ambition to transcend modernity itself, with Dugin's book serving as his "basis and inspiration".

The purpose of this preface is to introduce the reader to the world of Pyotr Volkov, to bring him closer to the world of his ideas and the problems we are talking about here. But before that, it should be said that Volkov strongly opposes any universalism, which tries to separate the world from its vital multipolarity: first of all, the universalism of the West, which possesses its resources and which is superior and thus more dangerous, because it tries to destroy any alternative, as which also opposes the universalism of the Vatican, which opposes Orthodoxy.

His considerations, moreover, come at a time when liberalism itself is dying, in the form of postliberalism and postmodernism, which destroys liberal rationality, giving birth to totalitarianism which seeks to destroy the very soul of the people. At a time when divisions like the left and the right are already obsolete, when their fall marks the arrival of a new era for the whole world and in which old ideologies must also be overcome, and societies need to understand themselves in a new light. And that is the breaking point. At that point, it is necessary to reject the old paradigms of civilization and establish new ones. It is necessary, in one word, to establish a "new Nomos of the Earth", and that is not an easy task. It will be the "Fourth Nomos of the Earth", a new relationship with the Earth and a new "agreement that will be valid for all the peoples who inhabit it".

In this regard: "The challenges of the 21st century will not be faced with a completely new way of thinking or just an ancient thought, but with a synthesis of both." The author's proposal, which goes in that direction, is "Normativism": normativism as a "synthesis of diverse ideas and systems of history, without representing an impossible utopia, but on the contrary, a valid alternative." "It can be understood as an ideology that reconciles mankind's thoughts. It is a synthesis of an asignificant part of the world's political and philosophical thinking and possesses the capacity to represent a synthesis of everything and at the same time a denial of a large part of the whole. Because, finally, do nations want their own ruin (because that is exactly the path that leads to ruin) since old ideologies do not understand conflicts and misery in those societies, the loss of power that the people possess? The people are the "strength of its workers, owners, culture, overall economy, values and spirituality", which is opposed by "international capital", leading to erosion and destruction, but only to a point: the one where the collapse of society will deepen. That is the point at which prosperity will disappear as a result of the work of generations. The struggle for prosperity is a struggle for the welfare and preservation of many and diverse peoples. It is a struggle to open the horizon of our past, present and tomorrow. "In a world as globalized as today's world, global prosperity is possible only if it is based on the well-being of societies in each country, so by contributing to the well-being of our peoples we help the well-being of the world by maintaining and repairing its essential part."

Volkov's considerations range widely: from the fall and rebirth of Russia, to the beginnings and foundations of capitalism, from the failure of communism to the history of the Roman Church in the fight against "Eastern schism", all the way to Hitler and the "new schism of 2018", Including the ancient beginnings of Russian civilization. The second part of his book has an intriguing title: "Geopolitics of the Apocalypse"....

Eurasianists (as myself) do not have to agree with Volkov in everything to enter into a special dialogue with him. One of the points where Eurasianists will disagree with Volkov is the question of Eurasianism versus Faye's "Euro-Siberian paradigm". The author stood upon the later paradigm, and therefore, in this book Russia is understood as "one of the last strongholds of true European identity" while China and the United States are regarded as "thalassocratic entities".

This is certainly not the place to dispute the author's conclusions. Let's just say that Volkov's claim that the civilization of Eurasia is an "artificial construction" opposes a number of dedicated researchers of Eurasian heritage in the so-called West and East, such as Danilevsky and Leontiev, who emphasize Russian "eastism" and "asianism". Such disagreements with the Eurasian paradigm are perhaps inevitable, because the author of this book set himself a huge task: to go "beyond the horizon" and "beyond the past, present and future." Perhaps the differences between Western Civilization and Russian (Eurasian) civilization, after all, are evidenced by the long-lasting and tenacious Russophobia, having its roots with the schism of 1054 and which occurs in various variants and with various inspirations, starting from the theological ones, creating a situation in which "Western Civilization" and "Russian civilization" are by now two different projects instead of one identical civilization.

Pyotr Volkov's book should be read first as an open call for dialogue: a dialogue that is conducted above established ideological divisions, such as the one on the left and right, dialogue with the past and the future, who want to have a future, not to dissolve and disappear forever in the sea of liberalism. It is, above all, a call to reconsider "one's own definitions of economic, political and cultural systems." It succeeded perfectly in that: it undoubtedly makes us more aware of the main political problems and helps us to search for their solution. It is, in a word, a book intended for those who intend to search for the truth.

VOLUME I:
HORIZONS OF THE FOURTH POLITICAL THEORY

INTRODUCTION

After the collapse of collectivist ideologies, there has been the statement claiming "the end of history": capitalism and globalization were displayed as insurmountable things. Most people stopped pursuing true alternatives, and those who continued to do so, anchored their thinking to existing alternatives, with the bitterness of not seeing those alternatives come true, or with the disappointment of seeing it wasn't what they were waiting for. We need a State and People capable of facing the problems regarding globalization, religion, immigration, and financial markets, but for doing so we must rethink our definition of economic, political, and cultural systems, and face dogma from liberalism, false religion, communism, and neo-fascism. This book aims, among other things, to help create an ideological approach that overcomes modernity, hence its title, so that the most fundamental political problems can be addressed and make people aware of them. This thought arises from an expansion of what was proposed by the Russian intellectual Aleksander Dugin. He had the decision to develop a fourth political theory to overcome modernity, opposing the three previous theories, liberalism, Marxism, and the third political theory (fascism and national-socialism).

Dugin served as a basis and inspiration for me to capture in this book what I believe should be the final structuring of this fourth political theory, a structure that I have decided to name "Normativism" since the purpose of it is to set standards in society, that is, ideals so that social sectors and economic, religious and political structures function as an organic body. The Fourth Political Theory must be, as Aleksander Dugin has said, something that does not belong to the left, neither to the right nor centrist political spectrum, but being something syncretic that integrate the useful thoughts of each one of the diverse schools of human thought. The Fourth Political Theory is an attempt to overcome the other three theories that have already revealed their nefarious consequences, that is liberalism, fascism, and communism. It is also an attempt to create a political theory to fight against the hegemonies that seek to strengthen the different universalisms in the world, and which try pulling the world aside from its vital multipolarity since they seek to create enormous centers of power and universalize doctrines, considered as the only possible truth. The universalisms that inevitably remain the main enemies of the Fourth Political Theory are the liberal universalism that comes from the West, and the universalism of the Vatican, from which everything possible has been done to expand the creed of the Roman Catholic Apostolic Church, with the Eastern Orthodox Church as one of its principal obstacles. Of these two universalisms, the most powerful and therefore the most dangerous is liberal universalism, which possesses the resources of the West, trying to destroy any alternative to its economic, political and cultural system which they want to make see as the only possible alternative.

This book will show essential guidelines that can help in the historical evolution of politics, religion, and economics, accelerating this evolution with thoughts and reflections on various issues that affect the lives of Russians and other peoples around the world. We must consider as very important the classification of the popular will in authentic will and manifested will while posing a different economic system to both capitalism and communism, new anthropology based in spiritual races instead of merely biological and material classifications, a new form of government and a reborn spirituality. Through these concepts, Normativism aims to represent an alternative to the ideologies imposed by liberalism, like materialism, capitalism, and liberal democracy. According to Dugin, in a framework where there is no competition from communism and fascism, liberalism is presently dying in the form of post-liberalism and post-modernity, which destroys the liberal rationality itself and that of the modern world, giving rise to totalitarianism that tries to be a transgressor of everything, in an attempt to destroy the very soul of the peoples.

The parties calling themselves leftist and right-wing have become obsolete, their decline marks the arrival of a new era for the world, an era where the old ideologies must be overcome in the light of a new analysis of society. The intervention of the State will be crucial, in the context of new rules in the playing field among institutions, rules whose purpose is to determine the way in which the State itself establishes its relationship with the sectors of society and the world, in its civilizing role. But the role of other agents, different from the State, will be equally crucial, so that we can follow an ideological path that fills true popular expectations, without mortgaging the future of following generations or plunging us into the false conceptions which led to dead ends. The book mentions the economic, spiritual, and philosophical aspects on which the Fourth Political Theory is based, including those that concretely define the Normative ideal.

In addition to healthy protectionism, through a simple system which I propose, the book shows how supply and demand can be leveled aimed at building an economic harmony based on the suppression of free mobility of business capital and the end of crises caused by capitalist accumulation. The concept of freedom is more appreciated in capitalism than the notion of equality, while in communism the concept of equality is more appreciated than the concept of freedom. We must put into practice a system where neither of the two concepts is more appreciated than the other. The last half of the book is devoted to spiritual concerns, including the existence of spiritual races and the mission of the Russian Orthodox Church. Patriotism, as stated in this book, is not the same as the nationalism of the third political theory, but a thought aimed at the cooperation between different peoples to fight against liberal universalism and the other universalisms.

The history of the prolonged conflict between the Eastern Orthodox Church and Rome is also reviewed, and reasons to defend and clarify the theological thought of the Russian Orthodox Church are shown, together with contributions related to theology, spiritual anthropology, and a new focus for explaining World history. The Normative model and project consist of seven pillars, the first is a new economic system that differs both from capitalism and communism, which appears in the first part of the book, the second is a protectionist economic policy based on patriotism, the third, in the case of Russia, is the reconstruction of Russian international power, the fourth is the strengthening and protection of Russian traditions and ancestral values and beliefs, the fifth is the expansion and reform of the Russian Orthodox Church thought, the sixth it is the establishment of a new calendar different from the Gregorian calendar established by Rome, and the seventh and most important is to create a new consciousness in humanity.

This book is among other things an attempt to discredit liberalism, which is totalitarian because it coercively dominates the whole of society by imposing ideas and actions related to the chief idea of liberalism, which is that the concepts of liberalism must be accepted by all. The challenges of the 21st century won't be faced with totally new thinking or merely ancient thought, but with a synthesis of both. Normativism is a synthesis of the diverse ideas and systems of history, without being an impossible utopia and being, therefore, a valid alternative. It can be understood as an ideology that reconciles mankind's thoughts. It is a synthesis of a significant part of the world's political and philosophical thinking and possesses the capacity to represent a synthesis of everything and at the same time a denial of a large part of the whole. I have proposed to myself the task of sustaining a clear alternative to liberalism, fascism, Roman-Catholicism, and communism, and not rest until these phenomena stop disturbing societies because these phenomena imply conflict and misery within those societies, the ruin of their peoples, the betrayal of laborers, and long-term harmful effects not only for workers.

The inevitable result is the loss of strength that a People possesses, the strength of their workers, their owners, their culture, their entire economy, values and spirituality, and the struggle against the People and against the basis of that same People, a fight against greatness, honor, and freedom. This struggle will inevitably lead to the destruction of the elements that serve as the basis for our individual and social life, to the dissolution of people's strength, and to the degradation of life in them, where hundreds of civic organizations, ethnic groups, philosophies, and false religions will generate more and more division, along with confusion and political disintegration.

But international capital will rise above these divisions and establish itself as the only one that may have some benefit from this, but only for a moment, at least until the moment when the collapse of society deepens. The welfare resulting from the work of generations will continue disappearing, and we will continue perceiving how we gradually sink if we do not open a horizon from our past, our present, and our tomorrow. Our struggle must be for the well-being and preservation of many peoples, and this struggle is one of the most significant reasons for our life, it is what makes it possible to work and build in the task of providing a new heart to our societies. In a world connected by globalization as today's world, global well-being is only possible if it is based on the well-being of societies in each state, so by contributing to the welfare of our peoples we are assisting the welfare of the whole world, maintaining and repairing an essential part of the structure of it.

We must gradually eliminate the processes that lead to the disintegration of our societies, and we will adhere to whatever is necessary to prevent our societies from degenerating thanks to civic associations and individuals who disintegrate them based on poisonous doctrines that must be fought with all our efforts, in the context of a gigantic ideological struggle. What makes lofty an ideology or a religion is the truth, and before sacrificing oneself in the struggle for justice, first, we should know what we must fight for. The sword of freedom is one disguised as many, and by service to it and God is that I write this book, being the service to God's laws. Justice remains an idea that obsesses human societies, but there can be no justice without the strength to carry it out, and to be stronger, our ideals must possess a firm basis.

Those who every day create the vital rhythm of human societies can do it where they want, but they must not forget that societies do not exist purely by the work of a government, a religion, of laborers or owners, but they depend on the creative capacity of each person in the different sectors of society and institutions. The belief in Normativism is the belief that man must not do any other thing than his authentic will. The Normative ideal represents not an ephemeral ideal that can disappear, it is an ideal that has always been within us, as far as we have wished that societies function on the basis of authentic will, that's to say the will to achieve true freedom of our self. The Normative ideal is achieved by mixing instinct with experience, experience with knowledge, knowledge with action, action with delicacy, and delicacy with devotion. The basis of this ideal must endure even if today it's arduous for millions to find themselves above narrow minds and false notions. We have already structured a belief that allows us to easily travel this road to make our authentic will, now it depends on the choice that each one wants to make.

Normativism is much more than an idea, a political movement, or a form of State, it is the expression of the desire for freedom embodied in an ideology. The Fourth Political Theory is neither left, nor right, nor center, since human beings are extraordinarily complex, we are more than a sector in the political spectrum. We mix to a greater or lesser extent the parts of different thoughts when the situations and morality dictate that pragmatism must displace labels that are useless, that only cause division. I believe with total certainty that a good ideology should be based on a vision of as comprehensive and transmissible of reality as the thinker can achieve, as improving the knowledge of things opens the door for improving the power to create.

With the worthwhile goal of fighting against the ruffians within politics and false doctrines that head us to the abyss, a fighting front must be set to create a political and economic system superior to capitalism and communism, and to safeguard traditions, including Christian values, currently threatened by liberalism and its decadent materialism, and even by the Vatican.

The decadence of our society can only be resolved if the rulers act to make authentic popular will a reality, not merely the manifested popular will, being concepts that I will explain in detail. For the authentic popular will to become a reality, we must fight against the attack and silence imposed by pro-western media, against an attack that also begins in the education that the youngest receive in their mind. Nothing that helped make our peoples great and make them joyous is safe from this attack, starting over that which makes us strong in the spiritual, economic, and military aspects, including the symbols and thoughts of exceptional persons in our history. Only one way can ensure the welfare of our People, and this is to generate the organic cohesion we need if we want to avoid falling into the abyss. That can be achieved only in a society whose essential parts do not collide with each other due to division by the economy, culture, ancestry, or misguided doctrines.

PART I:
THE REASONS
FOR AN ALTERNATIVE

INTRODUCTION TO THE FOURTH POLITICAL THEORY

THE LANGUAGE OF THE FOURTH POLITICAL THEORY

The Fourth Political Theory is an attempt to overcome modernity, starting with overcoming many of the words and concepts that emerged with modernity at the hand of liberalism, communism, and nationalism. Many of the words we use during social and political discussions and analysis are not ideologically neutral, words such as "individual," "class," "race," and "nation."According to Dugin, if completely out of ideological doctrines, those words lose their meaning or at least a significant part of it.

We can not display our attitudes to those words unambiguously, since the content of those words is modeled by context and semantics, and these three elements interact closely with each other. When we live in a state or a society with a clearly hegemonic ideology, it can be clearly seen how certain words are an indispensable part of certain ideological discourses. The meaning of words has an intimate link with ideology, transmitted through education in different societies around the world and is often clearly supported by an ideological and also active State apparatus. The State gives content to words and language in general, directing a significant part of the discourses, and setting the limits and moral nuances of the most significant set of concepts in politics and social sciences, as given in different parts of the world. To provide a straightforward example: if we live in a society in which liberalism has been established in a hegemonic way, the individual, which is the chief object of liberalism, liberal democracy, the concept of market, together with the Western concept of human rights, etc., start to prevail in language, helping to implant the liberal ideological agenda. If we live for example in a society where Marxism has been established in a hegemonic way, the concepts of working-class, communism, and class struggle are imposed in language.

But words that acquire an obviously negative content also begin to impose on language, in the case of Marxism concepts such as the bourgeoisie, fascism, capitalists, etc., and in the case of liberalism "authoritarianism", "oppression", "terrorism", concepts that in addition to acquiring a negative connotation also acquire a specific meaning with which the liberals, communists, fascists, etc.; will clearly express disagreements. There is disagreement also when discussing the meaning of words in ideological discourses and social sciences. The way in which a communist sees a fascist or a liberal seems from the point of view of fascists and liberals as a distortion of reality created by the opposing side, and of course, vice versa, since for liberals and fascists it is natural to see communism as an evil of society, seeing themselves as radically different in comparison to their ideological detractors. For someone convinced of the universality of liberal ideology, communism and fascism are almost equally bad. The capitalist liberal does not consider himself being in the same way as the bourgeois seen through Marxism.

Speculation remains for that person a way to exercise their economic freedom seen as natural according to their world-view, and the system that such a person advocate is routinely considered by him as a society characterized by freedom and openness, where there are opportunities that in other societies do not come to be. Generally, neither the Marxist analyst who bases himself on the analysis of the appropriation of surplus value from Marxist theory, nor the liberal who bases his vision of the world on liberal universalist perspectives, neither the fascist who predicts his model of society as the only possible alternative in the face of communism or liberalism, can manage to convince each other of something.

According to Dugin, ideologies are in this respect quite similar to religion; therefore, within the framework of the strong ideological polarization that existed in Germany before, during, and after Nazism; the conservative ideologue Carl Schmitt used the expression "political theology." Everyone who defends their position believes it sacred based on personal values and ideals, and the criticism of those values and ideals, or the advance of numerous ones usually does not cause many effects. As a result of the above, before using one or another term, it is necessary to know what ideology this term is used in, even if the ideology or term is not completely defined. Someone could merely say that science must adopt a completely neutral position. That is extremely problematic or indeed impossible. In this case, science should become "an ideology of truth", from which in comparison all other ideologies would be distorted forms that start from the relativity with which human subjects perceive reality. But it is clear that developing such a thing is impossible and even the pretension to do so is insane.

As Dugin mentions, within the framework of religion, there are often teachings that start from syncretism, because according to different doctrines, "absolute truth" and the religions that were based on these "absolute truths" are only relative manifestations of various concepts that do not possess absolute potential. On the basis of this, one can easily intuit that these religions, as well as the ideologies that start from intellectual processes such as these, can not be adopted by the entire world and are necessarily limited to the belief of specific groups, which are considered by the rest as having wrong thinking. However, according to Dugin, we can not forget that which differentiate science from the main current ideologies:

1 - Science announces its position with respect to the ideological paradigms to be taken into account, since in fact people who do not have a complex academic education, often do not even suspect that what they consider their "personal opinion" does not arise totally as a direct fruit of them, existing discourse mechanisms of each ideology hidden for those people.

2 - Science gives its position with respect to the ideological paradigms to be taken into account, since in fact people who do not possess a complex academic education, often do not even suspect that what they consider their "personal opinion" does not arise totally as a direct fruit of them, existing discourse mechanisms of each ideology that are hidden for those people."

3 - Science can elaborate on a matrix to compare the similarities between conflicting ideologies, establishing the similarities and differences between separate discourses and the elements that make them up.

In that way, when considering any concept, there are two options when proceeding: to interpret it from the position of the relative truths of one ideology or another, and for doing that we will be incapable to deepen in its elementary bases and we will be incapable to make comparison with other interpretations of the same concept, or on the other hand pay attention to the scientific method, which does not necessarily prevent us from attaching ourselves to relative truths that start from conflicting ideologies, but at least it forces us to reason according to the scientific approach. The concept of "the individual" is not ideologically neutral, since from there the liberal doctrine is formulated, where the individual becomes its chief object and the aim is to atomize society as much as possible, with the individual as its basis.

The Fourth Political Theory rejects that the individual being becomes the main object of its theory because it considers that the person and his society must be intimately linked as a body, and in fact they inevitably are, only that the link can be more or less stronger, varying from each person. Dugin presents an emblematic example of the lack of neutrality in the discourse of social sciences, in this case, the use of a term frequently being present in those sciences, the concept of "class", to then emphasize in the least neutral concept of all, that is the concept of "middle class." The concept of "middle class" is crucially fundamental for the ideas of capitalist liberalism in its numerous variants, ranging from those located more to the right-wing to those located more to the left (the most "social" versions).

Although this concept appeared after the Marxist theory, centered in the antagonistic class struggle, even the meaning of the term "middle class" has a much longer history, and it originates from ideological elements of the bourgeois revolutions against the Ancien Régime. As for the concept of "class" in general, that is clearly a concept of social organization that arises with modernity. The political and social systems of the past were based on castes and estates. The castes originated on the basis of the belief that the nature of different people differs in the sense that there are divine souls and earthly souls, or even savage and malefic ones. The reason that castes constitute a system with such limited social mobility is the belief that people can not alter the shape of their souls during the course of their life. It is in the caste system that concepts such as "the masses" have their origin given that society was seen as something divided between people of a divine nature and people of earthly or malefic nature, and based on this conception, the former should be above the others.

Over time, in many places, the doctrine that gave rise to the castes was replaced by a doctrine that allowed greater social mobility based on the system of estates. While this doctrine also proposes that there are superior and inferior people in their nature, this does not mean that the birth of a person in a particular place comprise the only factor to be taken into account to determine the position of a person in the social hierarchy or its amount of heritage, since in estates the accomplishment of different feats is considered as a demonstration of spiritual qualities superior to those of the majority. The bourgeois revolutions that took place in Europe demanded the replacement of many of the privileges of the clergy, the military aristocracy, and the nobility, and frequently involved the physical elimination of the members of those sectors. But the bearers of the liberal bourgeois doctrine were not the peasants, who were connected to the traditional society, but more mobile citizens, that is, the bourgeoisie, who since modernity placed themselves as an ideal of how a person should be in the capitalist State.

The bourgeois revolutions partially or completely eliminated the power of the Church and the aristocrats, and the result of this is the model for the making of a society based on capitalism and liberal concepts. To this end, the distinctions that gave rise to the estates are replaced, except for those that are not spiritual, that is, material distinctions so that the notion of class emerges as an indicator of inequality. In sociology, which arises from the bourgeoisie, the basic thinking of liberalism regarding the bourgeoisie being always at the top, is manifested in how the stratification model is being made, since in the upper class there is always the high bourgeoisie. In modern sociology, society is divided into a higher class, a middle class, and a lower class, a division to which it is sometimes added the completely marginal people. Ironically, classes and their importance in capitalist society were not perceived as clearly by liberal theorists as by

Marx. In Marxism the fact that capitalist society is divided into classes is presented as one of the main ideas of this school, and that these classes are in struggle, until according to Marxists, capitalism is completely replaced by communism, which supposes the disappearance of what from Marxism thought is called as the contradictions of capitalism, and therefore the disappearance of the material inequality being a characteristic of that. According to Marx, in a class society, there are always rich and poor, and the rich always get richer, and the poor get poorer.

From Marx's position, there can only be two classes: the bourgeoisie and the proletariat. All Marxism is based on the belief that the struggle between these two antagonistic classes has been the motor force of history since the beginning of the capitalist system, and the difference between these two classes can not be relative but absolute from a Marxist perspective since each of these classes represents a different world. In capitalism, according to Marx, Engels, and later Marxist thinkers, the proletariat must acquire self-consciousness, to organize itself and put an end to the capitalist system, and to create communism in what according to Marx comprise the two stages of the communist system, whose first phase was called by other thinkers as socialism, and after all the remnants of capitalist society have disappeared, the communist society will enter its second stage, the stage called by subsequent thinkers as "communist stage", although Marx in his writings prefers to use only the terms of a "first" and "second" stages of communism.

From a totally Marxist perspective, a "middle class" can not exist, since everything that exists between the high bourgeois and proletarians, such as the petty bourgeoisie or the prosperous peasantry, is essentially part of the bourgeoisie, or part of the proletariat, or a class that one can clearly define as dominant or dominated. That is why from a purely Marxist perspective, the "middle class" is something that does not exist, and through Marxism, it even can be stated that this concept remains an ideological tool of capitalism to promise the proletariat a future integration in the capitalist class, which according to Marx becomes impossible due to the appropriation of surplus-value by the capitalists. According to Dugin, Marxists and liberal thinkers have in common the fact that they admit a transition has taken place from a society based primarily on estates, where the considerations of the spiritual as well as material differences were established, to impose an order where now only material inequalities are taken into account. Also, Marxists and liberals agree that a class society, that is to say, a society based only on material inequalities, is "more progressive" than a society based on estates. But it is clear that liberal thought advocate that material inequality is justified, but not the communist struggle, while Marxist thought it is the other way around.

For liberals, something like "the end of history" can only start with the triumph of the capitalist system and liberalism, and the total consolidation of the "middle class", while for Marxists, something like that only starts when the society of the proletarian class destroys capitalist society completely by establishing communism. What characterizes specifically the way of perceiving class in liberalism is the conviction that in a capitalist society, where liberal principles have been successfully established, there is only one class, and therefore the differences that may exist within that single class are relative and not as conditioning as conditional. While for Marx there are always two antagonistic classes, for liberals like Adam Smith there is only one class, the bourgeois class.

The poorer sectors of capitalist society are considered from this perspective as "incomplete bourgeois." The richest are the most bourgeois of all, and justifying this approach is based on the premise that workers can always aspire to one day become owners. For example, a worker is hired by an owner, and after working as an assistant, he grasps what is necessary to be an owner as well. After some time he borrows credit and launches his business, and eventually hires an assistant for himself, which from the liberal narrative leads to a cycle. In this model, we see the whole society is a middle class since it is not considered that anyone is so low to be classified as "low class", nor is it so different as to be considered "upper class", since there are no more estates based on the consideration of spiritual differences and at the same time it is considered that the owner also accepts economic risks that can lead to bankruptcy and make him descend within that middle class. From the perspective of liberalism, the working class only represents those who can one day become owners or complete bourgeois.

Capitalism is based on the belief that the growth in the wealth of all members that make up society is constant, and therefore, according to the liberal perspective, all humanity can become "full bourgeois." However, as

Dugin mentions, it is necessary to show that within liberal ideology there are two alternative approaches with respect to the middle class. The first approach is that of the liberals who are farther to the left in the political spectrum, the so-called "social-liberals", who insist the high bourgeoisie should share a part of its profits with members of the middle and lower sectors of the bourgeoisie, that is, those that are denominated from the modern sociological discourse as "the middle class" and the "lower class", since this according to the "social-liberals" leads to a more stable system and to the acceleration of economic growth for the whole society.

The second approach is characteristic of the more right-wing liberals, who reject the fact that the high bourgeoisie is hindered by projects aimed at distributing part of their profits among other sectors, and to justify that approach it is stated that doing the opposite contradicts the liberal ideology and hinders the economic functioning of the capitalist system since it is the high bourgeoisie that stimulates the growth of other sectors of society, for example, the middle bourgeoisie, which in turn stimulates the growth of the petite bourgeoisie. For that reason, the concept of the middle class is for the "social liberals" an ideological slogan used when advocating the expansion of the "middle class" so that all become "complete bourgeois" through interventions in the capitalist system, while for the other liberals the growth of the middle class arises due to the natural development of the capitalist system, and the middle class does not require special attention to be raised.

Finally, we must consider the perspective regarding the middle class according to the third political theory of modernity, which comes from nationalism and within which is, for example, fascism. Like liberalism, nationalism is a bourgeois ideology, but unlike liberalism, it insists the goal of bourgeois society should not be all of humanity, but the People who belong to a specific Nation-state, and because of that, the Nation is seen as the maximum unit that according to the third political theory allows the unity of the People who compose it. The market is allowed to be open but only within national boundaries, and this is in order to safeguard national interests, which legitimize protectionist economic mechanisms.

From the third political theory, the middle class is seen first of all as the middle class of a given nationality within the limits of a State. Nationalism, like liberalism, accepts the bourgeois as a standard figure, but places more emphasis on its appearance as a citizen and, above all, as a citizen of a given National State. Subsequently, according to Dugin, for the third political theory, the Nation becomes a synonym of bourgeois society, with the State as an indispensable element without which that bourgeois society could not exist. The Nation is seen as a community composed of the middle class, and the aim of nationalism is to integrate the lower segments in the Nation and therefore in the middle class, for which the nationalists even use the help of State measures. That's why nationalism has some features that also belong to the completely statist economic systems that have been called socialist or communist, but in this case, the ideological goal instead of being to put an end to the capitalist class is seen as pushing the economically weak sectors at the level that should be reached by the middle class, seen as a necessary task for national integration, and not as a necessary task for equality and material justice by themselves.

This resembles, for example, that which happens within the "social-liberals" regarding the fact that economic measures designed to push economically vulnerable sectors are considered necessary for the stability of capitalism, but the difference is that nationalists do not do so for the purposes of equality and justice by themselves, but for the strengthening of what is considered a National community with a historical mission. Nationalism has a negative relationship with some or all national minorities, especially with those who are immigrants, since, from the perspective of nationalists, these elements alter the homogeneity of the nation, and therefore the homogeneity of the middle class, or they are anyway conspiring against the Nation, as for example all Jews and Slavs according to the Nazi doctrine, who are, as in the case of Jews or foreign sectors of all kinds, blamed for hoarding too much material wealth due to their economic activity. Meanwhile, other minority sectors are blamed for increasing the number of people whose integration is hampered by the differences they have with those who make up a particular nationality that is the basis of a specific State.

Dugin rejects the class being the object of the Fourth Political Theory because the classes do not always manage to establish themselves completely and because the concept of "class" does not manage to properly explain the social reality and therefore does not manage to solve its problems. Dugin mentions that the transition from caste to estates, and from estates to classes is not a universal rule. This process may occur as it did in modern Western Europe, or it may not occur or occur only partially, as it is happening up to the present in the non-Western societies. Therefore, the concept of class experiences limitations in its applicability for the analysis of societies. Class and classes can be identified in modern Western European societies, but if they really replace the criteria for establishing inequalities that are based on spiritual grounds and human nature instead of material position, that is not obvious at all even in Western societies, where we see that certain inequalities exist because the nature of certain people or in some cases the nature of their spirituality are considered superior to those of the rest.

In addition to the concept of individual and that of classes, other emblematic concepts are not ideologically neutral. It is very important to clarify that I reject, like Dugin, the Western variant of the term called "race", since it is a purely biological term and therefore is the result of Western materialism, being used extensively by proponents of the third political theory like Hitler, but also by members of the promoter elites of liberalism, in order to legitimize colonial efforts or segregation. This term is unneutral since it takes only biological considerations and leaves aside considerations about the culture and spirit of each People. Furthermore, it can not be employed correctly in anthropology, since groups with many biological variations, such as sub-Saharan peoples, are grouped within the same race.

But those who try to tear down the concept of "race" without replacing it with something, leaving in their place a void that they intend to fill with concepts such as "ethnicity", or "phenotype", and not a concept like "spiritual race", are not ideologically neutral when making such thing, by promoting egalitarianism rooted in liberalism, which does not allow individuals and the People to be considered different, ignoring that taking into account variety is a key both for science and for politics and that human beings are not equal. That is why instead of using the term "race" or leaving a vacuum, the term "spiritual race" should be used.

With this term, I classify human groups that differ by spiritual characteristics and not mere material ones. A form of classification based on this is presented in the second half of the book, as a way for taking into account, not only people's biological qualities but also spiritual qualities that differentiate them from each other and which originate from birth. The term spiritual race, instead of being a materialistic concept, like the concept of "race" in Nazism and the eugenicists of the USA, is a concept also related to spirituality, since undoubtedly, the different individuals besides biological differences also have spiritual and cultural differences that make them adopt forms of life, world-views, and even ways of looking at themselves that give rise to a very diverse spiritual whole, and when I refer to the spiritual I mean those factors that determine people's willingness to interact with what surrounds them, and this will must be understood from the point raised by Nietzsche, that's to say a will to power that people use to outdo themselves.

The concept of "Nation" is also not ideologically neutral and is not used correctly, because within a territory or a specific State, for example, the current territory of Russia, or the territories that in the past were part of the Russian Empire and of the Soviet Union, several nationalities or ethnicities live, while collaboration between these different nationalities is important since a single ethnic group can not alone face the globalization of liberalism, the other universalisms or environmental problems. In contrast to the previous political theories, the Fourth Political Theory has neither the concept of the individual, nor class, nor the Nation or the western variant of the concept of race as the central object of its theory, since it is based on the imperative of overcoming modernity and therefore liberalism, communism, and nationalism which gave rise to fascism and national-socialism. The object of the Fourth Political Theory in its complex version is Dasein, a concept that is the basis of Martin Heidegger's philosophy.

Dasein is human existence, where its organic, cultural, linguistic, and spiritual history is present and closely linked. According to Dugin, the object of this theory in its simple version is the Russian concept "narod", which can be translated as "the People", but not in the sense of the People as "mass" or "masses", that is, not as a group of individuals dominated by their "masters." We can say that the Russian concept "narod" is, for example, the living presence of the Russians in a place with their specific qualities. Within the narod concept are included not only the Russians considered as ethnically Russian but also other peoples historically and culturally linked to Great Russia. The People and not the individual (as in liberalism) nor two antagonistic classes (as in Marxism), nor the State, the Nation or the race (as in the third political theory), is the central concept of the Fourth Political Theory so that the ideological concepts of modernity are overcome.

According to Dugin, in the Fourth Political Theory, there is no materialism, economism, neither recognition of the inevitability and universality of bourgeois revolutions, nor linear time, Western civilization as a standard, secularism, and also (in the form conceptualized in the West) neither human rights, civil society, liberal democracy, economic liberalism, or any other axiom of modernity. The Fourth Political Theory rejects capitalism, individualism, and the "cult of money" in liberalism, it also rejects materialism, atheism, progressivism, and the theory of class struggle of communism, while rejecting the fascist idea regarding the necessity of a predominance of certain nations and biological races over other groups. According to Dugin, both liberalism and communism and the third political theory are totalitarian, since in communism, it is claimed the predominance of the whole (society and the working class) over the individual, and the third political theory also proclaims the superiority of the whole, in this case of the State, biological race and ethnicity over the individual, and both in communism and in fascism this predominance is sought to be achieved through coercive and propagandistic means.

Regarding liberalism, this ideology is also totalitarian because it proclaims the individual as the most important subject-matter and places it above society, while the concept of the individual is used as a way to measure the character of all political, economic, and cultural thoughts, therefore liberalism tries to impose an element on society, in this case, the individual, using coercive measures that start in the State apparatus, that is, the State forces people to respect the liberal guidelines regarding the individual, and it uses propaganda, as well as the coercive pressure on the part of the people governed and influenced by the propaganda of liberalism over those who oppose this doctrine, while these influenced people generate their own liberal propaganda. The Fourth Political Theory is opposed to totalitarianism because this political theory does not propose the community being upon the individual or the individual being upon society.

From the Fourth Political Theory, people should neither be considered atomized individuals or just a sum in the whole, since a People integrates both the individual and collective reality of human societies and hence the importance of the concept of "People" as the chief subject of the Fourth Political Theory in its more simple version, being Dasein in its complex version, that is the human existence, where organic, cultural, linguistic and spiritual history is present and closely related between. However, according to Dugin, the Fourth Political Theory takes the ideal of liberalism regarding the value of freedom, although in this case, not individualistic freedom but the freedom of the community.

Dugin mentions that the Fourth Political Theory takes from Marxism the ideals of justice and equality understood as ethical ideals and the harmonious development of human coexistence based on the end of human alienation. Of nationalism, the Fourth Political Theory bears the idea regarding the value of the ethnic group, identity, religion, spirituality, family and State, although it does not pretend that some Nation or biological group predominates over others, but a harmonious coexistence between them, which can occur within the framework of the State and its People and in relation to the peoples which are outside political borders. While accepting components of the three previous political theories, the Fourth Political Theory proposes alternatives rejected simultaneously by liberalism, communism, and nationalism, and proposes a theory based on the essential knowledge of "narod", or in a more complex version, the fundamental knowledge of "Dasein", that is, human existence, where its cultural, linguistic, biological and spiritual history is present and closely linked to each other. In his works, Dugin also criticizes the view being held in the West regarding the process named as time, seen in the West as something linear and non-cyclical, and that only leads to a single direction, that is, the direction of modernity, the direction of the West's new world order, an order that is totalitarian in its very essence, despicable and promoter of the superfluous and banal, being destroyer of the People's essence, that's to say their soul.

In fact, what we perceive in time and space are cyclical processes that lead to divergent directions, with each region possessing its own history and its own direction, even though the West wants to erase all those history and paths, leaving only those of the West, and therefore imposing a single world model for civilization, i.e. West's liberalism transmuted into globalist and destructive post-liberalism. But I intend radicalizing Dugin's thought in this sense, assuming that we should not consider giving its definite start and ending to things, considering that time, at least understood as something with an existence of its own, in fact, does not exist, and it is in the mania to set a starting and ending point to everything that people in the West forget the explanation of their origin, an explanation based on cycles, cycles that necessarily leave an echo from the development of the universe as a whole to the development seen in that microcosm called mankind.

Human beings are used to giving everything its starting and ending point, and especially from the West a linear conception of time has been made which its marked beginning and ending, without seeing the Eternal through its cycles of constant return. People wonder where God or his creation comes from, as if both are in need of a beginning or end, having neither beginning nor end of days, since past, present and future are a simultaneous reality, and time does not exist, that being the way of explaining existence itself, by not attributing the origin and end indicated by the illusion of time. Time does not have an existence by itself; it does not exist as something tangible, and it is only the result of the conjunction between the seen and unseen world that gives it origin, a conjunction that allows the seen world to be created and manifested in our consciousness as time since our consciousness and identity exist on the basis of starting and endings points that in fact are not real. To comprehend this, we should observe the fourth aggregation state of matter, called plasma, which does not exist independently. Its particles are electrically charged and have no electromagnetic equilibrium, but not by the action of matter, but by what underlies it. In the same way, it has been theorized that one of the fundamental forces in nature, called the weak nuclear force, does not have an existence independent of electromagnetism, this being an example of how there is a seeming set of independences which in fact are illusory.

So far I have mentioned elements of reality that exist as part of groups of four aspects, time is called the fourth dimension by the Einsteinian theory, plasma is the fourth state of matter, and there are 4 fundamental forces in nature. By means of the Fibonacci sequence, it is observed how

"4" is absent in nature, it is always an illusion, with the sole exception of the 4 cardinal points. The origin of these points is the convergence between infinity and end, between seen and unseen world: therefore "4" is the connection between the seen and unseen world, between infinite and end, but it is neither the infinite nor the end, it is only that which connects both aspects, being the aspects of the unseen world always infinite, in the creative chaos and infinite smallness, or in the creative order and infinite largeness. This does not mean that "4" is something to be regarded as exclusively detrimental since illusion generates in human beings both positive and negative effects. Human belief, although it uses illusion, remains the origin and engine of human societies, and within this framework, we should distinguish the positive from negative time, for using the illusion of time as something positive, which is not possible within the Western conception of time and within the Gregorian calendar.

Another essential aspect of Dugin's theoretical approach is the call for a multipolar world where Eurasianism is destined to clash with Atlanticism, as an inevitable consequence of two different modes of culture, Eurasianism representing the living traditionalism of Dasein, and Atlanticism representing its antithesis, modernity and its consequence, post-modernity. Both exist alongside two different subsistence modes, since Atlanticism possesses as its domain the control of trade through sea lanes and waterways (thalassocracy), and Eurasianism has the domain over large landmasses (tellurocracy). A struggle becomes inevitable because these two modes of subsistence collide as large masses of land also need maritime routes and waterways, and these routes and waterways need vast masses of land provided with natural and human resources.

DOWNFALL AND REBIRTH IN RUSSIA

The fall of the Soviet Union as is widely known, was absolutely disastrous for Russia in terms of the loss of territories, and therefore disastrous for the Eurasian cause since this cause is the creation and preservation of a civilization that is the antithesis of the Western one. But it was also disastrous in the economic and social area in general. In 1990, the real Russian GDP fell by 3%, and in 1991 by another 5%. Between 1992 and 1996 the fall of the Russian GDP was stunning, by 43.5%: a catastrophe bigger than the great depression of 1929 in the USA. According to data from October 1996, by that time there was a situation where approximately 44 million people out of a population of 148 million had fallen below the poverty line, defined at that time as living with less than 32 dollars per month.

The Russian economy hit its low with the crisis of August 1998, in which Russia could not pay international debts, and where many banks collapsed, having a devaluation of the ruble of 75%, and a Russian government that as a result of the crisis entered bankruptcy, which among other things created a large increase in unemployment, especially among women. The suicide rate in Russia doubled in the 1990s, and deaths caused by alcoholism, which can be considered in some cases as another form of suicide, tripled in that decade. Infant mortality reached third-world levels in a country that was the Mecca of communism. The population's high mortality due to the destruction of economic welfare and social security, added to the fall in the birth rates, caused population decrease inside the Russian Federation, as well as in other countries that made up the former Soviet Union.

The most dramatic case was that of Ukraine, which went from a population of 52 million people to a population of 45 million people in 2013, just before the Russian annexation of Crimea. Undoubtedly the fall of the Soviet Union was like Russian President Vladimir Putin said, the greatest geopolitical catastrophe of the 20th century, not only because of what this meant for the peoples that made up the Soviet Union, but because the disappearance of a large part of the international Russian power, which was based on economic and military might, and on the possession of a large list of territories being now lost by Russia, meant for many other peoples the loss of a counterweight to brutal capitalism and globalist policies. The peoples of Ukraine and Belarus, as well as the peoples of Moldova and Georgia, are peoples where there are both Russian minorities and a Russian like culture for the rest and must be considered as essential territories for the defense of the current territory of the Russian Federation.

These peoples separated even though that meant becoming insignificant at the international level, both because of the smaller territorial and economic scale in relation to the Soviet Union as a whole, and because of the economic destruction that brought the disintegration of the Soviet Union not only in the territory of the Russian Federation but in those countries, as well as by the wars that broke out in Georgia and Moldova immediately after the fall of the Soviet Union, and the other wars in Georgia and Ukraine in subsequent years. In the case of the Baltic countries, while they are countries that in the course of history went in the opposite direction to Russia's wishes and are now part of NATO, they mistakenly believe that being independent of Russia means being truly independent as if living under the economic and cultural shadow of the globalizing capitalism of the West is to be independent.

Meanwhile, in former Soviet countries with large Muslim populations, there has been a resurgence of Islam with its consequent radicalism. In other Muslim countries that did not belong to the Soviet Union, the intervention of NATO has created an enormous growth of the power of extremist Islamic movements. In Afghanistan, the West's support for Islamic fanatics to defeat both the secular Marxist government in Afghanistan and Soviet troops that came to Afghanistan allowed the proliferation of such things as al Qaeda. In Iraq, Syria, and Libya, the interventions of the West and Turkey have created total chaos by overthrowing governments that were authoritarian but maintained stability in those countries, and the result now is that these countries are a nest of terrorist groups and they have been devastated by war. In addition to that, millions of people from those countries decide to go in the hundreds of thousands overflowing Europe and creating a humanitarian crisis and tension throughout that continent.

Completing the goal of building a mature Russian State in a Russian cultural space is absolutely needed today. A State that will not be part of an international network for the cultural decline and financial interests, but an entity of the People. Only by realizing the need for that is the way in which any decline of the Russian People can be ended once and for all, developing a strong basis on which the new State may someday exist in its mature stage. This is the first principle for Russia's rebirth. Not realizing that principle is why God did not allow the victory of the U.S.S.R. in the Cold War, but its downfall. The failure to identify the inner problems meant all attempts at preventing the collapse of the Soviet Empire were to no avail. At that time, the internal enemy remained unrecognized. Only a tiny fraction of the People's potential remained as a result of the liberal paralysis inflicted in the Russian political system.

In 1991, the fall of the communist society didn't give the way to strong People as inner strength disappeared. The U.S., Vatican, and NATO flags rose higher as inner strength and authentic will among the Russian People were suffering from a devastating illness. Both in the West as in Russian liberal circles, the enemies of mankind worked very hard throughout those years to destroy Russia and impose liberalism. The only resistance to liberalism came from some traditional sectors of Russian society and from competition between great and small oligarchs. The ruling communist class itself had no idea it was infected with the illness of liberal ideas. This was not only because of Western actions but mostly because the communist regents and the communist society already carried the seeds of liberal decadence within themselves. The successes in ending the communist regime had catastrophic consequences. The growth of liberal votes at legislative elections foreshadowed the imminent internal and external collapse. Despite all the restructuring that seemed to occur and promises of economic wealth, the general situation was turned into a tragedy. Anyone who has truly observed the Soviet Empire's line of political development cannot help but realize that even when the Soviet peoples were under one flag and with rising international influence, its internal decay was already there. The Soviets then ignored the root cause of the fatal disease in their society.

No matter what they did, their efforts were condemned to fail because they only saw the symptoms of general decay and tried to fight those symptoms instead of the cause... Naturally not that all of those who politically doctored the Soviet State were bad or malicious by nature, but regardless of that it is necessary to establish faith in an idealistic Russia to battle against the threat imposed by the present weaknesses of materialism. When the Russian People abandoned their ancient ideals to follow practical materialistic promises of the Revolution and exchanged the crucifix for a rifle, the Russian People found themselves not in a socialist paradise, but rather in a reality of unending hardships. People did not die just over concern for their food, but for love of the Motherland, belief in its greatness, and patriotism. If anyone can uphold loftier ideals, is easy to remind him of a time when courage was the testimony to the strength of patriotic sentiments. Not vainly the Great Patriotic War is called as such. We must never fail to uphold truly strong ideals. Failures must not distract us from that goal, for we cannot abandon basic laws simply because some errors are made in their application, and we cannot condemn all advance just because there are still mistakes and hardships in spite of the best efforts. For that reason, individuals and society as a whole must do the best they can and try to approach the authentic will of a People. Harsh reality will always limit what we seek to attain. But that does not imply the abandonment of the People's duty to fight against the faults they see, to overcome weaknesses among themselves, and to strive for their beliefs. People are not so naive as to believe that society perfect for earthly existence can ever happen as promised by communism. Achieving this perfect society is a premise that this world, including the Russian People, could never put into practice and therefore would never be outside the realm of human imagination. The best we can achieve is a wisely constructed civilization that will allow every honest man a decent existence as both an individual and a member of the People.

    The reconstruction of Russian international power, which must take place by means of growth and economic well-being, population growth, the increase of Russian armed power, and territorial expansion, is a fundamental task for the Russians. But it has been also important for all the peoples of the world, since Russia, with its enormous amount of raw resources, its human resources, and its military might, remains an elemental bastion from which liberal universalism can be fought. The difference between what we should call Russian patriotism and Russian nationalism is that Russian nationalism is based exclusively on the ethnically Russian people, while Russian patriotism defends the interests of ethnic groups living within the current borders of Russia, and within the old borders of what was the old Russian Empire and the Soviet Union.

Russian patriotism, to be effective, must be differentiated from nationalism, defending not only the interests of the Russian ethnicity but the interests of other ethnic groups living inside and outside the current borders of the Russian Federation, maintaining People's unity and establishing alliances with several countries of the world. This alliance has as its result not only to the strengthening of Russia but also establishing from Russia a counter-hegemony pillar that allows humanity to fight against liberal universalism as well as other universalisms, and to help other pillars in other regions to do the same. The Belovezha Accords of December 8, 1991, together with the subsequent Alma-Ata protocol, which put an end to the Soviet Union, must be considered as illegal and without any validity. The creation of a confederate entity, that is the Commonwealth of Independent States, instead of the renewal of the federal structure of the Soviet Union, directly violated the will of the voters who in the referendum of March 17, 1991, voted for the permanence of a federal structure. The President of the USSR Mikhail Gorbachev and all the other participants in the meetings of Novo-Ogaryovo consciously violated the fundamental constitutional norms of the USSR.

The law of the USSR of 27.12.1990 No. 1869-1 "Regarding national vote" (and therefore the referendum of the USSR) had an explicit provision in the mandatory nature of the decision of the referendum for all the republics of the Soviet Union, including the six republics of the Soviet Union that did not participate in the referendum of March 17, 1991. The Belovezha Accords were also illegal because the decision of only 3 republics (Belarus, Ukraine, and Russia) could not decide the fate of all the republics of the Soviet Union, this was allowed only to be done by the will of all the republics, and this will could only be called by a referendum such as that of March 17, 1991, or by convening the Congress of People's Deputies of the Soviet Union. This also makes illegal the later Alma-Ata protocol of December 21, 1991. The ratification of the Belovezha Accords, made on December 12, 1991, was carried over by a public authority without the authorization to do so (the supreme Soviet of the Russian Soviet Federative Socialist Republic).

Once the Belovezha Accords and the Alma-Ata protocol are declared illegal and without any validity, the current status of the government of the Russian Federation as the successor state of the USSR should be retained because this state concentrates the majority of the population and resources among the republics that belonged to the USSR, in addition to possessing a large number of nuclear weapons. As the following step, Ukraine, Belarus, Moldova, and the entire territory of the former Soviet socialist republic of Georgia must be annexed by Russia, due to its cultural proximity to Russia in comparison to the other former republics with large Muslim populations, as well as due to its importance for the security of the Russian Federation and the ethnically Russian people living in those territories, to which we must add the combined resources of all those regions, including human resources. The strength of the Russian state, made up of fewer than 150 million people, would be seen in the eyes of the world as smaller than the strength of a state of more than 200 million people. Once the regions are reincorporated, a referendum will be held for the entire territory of Russia, including the reincorporated territories, to ratify the annexation.

The independence of the other post-soviet states must be recognized by Russia in the framework of a new legal treaty, which also stipulates the continuity of the economic, political, and military ties with these former Soviet republics. The annexed countries should not be granted autonomy within the great union, invoking national security as a reason for this and considering the annexed countries as the result of an illegitimate process and therefore not recognizing their existence.

As for other states, the difference between Russia's cooperation with governments like Syria and India, and Russia's cooperation with China and Iran, is that Russia endorses the doctrine of the first two governments, which besides being based on close collaboration with Russia, is based on the rejection of Islamic extremism, and in the case of Syria, despite having a secular government, the Baath party led by Al Assad is dominated by the Alawites, a group with a religion which, as we shall see, is compatible with true Christianity. Meanwhile, Russia does not defend the ideological position of Iran, which is based on Islamic universalism, or the ideological position of China, similar to fascism and clearly expansionist. Russia's cooperation with China and Iran only has a strategic purpose, but it has no ideological purpose, so Russia is not an ally of China and Iran. The word "partners" should be used to refer to those countries that only establish ties for some specific purposes but do not defend the other's ideological position and therefore are not truly allies, since a partner is only the enemy of your enemy, but not a friend, as in the case of Iran, while an ally is like a friend that can be trusted within the framework of an ideological agenda. For example, during World War II, the Soviet Union was not an ally of the US and England. They were just partners, and this became very clear once the cold war began.

THE PHILOSOPHY FOR A CHANGE OF POLITICAL PARADIGM

SOCIETY AS AN ORGANIC WHOLE

I intend to analyze society as an organic whole, being necessary to confront the concept of economic development that comes from liberalism through the concept of human development. The concept of economic development, as its name suggests, only considers the economic factor, leaving aside other aspects that make human beings joyful, aspects that do not come solely from the economic and material realms. Economic development remains a concept where the change of society, in this case towards modernity, is linear, because it handles a single factor, the economy. The change of society based on human development is not necessarily linear since it handles various aspects that change in different ways.

For example, while one aspect advances another one goes backward, being the reason why social change is not linear in as much it supposes a set of variables transformed in different ways. Human development, unlike the concept of economic development, does not necessarily imply going towards modernity, since the different variables of human development change in diverse ways and we should take into account those traditional factors of different cultures and civilizations that are important for the happiness and freedom of different peoples. Human development can be understood as the social process by which the capacity of the individuals to live their lives in the way they consider most valuable is increased (A. Sen). In this way, the level of development of a society can be measured by the freedom which its individuals have, to live their lives in the way they consider most valuable.

The ideal of freedom is the objective that we must pursue, although this freedom is not only freedom in the political plane, it is the freedom of being against all the factors that prevent achieving its full satisfaction. To go behind the goal of human development, it is necessary for society to function as an organic whole, so we must take as fundamental the establishment of a Normative system at the economic and social level, and try to channel the various agents of society in a desirable way, in this time of globalization. Society is composed of social agents that can be interdependent regarding each other, and they can function as organs to fulfill socially necessary functions.

The work of certain social agents generates damage to the process of human development and makes society less organic, and depending on the case, the measures are simple institutional regulation towards the action of that social agent, and in case the first solution is not possible or it is not the best, then those negative social agents are suppressed, and for that reason, I speak of Normativism and not of integralism, since some agents of society obstruct the objective of its functioning as an organic unit. In this way, society should be as close as possible to an organic body, where the social agents interacting with each other are organic bodies that work in a manner in which the goal of greater human development is possible. In a system that functions as an organic body, the organs are not seen in conflict with other organs during their functioning, in such a way that the whole body becomes ill.

However, the objective of Normativism is not only human development, but its objective is also no less than human development in its sustainable version. A society must not only ensure its individuals are free, but it must also generate opportunities for future individuals to be free as well, and this form of social functioning is the most organic because the generations prior to the subsequent ones will end up functioning as an essential organ for their heirs, which is fulfilling the function of granting joy in the new generations. For the aforementioned reason, to the definition of human development of Amartya Sen, which as we have seen is to define development as the ability of a society to generate new opportunities that help increase the freedom of society as a whole in all realms regarding satisfaction, we must add the concept of sustainability, to have a definition for sustainable human development.

This is the social process that expands the freedoms of society without affecting the freedoms of future societies, that is, a process that increases the opportunities of the members of society so that they can achieve their dreams, but where the conditions are created so that future generations have that same or better chance of achieving it too. For this to be possible, factors like environmental care and not endangering future generations with current actions are obviously taken into account. The different agents in society defend different interests and can build antagonistic relationships, which lead to key phenomena in the history of humanity, such as the struggle between dominant and subordinated sectors, ethnic-religious conflicts, intergenerational clashes, and the struggle in the fields of spiritual, sexual and political pretensions in general.

These conflicts can represent an opportunity to channeling human development, or they can be the opposite. Within the social relations, the struggle takes place, and this takes place when the action is oriented for the purpose of imposing one's own will against the resistance of one or more opposing sides. Struggle provokes competition, this occurs when there is a goal by one side that is also sought by others. In its crudest aspects, the struggle establishes power, understood as the probability of imposing one's will within a social relationship, even against all resistance and whatever the foundation of power is. On the other hand, it establishes domination, which is the probability of obtaining obedience in a mandate with certain content, between given persons.

According to Weber's well-known classification, domination can occur in three ways.

Traditional form: it rests on the daily belief regarding the sanctity of traditions or customs which rule society from remote times.

Rational-legal authority: it rests in the belief regarding the legality of a right of command by certain rulers as to exercise authority, the law being the link between dominated and the dominating.

Finally, there is charismatic authority: which rests on the personal qualities of leadership to create sympathy and attachment among the People.

As for the State, in Weber's thinking, it is defined as an association of people with continuous activity and who must successfully maintain the claim of the legitimated monopoly of physical coercion, for the maintenance of the current order. But as I mentioned, we have that a society should be as close as possible to an organic body, composed of social agents that work in such a way that the greatest possible sustainable human development is achieved. Collective action is obtained when individuals obtain greater benefits by cooperating for a common goal than when the opposite occurs.

There are dilemmas emerging from game theory, like what happens when individuals decide to adopt a bad strategy because they do not know the preferences of others. In what is known as "game theory", Albert W. Tucker formulated the dilemma known as "prisoner's dilemma", where someone prefers not cooperating with the other although the situation dictates that both will lose by giving themselves away. In many cases, we are experiencing problems regarding limits in the information that people possess with respect to both the total and partial "picture", something analogous to the information problems seen in the economy when not all sectors of the market are seen. In other cases, we are faced with perceivable costs to inform ourselves or to participate, which individuals are unwilling to assume.

The cost of collective action is greater as the group is larger, therefore for better collective action groups should generally be of lesser size, and there must be selective incentives capable of causing the individuals to accept the cost involved in getting informed and participating in the actions of their groups. The totality of the social agents necessary for the greatest possible human development must be present to work within society, so the task of the State is to arbitrate around which of these agents should be present and how to regulate both the agents that should be present as those that should not. Some agents are structurally necessary, conserving that same condition as long as they are an essential part of the People's life.

The structurally necessary agents must act in such a way that the greatest sustainable human development is achieved for the population as a whole, while the agents whose action is between unsolvable conflicts with the previous objective are structurally unnecessary agents. In human societies, some social agents are sometimes not structurally necessary, and those which are, not always are working in a way that does not conflict with the goal of the greatest possible human development for society as a whole. Both structurally necessary and unnecessary agents can come into conflict with other agents and be eliminated throughout human history. An evident example occurred in the French Revolution when the French monarchs indeed constituted a parasitic estate that consumed more and more impoverishing the rest and without contributing anything for the welfare of the vast majority of that society. The result was the elimination of that parasitic agent in the midst of struggles with other sectors of society, in the same way that many monarchies have been eliminated around the world, disappearing socio-economic and socio-political forms of feudal systems, as they ended up being an obstacle to the development of human societies.

The scientist James Lovelock describes us in his "theory of Gaia", that the entire biosphere (the set of living beings of the planet together with the elements of the lithosphere, hydrosphere, and atmosphere with which they interact) can be understood as a single living organism, that is, a being where all its parts are interrelated and yet still are as independent as the cells of our bodies. So, when understanding humanity now as merely a cell in all this organic system, and therefore as a single entity, we must integrate the characteristics that make the best possible functioning of it. Even in nature, perfect systems are not found, since for example the components of cells, even those of our body, can stop working properly, causing the cell to get sick or die. The cells are adapted to the situations of the environment that affect them. As long as they can adapt themselves to a modification of the environment, they won't experience damage. Therefore, humanity must be in a constant struggle to adapt itself to its environment and survive, being the freedom to preserve life the basis on which other freedoms arise.

In the capitalist system and capitalist society, the regulatory intervention of the State is required, together with the intervention of other institutions, so that certain social agents (for example, the companies of an economy) comply in the best possible way with their function as organs of society, acting in favor of the maximum possible sustainable human development. Based on what was mentioned above, we can define Normativism as the ideology that advocates for society a tendency to function as an organic body through the placement of norms in that society, and we will understand that "function as an organic body" means that it does so in the best way for the sustainable human development of that society, and therefore in a way in which the State acts in accordance with the authentic will of the People.

There are situations where the transition from situation 1 to situation 2 is an improvement for all individuals in society, or an improvement for some, without the others being harmed. The Pareto optimality concept indicates a situation where someone's well-being can't be improved without somehow worsening the situation of others, for example, if 10% of the population owns 90% of the wealth, and 10% is distributed to the rest. It would be an optimal Pareto situation if the individuals have exactly as much as all the others, and the same can be said of many situations that are between one extreme (complete inequality) and the other (complete equality). From Pareto's point of view, no criterion allows one situation to be selected as preferable to the others. Then, we must establish an "optimum" where we can select situations that are preferable to others, an "optimal" that can be considered as a social optimum. I define the social optimum as that situation where you can reduce the freedom of one or more individuals and increase that of another or others in a way that at least compensates for the reduction in the freedom of the former.

Thus, for example, if a famine affects a country, violating the property of individuals with greater wealth (for example through taxes, expropriations, etc.) which constitutes a violation of their freedom, is obviously preferable to the loss of freedom that some individuals would suffer if they die of hunger. Or presenting a less extreme case: if 1% of individuals concentrate 50% of the wealth, and the other 99% of individuals keep 50%, but nevertheless that 99% have their basic needs met, what they do not spend on those needs will be spent exclusively on other needs. In this second case, it would still be preferable to take part of their wealth from the former, as long as access to more wealth for people in the 99% implies an increase in their freedom that goes beyond the decrease in the freedoms of the rest, taking into account that this freedom is only that of 1% of the population.

Individuals with lower incomes than that 1% want to satisfy needs in ways that can always be between a little and much more essential than those of that minority. It should also be taken into account that some individuals may make better use of the increase in their ability to access goods, services, and freedoms. Because of this, their freedom will grow more than those who do worse use. Finally, it should also be taken into account that distributive measures carried out incorrectly can have a negative effect on the economy and society. This makes the freedom of people within the 99% not increase enough or even decrease, including the freedom to access the goods and services they need, either because of the wealth of society as a whole decreasing or for other reasons. Individuals should not only have the opportunity to increase their capacities, but they must also possess the education to make better use of their abilities, hence education, both formal and informal, is so important for sustainable human development.

To be free to do his authentic will, a person must become a master of his body, that is, he must have a healthy body. He must also be master of his emotions, to control them with a properly educated mind and free of the memory of bad experiences, linked to social processes, being that an essential issue for joy and for making others joyful. Finally, we must be masters of our desires, since we must create, recreate and absorb all kinds of concepts with our minds and materialize them, to make more prosperous our life and that of humanity. I believe that the control over these realms leads to health, and it should be noted that the last one, regarding the desires, is important as our desires have a direct implication with our own health and that of others, and I believe this is a conceptual contribution that must be made if we really want to have a complete definition of what health and disease is. Regarding this, we can emphasize the role of education in health, but we can also frame education as something essential for health, without it health wouldn't be possible.

THE POLITICAL WILL OF HUMAN BEINGS

Since the means of production were developed enough to generate a surplus and exclude people from this surplus, and since the moment in which humanity started to leave its tribal phase as hunter-gatherers, certain individuals and groups tried to appropriate surplus and to exploit the work of others. We, humans, organize ourselves to manage scarce resources, and due to the scarcity of these resources, we must compete to obtain all the resources we can. The competitive nature of human beings means that we have an order in which those who are most apt for this competition enjoy privileges over others. As mentioned by Marx, the set of institutions that make up the State was used to exert the organized repression imparted by the dominant group over the rest of society, preserving certain production relations within the framework of the exploitation of man by man.

The political forms adopted by the State are not the same throughout history, being compatible with an appreciable development of democracy, a development that has manifested itself in the political forms of the capitalist State, affirming civic and political rights. In the case of political rights, these in the first instance were solely granted for the bourgeois and the male landowners, and in a second instance extended to the other male sectors of society, until finally, in a third instance, they spread towards women. Power is the ability to set limits in the freedom of action of social agents, making them act in a way that otherwise they would not. Political power can be defined as that power which is exercised directly or indirectly, thanks to the possession of what Max Weber called as the monopoly of legitimized violence in a given territory, in such a way that it can only be exercised by the State, or by private agents which firstly must be authorized by the State. Political power does not necessarily have to be exercised directly by the political authorities. Some different groups are capable of indirectly exercising political power.

This is performed by persuading or dissuading those who do exercise political power directly, and within these groups of persuasion and deterrence, we find companies, the public opinion, trade unions, human rights organizations, elites, religious groups, etc. We can speak of two different kinds of political power: direct political power, which is exercised directly, either by public authorities or by citizens at the time of voting, and indirect political power, which arises in the capacity of persuasion and deterrence that certain groups and individuals have to influence the designation of those who will carry the direct political power, or in the political decisions which the former will take.

Direct political power only arises from the political decisions made by public officials or those taken by citizens when voting, but indirect political power is the power that moves the direct political power from the shadows, since another way in which social agents can enter politics, is simply persuading and dissuading public officials or voters. By this definition, even the media is a tool of indirect political power, since it serves to persuade and dissuade agents who do carry direct political power. But even this does not capture the complexity of the political landscape, it should be considered that also indirect political power can be divided into two kinds: the active and the passive. The indirect political power which is also active arises from an action impacting or being received towards those who carry direct political power, which manages to persuade or dissuade them to do or not to carry out certain political actions.

The indirect political power that in turn is passive, arises from a persuasion of those who carry direct political power without any action being taken by the sectors that persuaded them. This indirect and passive political power occurs when those who handle direct political power anticipate in advance the reactions that the rest (public opinion and certain influence groups) will have, then model their actions according to what they anticipated. Indirect passive political power also occurs when those who carry direct political power shape their actions according to the wishes of those who follow their decisions; only because the first ones consider the satisfaction of those desires is morally good, and therefore they are convinced of a certain moral political agenda that they have set out to fulfill. We can define the State in a simple way: it is the set of institutions that structure the exercise of direct political power, that is, the set of rules of a game designed to structure the way in which direct political power is exercised.

Democracy is a word derived from the Greek meaning "power of the People", and throughout history, it has been defined in many ways. Democracy has been defined as "a form of organization", "a form of state", "government of the People, by the People, for the People", etc. For Robert Dahl democracy is merely a theoretical concept, regarding a government that is characterized by answering to the demands of the governed without discrimination. Adam Przeworski defines democracy as "a system of positive rights and responsibilities", and O'Donnell defines a democratic regime as that where "access to the main governmental positions (with the exception of the judiciary, the armed forces, and autonomous entities), is determined by fair elections." But in reality, democracy must be seen as a social process (as stated by John Dewey) with its advances and setbacks, and that it is not merely a theoretical concept, but develops in reality. Democracy is in fact a social process because it is constantly under construction and deconstruction as social agents play, determining through political power the way in which economic and symbolic resources are distributed among the sectors of the population.

Anyway, as stated, I think it is critically important to classify human will into a manifested and authentic will. Manifested will is the will being displayed by the People, taking into account that they do not necessarily have enough information to achieve the complete picture of the consequences that their desires would have. These can cause negative consequences that would oppose their other will: the authentic will. Authentic will is the true desire of the People, which consists in being free to achieve certain wishes or being free to not suffer what is undesired. Realizing this will is only possible if People had enough information as to possess a complete picture of the consequences that their actions would truly have. To explain this, a famous Platonic allegory can be used: that of the cave.

In that one, a group of prisoners is since their birth in a cave and they are subjected in such a way that they can only look towards the wall, without being able to turn their head. Behind them, there is a corridor with a wall where other men carry all kinds of objects, whose shadows are projected by a bonfire. These chained men consider as truth the shadows that they see projected since they don't know anything of what happens behind their backs. Now I will apply this allegory to my analysis of democracy, to conclude the manifested will is what men take as truth, even if it is not always true. But these men have a will to be free as to fulfill a certain yearning or not to suffer harm, and the will that they are capable of manifesting, sometimes ends up entering into contradiction with their authentic will, since people do not always recognize what it is better for the fulfillment of it.

The manifested will is simply the will expressed by the People, while the authentic will is what they would be willing to favor, that is, their freedom to satisfy themselves if they have perfect information about the consequences of their desires and hence the true consequences of their influence in politics. It must be considered that the manifested will is only a distortion of the authentic one, which is caused by the limits on the information that the People are capable of receiving or understanding. Returning to the issue of democracy, John Stuart Mill stated that opinion, even if it is invalidated by those who have the power to do so, or by a majority, does not lose what it is true in it. There are situations where the transition from situation 1 to situation 2 is an improvement for all individuals in society or an improvement for some, without the others being harmed. The problem is that not everyone has to state the same since individuals are fallible in the sense that they are not omniscient nor omnipotent, and sometimes, a minority may be right as more "excellence" and knowledge is reflected in those than in the majority.

The problem is to establish an "optimal" where situations and arguments can be selected as preferable to others, and here is when democracy, according to Mill, wanting to make individuals equal, have the risk of limiting the excellence of some Individuals in relation to the majority and even individual freedom itself, so Mill's views are similar to that which sees in a democracy the danger of the tyranny of the majority. Anyway, the ideal of freedom is the objective that we must pursue, and with respect to the increase of the freedom of individuals, understanding that individuals have understandable limitations, a man can not be infallible, insofar as he is not a complete master of his body, his emotions, his desires, and mind, in short, everything related to him. Sometimes what men take as truth is not such, since they are standing a reality that is unknown by them and sometimes is even unknowable no matter what they do.

Human knowledge, being subjected to limitations, opens the door to different paths, alternative visions of reality, which do not necessarily have to be harmonious. Sometimes they can enter into conflict, and in addition to this, as time passes, the views of men can change since they are subject to a modifiable context. Mill is skeptical with some points related to democracy, for the very same issue of the fallibility of man, and accordingly, he identified situations throughout history where this fallibility overlaps with the desire to curtail individual freedoms. Like Mill, I also consider that particular cases should be treated without bias since truth does not disappear because the individual is swallowed by the majority, neither disappear because they want to silence it, and it can be considered that in this view freedom is also a means for protecting the truth. Perhaps we could even make a comparison between what is held as truth in Mill's thought, and its opposite in the famous Orwell's novel 1984, wherein that dystopian vision truth is merely what a bureaucratic apparatus determines, in conjunction with a homogenized and ragged majority regardless of how absurd and puerile is the argument's structure which must be believed.

The considerations regarding what is truth are faced with the limitations of the subjective, of those angles of reality that the subject can perceive, but behind this subjectivity is the truth behind a veil. Democracy is, in reality, the social process that develops as the State's action is more akin to the authentic will and not to the manifested will: that is the essence of democracy. The State acts in part according to People's direct political power when voting, together with the indirect and active political power of the People, who carry out actions to persuade or dissuade the rulers and the voters. Finally, also thanks to the indirect and passive political power, which occurs when those who possess direct political power shape their actions according to how they predict what the rest will do, or when those who carry that direct political power shape their actions according to the People's true wishes, due to the fact that they are convinced of a certain moral agenda whose fulfillment depends on the satisfaction of those desires. In this way, democracy is a social process that emerges from the power of the People, the State being a conduit of that power…

A demagogic system is not the form of State to which we should aspire, since, as stated, it is based on the capacity of the State to respond to demands that stem from the manifested popular will of the People, but not the authentic one, and as I mentioned, this manifested will is nothing more than a mere distortion of authentic will, due to the limits in the information that people have at their disposal. Therefore, instead of a form of State based on demagoguery, which is what liberal universalism want to impose, a form of State based on what I call Normativism is desirable, and which consists in a way of government where the State through its norms aspires to satisfy the authentic will of the People (instead of the manifested one) and therefore aspires to be truly democratic. Like democracy, Normativism is a social process, which develops as the State satisfies the authentic will, and therefore it must aspire to a society functioning as an organic body where their different parts do not collide with each other bringing conflicts and inefficiency.

It is also possible to define Normativism and democracy as social processes that develop according to the State's ability to make its individuals freer, or more precisely, according to their capacity to promote the sustainable human development of society, being this individual freedom something which depends on the People as a whole. Normativism and democracy can be defined in that way since ultimately the desires of every individual are either being free to do something that is desired or being free to avoid unwanted suffering. Thus, according to a State's performance when able to better satisfy the authentic yearnings of the People as a whole, more democratic will be that State. Democracy should not be seen as a form of government characterized by the fact that the State acts only according to what it perceives from voices in the tribune, therefore it is a form of State where there is less room for demagoguery. Hence, demagoguery should be defined as a social process by which political groups direct the People by appealing to the manifested will.

HISTORICAL SITUATIONS AND THE DNA OF LIBERALISM

Normativism and democracy, as social processes, will inevitably have their points of lesser and greater development, as the State responds better to the wishes of the People as a whole, despite clearly existing factors that divide humanity and which are related to social order, religions, spirituality, sex, age, etc. Some systems are often instituted by coalitions in which even minority groups, whose strength is still unknown, want to be heard, and added to that, the desire to legislate without the necessary resources to promote new measures can have repercussions that disturb the economy, motivating the evasion of capital or reduction in investments. Delegative democracy, which should actually be called delegative demagogy, "is based on the premise that whoever wins an election is thereby entitled to govern as he or she sees fit, constrained only by the hard facts of existing power relations and a constitutionally limited term of office."

According to O'Donnell, the head person of government "is taken to be the embodiment of the Nation, the main custodian, and definer of its interests. The policies of his government bear no resemblance to the promises of his campaign." Therefore, another characteristic of delegative demagogy is particularism and clientelism, which seeks to benefit certain groups in particular, in addition to the fact that certain economic groups and Social organizations exercise power over political delegates. In addition, political delegates partake in forms of nepotism and create political plans whose purpose is based on gaining popular support at a given moment, and not on the efficiency and sustainability of the plan itself. Thus, the creation of irresponsible and wasteful governments is done, and the inevitable result is unstable systems, with sharp political and economic crises that sometimes end up in a scandal or the fall of the government.

Democracy is a social process that, as it develops, is adjoining to change in the form and action of modern states. There did not exist in the past, neither did exist in the present nor will exist in the future an absolutely democratic political regime, since a perfect response to the authentic will of the People is not possible, in the same way, a perfect response to the manifested will of that people is also not possible. It is extremely important not to dissociate democracy from the perspective of dominant and dominated groups. In the Roman Republic, decisions kept large sectors of the population in a situation of exclusion. Democracy throughout history was a democracy only for male slavers or dominant elites.

The so-called democracies of today are the result of bourgeois revolutions that overthrow the feudal order, where a fundamental change in the history of humanity occurs, being that unlike other modes of production such as slavery and feudalism, it is no longer necessary for the property owners to have themselves the legitimated monopoly of violence by their own means, that's to say direct political power as an indispensable requisite to take control of the economic surplus resulting from the exploitation of subordinate sectors of society. A just and efficient system could never rise above a society where that change has not been achieved, as for example in feudal society, where the feudal lords and the monarchy maintained economic exploitation as something completely dependent on their ability, specifically to exercise direct political power, having to unleash violence and war. A just and efficient system would be inadmissible in a situation like the previous one, in a framework of violent struggles for direct political power, which would grant the possibility of appropriating as much economic surplus as possible.

When the bourgeois market institution arose, where it is no longer necessary for the owners of the means of production to exercise direct political power, that's to say having a legitimate monopoly of violence by their own means, in addition to the fact that the capitalists are more numerous than the ever small group of landowners and nobles of feudalism, and representation mechanisms were necessary to distribute power among the numerous capitalists, the first semi-polyarchical forms of government in the West emerged. The representative systems of liberalism are therefore complex political systems in that they live on pluralities, competences, and antagonisms, trying in the midst of all that to maintain a certain unity of the community, which is usually fragile. To emerge, plurality needs factors such as the emergence of a developed market and property, a higher income and consumption capacity of certain sectors of the People, and the fact that the monopoly of violence is more clearly defined than in feudalism, in addition to the necessity of transparent institutions capable of rendering accounts.

For Robert Dahl, the trajectory in which a demo-liberal system is born and evolves is important to the extent that civil rights and political rights do not always follow the same sequential order, sometimes there are political rights first, and then civic rights. Sometimes civic rights emerge first and only then the political ones arrive. In the first case, the trajectory is from closed hegemonic governments to competing, inclusive hegemonies, and in the second case, the result is competitive oligarchical governments, as in the case of England in the 19th century, where an oligarchy monopolized political power while competing with itself. It has been seen that the second option is the one that has created more stable cases, by providing a political culture and economic bases that provide better shelter to a more stable political life. However, this path is no longer possible for most of the current countries, since it derives from a context where the monarchical and bourgeois power confronted each other for assuming political control of the State. In the current capitalist states, even in the most open ones, the social process of democracy finds severe limitations.

The current demo-liberal systems are essentially demagogic systems because they are based on the manifested wishes of the People, exploited and led by oligarchies that act in a selfish and irresponsible way. A system can be democratic if the leaders possess the capacity of answering to the concerns of a majority of the population as to favor them in many aspects. In the first liberal regimes, democratic decisions occurred exclusively to benefit the bourgeoisie and landlords, and the overwhelming majority lacked political and social rights. Not all states embarked on their transition in the same way, and for example, some states were forced by the pressure of others to adopt more pluralistic forms for their political systems. On the part of the capitalists, they no longer see their economic dominance mortally stricken by the People's access to polyarchy, due to the collapse in popularity of collectivist ideologies and the collapse of the former communist bloc.

When voting, the option of majorities remains an option that does not intend to radically change the existing political and economic structures, in the sense of a step towards authoritarian political forms or towards communist economic forms, as they feel distrust towards alternatives which they see as something that may well not bring the material well-being which workers seek. In addition, the threat of economic regulation and control by states and unions, detrimental to the goals of capitalist companies, is more tenuous in times of globalization, economic liberalization, and productive restructuring on the raise. Added to that, political elites find the cost of repression increasingly high, and if they do not repress it is seen as a sign of weakness, while if they repress, they lose their remaining legitimacy. For the above reasons, the dominant sectors of society are no longer reluctant to employ truly polyarchical forms of government, while they see polyarchy as a way to achieve greater stability in the wake of political crisis, stability which generates better investment and business conditions for the dominant sectors.

To understand how current political systems develop, it is essential to fully understand the processes linked to the functioning of the capitalist machine, in all its dimensions. Capitalism is a system linked to current political systems, in a way that its roots appear to be holding not only institutions but the psyche of people who must get used to a society based on the knowledge of money and on compulsive consumption. Usually, explaining how to establish projects of social restructuring within the limits of a capitalist system is not an easy task, since the very political and cultural institutions inertially push the exaltation of certain economic formulas. Not fortuitously, capitalism has endured so many ordeals throughout history, and it is because of its great adaptability that this system is so interesting. But in part, the survival of this system not only lies in its capacity for adaptation, but it also lies in the fact that alternatives formulated by people satisfied their manifested will, but not the true will that underlies them all.

THE ORIGIN AND BASIS OF CAPITALISM

THE DILEMMA OF A WORLD RUNNING OUT

Normativism aims to be a very comprehensive doctrine, and for that reason, standing from the Fourth Political Theory, I made a critique of the main current economic views, beginning with a brief conceptualization of one of the manifestations of liberalism, which is capitalism, along with a review of the history of this system and its limitations. After the first states were created, they grew in size and complexity throughout history, while the development of new means of transport and communication allowed overcoming natural obstacles that were once formidable barriers. The modes of production were not the same throughout history, as the productive forces developed and the characteristics of each region, based on culture, nature, etc., differentiated from each other. Mankind creates economic systems to manage human and non-human resources that each society has in order to obtain the goods and services considered as necessary by every society.

In order to develop our creative ability, we require a framework that determines the way we produce, acquire and distribute these goods and services, including the way human resources are organized and treated, and those frameworks are the modes of production. Capitalism is one of many modes of production, throughout history there have been others, and capitalism coexisted and coexists with other modes of production, but depending on the region or epoch it has done so as a predominant system in a society or as a subaltern system. In the first mode of production, characteristic of the tribal societies of hunter-gatherers, there was a scarce division of labor, given the limited development of the material productive forces of society. This mode of production, where there was no private property ownership of the means of production, was called by Engels primitive communism. In other times, man, as a hunter-gatherer, simply took what nature offered to him, and was not concerned with the regeneration of its natural resources. Humanity observed how everything was spontaneously generated from nature, and the mysteries behind life and death were unknown, leading to animistic explanations that gave a soul to natural principles and organisms. Later, another stage began, where humanity began to think more and more of ways to stimulate regeneration of the resources which nature granted them, leading to the beginning of practices such as agriculture.

The worship of mother earth was replaced by solar and patriarchal cults, where the individual conceives life on earth as a mere prelude to life after death, and power groups began to create sophisticated forms of domination. In Europe, primitive communism was replaced by the slave-owning mode of production, in which slaves were a commodity of the owners, and their workforce allowed the creation of abundant wealth for those owners, since the retribution that the slaves received was just so that they could continue working, and sometimes not even for that. The historical development gave rise to a system of estates, which was based on discrimination of individuals due to their hereditary or birth condition. But it should be emphasized that in the case of estates in slave societies, it was routine to use prisoners from the wars of conquest as slaves, and in other cases, they were obtained by voluntary sale to pay a debt, or by legal sanction, while the title of patrician or noble could be acquired by diverse circumstances. For that reason this system was not closed like a caste, existing anyhow very little social mobility in this order, which for example gave rise to the estates of patricians and plebeians in Rome, and to the establishment of slave ownership.

In some societies, including Amerindian societies, the so-called Asiatic mode of production was installed. There the communities were subject to estates and caste powers that demanded the payment of tributes to the communities, as they were able to oversee fluvial networks, nevertheless maintaining certain prosperity and unit. In this system, there was no private ownership in the means of production, but there was a division of society into estates or castes, and the different communities, often annexed because of war, were taxed in a way that can be considered as a primitive form of exploitation of man by man. In Europe, slavery gave rise to feudalism, although this did not happen immediately after the fall of Roman civilization (as commonly thought) since slavery had its climax in the late Middle Ages.

In Feudalism, the serf was no longer a mere commodity separated from his means of labor and lacking in rights, although he was bound to the land of his lord and had to work also for the landowners, the nobility, and the clergy, who demanded certain tributes from the peasants, having ownership of the lands, together with forms of coercion and a State. Feudal society was also divided into estates, a system whose social right, unlike castes, does not rely as much on religion and tradition as on the official claim of political power. Later, in capitalism, the wage earner enjoys more freedom than the serf did, since the serf was tied to the land of his master, while the employee enjoys the important freedom to change the company where he works, emerging labor institutions based on the freedom of contract.

The capitalists, that is, those who control the means of production and the State in the capitalist system, engendered what was called by the Marxists as the working class or proletariat, who agreed with capitalists the price and the conditions to sell their work in the labor market. In the capitalist system, within what should be regarded as the working people, are all those who can only sell their labor-power in exchange for a wage (not only in the industrial sector but also in the rural sector and in the service sector), including those who are unemployed and white-collar workers who act as officials in capitalist businesses. It is important to take into account that State actions aimed at addressing the situation of workers have as a critical objective the ensuring of necessary conditions for accumulation and concentration of capital, instead of merely having the objective of improving the conditions of the working people. The intervention of the capitalist state in economic and social aspects is necessary for the aid of business, being of paramount importance for the functioning of the capitalist system. This intervention has the objectives of generating both an economic climate that allows a greater accumulation and concentration of capital, as well as avoiding the radicalization of the conflict between capital and labor and even the creation of a situation that could pose a threat to the capitalist order.

The State can intervene in the economic field, with the aim of fighting against unemployment, granting certain minimum welfare standards, financing various undertakings, directing public companies, controlling monetary policy, collecting taxes, etc., and therefore being a key agent for the distribution of economic resources. The State also acts in other fields of the social sphere, such as culture, education, health, security, defense, etc. Several associations increase the direct or indirect political power of vast groups of the population in the performance of the State (for example political parties, trade unions, and human rights organizations) so that these groups of the population can obtain a better response to their aims. Economic power is transformed into a tool for constructing indirect and direct political power in favor of capitalist interests, which means that capitalist economic power exercises a marked influence on the State's actions, and influences the electoral processes, to the detriment of the political power of the workers and to the detriment of their desires. Even the concessions and alliances that dominant sectors make with the rest or that are made within dominant sectors themselves, serve to accelerate and maintain capital accumulation in the capitalist State.

Modern welfare states and State intervention in the economy have their origin in attenuating the contradiction between capital and labor. Different groups make considerable pressure to moderate the intervention of the State in economic matters or directing it towards the benefit of only a minority, with the attitude of these groups being anti-democratic. Due to the misnamed process of globalization, capitalist companies have acquired great mobility, being able to relocate their productive structures and investments to any part of the world, therefore forcing states to reduce regulation and taxes in order to generate an attractive environment for the investments of private companies. This implies an increase in the political power of the capitalists and a reduction of the political power of the workers since the first ones have the possibility of further conditioning the performance of those who wield political power directly, in the opposite direction to the wishes of the working class.

Another way by which capitalists control the performance of those who directly wield political power is that capitalists accumulate their capital to the point that it does not necessarily have to be productively invested. Due to not investing it productively, there is an excess of savings within the companies, which occurs to the detriment of the welfare of the working people. Therefore, the economy is highly dependent on the level of confidence of private investors, which must be maintained at an appropriate level by the State, taking into account that redistributive policies and trade unions make that companies tend to contract fewer people in the face of an excess of savings, without the sufficient increase in productivity. To this is added that such a system, in order not to impoverish itself, needs an indefinite and adequate growth to maintain investor confidence, and this growth is hindered by the cyclical capitalist crises. This also collides with the objective of the preservation of natural resources and the fight against climate change, since growth, to be indefinite, requires increasing depredation of natural resources, and pollution in the air, water, and land arising from processes of production.

The capitalist economy as a whole must grow indefinitely in order to remain healthy since the capitalist financial system is based on private investors that as John Maynard Keynes stated; possess their "animal spirits", which produce in them the need for enough confidence that when investing, they will obtain an adequate return for their investment, within the framework of the cost-benefit relation that every capitalist must face. If the capitalist financiers do not invest, the obvious result is unemployment, the fall in aggregate demand resulting from this unemployment, and eventually economic collapse. Hence, capitalism, to remain healthy, needs an indefinite expansion of consumption, and an indefinite expansion regarding the depredation of natural resources added to the known problem of pollution. In order to maintain a healthy system, at least for a while, capitalist states are even trying to make people buy products that they do not really need, and measures are taken at the level of financial and fiscal systems to maintain the health of the overall system in the short term but which in the long run have devastating consequences.

This reasoning regarding the relationship between capitalism and the environmental crisis in the future has been mentioned repeatedly by academic David Schweickart, as one of the ways to justify his economic model, which has both good and bad things, although we will analyze Schweickart's economic model later on. Some people, when we show them the previous reasoning, that of the incompatibility between the health of the capitalist system and the well-being of the environment, may think that the problem will be solved by colonizing other planets. But this argument is absurd, not only because habitable planets are several light-years from us, or because terraforming Mars remains a business of such colossal scale that we are very far from this, but because we do not even see at present a real effort by humanity in the field of human space exploration. The death of NASA's budgeting is notorious, together with the fact that Russia, which does not possess the great financial power which the United States has, but with technology and experience at its disposal, was able to monopolize the field of human space exploration thanks to the death of NASA's budgeting.

However, the technology that Russia uses was developed essentially by the Soviet Union many decades ago. Only because the Soviet Union created very effective technology adopted in the Soyuz rockets and spacecraft a long time ago, it can be said that human space exploration was saved from almost extinction in the present. According to Schweickart, and according to many data, capitalism, in order to stay healthy, not only needs the economy to grow, but this growth must be exponential. If an economy grows 3% each year, which is the average growth of the United States during the twentieth century, consumption doubles approximately every 24 years, which means that in a century consumption becomes 16 times larger. So, if 3% growth for each year is unsustainable, just imagine Chinese growth rates of 10% in a country with several hundred million inhabitants. In addition to the above, an increase in consumption does not even always imply an increase in the happiness of individuals.

Although persons in developed countries consume much more than they consumed in the mid-twentieth century, individuals do not feel satisfied with their lives. According to credible scientific studies, people want certain goods or services not so much for their intrinsic value as for the status that they give us, that is because they make us members of a type of "club" within a particular group, that becomes a point of reference in relation to other groups. This means that we can consume more and more, but if we do not perceive that our status increases, we can continue to be equally unhappy.

CONCEPTUALIZING THE CAPITALIST SYSTEM AS A WAY OF UNDERSTANDING ITS REALITIES

We can make a distinction between the most developed types of capitalism, where the financial sector has a much greater weight, and the case of a less developed country, where this financial economy is not so vast and important, which also limits the ability to transform or reorient the real economy of developing countries. Hall and Soskice mention two primordial varieties of capitalism, one based on the liberal market economy, and one based on the coordinated market economy. The second is an economy whose companies depend more on strategic coordination with other sectors of society, like other companies, trade unions, and the State itself through public policies. This system restricts the freedom of the market, through the construction of a series of economic and social pacts between diverse economic agents, which even involve the training and education of social actors. Other authors, like Stiglitz, affirm the great ideological division in the praxis of capitalism is between the neoclassical school, which proposes capitalism based on a free market that for many is not really free, and the successor schools of the Keynesian model, which propose a model where public spending has a broader role in the economy. This spending is used to create jobs, train professionals, or promote and create emerging industries in developing countries.

For all the aforementioned, capitalism is a contradictory system, which allows some progress of democracy in relation to the deplorable conditions of the People in feudalism, but which at the same time remains a deeply undemocratic system, due to its inability to respond to the yearnings of the People as a whole, no matter what kind of political system arises over capitalism, whether if a political system of multiparty nature, a bipartisan one, a dominant-party system, a single-party system, or one without parties at all. Capitalism can be defined as the mode of production where the value of goods and services originates primarily from the mechanical bourgeois property ownership of the means of production. By mechanical I do not mean based on machines, but mechanical in the sense that it produces clashes in society ranging from great to minor ones, making society look less like an organic body and more like a set of groups and institutions in conflict, and by the clashes with others I mean they enter into contradiction and these contradictions are the cause of the weakening of the capitalist system and the negative consequences inherent to capitalism, such as inequality, the conflict between sectors of society and the internal conflict within each of those sectors.

In capitalism, bourgeois property ownership is mechanical and not organic because it produces conflicting clashes with the rest of the social agents, and this, as I will explain later, has its origin in the fact that in capitalism there is freedom of movement for the business capital, and also the economy is dependent on the level of private investor confidence. It is worth clarifying that the previous freedom of movement can be moderated, but it is never completely eliminated in capitalism. The essence of capitalism is the accumulation and concentration of capital in the hands of the owners. The competition between the former occurs to satisfy the demand of consumers in the goods and services market. Capitalism is a mode of production, and as such is made up of a set of relations and forces of production. These originate in a certain historical moment, and as a consequence of the development and contradictions of a previous mode of production. Capitalism arose already in the XI and XII centuries in its form of merchant capitalism, as new forms of trade developed between the regions of Europe, and with the development of merchant capitalism, the owners of the capitalist means of production could emerge. But capitalism was not yet the dominant mode of production since it was locked in the fetters of feudal production, which was basically autarkic, based on land, while greater freedom of trade that wasn't allowed in feudal regimes is necessary for capitalists.

As the population in the fiefs grew, it was no longer possible to satisfy the demand for food and other goods with the production capacity of the fiefdom. The urban growth placed merchants with all kinds of products, together with small producers who abandoned the countryside in search of better opportunities. The capitalists became increasingly influential and ended up demolishing the structures of the Old Regime. Instead of production occurring domestically, as it did in fiefdoms, it became common to buy the production of capitalist entrepreneurs, who possessed the necessary means, and who employed people to participate in the productive process in exchange for a wage. Workers began to be assembled in factories that replaced domestic workshops, although they continued working with old methods of manufacturing. The industrial revolution made the production processes more complex, introducing machinery that cheapened production significantly. Small artisan producers of that time were ruined due to being unable to compete with owners, who possessed larger capital which was required to pay for the new machines. Many were proletarianized by remaining solely with their labor force to be sold to the capitalist in exchange for a wage.

The division of labor became increasingly heterogeneous and increasingly complex, decomposing the work of each worker in several repetitive activities carried out with the intervention of machines. Thousands upon thousands of workers were gathered in the modern factories to participate in the production process, which gives rise to the socialization of that production process, although the ownership of their means was not socialized. When developing an internal market based on the development of productive forces, the accumulation of capital and overproduction makes it necessary to turn to foreign trade and colonial exploitation, so it was necessary to search for potential markets to sell the new offer being created, together with the exploitation of the resources in the colonies. To highlight a straightforward example: imagine that in a craft workshop there are three workers, all dedicated to the production of a portfolio. Suddenly the owner brings a machine that allows making three portfolios, needing only one worker per machine. The owner will reduce their costs significantly, and when accumulating capital it introduces more machines.

Workers continue selling their labor force, but now they must do so for a considerably lower price and become impoverished, while the owner's profits increase exponentially since it produces many more portfolios than before, and can lower costs by increasing the exploitation of labor. The owner must find new markets to sell all the portfolios, as there is not enough demand from the impoverished population, even though the portfolios are cheaper. Bourgeois property ownership radically changes labor relations and the condition of thousands of people, while at the political level capitalists achieve important gains that make them possessing political power, in addition to possessing economic power. Economic growth becomes possible, this being a modern phenomenon that is generated by the accumulation of capital resulting from surplus, which was reinvested and thus led to more substantial development of the productive forces, and a greater centralization and accumulation of capital. Pre-monopolist industrial capitalism, characterized by free competition, develops into monopolist capitalism, where the business monopolies of capitalism come to conduct economic life, by concentrating and centralizing capital, while blocking free competition.

In monopolist capitalism, industrial capital merges with financial capital and financial intermediaries take on an increasingly decisive role in economic processes (for example banks, investment companies, and stock exchanges). Banks are transformed into capital traders and financial capital is used to purchase shares so that the financial sector has intense control over economic life. Within the framework of monopolist capitalism, the need for companies for a greater volume of capital to dominate the market gives rise to the need to expand and incorporate technological innovations or simply more resources. This vaster volume of capital was obtained through the financial sector and interest rates. Monopolies are made transnational so that among many them the world market is shared, while financial capital is exported to all parts of the planet and occupies all economic areas. The remaining capital, which can not be reinvested in the domestic economy in the absence of sufficient demand, is exported where there are other investment opportunities, both in developed and underdeveloped countries, and both in the form of loans to governments and for the investments of companies.

States can not escape the influence of capitalist economic power, which rules the economic and political life of States. Both capital and the global economy have globalized, giving rise to a global market, where economies and companies have become interdependent. In capitalism, competition does not disappear, being necessary to pull down prices naturally. In any case, monopolies and oligopolies, due to a lack of sufficient competition, and by establishing barriers on possible competing companies, can speculate with prices and production thanks to the dominance over the market, requiring the intervention of the State to correct market failures generated by imperfect competition. Financial and production services led to the construction of electronic networks in part because they allowed the development of electronic transfer systems for capital, which are the backbone of the international financial system, since it was possible for banks to transfer capital immediately to any part of the world in the face of certain news, to place arbitrary differentials in interest rates, take advantage of favorable exchange rates, and evade political storms (Langdale 1991; Warf 1995).

These networks gave banks the ability to transfer capital around the globe at a great speed. Freed from the gold standard, and traveling at the speed of light, global financial capital maintains even freer mobility that makes it dance around the world. This system of free mobility is one in which capital moves in a constant stream of speculative investments that never materialize into physical and tangible goods (Warf, 2008). Capitalism has a flagrant contradiction that becomes a fundamental enemy of human development. On one hand, the accumulation of capital and innovation allows for a substantial increase in the number of goods and services, but on the other hand, the fact that the means of production are in the hands of a few, the process of globalization, restructuring for productivity, and the nature of financial markets (even more so when these markets are not regulated) cause the value created to be distributed unevenly.

As we know, the State and union organizations can act to raise wages, impose taxes on companies and individuals with more resources, bolster social security, improve working conditions, reduce unemployment, and in some cases even allow certain participation of the workers in the profits and decisions of the companies. This was one of the factors that led to the economic golden age after the Second World War, being a sort of contract between workers and capitalists in the framework of the welfare state, Keynesianism, and also the Taylorist-Fordist production system. But due to economic globalization and the development of the means of communication and transport, the capital of companies has acquired freer mobility. A type of macroeconomic instability arises from the fact that capital can flow from one region of the world to another, and it can leave countries either due to changing demand or new technologies that negatively affect markets, because trade unions become too strong, because of social and infrastructure problems, etc., which makes a country or region less desirable for investment (The result is capital flight.)

If unions or the State push for better wages and working conditions, or regulation in other aspects such as environmental issues, companies can move to any part of the globe, for example to regions where wages are notoriously lower, where working conditions are worse for the workforce, and where regulation in other aspects is more flexible. According to Rafael Muñoz de Bustillo Llorente, the evolution of the welfare state in developed societies is primarily characterized by an increase in the presence of the public sector in the economy and social security, if we compare it with what existed during the XIX century. Public spending, in the opinion of many analysts, would be largely responsible for the social stability manifested by developed countries, as well as their good economic performance.

The freedom of movement for business capital makes it more difficult for the State to tax business capital, and workers are impelled to carry an even larger part of the tax burden necessary to finance public spending (Manuel Costa Vallés 2005). Since over- increasing the tax burden over labor generates an excessive reduction in the incentives to work, it is foreseeable that the government will be coerced to reduce public spending, and therefore social spending. Just-in-time production increases the vulnerability of capital against interruptions in the production flow, and thus increases the bargaining power of workers, as it is based on direct action in the place where it is produced. And this applies not only to the industries operating just-in-time but also to the sectors of transport and communications, on whose reliability this method of production depends. (Beverly J. Silver 2003).

In any case, the aggregate demand is pushed downward and overproduction is generated, since an insufficient part of the wealth is destined for wages (Workers are from the point of view of the capitalists both a cost to reduce and the source of demand for goods and services.) The capitalists must lower the cost of the labor force to produce more goods and services to sell in the market and must use part of the capital for the expansion of their companies since this makes them more aggressive and competitive in the market, which implies more investment for the production of goods and services (including capital goods) which does not go to the worker's wages. To this, we must add that productivity is increasing thanks to an increasingly dizzying technological development, which increases the capitalist supply more and more, while wages remain frozen. This gives rise to insufficient aggregate demand and overproduction since the aggregate supply can not be offset by the demand for goods and services, leading to the loss of the value of the goods and services produced in the economy, and the consequent increase in unemployment, freezing of wages and downward pressure on State revenues.

All of the above generates a vicious circle since it causes a new decrease in aggregate demand. By relying on private savings as a source of investment and interest rates on them, enormous amounts of capital are accumulated, that ultimately can not be reinvested productively by investors, generating excess savings. Given the excess of savings, the private investor can lose confidence related to obtaining the benefit rate that he considers adequate if he keeps investing, that being the primary source of instability in capitalism. Investor confidence is also dependent on consumer confidence, which if greater means that consumers make more purchases and save less, while if the consumer's optimism about the economic situation is lower, they will spend less and they will save more.

Private investors do not possess enough information to know what the willingness of consumers will be when it comes to spending, as well as consumers do not know what their dispositions will be in the future when it comes to spending. Given the excess of savings, investors have three options: lend funds to certain governments, who will return them with interest, employ it for unproductive speculative activities (as in the stock market, land prices, etc.) or simply keep their savings, not investing them. In the last two cases, the result is that the aggregate demand decrease because the investor does not have the expectation of receiving an adequate return on his investments, he does not invest in new productive projects and the result is the increase in unemployment, unemployment that generates a new decrease in aggregate demand, generating the aforementioned vicious circle.

It happens that investors must possess sufficient confidence to obtain an adequate return on their investments, and this confidence is affected by various factors, such as a changing demand, technological change, social and political problems, etc. The low aggregate demand, and the dependence on the level of private investor confidence, is what accentuate the economic cycles of capitalism, which ends up generating cyclical unemployment in the short term. This is due to the fact that in labor contracts wages do not adjust rapidly enough to changes in aggregate demand, and the health of the economy is left at the mercy of the expectations of private investors with intentions that collide with the sustainable human development of a country as a whole. As is well known, the same capitalist crisis gives rise to a new stage of long-term growth, due to the destruction of the productive forces generated by crises, by eliminating capitalist overproduction.

Anyway, in the long term, another effect is perceived, which is not enjoying the economic growth that could have been obtained if it wasn't destroyed by overproduction and the short-term crisis of confidence before a situation of adjustment by the market mechanisms themselves is reached. It is necessary for the economy to grow continuously and indefinitely to avoid generating a situation unfavorable to investment, in which therefore the capital for productive investments is stopped due to lack of confidence. If humanity maintains the growth rates to which it has become accustomed, by the end of the century it will consume more than ten times what we now consume, and this planet, with its need for environmental balance, and its limited resources, could not support such burden, with the impact of the ecological crisis remaining an extremely important one. Toyotism, as a new model of capital accumulation in the age of computers, supposes a more heterogeneous production linked to diverse types of demand, but also labor market flexibility and the rotation of jobs and roles at work.

In addition to the above, the demand for a workforce with a certain preparation and various functions increases the structural unemployment in capitalism, conforming in a minor scale the versatile and multifunctional workers capable of operating several machines or of exercising a work of intellectual nature. But there are also a large number of laborers who work in precarious conditions and who do not have the qualification of the first ones, working in many cases for partial periods, when they aren't unemployed. The changes in business organization introduced by the new accumulation model implied factory decentralization (a central core and a multiplicity of dispersed, subordinated, outsourced units) while stable workers mix with casual workers who work for partial periods, with many sometimes working in a deregulated way, laborers working under the table, or working in small units as in the case of autonomous work and work at home. A large periphery of workers who have discontinuous and less paid jobs and who work in precarious conditions is formed, which is linked to the expansion of forms of part-time work, flexible working conditions, the growth of the service sector, working in small units, the use of subcontractors, etc.

This dismantles the workers' movement with the atomization of the working people, a movement that drives mobilizations and demands, and an important source of pressure for the State and companies. Automation makes jobs in the industrial sector smaller, but there is simultaneously the growth of the service sector, with a type of proletariat linked to activities in this sector, which usually works for partial periods and in a precarious, deregulated way. Added to this, resorting to the work of women and children is usual, being more vulnerable sectors that must resort to working as a way of subsisting since in modern societies the traditional family model based on a deep division of tasks between men, women, and children is erased. Innovation and technological development are becoming faster, introducing new technologies capable of producing more quantities and at more speed, increasing the capacity to generate wealth.

The technological revolutions of the future, fostered by nanotechnology, artificial intelligence, etc., will aggravate the essential contradiction of capitalism. It seems that there are no boundaries for factories, which can relocate their capital to other parts of the world, and decentralize and restructure themselves. The maximization of individualism in modern capitalism seems to have atomized human societies, giving rise to individualistic attitudes centered on competition and the greatest personal benefit. In addition, it seems that humanity no longer embarks on major communist revolutionary processes. We can not ignore the role played by the fall of the Soviet bloc on the workers' movement and the communist political parties, which caused the alert of states towards "red danger" and to significantly enhance certain policies and rights to calm the struggle between capital and work, precisely because of this threat that destabilized and even eliminated capitalist power.

In this context, fighting with strength for alternatives to capitalism was possible, as anti-socialist and anti-Marxist beliefs were not so deeply rooted, nor the belief regarding the impracticability of alternatives to capitalism. Deregulation in the context of the era of neoclassical economics, after the crisis of welfare states characterized by the intervention of states in the economy, and after the beginning of the crisis of the Taylorist-Fordist accumulation system, profusely increased inequalities and led to the freezing and falling of wages, as well as the deregulation of working conditions. Wages were frozen while the productivity of companies continued growing, so the inevitable result would have been a too low aggregate demand and overproduction. However, the capitalists injected credit to consumers through bank loans and credit cards, so that they had broader access to the goods and services of the economy (mortgages, cars, appliances, etc.), although these consumers became increasingly indebted until they couldn't return the payments.

In 2008, the crisis began worsening in the US, to which was later added the crisis originating in Europe, although with the crucial advance of the Chinese economy and the economies of other emerging countries, as new engines for the world economy, despite some deceleration in them. Much earlier, the massive capitalist crisis which began in 1929 had devastating effects on the world economy, with the exception of the Soviet Union, submerging first the American economy, already the world engine, in a great crisis. Keynesian measures were applied to activate demand and reduce unemployment, expanding the role of the State on the economy, a role that was small until then. These measures implemented during the presidency of F. D. Roosevelt were of great importance, but they did not take the American economy out of the pit it was in. (By 1939 US unemployment was still at 17%.)

It was the second world war, with its massive mobilization of men, and its war production and sale, which generated in the US economy that necessary push to get out of the depression and significantly increase the volume of that economy, together with the consecration of the US as a superpower. With all the aforementioned, we can identify six essential components that make up the capitalist system. The first is that it is a system based on bourgeois property ownership of the means of production, and that is already known by the general public. The second, also known, is that it is a system where the institution called the market exists, in which goods and services are sold and bought with a price determined to a greater or lesser extent by the competition depending on the level of intervention that public agencies have in setting prices.

Thanks to this second characteristic, in capitalism there are always companies competing with each other to provide goods and services to the consumer, although companies periodically make alliances, on many occasions, they do not. The third component is a system based on the freedom of movement for the labor force (which did not exist, for example, in feudalism). The fourth component is based also on the freedom of movement for business capital, and with freedom of movement for business capital I do not mean free trade in the goods and services market, but the ability of capital to move from one region to another. The fifth element that characterizes the capitalist system is it is a system dependent on the level of private investor confidence related to obtaining an adequate return on his investments. The sixth element of the capitalist system, linked to the fifth is it is a system that, in order to stay healthy, needs an indefinite and exponential growth of the economy.

Later I will show the Normative system retains the first characteristic of the capitalist system since it is still primarily based on the property ownership of the capitalists over the means of production. In addition, it retains the second characteristic, which is the mobility of the labor force within the framework of freedom of contract, and the third characteristic, that is, the existence of a goods and services market where prices are usually determined by competition. But while these three characteristics are preserved, the other three characteristics of the capitalist system are suppressed. It suppresses a clearly evident characteristic of capitalism, which is the freedom of circulation for business capital, while the fifth and sixth characteristics of capitalism are totally eliminated since there isn't dependence on the level of private investor confidence and therefore neither dependence on an indefinite and exponential growth of the economy. Based on this, I consider that Normativism also arises a new mode of production different from the capitalist one, that is, the Normative mode of production. Normativism suppresses half of the key elements that characterize capitalism, and therefore we can consider it as a different system to capitalism unless we adopt the foolish position of labeling any system that continues to be based on bourgeois property ownership of the means of production as capitalist and as essentially the same thing.

This foolish and dogmatic stance is a legacy of Marxism and anarchism that must be overcome if we really want to develop a viable alternative to capitalism. It would be a mistake to define capitalism as just an economic system since it is also a political system inasmuch as the economic decisions made by the capitalists greatly affect the decisions in politics, and the political decisions that are made thanks to the capitalist states also affect the capitalist economy. If in some capitalist societies there isn't, for example, a system based on free elections, and in others there is, this does not mean that capitalism is not also a political system, because for example, in many cases the causes of a society having free elections or not having them have the nature of the capitalist system as the reason. The nature of the political system that arises on the capitalist system is not irrelevant insofar as the structuring of political systems tends to obey the requirements to maintain or restructure capitalism in different historical or geographical contexts.

Currently, the term market economy is used as a synonym for the capitalist economy, but this confuses people and distracts them from the real problems of capitalism, making them see only a positive side of capitalism, which is that there is a goods and services market, where prices are still largely determined by the competition of companies. An economic system can continue to be based on bourgeois property ownership of the means of production, it can be based on a market economy, and can be based on the freedom of contract, and still have quite important differences with capitalism. Therefore, if we do not want to fall into a conceptual error, to the three characteristics traditionally assigned to capitalism, and which are the characteristics that in Normativism are conserved, we must add the other three characteristics that are of utmost importance.

Globalization brings us new problems that did not exist in the 1929 crash. Today, even companies in China can relocate their productive activities and capital to countries where wages are even lower, especially in India and Vietnam, in a way in which the bargaining power of the

Chinese workers is diminished, already limited by the cancellation of the right to labor strike and to free trade unionism. As developing economies grow, the existence of a stronger domestic market inevitably becomes necessary to absorb the growing production of goods and services, decreasing dependence on exports. The more contribution the domestic market has in aggregate demand, as opposed to the contribution coming from abroad, the percentage of overproduction that can be absorbed abroad is lower, and the macroeconomic disadvantage that inequality generates is more serious. This is one of the reasons why countries such as Chile, China, and South Korea, which have relatively open economies, stood out both in terms of economic growth in the underdeveloped world, simply because a greater opening of the economy allowed them to absorb overproduction and thus increase their growth rates.

For countries such as China to develop, their domestic markets must grow, which inevitably must acquire increasing importance for their economies, amplifying the problem of overproduction, as the economy of those countries becomes too large to depend on exports abroad to the same extent. This is because the rest of the world can't absorb the same percentage of goods and services produced by countries such as China. Added to the above, to increase the size of the domestic market, higher wages are required, and this will obviously cause the prices of economies such as China to increase, and therefore their products lose competitiveness abroad, which would make them even less dependent on exports.

The growth of the markets requires every day the production of more outputs, which in turn faces a limited supply of inputs throughout the production chain. This occurs mainly with non-renewable inputs of mineral origins such as hydrocarbons, drinking water, and other kinds of resources. As stated, capitalism requires an indefinite and voracious growth to stay healthy, which implies the growing depredation of the earth's resources, and growing pollution. Economic models such as China or Chile are not desirable paths for human development. There is a myth that says that the Chinese model is about social capitalism. Those myths were built because these economies are not yet big enough so that the need for a larger domestic market makes overproduction a more serious problem, which happens for example in developed economies like the US. These rich economies are highly dependent on consumption in their domestic market, in addition to the fact that the capitalist systems of developing countries require increasing depredation of natural resources.

Capitalism is a system that has generated unprecedented wealth, but at the same time has created a situation in which a world where wealth unprecedented in human history is generated comes also with unprecedented inequality. More than proposing some sort of new capitalism, which is impossible, since the systems proposed by the so-called center-left parties do not represent anything new in its essence, it is my desire to propose something different after a task of many years that began in my adolescence, and that since then has led to mature thinking, after much time of research and reflection.

PART II:
THE NORMATIVE ECONOMIC SYSTEM

THE NORMATIVE ALTERNATIVE

STATE CONTROL OVER BUSINESS INVESTMENTS

Many people, although they are aware of the evils of capitalism and have engaged in certain struggles to change things, do not know a viable long-term alternative to capitalism, or adopt foolish positions that lead to dead ends. In this section, I show the reader how can arise from Normative thinking an economic and social model capable of providing an adequate response to the social problems we are facing today. For example, Great Britain's Brexit made the world listen to the voice of those who did not benefit from globalization and the capitalist economic system, especially those who live in small towns and who lost the most with the process of globalization and capitalism. Nevertheless, it is necessary to propose a viable economic alternative to the current system, as to be capable of confronting globalism without leading the country into a major crisis.

As stated, capitalism can be defined as the mode of production where the value of goods and services is generated primarily from the mechanical bourgeois property ownership of the means of production. In capitalism, it is possible to go from the very moderate intervention of the capitalist State, through versions denominated as "centrist", till versions with a more substantial presence of State intervention in the market (for example the current economy of the People's Republic of China). In the diverse types of capitalism, elites sometimes promote growth and sometimes they do not, but in any case, the high inequality and concentration of wealth end up affecting the economic growth and the stability of the economy, as a consequence of insufficient aggregate demand, as well as the nature of financial markets and commercial exchanges within and between countries, often also due to damages caused by problems like corruption, which mainly affect underdeveloped countries.

On the opposite side, and as the second mode of production, is communism, where different collectivist positions can be encompassed. Communism is the mode of production where the value of goods and services is produced mainly from State, communal or cooperative ownership of the means of production. I don't refer to economic models commonly termed as social capitalism as socialist because this has created a false categorization, since the main characteristic of capitalism, that is, production based primarily on mechanical bourgeois property ownership of the means of production is something that is still going on.

But besides communism and capitalism, I want to add a third mode of production, Normativism. Normativism, in addition to being an ideology, is a mode of production where the value of goods and services is generated primarily from the organic bourgeois property ownership of the means of production. In this system, the bourgeois property ownership of the means of production is organic because it has a greater harmony with the rest of social agents since it enables a higher level of sustainable human development. With regard to the word "socialism", it has been used by innumerable groups and philosophies of all kinds, from Hitler's National-Socialism to anarchism, the Stalinist parties, the Trotskyists, and by the "leftist" parties, that despite calling themselves in that way, propose to stay in capitalism. The term "socialism" is now used by all kinds of political sides which can have almost nothing in common but to call themselves as socialists, so I have decided to name the third mode of production in another way as to separate it from these sides.

The cause behind the bourgeois ownership of the means of production being organic in Normativism finds its root over the fact that in the new mode of production the freedom of movement for business capital has been eliminated, together with dependence of the economy on the level of private investor confidence. Elimination is not the same as moderation since capitalism can regulate the freedom of movement for business capital, but it never disappears. Changes are so transcendent that this system can be easily considered as distinct from the capitalist one, and at the same time as a system which rejects communism, opposing the value of goods and services from being originated primarily by state, communal or cooperative ownership of the means of production.

As I will explain later, ending the freedom of movement for business capital requires the investments of companies have their origin in State funds, a condition that I wish to summarize as "State control over business investment", which is also capable of solving the problem of excess savings. State control over business investment is a characteristic of the Normative system, which will always be linked to the total suppression of the freedom of movement for business capital. Capitalist and communist modes of production are equally antagonistic to Normativism, a system that I will describe in detail presenting it as a completely preferable alternative to the first two, as to achieve the greatest possible sustainable human development.

Normativism is a mode of production where, as in capitalism, the value of goods and services originates primarily from the bourgeois property ownership of the means of production. But as mentioned, this condition is added to the fact that the freedom of circulation for business capital has been eliminated, and also the dependence of the economy on the level of private investor confidence, therefore making bourgeois property ownership something organic. For bourgeois property ownership to be organic, there must be State control over corporate investments, a way by which the Normative State, which differs from the capitalist and communist states, remains the entity that centrally directs the process of capital accumulation of the companies. In capitalism, the lesser organic cohesion between those who own the means of production and those who have only their labour-power supposes that the functioning of society less resembles that of an organic body. One difference that evidently separates capitalism from Normativism is the latter clearly implies a level of organic cohesion between workers and owners that will be broader.

As mentioned, in feudalism the serf was tied to their land, so the free circulation for labour was obstructed, while the employee in capitalism enjoys the freedom of movement as to be able to change the company where he works. The transition from capitalism to Normativism is also partly related to the degree of freedom regarding circulation for one of the factors of production, but in this case, it happens completely the other way around, since in this case, it is not the circulation of the factor of labour, but rather the circulation of business capital, now moving in the opposite direction to that freedom for business capital, since it is in the direction of completely suppressing it.

The elimination of this freedom for business capital will always be accompanied by a distribution of significantly more equitable income since the aforementioned measure can only arise as a result of pressure from labourers and other sectors related to them. The implementation of the new system would indicate its advantages, and this system would be in any case defended by a large enough number of people to ensure the social equality that is considered appropriate by them. The Normative mode of production is based on State control over business investment, and first of all, I want to describe how it will be carried out, and then I will formulate the reason for it.

By Law, the State obliges companies to establish sinking funds, consisting of a part of the capital from the companies, deducted over the basis of the total capital of them, being separated from the rest to be sent to a central fund controlled by the State. The State indicates a maximum period for companies to pay all of their amortized sums, which will go to the central fund as public capital. A part of the central fund is obtained through taxes on consumption and other taxes, but not through the sinking funds, and the first part is responsible for financing expending related to the State's public investment at the level of the whole town, region or locality (for example, the construction of schools, hospitals, roads, etc.), instead of the level of companies. First, the expenditures that correspond to the country as a whole are deducted, then those that correspond to a regional level, and then to the local level. Finally, once the communities adopt the decisions regarding these levels, they send the part of their respective funds that are constituted exclusively by the sinking funds to a network of local banks to finance the new investments that the companies must make.

The local banks charge interest rates moderated by the State on the subsidies for companies, subsidies that as I have explained are obtained through the capital accumulated with the sinking funds imposed by the State, sent to the central fund in the form of public capital, and then it is invested by localities among local banks. The State determines how much capital should be allocated to each region, and the regions how much capital must be sent to each locality, and finally the localities send the part of their capital generated through the sinking funds to local banks in charge of financing local business ventures. The capital that was sent to a certain region can not leave it, while the capital that makes up the central fund and the capital of the local banks that originate thanks to this fund, is capital that is publicly generated, and it can not leave State frontiers, obviously to prevent investors from sending their capital out of borders to evade sinking funds, also preventing companies from relocating their capital to impoverished areas of the world where wages are lower and working conditions are worse, which, as mentioned above, makes it difficult to fight for better wages and working conditions in developed countries.

If a locality can not invest all the funds that were assigned to it, they are delivered to the regional level to be invested by other localities in that region or in more public spending at the regional level. The funds for the new investments of the companies are generated in a public and transparent way through the sinking funds imposed by the State, and these funds are reinvested from the State to a network of local banks that strive to grant efficient subsidies to businesses. The funds that will be allocated at the level of the whole People, at the level of a region, or of a locality (and not at the business level) must be financed exclusively through taxes on consumption and other types of taxation, but not through the sinking funds on companies, since these sinking funds should not be too high either, to the point of discouraging investment. The central fund grants its capital to local banks in accordance with the number and size of the companies to which each one grants funds and the level of efficiency of these banks when granting subsidies as reflected in the final results of its operations. In this way, banks that grant unprofitable subsidies are penalized, and those who withhold funds are also penalized.

The capital sent from the local banks to companies should not be returned by them (except for the sum related to what they charge for their lost interest vis-à-vis the local banks), although in any case the capital of the subsidies is added to the total capital of the companies and therefore to the base by which the sinking funds are deducted by the State and sent to the central fund. An investment mechanism like the one I have described has as its result not only the moderation of the freedom of movement for business capital but also its total suppression since it is the State that decides the direction of capital flows for the investments of companies, through a network of local banks. To increase the efficiency of the system, it is convenient the local banks towards which the funds are directed are competing banks in the private sector, as a way to ensure the efficiency of the system and that it does not fall victim to the problems of public management.

In any case, in the consumer sector, that is, the sector of the banking activity in charge of granting loans for the consumption of individuals (purchase of houses and other consumer goods and services, as well as in the granting of insurance), there is the necessity for efficient public banking that operates together with private banking in this sector. This is because there is certain prudence to lend among the private banks that lead to restrictions in the loan policy, which affect certain disadvantaged sectors of the economy, and this prudence increases during a crisis, where banks lose confidence, while the Public banks do not need that prudence since they have objectives linked to public policies. The State should moderate the interest rates of the banks that finance consumption so that the previous ones do not become a significant source of inequality.

The sinking funds are considered by the companies as a cost of production and therefore are covered by the cost of the goods and services produced. If the sinking fund of the companies is made smaller, the income of the individuals will grow, but making it more difficult to obtain funds for investment, while if the sinking fund is raised then money liquidity will be reduced but at the same time the offer of funds for companies will increase, in both cases having an effect on the income of individuals that will be small, because the benefits and burdens will be shared by all companies. As I mentioned before, the economic model that I am proposing is one where there is State control over business investment, but not a communist economy.

Both in capitalism and Normativism, investors must charge interest on their subsidies as a mechanism of capital accumulation in the face of overproduction and under-consumption, which is rooted in the fact that the capitalist owner is incentivized to invest in such a way that he can generate the expansion of a private company, increasing supply and promoting economic growth, money that won't go to the wages of workers, who with their income make up the main source of demand for goods and services. In capitalism and Normativism, the expansion of capitalist business is a necessity for its owners, who are eager to expand their businesses to increase their power and personal prestige. A greater size increases the capacity of the company to act aggressively against its competitors and resist its threats, existing the logic of "grow or die." This incentive to grow is not present in the same way in the cooperatives, since to grow in size would imply hiring more workers with whom to share the benefit, and the capital that would have been destined to expansion in the case of a capitalist enterprise would be destined to the workers' income.

In summary, companies will continue depending on interests as an investment mechanism even in Normativism, being that necessary for the process of capital accumulation of each company, because capitalist owners have the incentive to seek the expansion of their businesses. As mentioned, the process of globalization and the evolution of transportation and communication technologies make capital mobility even more free, which entails a series of macroeconomic problems related to it, giving rise to very important social and economic consequences that must be taken care of. In the first place and contrary to what the neoclassical school says, capital does not flow to the regions of a country where it is less abundant but instead goes to where capital is already abundant, and where opportunities for investment are easier to find. As a result of the freedom of movement for business capital, inequality arises between richer regions of the country where capital is concentrated and poorer regions where employment opportunities are lower.

The labor force is forced to emigrate where the employment opportunities are greater, this being a factor of destabilization over the life of communities. As already stated, the sinking funds imposed on companies go to a central fund controlled by the State, from which new industrial plans are financed. By law, funds allocated by the central fund to each region can't leave them, including funds sent to local banks. Because the new investments are generated through sinking funds centrally distributed by the State, the problem regarding freedom of movement for business capital, which among other things forces workers to migrate to those regions where capital is more abundant, is solved. The capital of the companies won't be able to move freely between one region to another since the amount of capital sent to each region will be determined by the State, and the State will condition the economic activity in each region, by limiting access to capital in some regions, by increasing it in others, or leaving it practically the same, and thus contributing to the human development of regions where little capital flowed. In the Russian case, this will be very important to help reduce the inequality seen between the different regions of Russia and to develop the Russian Far East, which contains most of Russia's vast territory.

Several criteria will be taken into account to determine the amount of capital that should be allocated to each region, but as Schweickart mentions in his "Economic Democracy" model, which also has a type of state control over business investment, it can be considered that regions have a "prima facie" right to receive capital on a per capita basis where X population receives X fund (Taking that criterion exclusively makes the distribution completely equal.).The above criterion must be violated in certain cases, where the concentration of industries and capital in certain regions requires more funding for them when certain enterprises must be located in certain regions for reasons of efficiency, where industrial activity and the work of labor have higher productivity, and when certain regions are backward and should receive a greater flow of capital to provide greater employment opportunities and infrastructure to its inhabitants.

As David Schweickart suggests in his "Economic Democracy" model, a completely egalitarian distribution to communities from a per capita base can be considered a "prima facie" right that can be violated by the State, but because the distribution to the regions is a zero-sum game where each region loses what the others earn, each deviation from the distribution principle on a per capita basis would need a solid justification. Regions should no longer compete to attract capital, so they should not offer tax exemptions or other incentives to businesses. Communities would tend to be more stable since by ending the freedom of movement for business capital at the regional level, people should no longer migrate from one place towards another where there are more employment opportunities.

The ability of states to regulate their economies has been hit by the phenomenon of free capital mobility (Harris 1994), as there are capital flows inside State borders and between states, and here we have the second problem that poses us the freedom of circulation for business capital. The funds for the new investments of companies, which are reinvested by a network of local banks, won't be able to leave the borders of the State. The financial capital granted by the central fund for the projects of companies (which is publicly generated) can not leave the borders of the country so that even the government is not authorized to allow private companies to withdraw it outside borders. That unless the State first changes the laws related to the basic mechanisms of the Normative economic system, which must be protected by legal instruments in a way that their modification or elimination becomes difficult.

Now unions and political groups can regulate and control the activity of companies without fear of capital flight by discouraging investments due to the struggle for better wages and working conditions, since publicly generated capital can not leave State borders, and therefore the downward pressure on the workers' income disappears, as well as the pressure on their working conditions by companies that could relocate their capital to other regions of the world, for example to countries where wages and working conditions are notoriously worse for the workforce. Thanks to this, it is possible to strengthen and expand the power of unions in a way that wages are higher and working conditions are improved. It is also possible to increase the taxes on the capital of the companies and the regulation on them, through the action of political groups. These no longer have the threat constituted by the freedom of movement for business capital, nor can they utilize it as an excuse to moderate the quantity and scope of policies that have an impact on better redistribution of wealth and more extensive regulation at the wage, labor, and environmental realms.

It is possible to collect taxes that no longer depend so much on the burdens on consumption, and therefore on the burdens over workers so that the tax policy will acquire a much more progressive character (more favorable for workers and people with lower income), also strengthening social policies and social protection networks of the State, all of which also have a redistributive impact. This increases aggregate demand, favoring stability, and growth, by avoiding an accentuation of economic cycles, since workers enjoy higher incomes and the State can raise public spending. As a result of this, the cyclical crises rooted in low aggregate demand and overproduction of goods and services are fought, and as it will be seen later, the problem of excess savings which generates dependence on the level of private investor confidence is avoided, being problems which create a vicious circle where the fall in aggregate demand causes unemployment and freezing of wages, which generates a new fall in aggregate demand. There is no need to worry about the problem of excess savings because if the central fund is too high, the State can cut the sinking funds and the capital remains with the direct producer, while if the funds are not enough, the State can raise the sinking funds on each company.

Therefore, in addition to denying private owners the freedom of circulation for business investments, which enriches them at the expense of workers, it is also denied the possibility of saving large amounts of capital to the point that they can't be invested productively, which also enriches private owners to the detriment of workers, who suffer most from the consequences of economic crises and the nature of financial markets. By preventing the problem of excess savings, there is no longer a dependency regarding the level of private investor confidence, confidence that tends to decrease if the pace of the economy does not satisfy them. As the funds for the new investments of companies are generated through their sinking funds, which consist of an amount of money that by law must be set aside from the rest of the capital of companies and sent to the central fund, there is no need to worry about the level of investor confidence.

Large sums of capital from private savings can be mobilized and sent to existing companies or companies that aspire to exist so that they can make the economy stay healthy thanks to their investments, and not only can do that, but also will be forced to do so for the sake of the system as a whole, since companies must necessarily establish a fund with a certain amount of money that is precisely the fund that will be sent to the central fund, and to create this fund, they must necessarily invest. If the sinking funds are too high, the State can cut them and the capital remains with the direct producer, while if the capital in the central fund is not enough, the State can raise the sinking funds of the companies and therefore cover the need to finance them. Wages set by states and unions, if they are too high without productivity rising enough, can generate unemployment, because in the face of excess savings, entrepreneurs would lose the confidence of an adequate return on their investments and would tend to hire fewer workers because they should pay higher wages. Faced with this situation, the State would only raise public spending to fight unemployment, which would cause it to enter into a deficit and it should issue more money to finance it, which has inflationary consequences.

The previous problem would become an inconvenience to raise wages through political parties, government boards, and unions, as long as we do not have a mechanism to address the problem of excess savings, and the only mechanism possible is precisely the same one by which State control is carried out over the investments of companies, and with this mechanism is enough. For that reason, if we want to avoid the relocation of the investments of companies to other parts of the globe, linked to the phenomenon of free capital mobility, and still want to preserve economic efficiency, we need to apply State control over industrial investments, and more precisely, a control carried out in the way I have proposed.

As Schweickart mentioned when presenting his own model, the sinking funds obtained from the pressure of the State fulfill the critical function of equalizing the aggregate supply with the aggregate demand and therefore reaching the point of balance between both. If it is desired to reduce aggregate supply and raise aggregate demand, the State should only cut the sinking funds, which allows private individuals' income and private consumption to increase, since individuals will be able to demand higher wages as sinking funds become smaller, while decreasing the part of the capital that is not destined to the payment of wages, all of which occurs to the detriment of aggregate supply.

If it is desired to increase the aggregate supply and lower aggregate demand, the State simply has to raise the sinking funds, since to face the task of accumulating capital and to set it aside to direct it to the central fund, companies should moderate both the capital that remains with owners as the one destined for workers in existing jobs, so that they can make greater productive investments, which increases aggregate supply. The problem of credit cards as generators of debt can be fought in a more efficient way, to enjoy an economy that to get up on their feet no longer is in need to in-debt their individuals with interest rates. Foreign direct investment, whose benefit lies in bringing infrastructure, new technologies and practices, and in the generation of new job opportunities, finds as its incentive the fact that State control over the investments of companies, by avoiding the macroeconomic instability that arises from the freedom of movement for business capital, and also the instability that is rooted in the excess of savings and the dependence on the level of private investor confidence, generates a more favorable climate for investment.

Macroeconomic stability provided by State control over business investment would stimulate growth, and growth would bring new investment opportunities for foreign investors. The majority of foreign direct investment continues being among the most developed countries even though they present higher wages and better working conditions (in 2007 the developed countries received 70% of the investment, the developing countries 25% and the economies in transition the remaining 6%.) due to more and better infrastructure, and also to a more educated population. In addition, capital flight, which has various causes, such as a changing demand, the development of technologies that negatively affect markets, social or infrastructure problems that make a region less attractive, etc., ceases to be a problem.

The application of State control over the investments of companies would imply the beginning of a financing mechanism that would rationalize the relationship between financial capital and the companies that compete in a goods and services market, among other things avoiding private capital flight, which decreases the savings capacity of governments to pay their debts. If the economy should remain in a stationary state, now this would not imply general impoverishment due to a crisis in private investor confidence, it only will imply profits remaining a constant, which is crucial taking into account that growth will find limitations rooted from the fact that we live on a planet that needs environmental balance and that maintains resources which aren't unlimited.

As long as growth continues, the industries of cities will compete for the demand for agricultural goods, and as pollution degrades the quality of the water, the distribution of available water supplies could decisively affect the prospects for regional human development. Changes in global climate and higher levels of carbon dioxide could adversely affect crops and yields, especially in tropical areas. This would exacerbate the longer-term problem of soil erosion, resulting from intensive soil exploitation, poor peasant practices, and deforestation. In addition, increasing demand for the limited supplies of freshwater and the increasingly deteriorating quality of water sources could cause conflicts between regions and countries. Keynes said: "We cannot, as responsible men do better than base our policy on the evidence we have and adapt it to the five or ten years over which we may suppose ourselves to have some measure of pre-vision..." (Keynes 1920).

Individuals, although they no longer perceive economic growth, and although some have to work more than others, clearly perceive when a society is more egalitarian, and this perception, added to the perception of having a certain level of assured well-being, and to the perception of access to all kinds of new technologies, serve as a counterweight to the perception that the economy has reached a stationary state, so there are no conditions for individuals as to rise to destroy the structures of the existing order.

In addition, unlike what happens in capitalism, it is no longer necessary for the economy to grow rapidly and indefinitely to avoid impoverishment, we must remember that stopping free mobility for business capital also allows for greater regulation of wages and working conditions, as well as greater regulation of companies regarding the protection of the environment. The struggle of individuals is no longer practically a struggle for subsistence as it was in the feudal order, the economic order would be a reasonably egalitarian one, and finally, social mobility would be considerably greater than that existing in the feudal order of the master and serf, all of which decreases social conflict. The institutional system must always favor the development of the Normative social process, and therefore favor the fulfillment of the authentic will of the People, instead of being based on their manifested will.

THE PATRIOTIC ECONOMIC POLICY

The Normative State is a collectivist one since work and direction must aim towards the collective aspect, therefore being opposed to individualism and seeking the greatest welfare of the People as a whole united in its organic parts, so each individual must be responsible for his actions. Normativism is a centralist doctrine since the decisions of higher bodies must be binding on lower bodies to make more equal the distribution of resources among regions and localities, as the distributive process is not left to the mercy of regional autonomies. For the decisions of higher bodies to be binding enough regarding decisions of lower bodies, decisions about the distribution of economic resources that each region and locality receives must be centralized, so the central State must control the capital flows for each region, and at a lower level, each locality must receive what each region determines for them.

In the context of applying the above principles, it should be noted that rulers will find more opposition if they are unwilling to raise wages or improving social security at the rate at which other candidates are willing to do so, thus the whole system will be considerably egalitarian. If the new model of the socio-economic organization demonstrates its superiority in achieving general welfare, this will have a profound impact on the political consciousness of a large part of the population, since many would stick to the new model and therefore would like to preserve it. If certain political groups prove to have an alternative which in practice proved to be a very positive one, which through coordination between states, unions and companies created prosperity and stability, it is logical that groups with still capitalist tendencies would tend to lose popularity, together with groups of communist tendencies. Once a Normative State is established in an economy based primarily on bourgeois property ownership, the question of preventing the degeneration of that State into a capitalist one becomes paramount.

To implement Normativism, we need certain favorable conjunctures, such as economic crises in the capitalist system, a fairly capable and committed leadership, certain political crises and weak points affecting rival political sectors, the adequate organization for the People, etc. A good situation, determined by certain conjunctures, may not occur easily and should be exploited to the maximum, and to take full advantage of it we must avoid the degeneration of the Normative State, a State which these conjunctures brought. No longer there will be an excuse to make working conditions and taxes more flexible towards companies to keep investments. It will be necessary to stand for wage increases, improvements in working conditions, a tax policy with an impact benefiting the workers and sectors with less income, and also the maintenance of the State's social networks, to preserve popular support in a context of stronger action on the part of political groups and unions which are defending the workers all over different regions of the world, acting within their states and outside of them.

To organize a process that will lead to the conformation of the Normative mode of production, it is of key importance that the paramount contradiction of capitalism has become untenable for the economic functioning of this system, a system that is only an expression of liberalism. This contradiction consists of the fact that, on the one hand, the development of the productive forces makes it possible to generate more and more wealth with the means of production, and on the other hand that wealth is distributed unevenly, giving rise to an economic and social crisis which generates a climate more prone to a radical change in the nature of the State. A process aimed at ending the capitalist and therefore liberal order will likely find its conditions of development while the economic crisis of capitalism is unleashed, being a product of the present conditions in this system, that were already pointed out by Marxism, and which create a resurgence of instability and struggle between the sectors of society.

As is well known, the capitalist State is under the control and influence of large corporations to act for the benefit of capitalist firms. The Normative State, being the organ of society with the highest hierarchy and the main entity in charge of maintaining the organic functioning of society as a whole, must aspire to make each part of that society as similar as possible to an efficient and complex gear for a machine made with parts of a more or less interdependent nature. A critical sector of the economy that should be in private hands due to issues related to economic efficiency must be under the strict control and surveillance of the State. The State, as a representative not only of the capitalists but of the workers and the rest of society, has a hierarchy which is above all other social agents, structuring the relationships between various social agents for the sake of sustainable human development.

We must avoid a misconception of freedom in general, one that perceives it as a set of freedoms that do not constitute an organic whole, but a mechanical whole of freedoms. This is a mechanical conception as it is stated that some freedoms should exist even though their existence generates more adverse than positive results for general freedom in society as a whole, which is composed of several freedoms, including those related to access by people to economic goods and those related to their health and safety. Sometimes the same inertia of an economic and social system generates the conditions for its downfall since this same inertia determines how adaptable a system is or how unstable it will be. The same inertia that dismantled the Soviet system is currently affecting the global capitalist system and, therefore, the universalist doctrine of liberalism. Contrary to what is believed by some people, patriotism is not always an evil doctrine, and its power to unite a People around common interests is fundamental, insofar as a country can only be defended from both it's internal and external enemies if there is in the People an emotional basis to defend what they identify with, as to achieve, among other things, greater government stability, the preservation of People's culture and identity, and greater economic growth in the context of a struggle against liberalism and other doctrines that are enemies of humanity.

Regrettably, some Russian patriotic sectors identified themselves with Fascism and National-Socialism, without having much idea of how the National-Socialist ideology really was, especially in its anti-Russian and anti-Slavic character. They also lack proper knowledge of how to develop adequate policies for Russia. It must be clarified that the fundamental basis of a patriotic economic policy is the economic principles of the Normative system that I have already detailed, that is, the principles related to State control over business investments, which imply putting an end to the freedom of circulation for business capital, therefore increasing the sovereignty of the country, especially of its workers. They also imply the creation of an economy that, because it is more prosperous and more stable, and because it does not suffer from a crisis of confidence having their cause in foreign economic downturns, or sanctions and other events originated abroad, achieves more independence from foreign economies.

We must not lose sight of the fact that a true patriotic economic policy, whether in Russia or in any other country, can only emerge and succeed in the framework of State control over business investments, where the mechanisms that I have proposed in this first part of the book are used, which are anti-liberal in nature. However, there are other principles and measures that must be put forward to create a truly patriotic economic policy, within the context of choosing between free trade or protectionism in the economical relationship between countries. Those who promote free trade believe it will bring unprecedented development to regions around the world. They want the more developed countries to open up to exports from the less-developed ones and vice versa, they want countries to liberalize their markets and let the free flow of capital, goods, and services do their job.

But as Stiglitz mentions in his book "Making globalization work", free trade is one of the most controversial aspects of globalization. Effectiveness, when economic liberalization is pursued without adequate attention to institutional structures, has been seriously questioned as a result of the Asian financial crisis and the brutal experience with liberalization in transition economies (Stiglitz 2000). Clearly, the years of free trade were not a cure-all for many countries lagging behind in their human development, being a case worthy of analysis that of Mexico when joining NAFTA, even though it is not convenient for the US to have a poor and unstable neighbor on its borders, from where thousands must immigrate, bringing social instability and immigration issues. Free trade has not achieved anything but the maintenance of a close dependence by the Mexican economy, without achieving a significant development of it in comparison to its northern neighbors, so that poverty along with inequality remains as the order of the day, as it happens for example with other countries of the region, after decades of liberalizing and free trade policies.

The fact that agriculture is no longer a primary activity in many places has led to a deagrarianization of productive activity, and to social and family disintegration, together with conflicts in the distribution and access to land, as well as to the emergence of new actors and new social identities. What makes free trade one of the most controversial aspects of globalization is obviously the effects it generates: a drop in wages and working conditions due to global competition, unemployment, and even the loss of State sovereignty due to the economic dependence of peoples on external markets, with the last thing being notably seen in the peoples with less economic development, where industries must still emerge and it is necessary to protect them so that they continue emerging, and where growth is still being generated by exports.

Russia did not get rid of being a country that continues depending to a large extent on its exports of oil, gas, minerals, and other abundant elements in the country. Although in recent years Russia has witnessed a great development of its economy, Russia has been until now an emerging country, therefore with emerging industries that must be protected. But even if Russia ceases being an emerging country and completely becomes a developed country, it won't escape the problems of a capitalist system, among these a loss of sovereignty that also occurs in the most developed economies, as imports of goods and services from countries with lower wages and worse working conditions unleash economic pressure that forces lower wages in more developed countries.

This is done for the companies that operate in the more developed countries to increase their competitiveness against the products of countries where wages do not reach the levels observed in the peoples with greater development of their economies. It is of paramount consideration that a drop in the income of the most developed countries would have a negative impact on those less developed countries that sell goods and services to these peoples. It can be a long time before workers in the developed world, who do not have jobs due to globalized competition find new jobs. Both in the developed and underdeveloped world, the situation in relation to employment worsens in the older sectors of the population, who decide to retire earlier, as well as in the case of the less qualified workers, who are the most affected by globalization. Even if the workers of the developed world do not lose their jobs; their income and profits will probably decrease, since their wages must be lowered so that the entrepreneurs place their merchandise at more competitive prices in relation to the goods from abroad. Therefore, even if the liberalization of trade is beneficial to the economy as a whole, a substantial part of the population of that economy will lose from that, especially the workers, and among workers who lose the most are the less qualified ones.

When companies must close because of global competition, capitalists are also affected, and this is the reason for the relative opposition to true free trade even on the side of developed countries. For all the above, developed countries must place certain barriers to free trade, as the more competitive prices of countries with a cheaper workforce would wreak havoc even in the industrial powers. Free trade has not really been put into practice, what has happened was a series of disparate agreements between the advantaged and disadvantaged, wherein the developing countries markets were open to the sale of all kinds of goods and services from developed countries, without reciprocity between both parties. A series of barriers have generated an asymmetric relationship in the commercial relationships between states, where states from developed countries can subsidize their industries with a vast amount of capital.

This unequal competition made worse the situation for the peoples with less economic development in relation to how they would be if a fair and truly free trade had been put into practice. But as Stiglitz mentions, even if trade agreements had been fair and free, not all countries would have benefited (or benefited a lot), and not all the people residing in the most benefited countries would have had their share of that benefit. It is easy for more developed countries to end the opportunities that opening markets can offer for developing countries, because the latter lacking the infrastructure to send their goods to the market, as well as the ability to achieve the quality that would be demanded in the markets of the most advanced countries, and among other things, the lacking of an institutional quality that would be of good help for human development. Trade liberalization exposes developing countries to certain risks arising from the lack of development of their industries, and workers in those developing countries, unlike workers in more developed ones, lack qualifications, compensation and bank savings which would allow them to face a situation of dismissal in the same way as workers in the developed world do.

In addition, and as Stiglitz's work mentions, although even in the case that the country as a whole benefits from free trade, not all of its members benefit in the same way, giving rise to rich countries where wealth is concentrated on top of the social pyramid. Globalization has not only led to phenomena like outward-oriented growth in the absence of effective regulatory measures, but it is also capable of generating large accumulations of capital within the economic elites of each People. For example, the fortune of billionaire Carlos Slim came representing 7% of Mexico's GDP. On July 3, 2007, he managed to surpass Bill Gates in fortune, becoming the richest man on the planet. It is estimated that his fortune amounted to more than 70 billion dollars in July 2007. For the aforementioned factors, in Russia, a patriotic economic policy based on the protection of the Russian economy must be applied, even if Russia becomes a fully developed country. Certain freedom of trade between countries can help human development, if done fairly and complemented by adequate protectionist policies and measures, considering that the most successful countries regarding the development of their economies achieved their success through exports. In the case of loans granted by international financial institutions, Russia, like any other country, must maintain the policy of moderation in the requests for loans granted to the domestic economy.

Loans from those institutions have come with interest rates and repayment dates, and for many developing countries the costs of accepting these loans from international private financial institutions, and also public ones (such as the IMF, the World Bank, and development banks) were more than the benefits. Cases for analysis are, for example, the Spanish-speaking countries, like Argentina, which was dragged into the crisis of 2001 by its external debt, or the countries of South-east Asia during the crisis of 1997, or more recently the case of Greece, where the external debt went out of control. Countries should adopt a policy of moderation in their loans by international financial organizations, especially if markets and governments do nothing to reduce the risk of borrowing. In this way, we can avoid the capital hemorrhaging that has occurred from indebted economies to parasitic international organizations, although luckily in Russia the problem of having a large external debt does not exist yet.

When countries are willing to borrow, they should make the loans in their own currencies and not in foreign currencies, in the prospect of modification in exchange rates. The costs and benefits of external debt are distributed unequally, with those who do well receiving much of the benefit, and those who do poorly perceiving much of the cost. According to Stiglitz (2006) "The hard lesson of the last fifty years is that even when there are high social returns on investments—say, in education, health, and roads— it is hard for a government to raise money to repay loans", which means that countries have to rely more on their own financing.

The governments' savings capacity is a very important factor to take into account, and also the savings capacity of companies, to cope with the repayment of loans and indebtedness. The savings capacity increases if governments adopt a policy of moderation in the loans requested from the domestic economy to non-residents and if at the same time, they make sufficient expenses and policies (in education, health, infrastructure, etc.) that will create internal demand. According to Stiglitz, countries often expect trade agreements to attract foreign investment and boost employment, but as this author points out, companies look at several areas before investing, including the quality of the workforce, infrastructure, geography, and political and social stability.

For this reason, the macroeconomic stability that would favor an economy relatively immune to economic cycles, coupled with adequate public investment in education, research, and technology, is much more effective as employment-creating tools than trade agreements alone, which anyway are usually unfair. Countries whose industries are developing, including Russia, must protect them so that they have time to develop, while countries must protect those industries of a strategic nature, being pillars of the People's economy. Developing countries should focus primarily on increasing the speed with which they acquire technology and knowledge that can equate them with the most developed countries, and not only focus on those sectors where they enjoy a comparative advantage, updating and diversifying their products instead of that.

The question of how to close the knowledge gap is answered by Stiglitz in the following way: producing what is yet unproduced. This author cites the example of the Republic of Korea, where at first the comparative advantage of this country was in producing rice, but when this country began to produce steel, it was noted that it was possible to continue on this road. In fact, protectionism for nascent industries remained a popular idea in Japan during the '60s and in Europe and the United States during the 19th century, so the most developed countries of today were covered under a barrier of protectionism to develop their emerging industries. Through the diversification of production, and through innovation, more and better exports could be made, in addition to making the economies more stable, being able to rely less on primary goods. If, for example, the Type A economies depended exclusively on the production of primary goods, the per-capita size of the most developed and diversified economies (the Type B economies) would always be larger than that of the Type A economies. This is partly due to the fact that Type B would have inhabitants with greater purchasing power who have sufficient income to allocate a higher percentage of consumption to goods with higher added value, so they will not continue consuming primary goods in an equal percentage to those that would exist in Type B, which is experiencing lower levels of development in their economies.

In addition, the characteristics of raw materials are they are homogeneous and easily substitutable goods, and that is why they give rise to volatile markets that at the same time lead to economic instability as a result of the vulnerability of external demand. It is very important to note a growing industrial sector provides additional funds that allow the government to finance education, research, and infrastructure, which in turn generates more growth, generating a positive vicious circle. The developing countries, including Russia with all its military power and a massive number of resources, should not expect significant concessions from the more developed countries since most certainly they won't obtain them, and this affirmation is based on the experience regarding the last treaties. Therefore, I have not even bothered making in this book a recipe for the things that developed countries should do for the least developed, as they will surely do little to reverse the current situation.

Emerging peoples like the Russians must take the initiative on their own, they should not expect gifts from the rest of the world, and they should aspire to sustainable human development, based on the Normative pillars, so that they will be able to break once and for all their chains of dependence on the outside. On the part of the US, Western Europe, and other economically developed regions, they would be uninterested in losing the benefit of their State barriers, as a way to accumulate capital at the expense of the economically underdeveloped peoples, being these latter peoples those with whom true integration would remain for the developed world a way to distribute the cake more than it is willing to do. We must analyze the case of the American Spanish-speaking regions, and the case of Brazil as examples of what should not happen in Russia. Graciarena, in the work "The reconstitution of the State", tells us the following about the emergence of these states: "The new kind of State that was emerging on the march of events generated by crisis, without a preconceived ideological formula to frame and orient it, was partly a hybrid product that combined diverse traits, some of which constituted a novelty in comparison to its European congeners."

These states could not be truly welfare states that responded to the demands of their individuals, and therefore they favored policies like "outward-oriented growth", the perpetuation of the agricultural model, ultra exploitation, and the extensive penetration of foreign capital instead of the development of industry originating in People themselves. In Russia, unlike what happened in those regions, there must be a marked preconceived ideological formula, and this formula can not be other than Normativism, with this doctrine implying the implementation of an economic system that differs as much from capitalism as from communism, having also the aspects regarding a patriotic economic policy which were just mentioned, and the protection of orthodox Christian values against liberalism in all its assertions, such as globalism, materialism and multiculturalism. With regard to integration among the countries of the developing peoples, many integration processes between developing countries and other developing countries have been failures, since these countries have their own State interests which defend fighting tooth and nail.

Some clear examples are what has happened in South America with MERCOSUR, the weakness of African integration, the rivalry between China and India, or between China and Vietnam, and the failure of the Commonwealth of Independent States, led by Russia, where the level of participation of the post-Soviet states that is desired by Russia is not observed in several economic projects. This is because the underdeveloped world and emerging economies, although they share their underdeveloped or emerging condition, are encompassing within them amazingly diverse ethnic, religious, historical, and economic realities.

Many modern analysts seem to forget that within the underdeveloped world there are many underworlds, and one could even speak of a third world of the third world if we take into account the dramatic reality of the most impoverished peoples of the planet. The underdeveloped world has a critical advantage over the developed world that will become increasingly evident in the coming decades: its enormous demographic importance, and as in the case of Russia, the fact that they concentrate the main natural resources. These advantages can be exploited correctly by developing countries, so they do not need a radical economic integration if these countries learn to employ the talent of their population and the rest of the resources that nature provided them with, as a raw material for building an economy that is not based solely on the above. Therefore, they must rely on increasing industrialization and diversification, for which a labor force with sufficient skill is needed, together with adequate public investment in education, infrastructure, and research, and a reduction in income inequality. Countries should be made more competitive through a more skilled workforce, capable of increasing simultaneously the size of the domestic market, industrialization, and the competitiveness of goods and services. This increases sovereignty and economic stability in the face of external shocks and competitiveness vis-à-vis other Peoples, and also to prevent the drop of wages in the less qualified sector, given the great labor demand by the poorest ones.

The expansion of the middle-income sector will inevitably generate an expansion in the demand for more qualified labor, to the detriment of the size of the sector of low-skilled workers who subsist in more precarious conditions. The most qualified labor sectors must be absorbed by expanding industries, and thus the higher qualification of the labor force will push wages upwards and therefore aggregate demand (the increase in aggregate demand will feedback the increase in wages) while the size of the internal market increases and, therefore, economic stability in the face of external shocks as a result of dependence on foreign trade. A good qualification of the workforce will make possible greater industrialization and competitiveness for goods and services, making economies stronger and competitive.

The creation of jobs that require low qualification, and that in modernized societies are notably in the service sector of the economy (which requires low-skilled labor) must give rise to the expansion of a sector of workers with specialist qualification, versatility, and multifunctionality, capable of special intellectual work. One of the elementary aspects of treaties is related to patents. Some treaties involve restrictions on patents, trademarks, industrial designs, geographical indications, and the procurement of plants. Foreign patenting is extremely risky, together with the treaties that involve increasing this patenting since it prevents copying and adapting the technology of other countries. Russia must create its own technologies, as it has done successfully in many areas, and must fight against the foreign patenting of technologies so that it can absorb the technological advances made abroad as quickly as possible. Russia, within the framework of the Normative system, must embark on an unprecedented technological development in the history of the country, taking advantage of the extensive education that the Russian People possess, where the literate population is 99.7%, according to the CIA, and where according to data from 2012, 53% of Russian adults have completed some tertiary stage level in their education, which makes Russia the most educated country in the world.

It is essential that in Russia the euro, the dollar, and other foreign currencies are abandoned more and more as currency in commercial transactions, being replaced by the ruble, and this is crucial in sectors like the oil sector, where it is absolutely clear that Russia must continue with the processes related to increasing the transactions made with rubles to make the Russian economy more independent regarding the influence of the dollar as a reference for oil prices. But nevertheless, this won't be enough at all if we demand genuine independence for the Russian economy. The confidence crisis within the Russian economy must be suppressed once and for all. The confidence crisis is giving Russia severe problems, as could be clearly seen in an economic crisis that began in Russia in 2014.

Overcoming the capitalist mode of production and replacing it with an alternative that unlike communism, is perfectly viable, should be a priority for Russia if it intends entering the world stage as a truly prosperous State and master of its fate. The public sector must provide certain essential services because the private sector alone does not have the incentive to pursue certain socially necessary purposes that could only be pursued outside the market. On the part of the State, it should provide the most efficient and extended coverage possible (and also free) in terms of essential services for the population. These services include education (at primary, secondary, and tertiary levels alike) health, and everything related to social security, of which the entire population should be provided for.

For service to the freedom of individuals, basic needs must be guaranteed, like food, decent housing, health, education, access to electricity, drinking water, and (Why not?) access to the Internet and computing, together with the ability to effectively use those new capabilities, with the importance which they will acquire more and more. When considering that a developing country did not have a reliable market price system, that the business offer was limited and that there was great political instability that did not generate a pleasant climate for investors, it was inevitable for many to see the State as that missing link that unified society to make it change. Currently, this issue is not only in developing countries, but even developed countries also face a crisis regarding how to make market mechanisms operate effectively, and at the same time promote the accumulation of capital, absorb labor, achieve competitiveness against foreign prices, and regulate the disparity in the distribution of economic development.

All these problems, having to be faced at the same time, generated a bottleneck in the escalation towards global development. Stiglitz (2001) mentions that "The effects of government intervention in agricultural pricing became a major concern. Numerous studies presented evidence that misguided agricultural pricing policies were having an adverse effect on the gap between urban and rural incomes, the incentives to produce food and export crops, the ability of governments to establish food reserves, and employment opportunities in farming, processing, and rural industries. The theory of rural organization was advanced through the use of information, risk, and contract analyses" (Binswanger y Rosenzweig 1981; Braverman y Guasch 1986; Stiglitz 1986). It was attempted, in the midst of great civil strife that also weakened the economic apparatus, to build State structures that encompassed various ethnic groups and territories that previously lived in separate areas and continents, and with massive differences in their living standards, so impoverishment and inequality were everywhere.

Countries that started from such backwardness, of course, did not have a reliable market price system, the business offer was limited and was based on monocultures and raw materials, while great political instability did not generate a good climate for strengthening the economy and basic institutions. The 1997 World Bank Report puts forward a set of measures that, in the strictly administrative field, appeal to the promotion of greater competition (for example, through a merit-based contracting system), and appeal to the opening of the "main government institutions" (to break the state monopoly). In line with these principles, the reforms undertaken by the OECD countries have emphasized (...) "organizing the government into groups of agencies and departments (...); in the adoption of strategic decision-making and aimed at obtaining results, using output objectives, performance indicators, payments in relation to results and measures to improve quality; in cutting expenses (...); in greater flexibility; in an improvement of efficiency in the provision of public services; in the promotion of competition in the field and among public-sector organizations." In this way, the reforms prioritize a series of transformations within the State, to improve the performance of the public sector based on the experience accumulated in the private sector. What happened in the theory of development had a lot to do with the ideological climate in the West.

As a result, the theoretical developments and the ideological climate in industrial countries strongly influenced the policy recommendations given to developing countries. This point is clearly seen in the history of the World Bank (Kapur, Lewis and Webb 1997). "Economists tended to regard the Big Push story as essentially nonsensical—if modern technology is better, then rational firms would simply adopt it! (They missed the interaction between economies of scale and market size.) Non-economists tended to think that Big Push stories necessarily involved some rich interdisciplinary stew of effects, missing the simple core. In other words, economists were locked in their traditional models; non-economists were lost in the fog that results when you have no explicit models at all. " (Krugman 1999).

The microcredit policy used to help owners of small and humble nature, including those in rural areas, is an example of how through initial help individuals obtain a base for which to expand their potential after overcoming the difficulties at the beginning. Models of this kind can be designed to reduce the great inequalities between the urban and the rural realms, the displacement of unskilled labor, the lack of support for women, the deterioration in the situation of the new generations in relation to the older happening thanks to the infantilization of poverty and even the crisis of social security systems. Future research on the sources of growth should also address the joint and interdependent action of the causes of growth. But the question is not as simple as it appears here since growth is subject to an unpredictable temporal dimension: the future. Social sciences are not a field characterized by their precise predictions: the collapse of the Soviet Union would have been unimaginable to many even in the '70s, and the failures of a system like this had long-standing roots, and therefore they don't appear just like that. Then, a good beginning would be to reinforce the methods by which State academics and planners can foresee the future, and for that, a valid theoretical framework is needed first of all since future predictions that can be drawn from the Keynesian theory are not the same to those that can be drawn from the neoclassical ones, or from other schools of economic thinking.

Finally, the State must invest heavily in programs that help the population to adopt a healthy lifestyle, while natural medicines and some alternative therapies must be institutionalized so that we can struggle against the terrible epidemic of obesity, cancer, heart diseases, and other physical ailments. But in parallel, the State must have policies that help improve the mental health of the population, having to create a type of formal education that helps the youngest learn to deal with their mind. The state must also institutionalize the use of natural medicines, good at confronting problems like addictions and mental disorders, such as ayahuasca and other medicines, which although psychoactive and hallucinogenic, are useful if a study is previously done related to who is fit to take these medicines, together with the medicine being taken in a place properly prepared and has the necessary rules.

THE FAILURE OF THE COMMUNIST MODEL DRIVEN INSIDE (AND OUTSIDE) THE U.S.S.R

In this section of the book, I make an analysis of the best-known communist model, being driven inside and outside the Soviet Union, as part of my analysis of the second political theory, that is, communism. The first criticism that can be made of this type of communism is clearly that of its strict materialism, and therefore its rejection of Christian values, of spirituality, and of God himself. But in addition to this criticism, a critique of the theory of class struggle should be made, since this class struggle does not achieve anything other than the division of society, while as already mentioned, society needs to function as an organic body, and this class struggle is made with the objective of establishing an economic system that can not work, so the consequence of class struggle is never a more organic functioning for the body of society.

For this reason, criticism of the theory of class struggle must be based on a critique of the different communist economic systems. In Normativism, companies must operate in a competitive goods and services market, having some freedom when interacting among themselves and consumers, and using the law of supply and demand as a mechanism to determine prices, although the market must be regulated by the State due to the phenomenon known as market failures, which occurs with the presence of imperfect competition, externalities, asymmetric information and the presence of public goods. Without a price mechanism regulated by the relations between supply and demand, it is very challenging for a producer or a planner to know what should be produced, how much should be produced and in what variety it should be produced; and at the same time, it is extremely difficult to know which ways are the most effective to carry out economic activities, including the types of marketing. Markets demonstrate an amazing ability to collect and synthesize information regarding all the above issues, and they also have the ability to motivate companies to respond to consumer demand. People do not have to plan their consumption in advance, neither State bureaucrats. Planning depends to a large extent on market laws that, although imperfect, are however useful. Thanks to the market, there is no need to decide which companies should request goods, or in which quantities and dates the delivery should be carried out.

In the market, there is the possibility of encouraging producers in such a way that consumer satisfaction is maximized. In a market economy, every purchase is to the producer a signal that the item in question is in demand. Producers are very motivated, not only to satisfy these demands but for the introduction of new or improved products that people may prefer. The debate between central planning and market economy is known due to its importance in the twentieth century, from the time when it seemed that the centrally planned economy was the economy of the future, until the time when it was seen as a resounding failure, as the clumsiness of economic systems in the Soviet bloc were observed. In the Soviet Union and other communist countries, agriculture was collectivized at the cost of many lives, and businesses were nationalized, market relations were abolished, and an immense state apparatus of central planning was created for running the economy.

For quite some time it seemed that this entirely new way of organizing an economy was the best way to organize human societies and shape the future. The Soviet Union industrialized with Stalin while the West was in an economic depression after the crash of 1929. The Soviet Union survived a German invasion that was absolutely devastating, she was the real responsible for the destruction of the Nazi army, mainly because of enough mobilization of material and human resources, and not only thanks to winter as it is believed by many, especially in the West. Then, without Western help, the Soviet Union was rebuilt after the devastating economic and human effects of the war. Then came the Soviet technological achievements in the field of space exploration and many other technological areas, like medicine and even achievements in computers. Many Western economists analyzed the growth rates of the Soviet Union and calculated the point at which the Soviet economy would surpass that of the United States.

But in an unexpected way, Soviet economic growth stopped, and although the Soviet economy did not collapse, which would only come with the restoration of capitalism, the Soviet model began to show its serious flaws, being unable to distribute the new technologies among the population, and sometimes unable to generate them, neither effectively exploit those developed in capitalist countries. As Marx stated, to fulfill its function of exploitation, capital has to dominate the worker in the process of work, but different forms of domination are coupled with economic formulas that vary according to what form of exploitation is desired. To this extent, the relationship of exploitation is, in addition to being an economic relationship, a relationship that gets inside the forms of political and even cultural domination.

Workers and peasants, and even the managers themselves, both in the Soviet Union and in the other Communist countries, knew how to use a series of instruments as a way to escape State pressure (such as black markets) in response to the continuous shortages and the lack of a market price mechanism for correct regulation of the productive activity. Another instrument was the rotation of personnel and the relaxation of discipline and effort when managing companies, in the absence of an economic incentive to management in the same line of that which private property ownership and competition in a market are capable of giving.

This lack of incentive to efficient management is the problem that makes it undesirable to place certain areas of the productive sector under the ownership and management of a State apparatus. This problem is exacerbated if companies, in addition to being under state managers, suffer from excessive centralism that cuts their autonomy and places them under excessive bureaucratization, in the midst of a State apparatus that can not correctly visualize all the details of the general productive panorama. In China, during the great leap forward, and also in the Soviet Union, many public officials feared giving real figures to their superiors, or invented imaginary figures to increase their prestige, inflating in many cases the real quotas of production with non-existent numbers.

The simple idea of the subordination of science to the requirements of capitalist production is also insufficient to explain "technological trajectories", since ways of satisfying needs are always changing, and this opens space for technological development as to generate an entire range of new fields that may be more important than others, as was in the case of the field of computers. The Soviets could not realize that the technological trajectory was not directed to fields like the steel industry, and they bet on heavy industries but whose tasks did not imply the complex accumulation of scientific knowledge necessary for modern electronics. Sometimes to know when some technologies are imposed instead of others must be left for the market, and to know which paths use new technologies to impose themselves, through the practical needs of a changing world. Undoubtedly the Soviets achieved great scientific developments, but the question is not only to achieve scientific developments (such as those achieved during the space race) but how to distribute this scientific development among the population. Undoubtedly, the bureaucratization of communist science and technology contributed to hinder the correct distribution of technological development or direct it towards unviable trajectories.

Without detailed information from consumers, producers can not know what people want. The fact of knowing when goods are bought is not enough indication. Producers offer different kinds of products, like clothing or any other item that can not please people. Although people want to buy types that can be changed in distribution centers, if nothing else is available, consumers take what they can get. Monotonous goods, poorly adjusted to preferences, were a familiar scene in the countries of the Soviet bloc. Producers have no motivation to find out what consumers really want. The producers of the Soviet Union had production quotas that they tried to fulfill with the consumers in the easiest way possible. Meanwhile, in Asia, the great leap forward, which began in the late 1950s, partly toppled Mao's reputation as China's leader, but not completely, due to his guerrilla past in the struggle against Japanese imperialism, and the fight against the Kuomintang, as well as the achievements in the literacy and unification of China.

The concept of the interventionist State in its simple form is not bad, but the problem is that the Chinese, as if it was deciding between two total opposites, took that concept to the greatest of extremes, only surpassed by Pol Pot's Cambodia, although, unlike the Polpotian vision, which was the return to the agricultural and quasi-feudal state, the task of the Chinese consisted in an abrupt irruption into the industrial world, even though it required an enormous sacrifice. As a result of collectivization, a large number of peasants lost their private property, but more important than that, many lost their lives. Attempts have been made to attribute the traditional figures that claimed tens of millions of deaths due to famine as a result of a strategic error rather than a political decision, but in any case, the failure of the model was evident, even in its initial stages, and even so, with manipulation of the real numbers and lack of transparency, the plans were continued.

In Normativism, companies must buy raw materials and machinery from other companies and sell their products to other companies or consumers. Normally, prices won't be regulated except by the price mechanism of supply and demand, but this does not mean that certain regulations on pricing should not be implemented in cases where there are market failures resulting from monopolies, and in cases where climatic variations affect agricultural activities. Naturally, antitrust laws must protect the market system itself from falling due to its own weight, but added to these laws, there must be harsh penalties that punish economic fraud, which can get out of control and come to light especially during times of crisis. In the case of asymmetric information, the State must intervene to provide the actors in the market with information they need to operate in it more efficiently.

Let's imagine the companies as identifying the whole tree, and the State sees a whole forest but does not distinguish all the details of each tree, then the companies can determine details of the market that can't be noticed by the State alone, but meanwhile, the State can provide companies with certain details about what the forest is like, beyond the tree where each company is located. In addition to providing information about contracts, interest rates, working capital, nominal wages, real wages and the quality of products, the State must encourage companies to exploit new markets that companies could otherwise not exploit, due to not considering them profitable in the absence of sufficient infrastructure for those markets.

The only solution is financing first with the State these infrastructures, and to generate the institutions and culture that favor these infrastructures, since not everything is about money, it is also about institutions and a psychology in individuals that are like the essence of an animal or the essence of plants, without them they can not adapt or survive. In the same way that we must discover what vibrates in each one of these creatures so that they can adapt, in addition, we have to discover what must vibrate in each institution and in each mind to achieve the objectives that we set ourselves. We will have our companies or businesses, but it is not merely about money the question of how to adapt them, it also about what kind of infrastructure will create a sustainable human development, and what kind of institutions make individuals happier and more complete.

OTHER COMMUNIST MODELS

The flaws of central planning are not solved by the calls for a self-managed and democratic communism, since this kind of system, based on democratic management of businesses and democratic management of the market, experience their own inherent problems. Some of these self-management models are more radical than others, and one of the most radical is called PARECON, proposed by Michael Albert and Robin Hahnel. This model is based on work centres being non-hierarchical and therefore are self-managed by their workers. They all receive almost the same income, and there is no market mechanism for determining prices, production and competition. Instead of a market mechanism, consumers themselves determine what they desire to consume and in what quantities, but they need advice teams that reach agreements between consumers and producers to level production. In this model, there are also councils in charge of levelling wages among workers, rotating workers doing more remunerated tasks to those being paid less in the various companies.

These councils not only would give rise to a bureaucratic sector that will inevitably accumulate power, but will give rise to an economy suffering from similar problems to those observed in the Soviet model. In the first place, a scarce differentiation of wages would cause demotivation in the labour force, because different tasks require a different effort that must be rewarded. Demotivated workers could be monitored, but there would be problems related to how committees would be able to know if complaints are caused due to the mere personal issues among workers, and the moral burden when denouncing one's co-workers or even the impossibility of evaluating correctly cases in which someone works more than the others, since everyone would want to say that they work above average. In addition, because each one should be evaluated according to effort and not productivity, committees cannot evaluate correctly the cases in which workers make mistakes lowering company productivity.

With all that, only a significant reduction in People's productivity can be expected.

With regard to the mechanism proposed in this model for replacing markets, it would undoubtedly disturb individual privacy since a committee needs to receive lists of the products which persons want to buy, and in addition to that, making those huge lists would be too big a task, taking into account that they need several corrections to match supply with demand. Few individuals would have the motivation, time or ability to make intelligent decisions during the voting used in this model at the level of the whole community, to elaborate the final plans. Self-managed companies do not have the same incentives for expansion that capitalist companies, since hiring workers would imply in this case more people with whom to share the capital of companies. For this reason, workers would not be sufficiently motivated to carry out new hiring, which would generate a trend towards unemployment for a significant sector of the labour force.

The biggest problem of an economy based on businesses controlled by their own workers is the inability of these businesses to accumulate the amount of savings needed for investments, whether investments aimed at expansion and maintenance in those businesses, innovation, or hiring new workers, because workers who already occupy positions in the cooperatives would destine the money to their personal income. In Schweickart's model, the same mechanism of social control of investment is able to avoid the previous problem. The State would only need maintaining both the tax on capital assets and depreciation funds at an adequate level since in order to generate more economic surplus, workers should moderate the part of the capital destined to their personal income in order to face the tax and funds, which automatically makes them invest more in capital accumulation and hiring new workers. In this way, the tax on capital assets and depreciation funds linked to it, can be maintained at a level where sufficient employment is generated and the part of the capital that goes to the personal income of workers is moderated.

Nevertheless, Schweickart proposes the banks of his model have in their criteria also the generation of employment when granting subsidies to companies, combining this criterion with the criterion of efficiency, and this measure would be accompanied by the performance of the State as an employer of last resort. Whatever the measures we use, Schweickart's model has the problem that in a naïve way it does not take into account that workers, who now manage the means of production and unlike the capitalists make up a large majority of the population, do not necessarily have to accept the measures which the State imposes on them to cut the part of the capital destined to their personal income as to guarantee full employment. Being a large majority of the population, they can exert a considerable social pressure that will inevitably end up influencing the structures of the State, making impossible for it to put in place the measures keeping unemployment and productive investments at an "acceptable" level since these measures imply forcing workers to pay taxes and make funds separate from the part of the capital that goes to their personal income.

This would turn impossible models like that of Schweickart, at least within the framework of a polyarchy. Workers will push for lower taxes on their companies and the funds which they must establish, to increase their personal income. In a model like this, there will be plenty of opportunist politicians who, to attract People's support, will promise cuts in businesses taxes and funds, which of course means greater autonomy for workers when managing their companies. Therefore, self-managed companies would not generate enough funds for new investments (funds that can not be used for the workers' personal income). In addition to the above, regional inequalities will become wider, since workers from companies operating in different regions will push to the detriment of power held by the central authority, with the aim of reducing taxes going towards a centrally controlled social fund.

This social fund, being centrally controlled, also makes it possible to avoid the imbalances between the wealth of regions responsible for making communities more unstable. Anyway, workers would push to reduce the burden on their different regions, which benefits disadvantaged regions, causing an increase in the autonomy of the different regions with relation to the central authority. This happened in the Yugoslav case, where in the wake of the ideological onslaught, fewer taxes were charged and the State-controlled central investment fund was dismantled, giving rise to greater financial autonomy for regions and companies, and to self-managed banks that lent capital to cooperatives. Inequality was increased significantly between firms that operated within the same industry, between different industries, the one existing between cities and the countryside, and inequality between the different Yugoslav regions. For example, as for Slovenia and Kosovo, the difference was six to one respectively. Even in the Yugoslav one-party regime, with authoritarian mechanisms that delayed the natural liberalization and degeneration of a self-management model, a process of excessive liberalization was undertaken. This was the result of pressure from large sectors of society, both by workers who pushed for more autonomy of their firms in relation to the State and by the regions as a whole, which demanded financial autonomy from the central government.

To work, a system like the one proposed by Schweickart would need a non-polyarchical and authoritarian form of government, as in the case of Yugoslavia under the one-party government, so in that model, it is required to destroy democracy, and even in an authoritarian form of government, the survival of Schweickart's model would not be guaranteed. At present, in the political realm within parties and governing boards around the world, there is almost null support or interest for the collectivization of the economy in cooperatives or worker councils as proposed by some communist authors.

Another problem is there is a lack of real involvement of workers in the management of cooperatives, especially when they are of large scale since it is inevitable that the complex procedures and time spending needed, will end up generating a distance between delegates and the workers who elected them, while workers start to lose interest in management activities. If we take into account the problem of implementing economic models like the previous ones, which must destroy democracy, then its applicability becomes impossible. This applicability is trapped in a lack of political will that is a consequence of liberal institutions, the disinterest of workers, the intentions of capitalist owners, and the intentions of bureaucracies. In the case of bureaucracies, they take over the processes of changing the existing order and are interested in State and bureaucratic management of companies, instead of self-management.

For these reasons, the economic model proposed by David Schweickart, despite being economically viable while respecting their premises, is politically unfeasible, since people are not merely numbers that act rationally, Each one is representing interest groups that do not always think in favour of the collective, even if these interest groups exist within the workers, within each firm and each locality, and even if defending the particular interests of each of these groups supposes dooming the fate of society as a whole.

Anyhow, in Normativism there must always be a part of the economy composed of cooperatives, having to fulfil their work efficiently. The cooperative sector should be placed mainly in realms like the agricultural sector, housing cooperatives, financial and consumer cooperatives, as well as in many small-scale enterprises that emerge as the alternative for some people to enter the market. David Schweickart is the most remarkable modern anti-capitalist thinker I have read. Heinz Dieterich Steffan, promoter of the so-called socialism of the 21st century, does not even come close to David Schweickart. Although I do not agree with one of the three aspects of Schweickart's economic model, namely that of generalized cooperative self-management, I think that Schweickart's proposals regarding the social control of investment that an economy needs, and his defence of an economy where there is still a goods and services market where prices are largely determined by competition between companies, is something that in itself makes him one of the most valuable modern thinkers I have read in the field of economics.

The mechanism by which State control of investment is applied in my model is inspired by Schweickart's mechanism, based on a tax on the capital assets of companies that, like my model, is a part of the capital being separated from companies and sent to a central fund controlled by the State, thus avoiding the already mentioned problems of capitalism in relation to the dependence of the economy on investor confidence, the free circulation for business capital and the dependence of the economic system on indefinite and exponential growth. The only difference between my model for controlling investment and Schweickart's model is that Schweickart's is based on a tax on capital goods that completely replaces interest rates at least in what to business investments is concerned. My model, by continuing to be based on bourgeois property ownership of the means of production, needs interest rates in the process of capital accumulation of each company, because capitalist owners have an incentive to seek the expansion of their businesses.

I recall the joyous moment when in a fortunate turn of destiny I could have in my hands the English version of Schweickart's book entitled "Against Capitalism", in the library of a Uruguayan faculty, when I was only 19 years old. But before that, I had already made inroads into Marxist literature, and over time I carried out a rigorous analysis of the thought of Marx himself. Marx uses the term "first phase of communism" when referring to what Marxists today call as "socialism," and "second phase of communism" to refer to what the former call as "communism."

Marx does not directly use the term "socialism" to refer to any of these phases. The first phase of communism, according to Marxist theory, takes place in a period of transition between capitalism and communism, and this last phase implies not only the suppression of private property ownership of the means of production and suppression of wage labor. It also implies the extinction of mercantile production and the law of value, the overcoming of division between intellectual and manual labor, extinction of the subordination to division of labor in general, as well as a distribution criterion that was based on the principle "From each according to his ability, to each according to his needs."

On the political level it implies the extinction of the State after the suppression of social classes, and in the social level, the emergence of a solidary "new man" rid of alienation. The Marxist criterion "From each according to his ability to each according to his needs", the extinction of mercantile production, of the law of value, of anarchy in production, and even of money, purportedly would be reached in the second stage of the communist society, when scarcity disappears and there is enough common wealth to satisfy the needs of all. However, all of the above won't be desirable, since the ways in which individuals satisfy their needs are not static, but extremely changing and have been on the rise since Marx wrote "Critique of the Gotha program." The way in which people today meet their needs is much more complex, covering a whole new range of appliances, medicines, real-estate structures, vehicles, luxuries and amenities that were inaccessible in the nineteenth century, and to which it will be added different types of goods and services that today do not even exist or are too expensive for a certain part of the population.

In addition, in modern consumer societies, individuals will tend to renew their products and to acquire the newest, most advanced and practical ones. This renovation does not happen so often with products that are even passed on from generation to generation, such as a set of chairs, formal clothes, a wall clock, a mirror in the living room, etc. For this reason, the problem of scarcity would strongly persist, not allowing enough wealth to satisfy the material needs of all in the way that Marx believed when imagining the superior phase of communist society. Given the problem of scarcity, efficiency provided by the existence of a competitive goods and services market, and by material incentives at work, will continue to be essential for the proper functioning of an economy. One way to summarise Stimmel's theory regarding the ways in which social interactions try to satisfy variable human needs is to understand how, in general terms, human nature seeks continuous improvement. So much that needs in the satisfaction process are continually open to change, connoted by a subjectivism that is marked by the arrival of cultural values in each context and phase of social evolution, in such a way that satisfying a need becomes considered as a starting point to undertake new forms of satisfaction, aspirations and desires.

Therefore, cultural transformations, social changes and the new values that they entail must be considered at all times. Generally speaking, the appearance of new needs is usually discussed, when new conditions in permanent change should be discussed, which means that needs are met in different ways in comparison to previous, historical periods or non western cultures. The new relations of production and their nature affect the changing conditions that make us think of new needs when in reality it is about the new requirements necessary for the reproduction of the economic model. Thus, uniting the analysis of Stimmel with that of Marx, it can be said that the division of labour and the direction assigned to technological innovations in capitalism create the conditions that give rise to new problems and new ways of accessing human needs, while at the same time paving the way for a mind with unlimited desire.

And even if solving the problem of scarcity was possible, we must take into account the current limitations regarding sustainable human development and the billions of people who today have to share the world's resources: what environmental problems would exist in a future society where each one could completely satisfy his material needs? Marx evidently does not deal with this modern question that would become more notorious, as history goes by and the material productive forces of society unleash increasing potential. The subordination to the division of labour must continue because the contrast between intellectual and manual labour should remain, as there are individuals with greater skills and knowledge for certain tasks, while a large sector of people with jobs does not require special qualification, multifunctionality, or intellectual work, as opposed to a qualified and multifunctional sector of workers.

As stated by Marxists, in the first phase of communism there is still economic aspects of the capitalist mode of production, like mercantile production and the law of value, a distribution based on the principle "From each according to his ability to each according to his work", together with the contrast between manual and intellectual work, and subordination to the division of labour. If in the same way that Marxists we were to postulate the overcoming of a society characterized by what they call as social classes, then the existence of the State, which supposes effective monopoly and legitimate exercise of violence in a given community, could only be an end in itself instead of being merely an instrument for achieving the goal of establishing the communist society.

This is because material conditions which would lead to the abandonment of collectivism will inevitably exist even though what the Marxists call as "social classes" have been suppressed. Due to the impossibility of solving the problem of scarcity, which also makes necessary the existence of a goods and services market, and also due to the nature of human behaviour, material conditions would push in opposite direction to a collectivist organization if the State disappears. This is because, within the framework of scarcity, individuals would compete for resources, breaking with even basic rules of behaviour, while they would be tempted to hire waged labour and thus lower their costs and maximize their benefits, and in their search for profits, they will feel tempted to engage in a selfish behaviour, contrary to common good.

Due to the persistence of scarcity, that compels to compete for resources, the existence of the State, and therefore its monopoly of legitimated violence, are still necessary to enforce rules of behaviour, and also to distribute the resources that society needs, financing works and public services, undertakings and research. The State must redistribute wealth among regions, and put the rules of the game in the competitive market, and also have control over the way businesses invest. Anyway, it is important to recognize that the economism of which Marx has been accused could be a myth which arose from the circumstances in which Marx was involved. Marx does not tell us economics is the only factor that moves world's history, but he gave to economics its deserved place that was not recognized by many thinkers of the time, and therefore, the main struggle was concentrated on these thinkers.

In a letter to Joseph Bloch, Engels stated the original Marxist conception was distorted in such a way that the economy was given too great determinism in the analyses of society that were based on historical materialism. Although Marx's analysis and critique of capitalism are extremely valuable, Marx does not present any viable alternative to capitalism in his work. While Marx possessed enough data at his disposal to make an analysis and critique of capitalism, he did not have the data or events in his time to propose what should replace capitalism, and unfortunately, now unworkable and disastrous models that were applied in the Soviet Union, the other countries of the Warsaw Pact, Maoist China, and other regions, were based on Marx thought. One author that I consider as valuable within Marxism is Gramsci, since according to Gramsci, the power of the dominant "classes" over the proletariat and all the "classes" subjected in the capitalist mode of production is not solely given by the control of the repressive apparatuses of the State, because if such power was to be overthrown, only putting an armed force equivalent or superior to work for the proletariat would be enough. Capitalist and liberal power is given fundamentally by the cultural "hegemony" that the dominant groups manage to exercise over the subordinates, through the control of the educational system, religious institutions and the media.

Any revolutionary process would require a revolution of the cultural basis of the states, basis which relies on the dominant sectors. Gramsci was opposed to Bolshevik economism, economism that he considers a misinterpretation of Marxism, and instead sets a vision where culture is the life force that makes revolutionary change possible. Normativism is an ideology that takes into account the collective aspect, but also one that takes into account the individual, which is the basis of all collectives. It will be very challenging to cooperate and achieve a consensus due to our diverse points of view, although there are many things on which everyone agrees. Anyway, at this moment we have to unite simply to survive and live with dignity.

The People must generate a unity that allows managing society in a balanced way; cushioning the changes that are taking place and channelling them, and this is only possible with the existence of a common identity treated in a similar way for all. This homogenization facilitates a positive control both in the political and economic realms, being what a model of State needs. But we must avoid producing homogenization where there should not be, or heterogenization where that should not be present. It is necessary to know the nature of the People's thinking even before they begin thinking. Communism, even if we structure it correctly, is contrary to human nature, and that is why even if we structure it correctly, in the long run, the system will degenerate and lead to disaster. Communist thinkers do not accept or do not know that communism requires impossible altruism on the part of human beings to be viable, and the suppression of instincts deeply rooted in the consciousness of modern people.

THE THIRD POLITICAL THEORY

Many who claim today to be an alternative to liberalism and communism, defending the legacy of the third political theory, namely fascism and national-socialism, express themselves as if this third political theory did not have its own obvious flaws and dangers, and as if it was dissociated from atrocious crimes that did not even save the third political theory from being defeated militarily and ideologically in the hecatomb of the Second World War, where National-Socialism, Italian fascism, Croatian fascism, Hungarian fascism, Romanian fascism, and Japanese fascism were all crushed in what undoubtedly meant a dramatic end for the third political theory. It would be a mistake to say the birth of the key elements of the third political theory was only after the end of the first world war, since this movement has its true roots in very old thoughts that place special emphasis on territory, tradition, and war, and seeing it from its roots, the bulk of the third political theory is clearly previous to liberalism.

Dugin's fourth political theory has already been pointed out as being recycled fascism (neofascism), but these words surely come from ignorance. The Fourth Political Theory should not be linked to fascism or National-Socialism for several reasons. The first of them is that neither fascism nor National-Socialism had the objective of true destruction of capitalism since although they promoted social programs, they never managed to overcome the contradictions of capitalism. Although it is known that National Socialism was able to eradicate unemployment in Germany and that the German economy grew by 50% between 1933 and 1938, the German economy was driven by a loan policy that had mortgaged the future of Germany making necessary the wars of aggression. Unemployment in Germany had been eradicated, and the economy grew, but behind this is the fact that people capable of working had to do any kind of work that the government offered them or go to a concentration camp, the fact that workers could not leave their jobs without government permission, that working hours increased from 60 to 72 hours per week by 1939, and that by 1939 government debts had increased to 40 billion marks. In addition to the above, the real income for the German People in 1938 was actually the same as in 1928. For this reason, we can say Germany was not an economic miracle nor was there organic bourgeois property ownership of the means of production, since the bourgeois property in Nazi Germany continued to generate much exploitation and harsh conditions for workers.

Despite the image we have of Hitler as a kind of defender of whites, no one was able to commit such big crimes against whites than Hitler. His actions ended not only with a large part of the Jewish population and thousands of gypsies but also with millions of people in Eastern Europe who were considered inferior because they were from the ethnic Slavic groups, among them the Poles, the Russians, the Ukrainians, and the Belarusians. Hitler's racism was a racism directed against members of white European groups and that in the Second World War allowed the creation of a system of slavery based on the use of slave labor that was not only Jewish or composed of political prisoners, but which was composed of millions of people brought from Eastern Europe, which were considered inferior to the Germans by the fact of being of Slavic origin. The Nazi ideology advocated the colonization of Eastern European territories and the slavery, expulsion, and extermination of the peoples in these territories, and therefore the National-Socialist ideology was never the ideology of individuals being able to do their authentic will and having the freedom to do what they consider valuable.

Hitler is not the model to follow for a movement that is truly in a third position, that is, opposed to capitalism and communism. To proclaim the racial inferiority of the Russians, the Nazis propagated the myth that the Russians and other Slavic peoples are the result of a mixture with the Mongoloid Asian peoples, which is false, being now data from modern genetics that show a mixture with the Asian East genes of only 4% (according to the National Geographic genographic project). Even the Volga Tatars, who are living inside Russia but are not ethnically Russian, have a Mongoloid genetic component of only 16% in relation to 84% of the genes present in Europeans (Malyarchuk et al, 2010) while the Chuvasians, another People with a Turkic language, have a component of genes present in Europeans that is 89.1% (SA Fedorova et al, 2003.) Finally, the Balkars and the Kumyks, with also Turkic languages, present genes from East and South Asia that reach only 11% and 12.9% respectively, according to the Dodecad ancestry project. Thanks partly to Hitler is that the entire brainwashing campaign to promote liberal concepts like multiculturalism is being carried out for several decades.

Multiculturalism would probably not have been implemented if the actions of the Nazi party had never occurred, since with their actions they tainted the conservative thoughts that advocated the preservation of the human groups and the culture with origins in Europe, dooming the movements that advocate for this preservation. If it were not for Hitler, we would have a very different Europe with monocultural policies like we can see today in some Asian countries. There are still people who claim that Hitler was a kind of messiah sent by God, but the truth is that his actions were what drove today's world into the current situation. Due to the above, Normativism will have to face the whole propaganda campaign seen in the media, where Hitler is put as an example of a leader who promoted monoculturalism, and all movements that oppose multiculturalism will have to continue fighting against that tool made to promote multicultural policies. Hitler's genocidal thoughts made the patriotic doctrines needed to establish policies of monoculturalism to be seen as maleficent in Europe, North America, and other parts of the world, thus destroying the spirit of many peoples. It is important to clarify that another of the failures of the third political theory, mentioned by Dugin, is the very basis of that political theory, that is, nationalism.

By emphasizing the defense or supremacy of a given nation, the potential for a joint struggle against liberalism, other universalisms, and environmental problems is lost, a struggle that requires the collaboration of several nations since these phenomena of modernity transcend national barriers and are more powerful than what is strictly limited by them. In the case of Russia, within its territory, we can find several nations within a State, like the aforementioned Volga Tatars, the Chechens, Caucasian peoples in general, essentially Mongoloid peoples, and other minorities. As I mentioned, a true reunification of the territory of the current Russian Federation with Ukrainians, Belarusians, Georgians and Moldovans is necessary, and also the collaboration between the different nations is necessary to establish a united front of many peoples against liberalism.

In this alliance, Russia's main allies who are not yet members of the Collective Security Treaty Organization must be undoubtedly placed, these are India, the government of Syria, Algeria, and Vietnam. It can be affirmed, as Dugin has stated, that the second political theory and the third political theory have died under the weight of their failures and horrors, and one can not engage an enemy with something that is already dead. However, some values of the political theories described, which clash with the crucial points of liberalism, are advocated by the Fourth Political Theory, but in a new way that allows us to fight the great enemies of mankind.

PART III: THE STRUGGLE FOR WHAT IS SACRED

ROME'S UNIVERSALISM AGAINST THE ORTHODOX CHURCH

FROM THE SCHISM OF 1054
TO THE FALL OF CZARISM

It is imperative to carry out a review of the long conflict between the Roman Catholic Church and the Orthodox Church, as well as a review of one of the various nefarious aspects of the Church being directed from Rome, which I call the Jewish-Roman Church, for not accepting the true creed imparted by Christ, while conspiring against the interests of Russia and other peoples in the quest to strengthen Rome's universalism. I want to make a special mention for Avro Manhattan, who died in 1990, as he was an author who expounded many of Rome's maneuverings, and although some of his sayings are exaggerated like as with every author writing about what is often referred to as "conspiracy theories", nevertheless Avro Manhattan gives us fundamental information about this nefarious institution called as the Catholic Apostolic Church, together with its relationship with Orthodoxy in the East and with Russia in general, to which more recent data can be added.

The Jewish-Roman Church, described by Avro Manhattan as the mightiest giant of ancient times who survived over the course of centuries, has determinedly acted to dominate the human race imposing its deviant creed and its universalist doctrine, destroying, subduing or discrediting rivals in their way, using certain populations of the world as their pawns in a sinister game, in such a way those even factors that at first sight would seem to be insignificant, end up totally shifting the balance. However, not all opponents of Rome have been destroyed or subjugated, and of all these rivals, the most formidable is the Eastern Orthodox Church, which embroiled it in intense fighting since becoming its great enemy in the year 1054, due to theological and ecclesiastical differences which led to a great schism that divided Eastern Orthodoxy with the Western Jewish-Roman Church. Even today, we should not think that the Jewish-Roman Church is an irrelevant actor, since it has hundreds of millions of followers in the world and vast economic resources, including the second-largest gold reserve in the world, only behind the US, and enough wealth to end global poverty, with in fact about twice as that.

Of course, it is gold stained with blood, from a Church which claims to be preaching for the poor and helpless while living in the most absolute abundance. In the US, according to data from 2012, there were 62 million Catholics in that country, and instead only between 5.2 and 6.6 million Jews. Added to this, Protestants and Anglicans from the US and other countries share with the Jewish-Roman Church the erroneous and disproved belief that the Holy Spirit besides coming from the Father also comes from the Son. This turns the Son of God into what he did not want to be, a demigod in flesh, therefore rejecting the existence of the Son of God, imparting the false message that there is divinity in human flesh and tempting others with this false message, leaving in essence only a Romanized Judaism which rejects divine word.

The supreme court of the USA, composed of nine people, had in 2019 a composition where six of its members belonged to the Jewish-Roman creed and 3 are entirely Jewish, being the Chief Justice, John Roberts, someone of Jewish-Roman faith. Populations of the Spanish-speaking regions of America along with Brazil, which remain regions under the Jewish-Roman creed, have grown and a large part of the world's Catholics live in those regions and therefore along the US border, bringing the Jewish-Roman faith with them while they became legal and illegal immigrants, increasing the power of the Jewish-Roman Church in the USA. Those words of Abraham Lincoln, stating: "I see a very dark cloud on our horizon. And that dark is coming from Rome" are becoming increasingly prophetic.

The struggle between Rome and the Eastern Orthodox Church produced what was undoubtedly the longest diplomatic conflict in history, as since 1054, countless plots have been made by Rome to decimate its great rival in the East, having this fight its first climax in 1054, when the Orthodox patriarch Michael I Cerularius, who the peace of the Lord he found, started the split with the Jewish-Roman Church. This climax ended with the fall of Constantinople in 1453. Between the offensives that the Jewish-Roman Church launched against Eastern Orthodoxy is the Fourth Crusade, when crusaders at the orders of Pope Innocent III conquered Constantinople and large areas of the Byzantine Empire, after which the Republic of Venice and The Latin Empire divided the conquered territory, although later these territories were recovered by the Byzantines.

To this is added the war against the Bulgarians, who between 1204 and 1235 proclaimed Jewish-Roman Catholicism as their religion. Rome commenced a war which is now almost a thousand years old, with the aim of subduing or destroying the Eastern Orthodox Church, or integrating it into Jewish-Roman Catholicism, and for this purpose, often they had no qualms when directly or indirectly slaying thousands of people. During the initial stage of this struggle, which ended only with the fall of Constantinople and therefore of the Byzantine Empire, all kind of intrigues were used to lead this empire and its creed to ruin, a ruin that became reality when the last Byzantine emperor asked the Jewish-Roman Church for the conversion of the Orthodox creed to Jewish-Roman Catholicism in exchange of help by the Jewish-Roman Church against the Muslim invaders, aid that did not arrive, causing the fall of Constantinople. This is how Rome made its first major attack on true Christianity, while the famous myth of Jewish-Roman Catholicism as a kind of barrier that protected Europe from Islam was put into effect when in reality it was the opposite.

Under the mask of crusades in which the outcome of the third one was the definitive loss of the Holy Land, they wanted to make the world believe that Jewish-Roman Catholicism was the great benefactor and promoter of Christianity. With the fall of Constantinople, the time for being orthodoxy's empire was now in Russia's hands, where Orthodox Christianity was strong. As for Russians, the idea of an orthodox empire became a central idea, to the point that the Orthodox Church and the Russian State, initially separated, were integrated. It was in Russia that Orthodox Christianity could be reborn in such a way that Moscow and

Russia were considered as the successor of Byzantium. With Czar Peter the Great, orthodox Christianity became a part of Czarism, being understood as the doctrine and governing system of Russian society, and becoming closely associated with it.

Until the Bolshevik revolution, orthodox Christianity, protected by Czarism, was immune against any attack, including the attacks from Rome, whether diplomatic, political or doctrinal. But nevertheless, the key strength of Orthodox Christianity, which was its union with Russian Czarism, ended up becoming a weakness, since, with the fall of the Czarist State, this State dragged the Orthodox Church with it in 1917. Even after the First World War and the defeat of the Ottoman Empire, Greece, an orthodox State, did not receive Constantinople from Turkey, partly because of Rome's protest, and with the victory of the Turks under Kemal Ataturk, it became impossible for Greece to rejoin with Constantinople. To ensure Constantinople wasn't returned to Greece, Rome was forced to support the Turkish State even though this State was being ruled by an atheist dictator and its population was Muslim. In 1935, Kemal Ataturk came as far as to transform the great Church of St. Sophia, the most important symbol of Orthodox Christianity, into a museum that mixed Byzantine art with Roman and Muslim art, under the auspices of the Vatican.

The First World War meant two great victories for Rome, prevailing over the crumbling Islamic caliphate after the defeat of the Ottoman Empire, and over the crumbling Russian Empire after the Russian Revolution and the defeat of Russia in the world war. The Russian Revolution, in overthrowing the Czarist State, also overthrew the Russian Orthodox Church, because both were closely linked, since in Czarism the Orthodox Church controlled great riches and lands, as well as thousands of churches and chapels, and the Orthodox Church was a central element to justify the figure of the Czar. The Russian revolution had to overthrow the Orthodox Church because it served as the ideological instrument of the Czar to justify his power (to the point that it was crucial for Czarism to be safeguarded by the Church) and also because of the great wealth and territories controlled by the Church. The Russian revolution separated Church from State, nationalized its lands, took control of its schools, and completely separated the Orthodox clergy from political power. The

Russian revolution, because of this, gave to Rome the possibility of finally reuniting Christian orthodoxy with Jewish-Roman Catholicism, so that Rome could definitively defeat one of its great rivals. The atheist policies of the Russian communist government offered the potential to strike a deadly blow at Russian orthodoxy, toppling it completely.

Through figures like Count Sforza, Rome's plans were clear: once communist atheism was overthrown, it would be the time for Jewish-Roman Catholicism to massively convert the Orthodox world. However, Rome was facing a problem: Russian communism, and therefore its atheistic policies, which prevented the conversion of Orthodoxy to Jewish-Roman Catholicism, refused to perish. That is why the strategy of overthrowing the communist regime began to be applied, beginning with the invasion from Poland in 1919, a Jewish-Roman Catholic country, against a Russia suffering from its civil war, together with the intervention of Western powers in that war. However, the Bolshevik regime triumphed, and in addition to its atheist policies, it began to grant religious freedom to protestant groups that rivaled Rome. To make matters worse, the Russian Orthodox Church refused to perish even under the pressure of the communist regime, partly because the new separation of the Russian Orthodox Church from the Russian State meant that the Russian Orthodox Church distanced itself from its czarist past.

FROM HITLER TO THE NEW SCHISM OF 2018

In view of the failure of peaceful attempts for the conversion of Russia to Jewish-Roman Catholicism, Rome was forced to modify its tactics, and the tactic adopted was to destroy the communist government in the only way possible: by means of a military attack. However, this goal was distant and could only germinate with the rise of Fascism and National-Socialism, which were anti-communist movements. National-Socialism inevitable became the Vatican's greatest ideological ally, since as Hitler had expressed in "Mein Kampf", one of the primary objectives of National-Socialism was the conquest of Eastern Europe, which logically entailed the destruction of the Russian communist regime, and also the westernization of the conquered territories, including, as it was later seen, policies of assimilation and extermination. The Vatican began supporting the different fascist movements and National-Socialism with the clear aim of a military intervention that would destroy the Soviet Union.

When Hitler began to take his first steps to conquer Europe, the Vatican asked the exclusion of Russia from the negotiations regarding the annexation of Czechoslovakia by Germany, which was crucial, as Czechoslovakia, with its fortifications, in conjunction with the rest of their allies would have been a formidable barrier for Hitler. This made the Second World War inevitable, and in addition, after invading Finland, Russia was excluded from the League of Nations, in a context of mobilization of world opinion against Russia, something that was instigated by the Vatican. After Hitler's rapid victory over the West, Germany was able to take control of the Balkans, which included Orthodox states, and in 1941 Hitler ultimately decided to attack the Soviet Union with the largest military invasion of human history. At the beginning of the war, everything seemed to indicate the Soviet Union would collapse and that Nazi Germany would win the war in a short time. However, this did not happen, with the advance of Germany and its allies first stalling out, and then the forced retreat of Germany and its allies until their annihilation, with the cost of 27 million lives in the Soviet Union, but also with a cost for the Germans which represented 80% of their military losses suffered throughout the conflict.

The plans of the Vatican were not only aimed at the destruction of communism, since with the destruction of the Soviet Union the objective was the destruction of a religious rival, in this case, the Orthodox Church. In 1929, the Italian fascist government and the Jewish-Roman Church signed the Lateran Treaty, granting the Vatican its political independence and the restoration of relations between Italy and the representatives of the Jewish-Roman Church, with priests having to take an oath of loyalty to leader Benito Mussolini in return, according to article 20 of the concordat. This supposed the alliance of the Jewish-Roman Church with the anti-communist forces of Europe, which did not finish in Italy, as it arrived in Germany. The Vatican helped the Nazis to take power in Germany, using the Catholic party in Germany, being told by the Vatican to vote for the Nazi party. This gave Hitler the electoral majority he needed to form a government in 1933. In addition to this, the Vatican gave orders to the Catholic members of the German parliament for assisting in pushing forward the decrees that allowed Hitler to stay in power, being able to destroy the structures of German democracy and establish a dictatorship.

Then Hitler, now with dictatorial powers, wiped out the German Communist Party, and the Vatican ordered the German Catholic Party to disintegrate, which happened in 1933, much as its Italian counterpart did in 1927. In June 1933, Hitler and the Jewish-Roman Church signed a concordat according to which the Jewish-Roman Church was to be loyal to the Nazi regime. According to article 16 of that concordat, "The bishops, before taking possession of their dioceses, shall take either between the hands of Reich lieutenant (Reichsstatthalter) in the state (Land) in question or between those of the President of the Reich an oath of allegiance according to the following formula: "In front of God and on the Holy Gospels, I swear and promise, as befits a bishop, fidelity to the German Reich and to the State … I swear and promise to respect the government established according to the constitution and to cause the clergy of my diocese to respect it. In the due solicitude for the welfare and the interests of the German Reich, I will endeavor, while performing the spiritual office bestowed upon me, to prevent anything which might threaten to be detrimental to it "

Shortly after, Catholic Franz Von Papen, who in 1933 was Vice-Chancellor of the new government and who played a key role in the rise of Hitler to power, as he proposed to President Hindenburg becoming Vice-Chancellor in Hitler's government to keep it "controlled", affirmed the following "The Third Reich is the first power that not only recognizes but puts into practice the high principles of the papacy." Franz Von Papen, leader of the later dismantled German Catholic party, was a personal friend of the then Secretary of State of the Vatican, and future Pope, Pius XII. The Jewish-Roman Church did not have its own armies, but it managed to have at its disposal the armies of Germany and Italy. However, Germany and Italy were not the only fascist countries of which the Jewish-Roman Church proved an ally. Archbishop Stepinac helped to establish a brutal Catholic dictatorship in Croatia, led by Ante Pavelić, leader of the Ustašas, allies of Nazi Germany after Germany invaded and fragmented Yugoslavia. Pavelić undertook a huge genocide against Serbian Orthodox Christians, as well as other Orthodox Christians who belonged to other parts of former Yugoslavia, and other ethnic minorities, including Gypsies and Jews.

There were forced conversions to Jewish-Roman Catholicism, and the establishment of concentration camps, the most famous being the Jasenovac concentration camp. Ante Pavelić's regime caused the deaths of between 172,000 and 290,000 Serbs, between 32,000 and 40,000 Jews, and between 25,000 and 40,000 Gypsies. Pavelić's regime would be defeated along with the other fascist countries in the Second World War, and Pavelić received asylum first by the Vatican, and then in Argentina, Chile, and finally in Spain, all countries under the Jewish-Roman creed. In the mid-'60s, a certain cordiality between the Jewish-Roman Church and Orthodoxy began to be seen, starting a dialogue that was unseen for several centuries, and whose most famous example is that of the mutual excommunication being erased In any case, the Orthodox Church still feared being absorbed by the Vatican, and the actions of the Jewish-Roman Church against Russia and against Orthodoxy did not end with the Second World War.

In 1979, Pope John Paul II decided to return to Poland (his birthplace), bringing together nearly three million people around his figure, being Poland a nation strongly under the Jewish-Roman creed, and which at that time was part of the Soviet communist bloc and was an essential bastion of the Warsaw Pact. Poland would no longer be the same, since in 1980 an organization aimed to initiating the destruction of the communist bloc, disguised in the form of a Catholic union, and known as "Solidarność", under the leadership of Lech Walesa, began to operate in Poland with the help of the Vatican, then with a Polish Pope, and the help of the West. Walesa did not hide that his principal adviser was the Pope himself, and John Paul II said that if the Soviet Union invaded Poland to end "Solidarność ", he would personally go to confront them. This union finally caused the overthrow of the communist government of Poland in 1989, generating a chain reaction that would culminate with the fall of the Berlin wall and with the fall of the communist governments of Eastern Europe that were under Soviet rule.

However, it was required not only the fall of the satellite governments of the Soviet Union but the Soviet Union's fall along with them. In March 1989, 36 of the 42 deputies of the socialist republic of Lithuania, at that time one of the republics that were part of the Soviet Union, were candidates of the Sąjūdis independence movement. On May 29 of the previous year, John Paul II had named Bishop Sladkevicius as cardinal, the first Lithuanian cardinal publicly appointed in modern times. In February 1989 Lithuanian Catholics saw the apparition of the first Catholic newspaper allowed in the Soviet Union, the Kataliku Pasaulis. In the spring of 1989 the Pope appointed two new bishops, Jouzapas Matulaitis and Jouzas Semaits, which raised the number of Lithuanian bishops to nine. By the end of 1989, the supreme Soviet of Lithuania changed its constitution giving the Church and other religious organizations the character of legal entities, and the Ministry of Education of Lithuania introduced religious education within general education.

Pope John Paul II was seen by the Lithuanians as a saviour along with the leaders of the Sąjūdis independence movement, linked to the Jewish-Roman Church. Lithuania, like Poland, is also a nation under the Jewish-Roman creed, only that unlike Poland, Lithuania was part of Soviet territory. On December 8, 1989, the Communist Party of Lithuania, under the leadership of Algirdas Brazauskas, decided to separate from the Communist Party of the Soviet Union. Lithuania became independent from the Soviet Union on March 11, 1990, being the first republic of the Soviet Union to do so, and this, of course, brought a chain reaction. On June 12, 1990, the "Congress of People's Deputies of Russia" adopted the Declaration of State Sovereignty of the Russian Soviet Federative Socialist Republic, which was the beginning of the "War of Laws" confronting the Soviet Union with the nascent Russian Federation and the other constituent republics of the USSR. That same day, Boris Yeltsin, the President of the Presidium of the Supreme Soviet of the Russian Soviet Federative Socialist Republic, resigned from the Communist Party.

The definitive fall of the Soviet Union occurred on December 25, 1991, that is, the date for Christmas in the Gregorian calendar established by the Jewish-Roman Church. With the resignation of Gorbachev, all power was conferred on the government presided over by Boris Yeltsin. In Yugoslavia, another process of disintegration instigated by Croatian Catholics was developed in alliance with Bosnian Muslims against the Orthodox Serbs, which culminated with the disintegration of Yugoslavia after a brutal war, and with NATO interventions, which bombed the Serbs first in the civil war against Bosnians and Croats, and then in the Kosovo conflict, a region now separated from Serbia. It can be remarked that the Jewish-Roman Church organized two great victories against its Orthodox rival, the first was to overthrow the Byzantine Empire, and the second was to prevent the return of Constantinople to Greece after the First World War. One could also speak of a third victory, which although it was not so forceful since communism promulgated atheism and was unfeasible as a system, it is however important, and that was the collapse of the communist bloc thanks in part to the extensive collaboration of the Vatican and the Jewish-Roman creed in the destruction of this block.

This block by expanding Russian power kept the creed of the Orthodox Church under protection against potential invaders and Western influences, such as Hitler in the twentieth century and Napoleon in the nineteenth century, two invaders who declared their loyalty to the Jewish-Roman Church. In addition, the existence of the Soviet colossus kept Russia as a threatening dagger that, if aroused, could put Jewish-Roman Catholicism in considerable danger. After the fall of the Byzantine

Empire, the Eastern Orthodox Church, as it is known, became deeply entrenched in Holy Russia, and Russia became the center of this creed, so that Moscow became the successor of Constantinople and heir for its world mission. With Czarist Russia being something of the past, and with the Soviet Union being something that equally belongs to the past, then it remains to be seen which new Russia is coming after the previous one, since although certain elements are already being shaped, surely many still remain to be profiled. In this framework, orthodox thinking is essential, and it must be strengthened, which is only possible by carefully observing the points that I will state later.

In 2018 destiny showed its face, with the schism between the Russian Orthodox Church and the Church of Constantinople, servant of the West, finally happening under political instigation from the Western powers and their lackeys Petro Poroshenko and Bartholomew I, who seek to dismember not only the Russian geopolitical space but Russian faith itself, in times when all the Ukrainian State has become the instrument of the West against the awakening of the ancestral consciousness and power emanating from the defiant Russian People. On October 11, 2018, the present Church of Constantinople, betraying its brothers of faith, decided to separate the Ukrainian Church from the Russian Church in a completely criminal action. Russia's response was rapid, causing the breakdown of relations with the Church of Constantinople and refusing to recognize the illegal institution that Constantinople seeks to support in Ukraine, a Russian land inseparable from the destiny of Russians. There is no turning back, the path is towards the survival of Christianity, and this path requires us to know a very ancient origin.

THE ANCESTRAL ORIGIN OF ORTHODOX THOUGHT IN RUSSIA

DOCTRINE OF THE TRINITY

Through thought and remembering which can be summoned as the Holy Trinity in its complete form, we can give firmness to orthodox thought based on the ancestral worship of the Most High God, whose names can be traced to forms that existed at the very origin of civilization. By the Doctrine of the Trinity, I intend resolving the great question which triggered the Filioque controversy, to determine if the Holy Spirit comes only from the Father, as Eastern Orthodoxy claims, or if it comes from both the Father and the Son, as the Jewish-Roman Church, Protestants and Anglicans affirm. It is not my intention to sustain these affirmations with unprovable facts or observations based on religious experiences that are unique to me or to others. My only intention is to apply something as basic as common sense and the study of the holy scriptures, respecting what has already been established by orthodox Christianity, to guide Russia and other peoples of the world towards a better understanding and greater wisdom.

As it is known, the only God, according to the doctrine of the Holy Trinity within Christian churches, is composed of three elements, which are the Father, his Son and the Holy Spirit. The Father sent a mentor and redeemer to Earth to save mankind, and he used the Holy Spirit to bring him to this world. Man, according to the doctrine of the Holy Trinity within Christian Churches, because he is made in the image of

God is also composed of three elements: his body, which is analogous to the Son, followed by the mind or soul, which is analogous to the Father, since the Father remains the mind that created everything, and finally the spirit, analogous to the Holy Spirit. However, regarding this doctrine, at least in the form in which it was presented by the Jewish-Roman church and other churches for centuries, it is necessary to explain many crucial points that these churches did not explain or would not explain. The discussions of the First Council of Nicaea, held in the year 325, and the first council of Constantinople, held in 381, centered around whether Jesus besides being a man was God or if he was not God himself, so that some less elementary questions were not faced, regarding what the nature of God was like, and only the question of deciding whether Jesus was fully divine or just an envoy and prophet was addressed.

The basis of the Doctrine of the Trinity is that number 3, in concordance that there is a Holy Trinity according to Christian churches, should be considered the basis of everything related to God and the domain of the divine, so it exists a Trinity made up of the Father, the Son, and the Spirit of the Son, as has already been proposed for centuries, but it must also be considered, according to the Doctrine of the Trinity, that there is also a trinity in each element that makes up the Holy Trinity, which implies a trinity in the Father, another in the Son and another in the Holy Spirit. We see how number 3, as a divine number and number of perfection, appears repeatedly in the sacred scriptures, firstly in the fact that there are 27 books in the new testament, a number that comes from multiplying number 3 by itself three times.

Three were the gifts that the wise men gave to Jesus: gold, incense, and myrrh. Jesus before his death resurrected three people, because although the best known is Lazarus (John 11.43-44) he also raised the Son of the Widow of Nain (Luke 7, 11-17), and the daughter of Jairus (Luke 8: 49-56). Jesus prayed three times in the garden of Gethsemane before being imprisoned. Jesus spent 6 hours on the cross dying at 3 o'clock in the afternoon, on the ninth hour of the Hebrew day. For the execution of the Martyrs of Golgotha 3 crosses were erected on calvary hill; where three nails held three men at crosses; Jesus, Dismas, and Gestas. According to the Holy Scriptures, 3 hours of darkness covered the Earth until the death of Jesus. Jesus was not resurrected until 3 days and 3 nights after his death, there were only three people who witnessed the transfiguration of Jesus into divine glory after his resurrection (John, Peter, and James), and also sacred scriptures mention the existence of three heavens. Three elements, "Spirit, water and blood" are the divinely perfect witnesses of God's grace on earth (1 John 5:18).

Likewise, the attributes of God are three, his omnipotence, his omniscience, and his omnipresence. In addition, in the Holy Bible, the names of three archangels appear, which are Michael, Gabriel, and Lucifer. There are more mentions to number 3 in the book of revelations as well as in the Old Testament. And if in the case of weak believers all these references to number 3 do not convince them, then they should at least take a look at the importance of number 3 in other cultures. There is evidence that man in the past could have retained counting systems composed of numbers one, two and three, and from there on the term "many", which makes these primitive counting systems a trinity. Primitive men had a word to describe numbers one, two, and three, but the other quantities were called "a lot." This phenomenon prevails among peoples of regions as far from one another as with the Amazon Rainforest in Brazil and Borneo's jungle. In Greek mythology, the children of Chronos were three: Zeus, Poseidon, and Hades.

In Hinduism, there is a trinity composed of Brahma ("the creator"), Vishnu ("the preserver") and Shiva ("the destroyer"). Meanwhile, in Taoism, there is the belief regarding the existence of "The Three Pure Ones", which are the three primary deities of Taoism. In the Taoist text known as Tao Te Ching, one of the founding texts of Taoism, it is stated that "The Tao produced One; One produced Two; Two produced Three; Three produced All things." As indicated by Pythagoras and the Pythagorean school, the number 3 is the highest of all numbers, because it is the only number that equals the sum of the numerical expressions below it and is the only number in which the sum of those numerical expressions equals the product of those numbers and itself. The triangle, composed of three edges and three vertices, is the most stable physical form, which is why it is used in several human works. In addition, as Gauss showed, every positive integer can be written as a sum of three triangular numbers.

Time is experienced on the basis of three aspects: present, past, and future; Man, in turn, is endowed with three elementary intellectual capacities: memory, understanding and will. In geometry, bodies are distinguished, by their shape, density and color; the decomposition of light reveals three primary colors: yellow, blue and red; the triangle contains three angles: acute, right and obtuse; there are 3 shapes in the classification of angles: rectilinear, curvilinear, mixtilinear; there are three kinds of triangles: equilateral, isosceles and scalene; the triangle is limited by means of three lines: two legs and a hypotenuse; we define figures in triangular, circular and quadrangular by their shape; bodies are classified as geometric, and three bodies with edges (the cube, the prism, and the pyramid) are known. The prisms are straight, inclined, and truncated, and a cube can be quadrangular, trapezoidal, and rectangular. The water molecule, essential for the existence of humans and the rest of life, is composed of three atoms, two of oxygen and one of hydrogen. One of the most remarkable things is there are three spatial dimensions: width, length, and depth.

The number 3 also appeared during world wars, since the alliance that would lead to the first world war was called the triple entente, formed by France, Russia and the British Empire, and the victors of the Second World War were known as the three big ones, being Stalin, Roosevelt and Churchill. Finally, the number 3 can be seen in the most remarkable buildings of antiquity, which are the pyramids of Giza in Egypt, composed of three pyramids which were amazingly aligned with the 3 stars of Orion's Belt, as discovered by Dr. James J. Hurtak in 1973.

The existence of a contradiction within the divine world (the unseen world) in such a way that a part of the divine is ruled by number 3 and another part is not, would make no sense at all. This number clearly appears as structuring all that is purely divine in ancient scriptures, and it also appears structuring the purely material realm, in addition to its very exceptional mathematical properties. Therefore, in the same way, that the Holy Trinity is composed of three elements, each element of the Holy Trinity assumes three different forms. Therefore, there is a trinity in God, there is a trinity in the Spirit of God sent to Earth, and there is a trinity in the Son. In the initiatory ritual of being born in water (symbolized by baptism) the three parts of the messiah, that is, the bearing body and the Holy Spirit are connected in a sacred way, that is, the third aspect, whose most important manifestation is the divine word.

The Creator, the God on high, the element that heads the Holy Trinity, in turn, is composed of three elements. These are an active force, which generates change, transformation, movement, that's to say a masculine force, added to a passive force, which generates the permanence of things in opposition to change, this force is a feminine force. According to the metal tablets found in West Bank, whose authenticity was demonstrated in 2016, and which in present times is the oldest document about Jesus that has been found (being about 2000 years old) Jesus knew that God's essence was so much as masculine as feminine. God contains a third aspect, his aspect as a whole and not as two separate parts, this aspect is simply the totality of his action and inaction with his passive and active essences, that is, feminine and masculine. Without this third aspect the universe as we know it could not exist since we see the active side and the passive side of God do not manifest independently of each other. There is nothing whose features are completely permanent or anything that is completely impermanent, so the forces of the divine world are united. In addition to the aspects of the divine world, a fourth aspect connects the divine world with the material plane, an essence that exists through the number 4, that is, the element of illusion. Human beings and the material world are originated by the conjunction of the three aspects of God plus the connection between these aspects and the material, and even though we are divided into different sexes, all human beings have some feminine aspect and some masculine aspect within them, as well as a force that primordially unites those two principles which emanate from God, and another force that unites us to that same God.

The doctrine known as Monophysitism, according to which Jesus is always present in a divine nature or in a synthesis of both, is erroneous because Jesus had a divine nature only after receiving the Holy Spirit in his baptism, so the doctrine now supported by the Eastern Orthodox Church and the Jewish-Roman Church, known as dyophysitism, is correct inasmuch as Jesus possessed two natures, one before his baptism, based on free will, and another after it, based on his direction by the Holy Spirit. The doctrine of both churches correctly rejects Nestorianism because after its initiatory baptism the nature of Jesus becomes divine. The Holy Spirit also consists of three parts, its feminine aspect, its masculine aspect, and its aspect as a conjunction of those two elements.

A BRIEF SUMMARY OF ORTHODOX TEACHING

It is necessary to explain why the teaching of the Russian Orthodox Church is not deviated from Christianity as for example the Vatican's teaching. One of the clauses of the Creed about the origin of the Holy Spirit stating "I believe in the Holy Spirit, the Lord, the giver of life, who proceeds from the Father" was modified in a Council that was only celebrated in the West in the city of Toledo adding to the clause, the words "And of the Son", for that reason, the complete sentence says "I believe in the Holy Spirit, the Lord, the giver of life, who proceeds from the Father and the Son." That Council did not have the presence of the Patriarchates of the East. In the Sacred Scriptures, the Lord says: "When the Advocate comes (the one who brings consolation), whom I will send to you from the Father—the Spirit of truth who goes out from the Father—he will testify about me." (John, 15:26).

Therefore, the Holy Spirit, as the Eastern Orthodox Church states, comes only from the Father and not from the Son. Understanding the Doctrine of the Trinity, we can assure the Son is only the body that receives the Holy Spirit. Although the body is one of the inseparable aspects of God, the Holy Spirit does not come from this body, because it is illogical to think that what emanated from the divine emanates from a man made from matter. When the Jewish-Roman Church claimed that the Holy Spirit came not only from the Father, but also from the Son, that is, coming from the body and therefore from matter, they created a doctrine where the material world began to be worshipped, thus the Jewish-Roman Church created a doctrine that was no longer strictly spiritual but also materialistic, and it is obvious that the worship of the material world is equal to the adoration of a golden calf, leading to the corruption of the sacred doctrine of God. It is the duty of Orthodoxy to unite to defend a strictly spiritual and divine doctrine. Orthodoxy, which still rejects the belief that the Holy Spirit also comes from the Son, must remain faithful to the direction of the spirit and therefore in the direction of God.

Fortunately, in the Orthodox Church there is no "original sin", what exists is "ancestral sin." God endowed the human being with "free will", granted him the power to choose and to carry out his own decisions. Therefore, he can choose between achieving what is good (living in God's love) or doing what is evil (getting away from God's love). The Apostle Saint Paul warned us about this: "I have the right to do anything," you say —but not everything is beneficial. "I have the right to do anything"—but not everything is constructive. " (1 Corinthians 10:23). The natural inclination to do evil (to separate from God) is what we call as "ancestral sin", natural inclination which can be linked even to the Nous (the eyes and mind of the Soul in Orthodox Teaching). There is no conclusive statement in the Bible nor in the writings of the Holy Fathers of the Church to sustain a "Doctrine of Original Sin." As stated by the Orthodox Church, it is not possible to inherit the transgression committed by Adam and Eve, because due to the existence of free will, no one can be charged with faults or errors of others, as it would be an influence on that free will of ours. Our responsibility from sin is not hereditary but individual, and arises directly from the free will that all human beings have.

The Orthodox Church also criticizes the absurd doctrine of Papal infallibility, being this popes mere imperfect human beings. In fact when Jesus is asked: " "Good teacher, what must I do to inherit eternal life?" "Why do you call me good?" Jesus answered. "No one is good—except God alone. " (Luke 18: 18-19) "...for they loved human praise more than praise from God Then Jesus cried out, "Whoever believes in me does not believe in me only, but in the one who sent me. The one who looks at me is seeing the one who sent me... " (John 12:44).

The Jewish-Roman Church relentlessly demands celibacy from its clergy. But the first Church never prohibited the marriage of the Clergy or that of the Bishops. The great theologian of the Church, St. Gregory, was the son of a Bishop, as were other great saints, but the Church later determined that the Bishops were not to be married so that they would move away from mundane obligations, thus being able to devote themselves to the spiritual. In many Orthodox parishes (especially those from the Slavic world) the parishioner demands that the parish priest be a married man, the reason for this being obvious: If a married man can preserve his home, he can maintain a parish. As for what statues are concerned, the Jewish-Roman West, against the word of God, placed statues in temples. The Orthodox East rejected them and continues to reject them inside temples, based on the Word of the Lord: "God is spirit; and his worshippers must worship in the spirit and in truth " (John 4:24). And so we are also told: "...Worship the Lord your God, and serve him only " (Matthew 4:10). Saint Paul tells us: "The God who made the world and everything in it is the Lord of heaven and earth and does not live in temples built by human hands..." (Acts 17:24)

The Orthodox Church does not have religious orders or religious congregational institutions and has never admitted them, because these associations give rise to the danger of becoming sects, and sects seek to achieve influence over people around them by their particular worldview while grasping for power and moving away from God. The Orthodox Church, unlike the Jewish-Roman Church, consecrates the natural bread made with leaven, since it considers the use of unleavened bread by the Jewish-Roman Church a heresy since it is clear that Jesus ate natural bread with yeast in his last supper, as well as the apostles consumed this type of bread to fulfill the Eucharist, together with the first followers of Jesus. In some Protestant churches, the same bread handled by the Jewish-Roman Church is also used.

We must consider fundamental the belief that Russia is a sacred land, but that it must completely distance itself from iniquity. Undertaking a process of more substantial return of Christianity to its sacred basis from the East, it is therefore necessary to deepen the attempt to take it away from the corrupting and desacralizing West, an attempt which started in Constantinople, turned into the imperial capital by Constantine the Great, later becoming Bastion of the Byzantine Empire and Orthodoxy. As for Islam, it is worth mentioning they do not even accept the Doctrine of the Trinity, since they consider God as an indivisible unit. To distance Orthodoxy from Western modernity, a different calendar from the Gregorian one established by the West is necessary, within the context of the schism that took place in 2018 between the Russian Orthodox Church and the pro-Western Church of Constantinople. This new schism, instead of supposing a defeat for Russia must suppose a golden opportunity to save Christianity and returning all its ancestral and divine essence.

THE NEED FOR A CALENDAR DIFFERENT FROM THE WESTERN CALENDAR

Jesus refers to himself as the Morning Star, which is a clear reference to the planet Venus. Melchizedek's kingdom, Salem (Shalim) was the name of a god that symbolized Venus (van der Toom et al 1999) and although it symbolized it in its aspect as the Evening Star, it can't be ignored that from very remote times Venus was always having its place on the Biblical account, while not Sirius, which was a star adored mostly by Egyptians, and now by Freemasons, although that does not prevent some from speculating that Jesus referred to himself as the star Sirius and not as Venus. Shalim symbolized Venus in its appearance as an evening star and Shahar in its appearance as a morning star. It is necessary to get rid of the current Gregorian calendar established by the Jewish- Roman Church and move to a Venusian calendar, based on the 263 days which is the average time for the planet Venus from rising and setting as the morning star, as well as the average time of its rising and setting as an evening star, to which is subtracted the 3 days which passed from Jesus' death until his resurrection.

They are 3 days where the Holy Spirit is unmanifested on Earth, therefore, the time from the birth of Jesus will be counted by a cycle of 260 days, which curiously is the same cycle used by the Mayans in one of their calendars, namely that which they considered as sacred and as the oldest, the tzol'kin calendar. One of the widely known things about the Mayans is the precision and symbolism of their calendars. The relationship of the Holy Spirit with the 260-day cycle is due to the fact that Jesus surely received the Holy Spirit 260 days before his crucifixion, at his baptism, as stated in the Bible. In the Akathist hymn to Saint John, Forerunner and Baptist of the Lord, Saint John is called as the Morning Star of the never-setting Sun, and therefore by baptizing Jesus he makes him the Morning Star and his successor.

To divide the 260-day cycles, we must employ a system with the meanings attributed in the Bible for each number. Fortunately, the Mayans utilized a calendar that reflected everything necessary, since their 260-day calendar is divided into 20 periods of 13 days each. The 20 is in the Bible the number that symbolizes patience. For 20 years Jacob waited to take possession of his wives and property and be released from the control of his father-in-law Laban (Genesis 31:38 - 41). For 20 years the children of Israel hoped to be freed from Jabin, king of Canaan, who oppressed them (Judges, 4-5). Other numbers, which could be seen as patience numbers have other meanings, like number 40, since "40" also represents the number of days in positive events not only related to patience, such as the instance in which Moses was with God, the instance when The Earth was allowed by God to rest, and the instance when Israel received manna.

According to the Bible, number 13 possesses a specific meaning. And this meaning is perfectly illustrated first by the symbolic aspect of the Last Supper, the last meal of Jesus with his 12 disciples (Judas was the 13th apostle, the one who betrayed Jesus). The Bible leads to the following interpretation: the number 13 is connected with the suffering of Jesus, who was crucified the next day. The number 13 represents darkness since it symbolizes Nimrod, known in ancient Sumer as Enmerkar, who was the 13th son in Ham's line, and who was the founder of the first kingdom after the flood, founding the first kingdom of evil by opposing God. That's why "13" represents the wicked governments created by man. Nimrod was according to ancient tradition the one who established a vast evil empire, building (according to Genesis) Babylon, Uruk, Akkad and kalneh in the southern region of Mesopotamia, and Nineveh, Resen, Rehoboth-Ir and Calah in the North, so Nimrod represents the governments based on wickedness. In addition to the references in the Bible, "13" appears in many important instances throughout history.

The pyramid of a dollar bill has 13 steps, and the eagle has 13 leaves in the right foot and 13 arrows in the left. The shield on the eagle's chest with the US flag is 13 stripes because these represent the 13 colonies that became independent from the British Empire to become the United States. On the eagle is the star of David composed of 13 small stars. Pope Francis was elected on the 13th day of month 3 of the year 2013, adding those digits the result is "13". As for Freemasonry, one of their texts, the

York manuscript number 1, states that Freemasons commissioned by Nimrod were involved during the building of the Tower of Babylon and that even Nimrod was a freemason who cherished them, and despite this text being placed under the category of a speculative and non-operative text, it clearly shows certain sectors of Freemasonry followed the path of darkness.

By having the calendar number 20 above number 13, the triumph of patience over darkness is represented at the end of each 260-day cycle, and therefore the triumph of good over evil. For the triumph of good over evil to be fully represented, there must be a week of 20 days with different names, such as the 20 days of the tzol'kin, putting again "20" over "13" and creating a double triumph of good over evil, in the same way that the birth and resurrection of Jesus supposed a double victory of good over evil. Due to a transcription error, the number 666 in the oldest manuscripts is number 616 in the original Bible, so the real number is "616". If we add the digits of "616" it gives us "13", the number of darkness. A trinity in this calendar can be seen, composed by "13", "20", and "260".

The fact that there are also 13 cycles of 20 days in addition to 20 cycles of 13 days represents a victory of darkness over light, which if we add it to the above we have both a victory of light and a victory of darkness, and if we add to the aforementioned the other victory of light, being the cycle of 20 periods of 13 days (the cycle 260 days) then we have a representation of the cosmos, the trinity, by including the final triumph of light after the struggle against darkness. Thus, the year would be comprised simultaneously of 20 cycles of 13 days and 13 cycles of 20 days occurring in the 260-day cycle. The days of rest will be placed as one after every 6 days, so as not to go against God's command. At first, we could think that the way we count time is unimportant, and this is one of the great flaws of modernity's thinking. The way in which we measure time exercises a profound psychological influence that in the long run affects our relationship with others, with nature, and with ourselves. In the words of Aleksander Dugin "Time is what is inside us and what makes us who we are. Time is the uttermost identity of man."

This calendar is intended as a reminder for mankind of the two victories of light over darkness, as well as the only victory of darkness in order that people keep in mind their errors and threats. In addition, being a cycle shorter than the Gregorian calendar, people will have the feeling that their life is longer in a world where time is absorbed by communication technologies. 260 days is, in addition, the time which lasts the pregnancy for human beings in a mother's womb, taking into account that the gestation for human being starts 14 days after the beginning of the last menstrual rule, because of implantation of the blastocyst into the endometrium. This reminds us of our own evolution and of respect towards mother nature, including those beings which are part of it, human or not. The 260-day cycle also amounts to 9 months, since dividing that amount by 9 results in 28.88888… That is equal to approximately one month (the movement of the moon around the Earth). The month is thus multiplied by the number that represents both end and infinity, since number 9, which arises from number 3, that is, the number of the elements of creation repeated on itself, is the number of infinity, and for being infinity is logically the number representing end. The 260-day cycle reminds humanity of the arrival and reappearance of the Holy Spirit and should be considered as a sacred cycle whose calendar is above any other calendar.

Number 20 and 13 are the binary bases of the tzol'kin and they are chosen to establish the start and the end of the following code of equations. The number 72 appearing in the following descending sequence is curiously the angle of 72 ° in which planet Venus appears after its synodic period of 583.92 days (in relation to the previous elongation) after eight years which is precisely the amount of binary digits present in the sequence which will be shown here, although the finalized equation has nine values, as the equation is composed of two parts. 7 + 2 is number 9, that is the end of the system and at the same time infinity, while "65" is the albedo of Venus, which is the percentage of radiation that its surface reflects in relation to the radiation that affects it, and multiplied by 4 it gives us the days of the tzol'kin, the number 4 being only a connector between the visible world, which tends to the masculine aspect as to have change in it, with the reality of the unseen world which is eternal (changeless).

The equation: 01011000

$(0×20)+(1×19)+(0×18)+(1×17)+(1×16)+(0×15)+(0×14)+(0×13) = 52$, which added to 13 gives us 65 and added to 20 gives us 72

Turning the first equation we have the following:
10100111:

$(1\times13)+(0\times14)+(1\times15)+(0\times16)+(0\times17)+(1\times18)+(1\times19)+(1\times20) = 85$, which by subtracting 20 gives us 65 and subtracting 13 gives us 72

Turning the equation allows us to appreciate that each value from "20" to "13" or from "13" to "20" has a binary relationship with astronomical concepts that are not obvious at first glance. Reducing the final figures to a single digit for seeing the result yields interesting conclusions. In the case of "65" results in "2", and "72" gives "9". But more important is that "65" is the system's starting point and 72 represents its end. In addition to number two, by reducing "65" we previously have number 11, so we can see that "65" is the starting point of the system, since number 11 reflects the two creative poles and therefore the origin of creation. Number 72, reduced to "9", indicates the system's end, since it is number 3, the number of the creation, multiplied on itself, thus being infinity and end at the same. In both cases the final results are obtained by adding or subtracting the two opposing numbers within the equations, that is, "13" and "20". Number 52, which is the value that we see as a result in the first part of the first equation, is the number of years it takes to repeat the Mayan calendar, that is, 52 times the 365 k'in units used, due to the coincidence of dates between the tzol'kin and the Mayan solar calendar after that time, which is equivalent to 73 completions of the tzol'kin cycle.

The Mayan long count calendar used a 20-day cycle called uinal, a 360-day cycle called tun, a 7,200-day k'atun, and a 144.000-day cycle called b'ak'tun. The long count comprises 13 periods of 144,000 days, or 13 b'ak'tuns, which equals 1,872,000 k'in (days) which in turn equals 7,200 tzol'kin cycles or 5,200 tunes, or 20 ahaw cycles of 93,600 days. An ahaw is in turn 360 tzol'kin. The figures in k'in (days) expressed in the cycles possess the peculiarity of all being able to be reduced to number 9: "360" $(3 + 6 = 9)$, "7,200" $(7 + 2 = 9)$, "144,000" $(1 + 4 + 4 = 9)$, "1,872,000" $(1 + 8 + 7 + 2 = 18, 1 + 8 = 9)$, "93,600" $(9 + 3 + 6 = 18, 1 + 8 = 9)$. The same is for the longer cycles not used so often by the Mayans: piktun, kalabtun, k'inchinltun, and alautun. Twenty b'ak'tuns would form a piktun of approximately 7,890 years and twenty piktuns generate a kalabtun of 57,600,000 k'ins, approximately 157,810 years, and we observe the following: $5 + 7 + 6 = 18; 1 + 8 = 9$. The number of Venus' albedo (65) multiplied by number 4 gives us the number of days of the tzol'kin, and as has been observed, if we add the numbers of the four corners that we can observe in the tzol'kin synchronicity scheme (1, 7, 7, 13) we will find it gives a total of "28", which is the approximate number of days in a month, with this being repeated also in the inner corners.

If we multiply number 28 (which was obtained by adding the corners) by number 13, we obtain the number 364. Taking into account that the Mayans counted starting from zero, we can adjust this to our counting mode, so we can add a digit to "364", giving "365", that is the number of days in a solar year. With the Mayan cycles as a basis we can calculate the amount and hierarchy of the different prophets. The Mayan uinal, composed of 20 days, represents the duality that creates good and harmony, being Christ there. Christ is therefore in the highest hierarchy, and we can see that the tzol'kin consist of 13 cycles of 20 days, which means there is a second hierarchy consisting of other 12 prophets. In a third hierarchy there are 347 prophets, that when adding the previous 13 prophets total 360, which is the number of uinals in a K'atun. In a fourth category, there are 6840 prophets, which added to the previous 360 gives a figure of 7200, which is the number of uinals in a b'ak'tun. Christ said: And what was God's answer to him? "I have reserved for myself seven thousand who have not bowed the knee to Baal." (Romans 11: 4) Finally, there is a fifth category, composed of 136,800 prophets, which, when added to the 7,200 prophets of higher hierarchy add up to 144,000, which is the number of uinals in a piktun, and the number of people that according to the Bible would be chosen by God from his 12 tribes, to put forward his plan. The 12 tribes are a reference to 12 people from which the rest of human beings are descendants, by creating 12 ancestral lineages.

A new calendar would mean a new step towards a completely independent Russian Orthodox Church, free forever from the nefarious control of the now pro-Western Church of Constantinople.

THE ANCIENT ORIGIN OF RUSSIAN CIVILIZATION

The origin of the tzol'kin calendar is a mystery, but it is tempting to analyze if the Mayan culture inherited all kinds of knowledge from a previous ancient culture, mother culture not only of Mesoamerican cultures but of many cultures around the globe, like the Ancient Egyptian culture, Mesopotamia, the Indo-European-speaking peoples, Semites and the cultures of India. The chief deity of this mother culture can be traced due to the survival of its name in several places in the world. In that way we have the name Anu by the Akkadians from Mesopotamia, Danu and Vishnu in India, Danu also in Ireland, Jnum (Khanum) and Nut by the Egyptians, etc. Anu was also identified with the Semitic god Ilu or El from early on (Pope 1955). According to Akkadian belief, Anu had a son named Adad, fulfilling the role of the main Son of God, and related to water and rain. From there the name of Adam could be derived.

Adad, which is also pronounced as '' Haddad '' was called by the Akkadians as ''Rammanu '', meaning "the one who thunders", Manu by the Hindus and Mannus by the ancient Germans. In Hindu mythology and German mythology, Manu and Mannus, respectively, are considered the first human and progenitor of the rest. In the English language, the word '' dad '' is used to designate the paternal figure, and '' man '' is used to designate human beings. From the mother culture is that all European peoples adopted a Trinitarian thought instead of just a dualistic thought. The ability to transcend dual thought and realize trinities is born in that ancient civilization, because although without duality there can't be good, without trinity there is not the possibility of recognizing the divine as the reconciliation of the duality expressed in number 3.

Enlil is a Sumerian title for Adad, showing that currently, on the internet and in documentaries, there is a clear attempt to misinform and to attacking Christ, since it is wished to put into people's minds the idea that Enki (which is also known as Ea and as Nimrod) being the serpent of Eden, is the savior of mankind and Enlil the antagonist, when in fact it is the opposite. The storm can bring life or death, therefore Jesus is severe, his mission is to create the confrontation between men so that light is brought forward, being the masculine principle the main aspect directing Christ, the rest being only a mask that adjusts divine light to the capacity of men.

"Do not suppose that I have come to bring peace to the earth. I did not come to bring peace, but a sword. For I have come to turn ''a man against his father, a daughter against her mother, a daughter-in-law against her mother-in-law — a man's enemies will be the members of his own household ''. (Matthew 10: 34-36).

Remember that darkness, being the feminine aspect, although an inseparable part of creation is the only source of inertia, and light is the source of change, of conflict and finally of salvation. Adam and Jesus are one and the same, made in the image and likeness of the creator, the first being the severe side of the Son of God, the one that allows the entrance of sin to confront mankind, and the second the redeeming side, the one that comes to rid man from sin since there can be no life or resurrection without death and descent.

''So it is written: "The first man Adam became a living being"; the last Adam, a life-giving spirit. The spiritual did not come first, but the natural, and after that the spiritual. '' (1 Corinthians 15: 45-46).

''For since death came through a man, the resurrection of the dead comes also through a man. '' (1 Corinthians 15: 21-23).

"Nor can the gift of God be compared with the result of one man's sin: The judgment followed {arose because} one sin and brought condemnation, but the gift followed {arose because of} many trespasses and brought justification. " (Romans 5:16).

In the Holy Bible, we see Jesus announces his pre-existence: " Very truly I tell you," Jesus answered, "before Abraham was born, I AM! " (John 8:58).

"But you, Bethlehem Ephrathah, though you are small among the clans of Judah, out of you will come for me one who will be ruler over Israel, whose origins are from of old, from ancient times. '' (Micah 5: 2).

"The Son is the image of the invisible God, the firstborn over all creation." (Colossians 1:15).

"And now, Father, glorify me in your presence with the glory I had with you before the world began." (John 17:15) "I am the Alpha and the Omega, the First and the Last, the Beginning and the End." (Revelation 22:13).

The passage from Genesis 2:21-23 narrates: " So the Lord God caused the man to fall into a deep sleep; and while he was sleeping, he took one of the man's ribs and then closed up the place with flesh. Then the Lord God made a woman from the rib he had taken out of the man, and he brought her to the man. The man said, "This is now bone of my bones and flesh of my flesh; she shall be called 'woman,' for she was taken out of man.". This means the first truly human women are created from the seed of the Son of God and their union with earthly females.

The Nephilim were sons of God who descended to Earth, and who lacked female companionship and mingled with the women of Earth. Like Angels, they could teach humanity truth and justice.

"The Nephilim were on the earth in those days—and also afterwards—when the sons of God went to the daughters of humans and had children by them... " (Genesis 6: 4).

The Nephilim were taller than earthly humans but not necessarily giants by modern standards, because for example, when the Europeans discovered the Patagonian native Americans they thought the southern portion of South America was inhabited by giants just because Europeans were shorter in those days. The Holy Spirit is the Son of God and the principal of these celestial beings, and he became the father of Humanity, the first Adam. When in the Bible it is stated that Amalek is "first among nations" it is a reference to the ancient Nephilim. Adam had offspring with earthly women who were not yet truly human because they did not possess the divine seed that their offspring would have. Those earthly women and men were Homo Sapiens without divine spark, without Adam, that is why Homo sapiens has about 300 millennia living over the Earth and only in the last 50 millennia, since the start of the Upper Palaeolithic, they could manage to evolve their culture. As with species of marsupial animals, the original Homo Sapiens survived only in Australia because of isolation. The morphology of the earliest human remains discovered, those of Jebel Irhoud in Morocco, which are 315.000 years old, is identical to the morphology of Aboriginal Australians.

Amalek is described in the Jewish tradition as its main enemy, and the reason is obvious, the Jews did nothing but steal the knowledge of the Nephilim, and then distort it by creating their new tradition. Moses and his people roamed 40 years in the desert; Moses himself could never enter the promised land, dying in exile. Moses attributed to himself a miracle from God:

"Then Moses raised his arm and struck the rock twice with his staff. Watergushed out, and the community and their livestock drank. But the Lord said to Moses and Aaron, "Because you did not trust in me enough to honor me as holy in the sight of the Israelites, you will not bring this community into the land I give them." (Numbers 20: 11-12). Thus Moses, a genuine prophet of God at first, became an exile until his death and the creator of the great lie within Judaism, which rejects Amalek in its ancient writings and declarations, and therefore Ammanu-El, which is called Christ.

Ammanu-El is in Aramaic the other name of the Son of God, as is perfectly verified by the Bible itself.

"Therefore the Lord himself will give you a sign: The virgin will conceive and give birth to a son, and will call him Immanuel. " (Isaiah 7:14). " All this took place to fulfill what the Lord had said through the prophet (Isaiah): "The virgin will conceive and give birth to a son, and they will call him Immanuel" (which means "God with us") " (Matthew 1: 22-23).

In addition, the Melchizedek priesthood precedes the Hebrew one. Melchizedek was King of Salem and Priest of El Elyon, meaning God Most High, who, offering wine and bread, blesses Abraham saying "Blessed be Abram by God Most High, Creator of heaven and earth. And praise be to God Most High, who delivered your enemies into your hand." Then Abram gave him a tenth of everything. " (Genesis 14, 18-20).

In Christianity, according to the Epistle to the Hebrews, Jesus identifies himself as a "priest forever according to the order of Melchizedek", and thus Jesus assumes the role of high priest and King, continuing the task of Melchizedek, a task which implies being both High priest and King. As for Venus, its importance can be attested in antiquity, since in Sumerian mythology, the Anunnaki were a pantheon of "gods" and "goddesses" that came to Earth to create the human race. According to ancient sources, these gods lived in Neberu – translating to "point of crossing" in Akkadian language, "Nebheru" in Egyptian language (which means house of Horus and was the name given to the planet Venus). As it can be observed thanks to modern space research on Venus, of which the Soviet Union had much contribution, the atmosphere of this planet seems to have suffered a cataclysmic event, hence the seed of its civilization went to the planet Earth, which is a twin of Venus, as it is of a very similar size and composition.

The civilization in Venus was called "Nippur" in antiquity, portrayed as the home of the gods and as Enlil's abode. Nippur is a corruption of the word "Nibru" which in turn is a corruption of the word "Neberu". The metonym for Nippur was "Kur-Gal" which means "Great Land" and "Great Construction" in Sumerian. Kur in addition to being the word for "mountain" also meant "land", "underworld" and "build". Linked to the word "Gal" meaning "Great" the Sumerians employed the name "Kur-Gal" to designate simultaneously their land, their creations, and the underworld, and therefore the land, creations and underworld of those who were before them. "Kur-Gal" is all that which existed above "Ma" the name that the Sumerians gave to the primordial land, in other words, the concept of the planet. Above Kur-Gal was the "Abzu" which represent the primeval sea (outer space). The term Kur-Gal was even employed as a name for the God Enlil, so the great importance of this term in ancient times is evident.

The groups named by the famous Lithuanian archaeologist Marija Gimbutas as the Kurgan people, being the cradle of the Proto-Indo-European language and who lived in southwestern Russia, near the Caspian Sea, buried their dead under tumuli, this may explain why the word "Kur" which was used for "mountain" and for "land" also was used as the name of the underworld. The mother culture in Venus, also the basis for the Kurgan culture, included the costume of burying their dead and constructing temples in mounds, mountains, and pyramids, which later would be reflected in the pyramids of Egypt, the ziggurat temples of Sumer and pre-Columbian era constructions in America. The term kurgan comes from a Russian word (of Turkish origin) that designates a burial provided with a mound, under which is the burial chamber.

Something important remains to be said, and that is the need for an alliance between the Russian Orthodox Church and the Alawites in the Middle East, a crucial strategy for both Russia and Syria. Contrary to what is believed, the Alawites are not Islamic, they remain rather a syncretic religion that considers several prophets around the world, including prophets outside the Middle East. The Alawites are monotheistic, and they revere al-Khadir, who by his supreme wisdom and devotion to the supreme God, he is no other than Hadad himself. The Alawites also do the consecration through wine and bread, while they revere Jesus among other prophets. Al-Bashar, the current leader of Syria supported by Putin, is an Alawite and maintains control of the Alawites over Syria through the ruling Baath party, with Alawites accounting for approximately 11.3% of Syria's population. The survival, expansion, and renewal of the Orthodox creed are important enough to put an end to Russian secularism, including the separation of Church and State, so that Russia becomes the center for the preservation of true Christianity and the center of a spiritual revolution.

THINKING IN SPIRITUAL RACES INSTEAD OF BIOLOGICAL RACES

TWO SPIRITUAL RACES

The lesson regarding the tree of the knowledge of good and evil of Eden is that a tree born twisted never grows straight, and the seeds of its fruits will eventually generate more twisted trees. The twisted tree is the race of the times before Adam, that is the race of the descendants of Enki (the serpent in the Garden of Eden) which intermingled with the godly race of Adam, also known as Adad and as Enlil in ancient times. Eve eating first from the tree signifies that she was from the generation after Adam, because Eve is Adam's daughter and the result of mixing between the primitive first humans and the Son of Heaven. Adam's rib, as pointed out by scholar Ziony Zevit, is a reference to a bone called baculum, which is present in the penis of most mammals but not in man, and therefore, a reference to Adam's procreation with the daughters of the first humans. Instead of making foolish biological and therefore material racial considerations and world views, we must have considerations and world views regarding the spiritual races, not biological ones.

    Any fool incapable of realizing that the problem of mankind is in the material realm and not in the spiritual realm is badly mistaken. Therefore, we must conceptualize and make a good understanding of which are the current spiritual races and what is the difference in their basic structure. As I already described, the masculine principle is the main aspect directing Christ, being the rest only a mask that adjusts divine light to the capacity of men. In that way, the Holy Spirit consists of three parts, its feminine aspect which is a mask of darkness that adjusts divine light to the limited capacity of men, then its masculine aspect, which is light itself, and its aspect as a conjunction of those two elements. The structure of a soul of divine inspiration must follow that same principle, that of an inner part of divine light which has in its front a feminine mask of darkness solely to adjust that light to the lower capacity of men. With earthly souls, who inhabit the Earth since the times before Adam, it occurs the opposite, because both in earthly women and men, the masculine part is in front and the feminine part is the inner nature behind. This means that the deepest nature of their souls is darkness (the feminine part) masked by false light (the masculine part).

The souls of divine inspiration are those which I call as the Righteous spiritual race and the earthly souls are those which I call as the Fallen spiritual race, who are Fallen because they moved away from God and therefore away from Heaven. In that way, the Nous (the intelligence and eyes of the soul in Christian Orthodox teaching) varies according to the structure of the soul, and it can reach obedience towards God in the case of the Righteous ones while in the Fallen ones it never can reach it. If it cannot reach it, it will never do so, because the Soul and therefore the Nous cannot be changed in the same way that we cannot change God's decrees. When the race of Adam intermingled with earthly stock some of the offspring inherited Righteous souls and some not, and the result is clearly seen today. Animals don't do sexual identity, they just do sex. Before Adam, no such thing as a sexual identity existed, and because of that, one characteristic of earthly souls is bisexuality.

Homosexuality is always the result of latent bisexuality no matter how early it developed and in the same way bisexual preferences can move toward heterosexual preferences in latter stages, but the latent bisexuality is always present, regardless of how heterosexual or homosexual the Fallen ones appear to be. The Fallen race can metamorphose their sexual identity, and the Fallen ones use that ability to sneak into the Righteous race, even as sexual companions in apparent heterosexual relationships. Because of that, the better way to distinguish a Fallen one is not sexual identity but political identity. The Fallen one is always extremely liberal in the political spectrum, sometimes that extreme liberalism is manifested in all aspects, but on other occasions only in the aspects regarding culture when manifesting a non-liberal and even a Marxist economical approach.

Sometimes liberalism is manifested by the Fallen one in the features involving purely economic matters, but regardless of what features of liberalism are manifested by them, the Fallen race knows that the decaying result will be the same because one sphere affects the other. The same Fallen race became the priesthood and leadership of their so-called Christian churches, and the result is not only widespread homosexual preferences in their clergymen but also child abuse and any perversion imaginable. The fact that women are three times more likely to be bisexual than men (McClintock 2015) is not a surprise. Women are the most affected in the racial contamination with the Fallen race, because the members of the heavenly race of Adam came to Earth as males, mating with earthly primitive women instead of the other way around. " The Nephilim were on the earth in those days—and also afterwards—when the sons of God went to the daughters of humans and had children by them... " (Genesis 6: 4).

The Soviet Union and that entity which made it possible, the State, failed to build inner strength because they were unable to recognize the spiritual problem. Therefore, all attempts at economic and political reform, all social work, all the early economic advancement, and all scientific advancements ultimately failed to save the Soviet Empire... The strength and value of Russia come from the number and proportion of Righteous among its ranks when other countries are already fatally ill with the Fallen race plague, who are there in enough proportions to demolish the basic spiritual and cultural structures of a People. Regardless if the reasons for the fall of the U.S.S.R. are divine justice, its massive economic problems, its cultural contamination by materialism and other ideological flaws of Marxist thought, or foreign actions, the source of all that problems is that the spiritual illnesses in Russia and other countries weren't faced.

All the symptoms of the decay of Soviet communism first emerged from basic spiritual issues. The symptoms which put an end to the Soviet Union were all limited in space and time, but the source of those symptoms, which is neglecting the preservation of a People's spiritual purity, continues today and will continue as long as God's plan for mankind is unconcluded. Realizing not only the symptoms which destroyed the great empires of the past but also the source of those symptoms, which is within the nature of spiritual races, provides us an entire new perspective when trying to understand human history. We no longer see separate events disconnected from each other but one single long event: The fall of the Righteous men. A physical disease can be easily eliminated from a human body, but a spiritual disease cannot be eliminated nor treated in any degree.

By his dark nature, the soul of Fallen ones will forever destroy their inner happiness and will negatively impact on other individuals, lowering man to the condition of a beast who bears the pain of having self-consciousness and reasoning. Spiritual rebirths don't come from anywhere, they are possible as long as the spirit of a People is kept pure with the existence of the Righteous spiritual race in good numbers and proportions. For the Righteous ones, the stress they suffer inspires them in their approach to man's authentic will. Their lost wars are the cause of their future victories, and their drawbacks are the cause of their future advances. But for the Fallen ones, the stress they suffer inspires them to acquire destructive behavior toward others and toward themselves, and their stress doesn't make them closer to authentic will but farther from it.

If a People is losing qualities imparted to it by God, qualities deeply rooted in their spirit, they lose their divine spark, which cannot obtain a replacement in the same way that neurons in our brain. As a patient suffering from Alzheimer's disease, the quality of the People's spirit can start to fade away as with a dying Brain which is unable to repair itself because of the divine inspiration behind its design. Peoples who don't care about the purity of their spirit and allow themselves to be lowered until reaching the level of animals are always punished by some calamity because they have sinned against the will of God. By neglecting their responsibility to guard the spiritual basis of the Russian People, the old Soviet Empire also discarded the only reason that can give an empire and its people their divine right to achieve progress and final victory. Communism, despite achieving early material success and victories, impeded the Russian People from strengthening spiritual and ideological forces that would have made them the winners of any competition with the liberal west.

When the reason for Communism's existence ended, which was preparing the basis for a modern economy and thus achieving victory against the Axis, then Russians and their empire were brought down by a superior power. That power wasn't a foreign intervention, even if foreign powers were preparing for a war with the Soviet Bloc for decades. It wasn't military defeats that caused the Soviet downfall. Any military drawback suffered by the Soviet Union was nothing when compared to the victories of the Soviet Union when waging wars. If we review all the causes of the Russian collapses of both 1917 and 1991, the failure to recognize spiritual problems, which inevitably lead to psychological and political disaster, and failure to acknowledge the way to solve them, were always the factor which sealed the destiny of Czarist Russia and its successor the Soviet Union. The main spiritual problem was and up until now is the need to satisfy a nest of fallen race bandits and financier leeches. The most terrible example of Fallen race tyranny is modern-day U.S. and most of the Third World, where the Fallen race assures complete domination over great masses of people.

Within some decades, they achieve the elimination of vast portions of the Righteous leadership for the People, and by eliminating the spiritual and therefore political leadership of the Righteous ones, the Fallen race prepares for them tyrannical dictatorship, often under the mask of the so-called liberal democracy. The liberal and socialist fallen ones reveal themselves as leeches and tyrants when they are just a few steps from cultural, economical and political domination. That domination is always destructive, not just toward the human race, but to the entire planet. Now, after they no longer need most of their veil, the Fallen race is making its great and final Revolution: that of destroying our planet, even if as the parasites they are, all of them are going in the direction of dying together with their victims.

Naturally, the attack of these parasites is aimed not just at economic targets but first of all toward the spiritual and cultural foundations which the People need for healthy existence. Religion, correct behavior, and traditions, in general, are weakened and also they are shown as ridiculous and obsolete. The Fallen race is an expert in lowering the Righteous ones into the swamp of their own primitive nature. They made patriotic sentiment look as stupid and irrational, and try to impose their own disgusting ideas regarding what should be considered as "good", "beautiful" and "worthy." In this way, the Fallen race corrupts culture in all of its forms, including ideology, religion, literature, cinema, theatre, and educational values. In the economic realm, they promote liberal capitalism with some superficial concessions for the masses. In the political realm, they are always trying destroying the basis of any resistance, starting with the destruction of true Christianity, then the destruction of Righteous leadership, and finally they falsify world history putting insignificant events and personalities as significant, and putting true important events and personalities into oblivion.

They are even capable of erasing the history of entire peoples putting in place the history of civilization from the liberal and western standpoint. Sometimes, they put some military or single-party tyranny when the culture of a People and its spirit is not broken enough. When the Fallen race becomes the financial elites, they are so greedy and selfish than to parasitize the entire world they dismantle State control as much as the intrinsic limitations of capitalism allowed them to do so. In that way, they place gigantic amounts of wealth under their own financial control, regardless if those leeches are of Jewish or Arab origin, or if they are sitting in the Vatican, or in some Chinese skyscraper thinking that money can buy everything. In the poorest regions of the World, as for example in sub-Saharan Africa, the international finance carried by the Fallen race is parasitizing the already delicate victims until all sorts of welfare and stability vanish completely.

That's how even hell was brought up to earth, with more and more slums full of misery and death. When more and more states are put into the control of international finance, this forms a ring of both wealthy and poor countries whose puppet governments sent coalitions of military and financial armies which are sparking wars and inner instability into designated targets. After order is gone in that targets, the Fallen race comes out with the flag of their so-called democratic revolutions, which in fact represents just a strategy for enslaving peoples and controlling their resources.

If a People with a strong State is able to resist foreign attacks even repelling them with military actions, after the victory of the People is temporarily achieved, that People become surrounded by the puppet States which are composed of those peoples which already were put into subjugation. That subjugation is achieved by the Fallen race with a persistent work aiming towards the destruction of culture, economy and leadership, with the final result of a People's spiritual and material decadence. In the controlled masses who follow the different versions of liberalism, the Fallen race finds the way to possess a system without a real democracy based on authentic will, and to have instead a system to conquer and rule the People through a masked dictatorship. To make this process more easily, they are lowering spiritual quality by ruining the culture and the blood of the targeted peoples. The Fallen race wants a bastardized and therefore weaker humanity.

A spiritually pure People can never be defeated by the Fallen race, because that People protects a higher form of culture and has better blood allowing them to carry better souls. Certain forms of culture and certain lineages perform as better carriers for Righteous souls, in the same way that certain red blood cells are better carriers of oxygen than defective ones. The present corruption is a form of fatal spiritual anemia, ending culture and good leadership and raising the fallen race up to remain the rulers of a world made sick by these parasites. They continue bringing non-white immigrants as a flood and by forcing the mixing of blood and culture, they destroy the Righteous spiritual race. They want to destroy the hated righteous spiritual race through a bastardization possible because certain human groups have lesser proportions of that spiritual race than others.

It was the Fallen race who brought multiculturalism with the help of Hitler's madness and consequent demonization of nationalism. The fallen ones are always working to ruin the spiritual and physical quality of women and girls to break down mankind propagating themselves and therefore creating all types of low life bisexual degenerates and drug addicts. The Fallen race will attempt to undermine the spiritual foundations of the People using all the means available. The Fallen race boy and girl are ready for corrupting the unsuspecting Righteous human with their lower form of culture, their lower blood, and their dark spirit, using seduction as a weapon when stealing men and women who still are Righteous, separating them from their spiritual brothers. The toxic way in which they engage in all kinds of relationships with people of higher virtuosity is because they believe that no God and therefore no destiny can reach them. They don't care about any country; they just want headquarters for their international robbery and deceit, headquarters skilfully prepared to be beyond interference from other states, such headquarters are, for example, the Vatican, today's Zionist hijacked Israel, tax haven countries and places, the global financial network and secret clubs and lodges. One part of the Fallen race openly admits they are degenerates hostile towards the spiritual and cultural foundations of all peoples.

The Fallen race's corruption of culture and politics is now so strong they can now openly admit and teach their basic philosophical and political beliefs with their detractors' opinions being branded as politically incorrect. In the hands of the Fallen race, liberalism and its political correctness gradually become constant psychological weapons for sparking fear of the majority and lack of confidence in the minds and hearts of Righteous people. That's the best procedure for crushing opposition, which is necessary to safeguard stability and peace in the eyes of the clowns being in charge of the political bodies of the West. The State authorities either are silent or prosecute victims of unjust attacks who just wanted to put an end to the machine of lies (as occurred with Mr. Assange), attacks which include defamation and lies. Stupidity or ignorance causes many persons believe everything that mass media places into their minds.

As a result of this, we shouldn't be surprised if some people nowadays think that the personification of the Devil, Enki, also known as the serpent of Eden (and who later came as Nimrod) is a savior together with his disgusting Fallen race of degenerates. The Fallen ones are clever enough to see their enemy not only in the ones who are attacking them but also in anyone who is capable of eventually resisting them. That's the reason for their hostility toward anyone who disagrees with their ideological and cultural rubbish. All those who disagree with that are made seen as evil and as ignorant. Because of thousands of years of training, the Fallen race has a great capacity for perceiving all those who can pose a menace for them, and therefore they can distinguish some of the qualities of superior souls which allow the Fallen ones to seek a first strike or resist the Righteous race even further. As with animals, all which is need for sparking suspicion in a Fallen one is some clue that a superior force is coming, the superior force of the sons of Heaven, with their superior genius and superior spiritual abilities in general. So, to find the hostility of the Fallen race, it is not necessary to attack them, they will challenge the Righteous because they can perceive that with may pose an eventual threat, and therefore that which is more elevated than earthly souls.

All those whose innate skills are above the primitive nature of the Fallen race are targeted sooner or later. Mass media is aimed at the designated targets because the objective of mass media under the control of the forces of darkness is striking any element which may be useful in the fight for doing away with the control of Fallen race parasites. Those elements under attack are religious and cultural values, workable ideological teachings, or anything constructive for the betterment of mankind. The attack proves to be more efficient if the People under attack is already weakened by spiritual and cultural contamination for all sides because that contamination generates selfish and lazy individuals incapable of posing a real threat, and of course more Fallen ones in the ranks of humanity. Mass media is tasked with lowering human culture and emotions to those of the animal kingdom, and in that way, western mass media does not promote any positive behavior or higher knowledge, just promote the most lower parts of culture and attitude, making more difficult for the individual mind and his spirit to raise from animal nature.

PROTEST MOVEMENTS AND THE FALLEN RACE

Through the unification of mass media and protest movements, aimed at the least educated people and the least intelligent ones, the political and protest movements pretend to spark instability among Peoples by driving those in the lower levels to commit destructive acts and provocations. As for the unauthorized public demonstrations in Russia, many of these are performed with the clear objective of damaging the government and deliberately causing instability, so it is obvious that the current Russian policy prohibiting unauthorized demonstrations must continue. When they finally show the true intentions behind them, protest movements abandon any interest in social or economic problems and pave the way for political organizations whose orders are to destroy the State with violence and refusal to cooperate. The goal of protest movements under the control of the Fallen race is creating mere instability by mass strikes, armed insurgency, vandalism, etc. Protests are used for controlling the political activity of the protestors themselves and recruiting new protestors who eventually can start more massive political demonstrations.

Protest movements, in addition, obtain financial sources which political organizations and powerful economic actors use to feed a machine aimed at causing instability. Protests also spark in the masses the will for structuring the political organization, but that spark is achieved by exercising pressure, which forces some people to join protests and finally political organizations that operate hand in hand with protests. By using protests, the Fallen race actually destroys the foundations of the economy and the institutions for the targeted peoples. The instrument of protest, which in the hand of righteous individuals can exert positive influences, now is a weapon used not for achieving justice but for achieving destruction and enslavement. Protests are used to break the determination of the ones which still have the ability to resist the constant deceit of the Fallen race and their constant use of violence, intimidation, and seduction with their economic and political resources. If a People is unprepared and, therefore, if its State is weak enough, protest movements can have a disastrous effect over those targeted by the selfish and despicable interests of the Fallen ones, which use their inner dark nature to instigate into the protest movement its evil destructive capacity.

Due to their dark and manipulative nature, the Fallen race is capable of driving away those in protest movements who can challenge their dominance over that instrument. Because individuals within a People do not always have the knowledge and ability to understand certain matters, and because there are plenty of individuals and organizations capable of using those who are more vulnerable and those with lower nature, the State should not remain indifferent in any way regarding protest movements and unauthorized protests must be stopped as soon as possible as it is already done today in Russia. Any attempt in Russia of doing away with the current attitude shown by Putin's government toward unauthorized protests represents ultimate stupidity as long as there is a lack of skill within the People to push for their authentic will and not for a mere manifested will which is brought by demagogic and unrealistic promises being made time after time.

The Fallen ones are masters in the use of demagogic skills because of their lack of morality and their innate destructive skills which avoid any hesitations in them. The leadership of the Fallen race in protests will continue until a persistent education campaign avoids the manipulation of the sectors of the People teaching them the underlying causes of current or eventual problems, together with states, especially the Russian State, leading the way for fighting the Fallen race, therefore avoiding their misdeeds. Current unauthorized protests, at best, would create nothing but instability and confusion among the People instead of any improvement in their living, because first of all the demands of protest movements either cannot be done or are harmful.

If there are some realistic and useful demands, once the real intentions behind the creation of protest movements are shown, those demands vanish from the discourse of the political arm which leads the protesters, because the intention of that political arm is never to achieve positive changes. Because the real objective is the weakening and destruction of the Righteous individuals and their peoples, the Fallen race makes deceitful and even absurd political or economic demands. But a People with enough inner strength cannot be put into submission. A corrupted spiritual and cultural reality must be prepared if the Fallen ones are to achieve any advance in their goals. Any strengthening of the Righteous spiritual race implies fewer persons will allow themselves to follow the goals of the Fallen ones. Demands which are impossible to achieve can be more seductive than realistic ones, and that's another reason which makes protest movements even more dangerous because the real desires of the leadership of protest movements are kept secret while seductive demands are used for the poisoning of vulnerable minds.

The Fallen race does not want to preserve Peoples' independence and therefore any action aimed at truly increasing sustainable economical prosperity and both political and cultural independence is challenged by initiatives to destroy them or made them more difficult in its eventual implementation. Instead of prosperity and freedom, the only goals for the Fallen race are aimed toward the destruction of all which is useful when trying to find a real purpose and freedom in the People's living. Because there is not a genuine interest in ending injustice and elevating human life toward new levels of freedom and joy, masses are used for putting real sovereignty at risk because of leadership for the protest movements, composed of the lowly spirits which gradually escalate into more prominent positions. All around the world, in places like Ukraine, political movements and the protestors used by them do not make any attempt in shortening terrible long working hours and attending other social and spiritual needs. Instead of that, the social and economic elites are generating wealth at the expense of the oppressed masses.

One problem arises, and it is when even individuals who were born with a Righteous soul are infected by elitist attitudes toward their spiritual brothers. But that's the result of an incorrect education which a Normative State must replace to end the inner fighting between those who are of the higher spiritual race. That inner fighting arose because the selfishness and lack of vision of the Fallen race are contagious to both employers and workers. The dangerous inner fighting between those of higher souls acts like a fuel that makes possible more demagogic demands by protest movements and their political organizations. A logic based not only in assembling recruits but also in dividing and conquering is used by those who are against God's plan with his Righteous humanity. The Fallen ones know that by dividing Righteous humanity and consequently making them fight against themselves their opponent can be weakened and conquered. In that way, social elites and the working class are put against each other; the State officials are put against the citizens, and the citizens are put against the State, religions are corrupted and put against each other, and so on.

The Fallen race needs division and a government which appreciates division between the chosen sons of heaven and unity among the fallen sons of Earth. Ideological, social and ethnic differences are used to allow the destruction of loftier forms of culture, including the highest forms of economic and political systems. Division among the sons of heaven is one of the key reasons which are allowing the surrender of states and their peoples to liberalism or the other flawed ideological thinkings. The art of social, cultural and political division is not carried towards the betterment of the human spirit but towards the individualistic attitudes which are the germ necessary for setting liberalism and for setting protest movements and political organizations which made liberalism possible. Individualistic attitudes inherent in the Fallen ones and contagious to Righteous souls can only lead to social and spiritual disintegration.

Protest movements and disintegration are sustained due to the mental and ideological poisoning aimed at both workers and elites with powerful and persisting use of mass media when that instrument is in control of the Fallen race. Protest movements and their leadership will try their best when deceiving individuals with the impression that a better future is possible with lies or harmful promises. In that way, the manifested will generated by demagogic skills and emotional fervor is able to produce enslavement and long-lasting destruction. To feed protest movements and their political organizations, groups of so-called intellectuals are tasked with creating or communicating senseless theories which prevent intelligent people from supporting the causes which they should stand for, while those with the lowest intellect are used to fight for those senseless theories because they lack the intellectual ability to understand how absurd is the nature of the economic and political theories of liberalism.

The destruction of true spirituality with the attack of protest movements and their political organizations, aimed against the Righteous spiritual race, is allowing the chaotic rule of the inferior Fallen race, which is the true objective of liberal ideology. The nature of Liberalism is criminal negligence towards the spiritual value within the peoples as carried by their most outstanding members. That denial will eliminate the fundamental elements which all the human civilizations need for their creation and preservation. Liberalism was born by mixing human weakness with the human capacity for basic reasoning because when human weaknesses and basic reasoning are put together the practical result is that those weaknesses are justified by limited human logic.

That ideological poisoning, because it does not require profound minds to propagate itself, can be presented to the broad masses because of the simplicity behind the liberal political theory. Under ideological simplicity, a simple intention can be masked, that of the evil attempt to allow human selfishness and short-sightedness to provoke the ultimate destruction of mankind, despite the opposition of Righteous persons who are able to recognize the flaws of absurd theories and the manipulation used to promote them. The Fallen ones are able to spread their lies and manipulate the People with the social and political demands of protest movements more easily because once the spark for chaos is started, the Fallen race turns it into hatred toward the ones discovering the truth. Only by manipulation and chaos a philosophy designed for injustice can be spread: the liberal doctrine.

Protest movements, because they urge for change, reflect the innate feelings of all the Righteous souls, and to manipulate those feelings, they carefully collect all the data at their reach, about various aspects that could have an impact on the People's living. After a thoughtful study is done, the lowly souls start to seduce the masses to gain their support, pretending to be worried and angered at the limitations suffered by some sectors which are controlled by the idea that they are in a battle against daily injustice, when in reality they are led to fight for injustice. The oppressed are put to fight in the side of those who cause their misery, without being aware of that. In that way, the Fallen race uses the People's daily struggles as the instrument for their global power. Common persons do not possess the knowledge or time necessary to become closer to their authentic will, because of the complex reality we live in, including constant transformations of the social, cultural and economic structures, transformations that make reality more and more complex. When a lack of understanding is affecting the common individuals, the Fallen race uses their innate skills for manipulation and destruction to be recognized as the ones bearing the ideas and determination necessary to bring human progress.

Since those skills are very powerful, such a big fraud as liberal thought can be instilled while the ones causing misery are able to make themselves seem as saviors and innocent, accusing others of being the source of daily problems. That's how the Fallen ones became the leaders of protest movements so easily because they are experts in winning the supports of their victims, expressed as manifested will. In order to exploit manifested will, the masses are studied to the last detail and their elites work to promote human weakness by poisons as individualistic and feminist thought, materialism and all kinds of ideological and cultural instruments that have destructive effects in complex modern societies. Without that poisoning, no Righteous person would accept the trouble makers of the lowest portions of society. But that trouble makers arose from obscurity because inner division in the side of the best portions of society is not ended by the economic and social changes but on the contrary, that social and economic chances are creating more and more a type of worker which is at the service sector and whose necessities are very neglected.

The People and its State must maintain the determination and capacity to create a better living for them, avoiding the economic and social differences which the lowest elements of society use as their instrument for even more misery. By giving welfare and motivation for civil laborers and soldiers, the old Soviet State instilled in them an unselfish attitude towards their duties, which was the most critical characteristic of Russian officials in extreme situations as saving Europe from the Chernobyl disaster. It was the volunteers, officials and professional employees of the already shaking Soviet State. The disaster urgently demanded a solution and so one was found. Of course, the Soviet Union encountered a similar situation before... in the carnage of the Great Patriotic War, with its old images and writings showing a fearless but always kind and devoted soul. The nature of the Fallen race includes admiration towards the liberal west and its countries. The Russian People, whose heroic ancestors fought against Western aggression do not fall into their trap so easily, but there are still some fools who are the first to be deceived as in any other country.

To disguise the destructive nature of their protest movements and promote their political agenda, Fallen ones talk more and more about liberal concepts as the necessity of some human rights while neglecting others, liberal democracy, and the false concept that all man are born equal while in reality, they don't because of the profoundly different spiritual natures in them. Human beings are more than a pile of flesh and bones. If that was the case, and this material plane is the only existing one, then Human existence would have no purpose at all, nor a real explanation for it. The Fallen race steadily use materialism as a poison for deceiving and confusing existing intellectuals and future ones to deteriorate the minds and culture of their enemies and promote their own concepts, which are lower imitations of higher concepts as freedom, human development and so on.

They are able to constantly steal knowledge which they had learned from others and adapting that knowledge for their destructive action in public life and also for the practice of absolute wickedness and depravity behind closed doors. The leadership of their protest movements and their political organizations, when they see their concessions being given to them, finally show their true nature as enemies of God and therefore as enemies of the Righteous mankind, because they will always have their primitive hate against higher forms of culture and spirituality. They promote cultural forms, including ideological ideas, only in accordance with how much all that can give advantage to them, while ruining others, and in the long run, they end up even ruining themselves.

Protest movements are created and directed by a force that is more familiar to us today than it was in Russia in Soviet Times and which is called "public opinion." Public opinion is manipulated by the skillful mixture of mass media and protest movements. As long as mass media is under control, protest movements are also put under control. The cultural build-up of the People always rests on the foundation of a State. One of the most important factors that can shake that foundation is the

People's misinformation by the work of unscrupulous individuals who manipulate information at will through the media. It is the media, whether television, newspapers, certain Internet sites, etc., which propagates a social illness that dilutes the People's potential to have a wise opinion regarding matters of the utmost importance. In Russia, the State has the logical precaution of maintaining a close monopoly on mass media, as to allow a message that with the latest events have become increasingly contrary to the interests of the powers behind NATO.

We do not need massive and dangerous mass media that seek to misinform people with propaganda efforts while being protected by the so-called "freedom of expression." Some of the individuals behind this machinery aiming at hiding the truth are true traitors to their own People; they do not deserve any space in the media because they do not give space to the truth. Today's media is making news without real importance seem important issues, and issues that have crucial importance are thrown into oblivion or ignorance from the beginning. Even worse, fake news is on the rise and staged events like the 7th April 2018 chemical attack in the Syrian city of Douma, and the poisoning of Sergei and Julia Skripal, all of which was staged and directed by British intelligence, serves as a warning of how even staged events can damage the global image of Russia and its allies by the use of mass media as a tool for deceit.

Modern heroes like Julian Assange are incarcerated for allowing the world to know the truth and betrayed as happened with Assange thanks to the pathetic new government for Ecuador. The media makes an incompetent with the necessary support and money to be relevant in politics, and sometimes, unfortunately, some of these individuals manage to catch many people thanks to knowing how to speak in an attractive way for them. It is critically important to reflect on how propaganda and disinformation resulting from the media, under the so-called "freedom of expression", pollute people's minds through different methods, including slander and defamation of those with good intentions while embellishing charlatans, cowards or the unscrupulous as figures that represent some kind of preferable alternative to people who have the intelligence, knowledge, strength, and spirituality to carry out a project seeking to establish a change in social structures and even global structures. To destroy the figures carrying change or the messages useful to society, the media appeals to minor events in the private life of these figures, or focus on statements that are only part of the total message that these people want to give.

If nothing is found that can be used to throw these figures down, lies can be invented and statements twisted, nothing escapes unscrupulous methods to manipulate information and drive protest movements. The ones behind the manipulation of information sometimes try making believe others that their work is done under the duty of reporting information, but in fact, they do it with the need to obey certain sectors of society or sometimes they do it looking for sensationalism to win over the public. Even the Internet is not safe from the manipulation of its information, because for example, during the campaign for the US elections of 2016, in June of that year the editor of Wikileaks, Julian Assange, said that Google was "directly committed" with the Clinton campaign, which was confirmed by a series of leaked emails. Numerous reports have also concluded that Google manipulated search suggestions to favour Clinton, opting to eliminate the negative but popular suggestions that appeared when the searches were done.

In November 2016, the European Parliament voted in favour of a resolution on its "strategic communications" to struggle against alleged Russian propaganda against the European Union. Of the 691 deputies who participated in the vote, 304 voted in favour of the document and 179 against, while 208 abstained. The project, prepared by Polish MEP Anna Elzbieta Fotyga and debated in the European Parliament, calls for a response from the European Union to what it considers "propaganda and misinformation" from Russia. The document mentions the Sputnik agency, the RT television network, the Russkiy Mir Foundation and the Russian cultural cooperation agency Rossotrudnichestvo. Controlling both the mass media and protest movements remains the only way in which the Fallen race can be put in ruling positions of politics and culture. That would be impossible if it wasn't by masses driven like a herd by mass media and protest movements instigating large numbers of individuals as long as they are unable to become aware of their authentic will, and of their real nature when they higher spiritual quality makes impossible the deep control of the Fallen ones.

To make their political and economic position stronger, the Fallen race tries to destroy all ideological and cultural elements which could serve as barriers against their misdeeds. When performing this, they always are promoting laity and religious tolerance, and with that, they start to erase the most basic elements of Righteous traditions. When eroding the ideological and moral basis of a People, they also destroy the pillars of the economy, creating economic chaos with their greed and short-sightedness. Unfortunately, some still believe the lowly souls are emissaries for a better age of humanity, the age that we call as modern age, with all its liberal values, its materialism and also the false spiritual teachings within new age nonsense and corrupted western Christianity. The Fallen race will always show themselves as wise persons and then they will start to spread their lies regarding the progress of humanity by distorting facts and totally omitting others. People give them much more credit for human progress than what they actually achieved. That which they achieved was purely made for serving their selfish goals and cannot be compared to the contribution of the race which God made in accordance to His own image.

Protest movements and mass media can manipulate the People to make them believe those of lower souls are victims of what they call an unjust society for them, because what they call unjust societies are those capable of strongly fighting against the Fallen ones and their ideas. Anyone who does not believe that Fallen ones are victims of unjust societies but instead the destroyers of societies is treated in an unjust way and with hatred. Using their manipulation skills, the Fallen race puts into the mind of a People that the lowly souls are the best drivers of human progress until many believe all that as true. They make seem themselves as very worried by the hardships of the People and that important actions are made by them for ending those hardships. We must remember that all that they want is having full possession of the rights which can allow their misdeeds. Their inner nature will never change.

The Fallen ones are an absolute disease that is hastening the decay of the unfortunate people who cannot defend against the source of that spiritual illness, which is made worse when lower souls achieve the concession of more freedom for the spreading of cultural and economic misery. When the power of ancient elites was established, the Fallen race was smart enough to find ways of being close to them, for example within the occult and satanic circles of the elite, which are nothing new, as they have existed since very ancient times. To prevent the world from falling entirely into darkness, sometimes the peoples reacted and the Fallen ones were burned at the stake, beheaded, etc. But every time the Fallen race faced struggles and was put away, they soon returned and peoples were subject to the same dark forces again. No matter how much time passed, sooner or later, as with endemic disease, no attempt was strong enough to do finally away with the dark forces of the spiritual race whose inner nature is darkness itself.

The reason for explaining that even high levels of persecution never changed their nature is because that nature can't be changed. As the dog barks and birds sing because of their inner animal nature, the lower ranks of humanity will continue to take advantage of others. Even though the Righteous' resistance and natural dislike against their common enemy, the Fallen race, they return because any inner weakness in the Righteous persons, including the fact that they are put against each other, is exploited all over again. In order to set up their influence and their deceit, the Fallen ones put their resources in so-called aid to governments and communities, but of course, that aid is, in reality, an instrument used to rob their victims because any lack of intelligence and vision, any suffering and any weakness, in general, is enough to set the trap of so-called humanitarian and social aid together with protest movements and the use of mass media to attack certain governments, organizations and persons, including their ideas.

The detection of the Fallen race and their activities must be done before times of great public distress when it may be already too late. People must be educated to detect the traits that will allow them to recognize the nature of the real threat earlier before the power and poisoning of the Fallen ones is consolidated. A People and its State must be able to act promptly, before the economic and social crisis, and before the action of protest movements and mass media create instability and finally domination. When unfortunately that domination is achieved, the Fallen ones force the Righteous to live in states governed by nefarious individuals and institutions which made evil and coercive demands.

They regard the planet only as their possession for achieving selfish goals regardless if they destroy it at the end. In that, they don't have any consideration towards our planet more than mindless exploitation of their resources and their peoples as much as they can. Anyone who becomes aware of the revelations in this book will instantly understand why mass media and some individuals are so aggressive towards the Fourth Political Theory and Aleksander Dugin, distorting his image and the perception of his thoughts. The best way of proving the value of this book is by studying current problems. This book show how is the inner nature of the Fallen race and of their protest movements and mass media, which use tricks characteristic of that spiritual race. In that way, it is possible to know their real goal and how they make both unconsciously and consciously their actions. When they speak Russian, their thinking is of their fallen race.

THE RIGHTEOUS SPIRITUAL RACE
IS THE ONLY BEARER OF CIVILIZATION

The biggest lie is the Fallen Ones are not a spiritual race but just a way of living and a personal choice. With that, the Fallen race builds ideological tools that allow them to make subsequent lies based on the biggest one. Jesus made clear his attitude toward the enemies of God, the Fallen Ones, using a whip to drive them out of God's temple. The only concern of the Fallen race is related to the material world despite sometimes they pretend to have some higher spirituality. They are enemies of true Christianity as they have been since the very beginning of it in the time of Jesus Christ, and in the same way, they have been carrying their misdeeds since the very beginning of mankind's existence. Detailed studies of Righteous individuals have shown the real moral nature of Fallen race philosophical teachings, which is always destructive or consist of very little philosophical teachings which do not cope with the real problems being faced by mankind. The Fallen race philosophical teachings consist of ways to deal with their enemy, the Righteous, and ways to have some coordination between themselves, and in that teaching, we can see every idea was stolen or distorted because they don't even have the capacity to create original thinking. Philosophical schools are created to promote the advance of false teachings and therefore for widespread cultural and spiritual decay.

Philosophical schools and modern "Gender studies" serve the Fallen ones as a method for creating confusion and corrupting societies. The Fallen ones were always a spiritual race with specific characteristics shared by all of them, therefore they belong to a separate spiritual race and not to a simple "way of living" or "personal choice." In their philosophical, anthropological and sociological circles, creative and independent thinking is often considered a sin against their political correctness and their ideological schemes that determine who is promoted and who is not in their academic world. Government offices are among the first victims of that academic and cultural poisoning because many State servants and bureaucrats have little knowledge regarding true philosophy and science and only are familiarized with a small part of real knowledge. Ideological and cultural poisoning is capable of convincing some sectors of the parasitized People that the Fallen Ones are just persons of a different political, sexual and philosophical orientation. The degree of destruction which they cause is determined by how skillful the individual Fallen is when continuing on his actions as a parasite among other peoples.

As happens with the Righteous race, their inner nature also varies from individual to individual, according to innate dark skills which make some of them more dangerous than others. The Fallen ones need lying continuously and with the use of sophisticated methods for sustaining their existence as a parasite within the body of states and peoples. The use of their tricks is as important and normal to them that the only possible explanation is that it is also part of their inner nature. Once their influence is strong enough, they no longer need hiding, dropping the veil and suddenly all can see their real character, which only some were capable of truly perceiving instead of ignoring evident signals. A new State which begins as a State within the original one show itself with the colors of the LGBT movement, liberal political parties, feminist movements, together with satanic Vatican deviants and child rapists, and that State will continue to exist as long as it is not exiled from Public institutions and culture. The Fallen race has always tried creating their states consuming the previous ones which were created by the other spiritual race, and they start by creating within those states the seed for their own. The effect of the Fallen parasite is the collapse of the civilizations created by their victims and even the impossibility of creating new ones. Like dangerous bacteria, they spread in all those places which are the best for their proliferation until those places became so full of illness that even the parasite is unable to sustain itself. To spread, they pretend to have some loyalties towards countries and their traditions, but only because those countries and those traditions created the body which they feed on.

Because of that, the Fallen ones are nomads eternally wandering, because the Fallen ones have no true loyalty to any country, not even to the planet Earth, which in case of being totally controlled by them would get uninhabitable and replaced by some other planet if they manage to do so, as their dark spirits just wander from one place to another. Like any parasite, they will always need new places and therefore new lands and peoples for their destructive expansion. Therefore, the Fallen race has always been wanderers feeding themselves on the body of their victims. Their inner nature may be unacceptable to the Righteous race, but it is acceptable to them. While the Fallen ones are eternal wanderers, the Righteous race despite being wanderers at the beginning, over the course of time they were able to create a permanent settlement in one place.

But the most important thing is they never were just an earthly fallen creature. As soon as better numbers and technology made possible to endure natural hardships and resist the earthly native souls, the Righteous was able to establish more and more permanent settlements for human civilization. Only at the beginning, they were just nomadic wanderers in small clans constantly moving in the search of new resources. We must remember that at the times when both Russian territories and the American continent were being settled, many Righteous people struggled for living moving to pristine lands. After years of technical developments and demographical growth, that hard life became something of the past.

If they did not have their innate creative and spiritual capacity, they would have to avoid unexplored or lest favorable lands and also they would need to live as eternal nomads. The world has plenty of places where human development was and currently is the product of the cultural and therefore technological achievements of the Righteous race, who was born with the skill of making more sustainable and productive use of large territories, fructifying and multiplying in them. The reason for the Fallen Race wandering is that the Earth and Earth's civilizations are still too infertile for their inferior spirituality and intellect, therefore they cannot support a permanent settlement of their own. Also, they are faced with the lack of a civilization based in space exploration needed to compensate for the limited resources of a single planet. Instead, they feed on host peoples and their lands which suffer from very negative effects as they wander from one place to another.

They don't cultivate higher forms of civilization and therefore sustainable development; they just parasitize. Since the Fallen race could never create a civilization by themselves, the only thing which they can do is to influence peoples and states as much as they can, by the combining forces of domestic and foreign action. The only logical conclusion is that the Fallen race does not assist in the progress of mankind, on the contrary, they are an obstacle for it. In some cases, their intellect may appear as a positive and original influence, but doing a more profound analysis, we can see that the ultimate result of that influence is always negative despite appearing to have some good effects in the short term.

In that way, their intellect is always destructive because of the dark inner nature which drives the creations of that intellect. That dark inner nature is incompatible with true spirituality and with the true creativity associated with it, which are necessary for the sustainable development of civilization. If a spiritual race does not have the abilities required to build sustainable development for mankind that means they do not possess any power for creating and strengthening civilization, not even for themselves…

Mass media make them look innovative and impressive to generate a false image of them until the masses think they are truly brilliant minds with remarkable souls, but they are nothing more than good imitators of true genius and spirituality. The Fallen race mass media promotes and helps untalented and crooked persons, no matter how poor their true abilities are, as long as they are from the low spiritual kind. They will never be original and positive creators, and to appear being so, they made some distortions or unimportant contributions that may impress those who can't identify that which is genuinely of a loftier and original nature.

They don't have the innate divine spark within them which is the sole way in which a truly exceptional achievement can be produced. They merely employ tricks to steal and distort the achievements of others. We can see how the Fallen ones steal and destroy human achievements in those areas where these lowly souls are seen more often, which are degenerate or empty television shows, films, stupid music and corrupt literature, which does not require the spark of divine intellect and creativity. While the Righteous race possesses qualities that make them able to found civilizations and made them stronger, the Fallen Race has those qualities necessary to destroy human civilizations. What the Fallen ones propagate in cultural fields are inferior versions of the achievements of those of higher nature, complete imitations or cultural poisoning.

All elements of civilization which the Fallen race possesses come from the achievements of the Righteous ones, including of course all those who suffered from the actions of the first. Despite the Fallen ones are masters in pretending to possess spiritual and intellectual skills, they aren't capable of creating the basis for civilization nor even the strengthening of it. To create the basis of civilization and the strengthening of it, not only the intellectual skill of true higher spirits is required, but also the Righteous' attitude towards labor and spirituality. If that is not possible, then chaos will make impossible any advance towards higher forms of living. For that very reason, the cultures, states and economic institutions permeated by the Fallen race have poor boundaries and barriers, being those boundaries and barriers of vital importance for the well-being and conservation of a People. That is destroyed or made more difficult because the Fallen race is guided by nothing but individual selfishness and therefore liberal universalism and globalization are promoted regardless of its consequences. If the Righteous spiritual race did not arrive, or if it became extinct, the Fallen ones would return to the most primitive forms of life and will fight against each other as apes in a jungle.

The only reason behind some degree of unity among them is because of their struggle against the sons of heaven. If we take that from the equation, their already fragile unity will vanish completely and they will resume their selfish inner nature in all its magnitude until they fight against each other like a plague of hungry rats set over a piece of food. Only when a common peril or a common victim force their primitive will to some degree of unity is when the Fallen ones aren't fighting between themselves. In the same way, their false self-sacrifice is masking their individual self-interests, because a big act of sacrifice, even if it is made only for individualistic and selfish reasons easily appear to some as something impressive. The same can be observed in other earthly creatures. A group of wolves only are united when they need to destroy their prey, and when they achieve their goal they will only show the mindless individualistic nature typical of many animal species. When knowing those essential facts, it is easy to see why the intentions and sacrifices of the Fallen do not go beyond primitive animal self-preservation.

Even if their intellectual powers were comparable to those of the Righteous spiritual race, which is not the case, despite it appear so to some, they will never have the other spiritual qualities of higher souls as embodied in true solidarity and true self-sacrifice. Because of that lack of true solidarity and true self-sacrifice, the authentic will is absolutely far from the Fallen race, instead, a primitive manifested will takes place within them. Those limitations forced them to use the tools and benefits of the civilizations surrounding them. Before the arrival of the sons of heaven, they never produced a civilization of their own even in the span of hundreds of thousands of years. Even now, if the already created civilizations were left completely at the mercy of them, they would get destroyed sooner or later because civilizations need peoples capable of developing a culture of their own, and the Fallen ones never will be capable of that, they are only capable of stealing some degree of knowledge from others. If a genius from 1920 was able to travel in time to the present, he would encounter an enormous exponential advance which will absolutely shock him, even if he is just one century behind us and human existence developed through thousands and thousands of years. The Fallen ones feed on these exponential advances which only a century ago were unimaginable to people back then.

A dangerous threat is more and more strong, which is that the Fallen race of today has more achievements and knowledge to feed on that in any other time of human history. Today, the individual and its community are surrounded by many technological and also spiritual creations, and the enemies of God and of mankind made at God's own Image can use all the exponential advance of higher souls against their original creators. To exploit that exponential advance in the most skillful way possible for lowly souls, the Fallen ones are cunning when parasitizing others and destroying the products emanated from others. The intellectual qualities of the Fallen ones, which serve only their dark inner nature, have been feed through thousands of years of the exponential growth of their adversaries and the need to fight against them.

Because they focus entirely on preserving and increasing their selfish happiness, they fall from spiritual Heaven to material Hell, hence their destiny is being fallen souls and it always will be so. They even spread their attitude toward the Righteous' ranks, and that is very dangerous since if mere individualism becomes the guiding principle of a People, all attempts for higher forms of living by a necessary social order are made impossible. When the guiding principles needed to form a civilization are lost, the only outcome possible is the destruction of civilization. When the authentic will is put far, because we approach it only with high guiding principles, and manifested will reach the levels of mere animal self-preservation, the inner force and social order that maintains the People's well-being is lost. The well-being of the People rests on those whose innate spiritual quality are making possible real self-sacrifice and therefore true solidarity, not on the dark intentions and deceitful ideas of wicked and pitiful individuals who pretend to know more than God, violating his eternal laws.

The Righteous souls will always disagree and struggle against the nonsensical ideas and actions of evil products of modernity, such as liberalism and feminism, whose proponents try to deceive the People by a mask of wisdom and solidarity which is useless against those who can see their inner dark nature as selfish degenerates, constantly violating God's laws which constitute the basis for authentic will. The Righteous are able to come closer to authentic will because of their Nous (which is the intelligence and eyes of the soul in Christian Orthodox teaching) is developed enough to obey divine laws and understand their importance, at the expense of individual selfish interests when serving God and his true sons as a whole is deemed as the intended purpose of existence.

The Righteous even being just a very young boy can listen to the nonsense of liberals and feminists without paying attention to that at all but accepting immediately an inner authentic will which makes him ready to do what he must and not just what he hears and perceives in the rants of dark souls. The true wisdom and authentic will of the Nous become manifested when the time for the Righteous individual to manifest it finally comes. Authentic will, which comes from the Nous, and therefore from God, leads men to willingly recognize God's power and act accordingly, being the individual human just a particle within God's creation. Any human individual, any human organization and the development of them absolutely depend on that understanding and the authentic will associated with it. Normativism, as the true Christianity which is, should be no less than acting in accordance with the will of God.

Without reaching authentic will, all the superficial mental and physical capabilities are useless and do not serve any other thing than darkness, regardless of how brilliant and powerful some humans may appear to be. All those capabilities will retain no real value and cannot be used for creating civilization but for destroying it instead. Only the Righteous spirit is capable of having a true creative influence which only comes by having a higher form of Nous, in order of creating human development through the ages and therefore sustainable civilizations... From his soul and the Nous associated with it is that the Righteous owes his position over Earth. It is necessary to realize that authentic will and acting according to it have no relation at all with the superficial and stupid idealism behind what is called by some as "solidarity" and "humanism", which sometimes enters into contradiction with the necessary basis for creating human civilization. Authentic will means exclusively the ability to achieve anything necessary in God's plan with his true sons. Despite a pure authentic will is beyond human reach, approaching it is possible and a necessity, and doing it is the opposite of liberal thoughts and individual selfishness.

Only by approaching authentic will we can assure that a People's existence and mankind's protection as a civilized race are assured instead of being destroyed by Nature and earthly spirits. Only the Nous of Righteous souls has brought human achievement, because those souls are the only ones capable of placing God and his true sons above selfishness and stupidity, being then the principal and founding element for every truly civilized culture. Manifested will whose only goal is mere self-preservation disregarding any other thing does not differ from the will of primitive animals. The Righteous persons understand their actions should aim not only for the petty interests of individualism but above all for the health of the People and therefore the health of a higher mankind. Demonstrating a divine spirit is through tasks that are achieved by true self-sacrifice and real capabilities. In that way, the individual is able to make a correct place from himself in the People's body, for the sake of the benefit of that body as a whole. Only by serving God and therefore those made at His own image is that any true reward is possible instead of suffering and death.

Even the human ego must be put to work for the interests of the People as a whole and not the opposite, overcoming personal opinions and selfishness and putting the individual capabilities at the service of a higher entity, that of true human civilization as expressed in its peoples and states. If individuals have only earthly intellectual abilities, and their Nous does not have the qualities of higher souls, that intellectual abilities will be used merely for destructive purposes and would make impossible loftier forms of human organization and wisdom. The reason for the Righteous' ability when building and strengthening civilizations is not only the intellectual abilities of the earthly mind but also the will necessary to overcome problems to attain higher forms of living while understanding consciously or unconsciously that the only reward is achieved by doing so and not by acting only for self-preservation and individual short-sightedness. When the acting provided by uniting Nous and the bodily mind is carried out for approaching authentic will instead of the actions aimed at the individualistic intentions done by the lower forms of manifested will, so the human capability for building and protecting higher forms of living increases exponentially.

In that way, peoples become prosperous and expand their political and cultural influence. That is the absolutely essential basis required for the welfare and influence of a People in any degree. Once the partnership between humans and their souls become a true partnership to achieve a higher common goal, not just for the purpose of ephemeral self-interests, then it requires the need for self-preservation to evolve into the need for a higher preservation, that of the Soul, which only is possible with the common preservation of brother souls and God's gifts to our planet. If the need for self-preservation does not reach this level, there is no civilization possible, not even a functional family. The individualistic attitudes are not just selfishness aimed at struggling against others for one's personal interests. The individualistic attitude is also short-sightedness regarding time. In selfish individuals, as they inevitably put the immediate moment as their only priority, lust for an immediate result is too great to plan things for the future or ever for seeing the prospects of that future.

This kind of selfishness is the one that causes danger to future generations due to the misdeeds of previous ones, and the one that puts the individual itself in danger inasmuch as he does nothing for his own future. As stated in a previous chapter, time is an illusion, but an illusion which man cannot escape and will not escape. Pretending to escape that is like pretending to escape God, and therefore pretending to be God. The reason why the Righteous is so important is discovered in how his will is expressed with his Nous and finally his bodily mind. Every human that is unable to reach the higher will required for him is a useless pile of meat and bones which is shattered by time until becoming dust. Civilizations are not destroyed by merely human conflicts and natural disasters, but also because they lose the kind of souls present in good bloodlines and which are the ones demanding a healthy culture.

The main reason for the demise of ancient cultures and civilizations is the disregard for the spiritual quality of a People, which is carried by the vessel of bloodlines, and which is in need of higher forms of culture correlating to their higher inner nature. For some time, the structures which the most capable souls made are capable of sustaining the individuals whose ancestors and themselves disregarded the value of inner spiritual nature, but after a period of stagnation, the collapse of that structure is unavoidable if the ones who truly created it aren't with it.

Adam's spiritual purity declined as it mixed with earthly humans until finally, the product of that mixture was a culture that resembled more the earthly ones than Adam's nature, both in intellectual and material results. The Righteous surrendered the purity of his spirit by intermingling and lost the right to the Paradise which God has made for his true creation. Therefore, the Righteous have to follow the road signaled to him by God and Righteous ancestors, not the suicidal road of individualistic madness and short-sightedness present in all the variations of liberalism. When the time arrives, destiny imposes the conditions which made the Righteous arise from a previous level to a level in which his innate spiritual qualities and his innate genius are evident, both in intellectual and material work and therefore in the results of human culture and true human freedom. This phenomenon will be by far more evident in the spiritual race which in all the periods of time was and still is the sole bearer of true human development and civilization: the Righteous ones.

The innate abilities of the individual only appear as truly manifested when hardships and exceptional conditions made those abilities necessary. In that way, those innate abilities are manifested when they have to. The same is true in the level of a People and in the level of a spiritual race as a whole, their true abilities aren't seen until specific conditions stimulate the People's ability and that of the spiritual race, putting the

Nous, the bodily mind and finally material strength into action when is necessary, and into inactivity when it is unnecessary to rush things. Even when things are accomplished, individuals and their peoples fail to identify the true force which made possible individual and collective achievements. That's because they only are able to see the most visible expressions of human achievements. All inner forces which are behind that remain unseen, and also other achievements which are related to the People's cultural and spiritual preservation. The true genius coming from the Nous is innate of every individual and every People and it cannot be taught or learned in the same way that the nature of a human soul cannot change.

Even considering creators themselves do not recognize the greatness of their creations until that creation shines over the human world, it is a mistake to think that special conditions created existing capabilities. Those capabilities were already present, and they manifest only when they have to. Challenging situations and stress are needed to awake hitherto unseen capabilities. All rewards come with a cost, but the cost is nothing compared with the reward when the Righteous is doing what he must do. Some individuals will fail at their task, others not, and some individuals will never witness what being created at the Image of God truly is, and with the later, I am referring to the Fallen ones. Someone who at the beginning appeared as selfish or as a mere madman one day show his true inner nature by putting all the might of his will in situations which others are unfit to face, generating astonishment and sometimes jealousy in the rest. Higher souls do not reflect the rest of their families entirely, but if mighty ancestors are present, that ancestor will put the necessary drop of blood which will make an outstanding individual possible. The same is true in the higher levels of peoples, civilizations and spiritual races. All their creation, development and destruction reflects how mighty their ancestors were because bloodline is the vessel of higher souls, but vessels do not always are of a good bloodline due to the intermingling between diverse individuals and peoples.

The loss of the divine spark of higher souls is the ultimate cause of the stagnation and destruction of human civilizations and Righteous' legacy because the founders of all that are Righteous themselves and in their same spiritual race some are of loftier nature than others. The ones who carry human achievements and are able to create and sustain a civilization are replaced by new generations, each one more contaminated than the previous ones until a civilization stagnates and then disappears. When a new People arrives whose bloodlines and culture are still the vessels for higher souls then a new civilization will start, and the previous cycle will be repeated if nothing is done about it. Throughout history, various lands became the home of the same Righteous spiritual race who inhabited them at different times. Those lands experienced a second contact with the sons of heaven, and then even other waves arrived as the described cycle restarted. The problem with doing nothing to avoid that cycle is that the spiritual race that already brought civilization to those lands lose the memory and knowledge of the past, and without that memory and that knowledge is like climbing the same ladder repeatedly until it finally crumbles. And mankind now has the destructive creations and economical power which can destroy that ladder, and that ladder is, of course, planet Earth.

Some shaking states, whose original Peoples and cultures have already been adulterated and whose original spirits departed from them, may appear as shining examples with their creations seeming as their own creations. But they are enjoying the product of the past work of their predecessors, and the states and civilizations which do not have their true founders any longer are like cancerous cells who lack the original DNA sequence and eventually die killing others. If the original bearers of true culture aren't there, then the original DNA will be stripped from the cells which are the elements of culture, and the elements of culture will become defective and fatally ill. With the destruction of the spiritual aspects of the Righteous sons of heaven, as carried by their bloodlines and their culture, the engine for human development and achievement is destroyed in the corroding waters of the Fallen race.

Even for Adam, after his ancestral sin, the punishment was the expulsion of the paradise which God has made with him and by the joy of the sons of heaven. Since those times, the Righteous has interacted with earthly souls by intermingling with lower bloodlines and cultures, and by doing so, they have been destroying the spiritual existence of those made at God's image. The Righteous race ignored the first divine law, that of keeping their bloodlines and their culture pure instead of making that bloodlines and that culture the room for the Fallen race parasite composed of lower earthly stock, which began tempting the sons of heaven since the union of Adam with earthly, fallen women. Because the DNA and the culture of the Righteous ones made a room for further development of the primitive earthly humans, the abilities which the Fallen race exercise today were not possible until the Righteous spiritual race appeared.

The Righteous race caused the primitive intellectual and cultural skills of the Fallen race to develop and doing so, and evil half- breed was created. The result of mixing, as it is controlled by mere chance, made that the current Homo Sapiens, which is a half-breed between the sons of heaven and earthly humans, have in its ranks individuals who inherited Righteous souls while others not, in the same way that individuals inherit some specific genetic traits while others do not inherit those traits. The part that is missing in current anthropology is DNA is not only the carrier of physical traits but also spiritual ones, which currently aren't restricted to any visible physical phenotype. Development through centuries made the whole of Russia, for example, could form a Eurasian civilizational sphere of her own. However this culture not only was built on the foundation of the Byzantine Empire and Western powers, but it was also built with native Russian spirits and creativity.

As everything sooner or later encounters its opposite, the founders of civilization encountered the destroyers of civilization. The sons of heaven encountered the sons of earth. Take the Righteous spiritual race away, and undoubtedly within a short time, ultimate darkness will descend upon this planet, all human civilizations will be destroyed, and the world will become a desert. Adam and his race are the Prometheus of humanity whose higher Nous is the fire to ignite the bodily mind to be the carrier of light, in the form of more superior knowledge, happiness, spirituality and material achievements everywhere, including the fact that humanity is today the master of the others species living in this planet. God used his creation, the Righteous race, to make a superior form of human life and without it the lower earthly human inhabitants would be only slightly above the level of apes.

Asphyxiated with liberal concepts and false humanitarian intentions, the sons of heaven are in the presence of a grave made for themselves and their destiny, as their progress is blocked by false teachings and stupid sentiments. It will be an even harsher destiny which awaits to all those who believe that they can defeat God, while they only destroy themselves. Any man who will not fight for God in this world made by him does not deserve living. The many, who would desire to live in his creation and his paradise, must fight their road. This road is dependent on the inflexible divine law, necessary and just because the Righteous man is destined to be a triumphant member of God's Kingdom. The ultimate outcome of the struggle against the forces of nature and against the earthly human spirits is determined by God and by the inner natural tendencies of his sons which are present all along with this planet.

That inner divine nature is what determines if peoples bear cruel hardships and disasters with all the suffering and death brought by that. Someday, God will carry out his severe punishment again because people abandon God's laws after they though that achieving a higher level of comfort is all that is needed in human life and human civilizations. Atheists will laugh at declarations like this one, but our planet moved through space for millions of years without men walking on the surface, and that can easily be a reality once more. Some will try battling constantly to see if liberalism, feminism, and Marxism are able to work. At least those ideas cannot cause harm which goes beyond the realm in which they are possible, which will become scarce and then inexistent once the Righteous spiritual race, led by his Saviour, has attained sole rule. All the false teachings of the past will then have no possibility to cause harm. Liberalism, feminist rants, Marxism and even die-hard classical western fascism may be perfectly good ideas if the Earth ceases to be suited for human life because it will be no longer a place to apply them. Looking into past decades, the mingling of all those ideas was intended by the Russian world savior wannabe, Gorbachev, or at least what the Soviet prophets thought he intended, and they believed that through his plans their ideals would be attained.

Anyone who seriously intends to protect liberal ideology would have to change his mind before he desires to wage the Third World War to keep liberalism alive. I say this because a big part of mankind living inside and outside Russia has not been completely fooled by this liberal nonsense. If this wasn't the case, and Russia's destiny is to disappear, the last liberal would very likely die out with the last Russian. Those who truly want liberalism and the destructive products of modernity to be the ultimate conquerors of this planet would have to do all they can to impede the Russian Orthodox Church and the Russian economic and military power, of rule over a bast cultural sphere. The preservation of a spiritual race and its ranks remains the most important element behind the ideas which emanate from man. Ideas as those of liberalism and the Pope represent the feelings and concepts of the man who created them. In that way, ideas cannot be separated from man, and in turn, man cannot be separated from his spirit and from the divine laws which govern existence. In the same way that without humans there can be no human ideas, without a spirit there can be no humans.

An idea cannot destroy nor conquer by itself the basis of mankind's well-being since ideas themselves come from mankind. In the same way, mankind cannot conquer or alter what is of their spirits since mankind completely comes from them. And finally, human souls cannot change what it comes from God since God is the ruler of existence. Thereby, ideas cannot conquer man; man cannot conquer souls, and souls cannot conquer God. All men, even aided with their ideas and their spirit, never defeat God, they have merely learned to dominate some of God's gifts who came as the resources and creatures of our planet. Although man can grow in knowledge and manipulate his surroundings, he never will be able to create in the way God does. Neither man and his ideas, nor his soul have never once surpassed God, but just lifted one little part of his giant veil behind which there are eternal secrets.

Today millions mindlessly imagine themselves as the materialistic and atheistic conquerors of God's realm, but their only true weapon is their soul, and the ideas which they have are childish and pretentious when one ultimately realizes how flawed they are. This is always contested by the arrogant statements of the modern atheist whose ideas can be purely from the Fallen race in its origin, and therefore nonsense: "But, God is an invention of man!". That defiance of God will ultimately lead to the downfall of those who do were unable to accept grander truths and show a higher will.

When pretending to defy God's laws man only comes into a struggle with the same laws to which all humans and the Universe owes their existence and preservation. That defiance will be met only by self-destruction since such a deviation as atheism and materialism is an attempt to disregard the basic principles from which mankind and their world emanated, and therefore is a sin against the will of God. The Righteous ones will remain in control of God's gifts as long as they do not doom themselves with spiritual degradation resulting from the intermingling and corruption of the Righteous spiritual race with the lesser spiritual peoples and individuals, that's to say, peoples with more Fallen ones as a proportion of their ranks and individuals who aren't the bearers of a Righteous soul. God does not desire the mating of his true sons with earthly individuals unless a severe lesson is needed to be taught. Destiny will show no mercy to human and spiritual weaknesses and only the most Righteous souls will shine in their path. Those chosen in the highest level must rule, with God's will being accomplished by complete victory of his true sons, not by a sexual and cultural intermingling which runs counter to God's will to elevate his creation. Chaotic families emerge when all or some of their members are of a lower spiritual nature, creating contagious social dysfunction and toxic relationships.

Every breeding between two humans that are not from the same spiritual level produces a result directed by chance. The offspring could be on a higher level than the spiritually lower one of its parents; it could be better than the two parents, or worst than both. Being under the rule of chance is being under the rule of chaos.

GOD'S RULE AND THE IDEA OF THE THEOCRATIC STATE

THE POLITICAL SYSTEM

The tasks of the Fourth Political Theory are to think about the day when the People will receive what is necessary for a dignified existence, and also having the will to uphold the premise that persons do not live only for material pleasures. The People's economy and culture should be productive and provide a valuable service to the community, but it will gradually become involved in inevitable decline as the power of wisdom is replaced by the influence of the manifested will from the masses instead of their authentic will as a People. The new State can best care for the well-being of its People by recognizing the importance of Christianity and the spiritual race concept in everything relating to the operation and leadership of the community. If the program of the Fourth Political Theory, in what is related to the leadership for the People, sought to crowd out God and replace him with the manifested will of the masses, that would mean that the Fourth Political Theory itself was already assimilated in the poison of liberalism, just as the world of Western political parties is today. It would no longer have the Dasein as an object of its ideology.

If the Fourth Political Theory failed to understand the fundamental significance of God's rule and instead only patched up the present form of the State or actually considered mob rule of the mere manifested will, instead of the divine authentic will, it would then be nothing more than another fraud competing with liberalism or even worse, it could just renovate that ideology and give it some more time for its existence. These are the most important factors in order of the Fourth Political Theory to have Dasein as its object and only center: what most clearly distinguishes a spiritual ideology from liberalism is the fact that a concept based on spiritual races is able to recognize the value of spiritual race and the importance of Christianity and makes these the pillars of its whole existence. When it had the chance, the Fallen race was forced to almost quickly make concessions and return to the ideas of just rule. It cannot do without these principles even in its own wicked organizations. Regardless that, not only they have never succeeded in creating a civilization or even a real economic structure, but they also have never been able to maintain the operation of existing structures without some of God's principles. If liberalism and thus the Fallen ones were to take over and continue with the present world economic structures under their absolute leadership, even if they tried a thousand times over and were successful in gaining total control over the planet every time, they would prove nothing.

Liberalism and the Fallen ones would be unable to employ God's principles to create a system like Normativism, not one that works in any way. Liberalism and the Fallen race themselves gave practical proof of this. The reliability of God's principles is not determined by the ability to take over, manage or patch up an earthly system that already exists. The only valid test for the already known result of God's infallibility is whether or not we possess the spiritual and mental power to establish a culture based on his own commandments. It would not matter if liberalism was able to implement its mass-rule theory and assured absolute control over today's existing world economic structure, because it would not prove anything, on the contrary, they will prove that God's principles were right instead of them. The People will only be satisfied when they receive the elements necessary to carry on both their earthly and spiritual existence, and through this process, they create a shared conviction among the People's community that results in the interests of the People being guarded by the Righteous and the interests of the Righteous being upheld by the People as a whole. The members of that People cannot be satisfied in the long run by worthless ideas and materialistic phrases. The economic system must be productive and provide a real service to civilization, but it will gradually become involved in inevitable decadence as God's principles and thus authentic will is replaced by the influence of the masses and their mere manifested will.

That influence is for example in the protest movements, which do not serve the true interests of the protesters, but only the destructive objectives of the Fallen ones. Liberalism embody the pure essence of the Fallen race's attempts to eliminate the importance of God's principles in every aspect of human life and replace them with the material power of the masses imposed by manifested will. Its consequent result is plutocracy instead of theocracy, and demagogy instead of democracy, creating a form of government whose disastrous consequences we can see going on all over the world. The result of a sound theocratic government will be true democracy based on authentic will. Democracy and theocracy aren't opposite forms of government, on the contrary, theocracy is the fundamental ingredient to achieve the authentic will which true democracy requires. Therefore, theocracy can be a form of government within a form of government, the nucleus of democracy. We can observe a system resembling that in today's Republic of Iran. Despite that country isn't part of the Christian orthodox world but of the Islamic world, Russia could draw good ideas of the Iranian form of government. In Iran, theocratic government bodies coexist with popular elections to decide a Prime Minister and a Parliament.

A theocratic government within a democratic government can be established in Russia in the following way: the office of Prime Minister (Russia's second most powerful political figure after the President) will remain and will be elected through popular elections and the political parties. The office of the President of the Russian Federation will be replaced by that of the Righteous Leader of Russia. The Righteous Leader of Russia will be the head of the Russian State as well as the ultimate political and religious figure. The Righteous Leader of Russia will be in control of the Russian Armed Forces, State media, and censorship of the means of communication when required. The Righteous Leader will appoint, as the office of the President does today, federal ministries and other State officers, and it will be in charge of Russia's foreign and domestic policies. In the way the current office of the Russian President does, the Righteous Leader will be empowered to grant federal pardons and reprieves, and when extraordinary circumstances require it, the Righteous Leader of Russia will convene and adjourn the Federal Assembly.

But in addition to all that, the Righteous Leader of Russia will be the head of the Russian Orthodox Church. To establish the office of the Righteous Leader of Russia, the office of President of the Russian Federation and that of the Patriarch of Moscow and all Russia will be merged once the Patriarch dies. The last Patriarch of Moscow and all Russia should be canonized by the Russian Orthodox Church immediately after his death. The Righteous Leader of Russia will be elected by the Holy Synod of the Russian Orthodox Church to hold his office of both Head of the Russian Orthodox Church and Head of the Russian State. A Guardian Council for the Russian Constitution will be permanently in charge of protecting the new Normative constitution. It will be composed of 12 members, who are six bishops of the Russian Orthodox Church appointed by the Righteous leader, and six members of the Supreme Court of Russia appointed by the Chief Justice of the Supreme Court. The Federal Assembly of Russia, including the Prime Minister, will become a 347 member unicameral institution. The Federal Assembly of Russia together with the Prime minister will be elected by popular elections as it is done in the present.

In this way, the higher 3 spiritual hierarchies, which I wrote about when describing the new calendar, will be numerically represented. By doing so, we avoid the organizing principle for Righteous humanity being replaced by the destructive organizing principles of Fallen ones. We stop the Fallen race from becoming the cancerous illness of the People and thus of the Righteous spiritual race, and in a larger sense, we can stop them from continuing their work as the destroyers of all human culture. Modification or removal of the fundamental mechanisms of the Normative cultural and economic system must be made difficult through their protection by legal mechanisms in the constitution, assuring the protection of laws necessary to maintain the struggle against liberalism and separatism, so laws must be instituted in a way that they can not be easily submitted to amendment (that is, changed or eliminated) with constant monitoring by those Righteous in the higher positions.

Essential laws for the permanence of the Normative redistributive economic system as the ideological basis for the operation of the economy must be created and protected within the constitution, and laws contrary to cultural liberalism must be protected, while in the case of Russia, laws against separatism and its promotion must always exist so that peoples are really protected by laws which safeguard an entire cultural and economic system that guarantees People's welfare and the well-being of future generations. In the same way, we must continue within the path started by Putin with his law against homosexual propaganda, to preserve a necessary moral and social order that should not be disregarded. What undoubtedly needs to be eliminated from Russian legislation is abortion rights when the justification is anything other than the incapacity of the mother's body, fetal disease, or rape, which supposes the conception of a human being in a way clearly contrary to God's love.

MAKING AWAY WITH THE POISON OF LIBERALISM

The problem of today's democracy is the need to satisfy manifested will make it slower or impossible to make certain political decisions oriented to satisfy authentic will. This happens because people do not have all the information they need, and in addition to all the bureaucratic obstacles involved in satisfying the manifested will, political systems sometimes become slow and inefficient. Those people who are now easy targets of media manipulation or those who have little notion of the complex concepts behind a functional ideology, do not realize the basic principles for the functioning of human societies are left to the mercy of the interests of groups that do not always work for the aims of society as a whole, even if it is the society where they were born and on which they depend. Politics became a prey to unscrupulous elements or to political ignorance and the stupidity of agents who contaminate societies with the poisonous doctrines of capitalism, communism, materialism, and liberalism in general, to the point that in a People's political life, the action of politicians, rather than being based on the product of creativity, solidarity and ideological genius, is based on negotiation and is being directed so that they act according to the manifested will of the majority in opposition to authentic will.

Many important and not-so-important leaders know that a system of mediocrity like the so-called democracy of liberalism is a system that does not demand the intellectual strength and character of a great leader. This is how it has been seen that really unscrupulous individuals or ones really lacking in intelligence, preparation, character, and even mental health, took a position of relevance in the political life of many countries and led societies to disaster. These individuals do not worry about being responsible or do not even know what they should do to satisfy the authentic will of the People, therefore they do not approach divine principles but go against them... The true Righteous leaders, who are intelligent, who have the right character, and the adequate preparation, will never serve the selfish, foolish, or cowardly interests of sectors of society that are powerful either because they have great economic power, religious and political influence, ability to shelter behind the ignorance suffered by those governed by them, or often for having an inexhaustible capacity for charlatanism, manipulation, and intimidation.

Putin, due to his great charisma and talent has managed to lead the Russian People using democracy and has saved it from total ruin. Undoubtedly, the rest of changes in Russia can not be implemented by means of silly and childish violent insurrections that some imagine, but with a process that in addition to receiving a great popular support does not incur in illegal activities forbidden by the current Russian constitution, relying instead on a popular process where a party and its allies have the necessary majority to formulate a new constitution. This party must obtain the support of large sectors of Russian society, and I think that nowadays All-Russia People's Front is in charge of this first stage, since it has a great support, to which is added the alliance with the LDPR, which is led by Vladimir Zhirinovsky, a deeply patriotic man and devotee of Russian traditions.

In the future, it will be possible to count on the support of sectors of the reformed Russian Communist Party and other patriotic organizations, which should form a popular front with the already existing All-Russia People's Front and the PLDR once the different parties have completed their ideological evolution. But the All-Russia People's Front and its allies must adopt the Fourth Political Theory and its final formulation, Normativism, and prevent Russia from being attacked by the unscrupulous, cowardly and incompetent that could lead it to ruin. Pseudo democracy imposed by liberalism is nothing more than the product of misguided and corrupt societies within the ranks of political parties, religious institutions, trade unions, and other organizations that destroy the cultural results from many years of progress, bringing chaos, corruption, instability, impoverishment, and crime.

This kind of individuals, who of course are Fallen ones, hide behind the majority during the popular vote to legitimize their nefarious power and avoid taking responsibility for their actions. The People understood as a great community must unite around a vanguard of workers, owners, students, men of faith, all those who can contribute to the community as structurally necessary agents while depending on it. The State must remain within the Normative general lines and precautions must be taken so that the poisonous and sabotaging elements of society do not get into the relevant positions of the State, taking down millions towards paths that already were shown to be flawed.

It must be guaranteed, of course, that those who occupy relevant positions are properly educated in the fundamental issues and have the character and decency to guide the People who, inside or outside borders, will depend on the strength of the Russian State and their allies to face the abuses of the capitalist world system and the doctrines that have as result the irremediable destruction of the force, resources and capacity within peoples. The process that has been seen in demagogic systems must be avoided, in which the intellectual impoverishment and the lack of character and decency by rulers become more and more evident until those that stand out only by the ability they have for attracting votes are governing, basing themselves on the demagogic skill to use the manifested will of the People for their own benefit and that of their cronies, which in turn is the mode used to justify these individuals occupying their positions of authority and, therefore, the position of the Fallen race. The Russian People has known since the beginning of its history many clearly unscrupulous, incompetent, or cowardly people, getting into the field of politics and acting as tyrants, demagogues, etc.

But this is not exclusive to Russia, a country that recently abandoned the single-party regime in 1990, and that had previously known only autocratic governments. The same situation occurs in countries that have operated under the system based on parties' electoral competition for a long time. My birth home, Uruguay, was one of the first countries in the world to apply this system and maintained this system for many decades only with relatively brief periods of interruption compared to the periods in which this system has been employed. There it is still possible to look as incompetent, unscrupulous and even perverse people climbed and continue to climb to important positions of the State through misguided popular vote and also put forward the degenerate agenda of the Fallen creatures... Only that can explain how a country as rich in natural resources as Uruguay, and with an appreciable cultural development in relation to other countries in that region, is still unable to become a developed country.

The fact that in many places where the system based on electoral competition between parties had only accomplish a fraction of the authentic will of the People, and that there are carried out even things that oppose their manifested will, is a fact which indicates that not only the ones being governed but also many of their representatives, do not possess enough understanding of the political issues needed to correctly managing states and to choose those individuals most suitable for the tasks that await them, some of which are of gigantic proportions. Even the destructive effect of the Fallen ones' activity, which we can see in all regions, results from their constant effort to undermine the importance of the individual person in those peoples hosting their presence. We must never forget the fundamental premise of the enemy, being, as I stated, that the Fallen race seeks to replace the power of the divine authentic will by the domination of the manifested will of the masses.

Currently, the area of politics has completely turned its back on God's principles, but our ancestors have already warned us about this. All of the creative power of human civilization is the result of the activity of chosen persons who direct People's destiny, and especially those who become leaders. But in politics, the most important principles instead of being God's principles become the ones based on the will and strength of the majority. That way of thinking trickles down the human race, it gradually begins the sickening of all life and finally destroys it. The same way of thinking is the governing principle of State administrators and therefore it is also tested in the might of the military forces of countries regardless of how powerful they apparently are. In all those fundamental areas, the idea of obeying God's will, which is the People's authentic will instead of the manifested one, is the way in which God's authority and the authority of his Righteous race is able to be over those of lower spiritual nature and those of higher spiritual nature have the responsibility to dominate and create with their divine power.

The process of selection which goes on today when educating in the areas of scientific knowledge and art, and in the area of theology, it is already subject to severe handicaps all over the world. Great minds are revealed with the daily battle of life itself. Many are corrupted and annihilated in that process, which proves someone is not destined for the higher ranks of responsibility within the People. Only the chosen ones, which are few, are fit to remain in the glorious path of God. The manifested will of the masses does not come from experts; the masses do not possess such an amount of knowledge to realize something as complex as God's authentic will, and we can assure the manifested will of the masses is not Divine in its nature. Just some chosen personalities enjoy the great power of coming close to authentic will, transforming mere masses into a People. Without a doubt, the People's authentic will is not satisfied by the rule of the manifested will displayed by the masses, but only by the chosen ones of those whom God has given special destiny and exceptional abilities for God's unknown purpose. The ultimate goal of the People is to make sure these men have a dominant influence to assist the People in their tasks. In that way, they should never forgive that the Divine blessings of mankind have never come from the ordinary earthly persons, but they have come from the authentic will of certain chosen ones. In the human world, these Godly minds are both the providers and founders of mankind.

The People's organization must put a favorable condition in order of these chosen ones to emerge from common people, therefore, removing all barriers that could possibly interfere with God's authentic will as expressed in the chosen ones. The State and its Righteous people must set leaders to guide them in the path of constant evolution, and consequently, we must make sure the People is guided by the highest Righteous leaders. By doing so, we can be released from the evil civilizations of mechanization, and replace that monstrosity by a civilization that is able to live in true freedom and honor. The greatest concern of the People's organization is to place the individual according to the position where he is most useful to society. It is a crucial task in any organization to lay down this principle into daily practice. Whether the result is practical or theoretical, the most important part of the process of leadership is spirituality and therefore character and intellect. People must be organized so that it assists as much as possible the work of their leadership to awake all the creative forces and make good use of those forces given to them by God. The common persons do not possess enormous creative capacity, and the manifested will of the majority do not create good organized actions or thoughts. But always the spirit of the wise and Righteous man and his authentic will makes possible for a People to advance as a whole.

Even the purely theoretical mental work being carried by good leadership is the exclusive product of those specific persons. Their contribution is impossible to measure with precision, but we can be assured that their work is indispensable for all further progress in the path of the People's destiny. Since the start of the current materialistic civilizations, we have seen individual persons creating scientific and technical achievements and complementing that with the work of previous or future persons. The same can be said about Christianity. Christianity resulted from the supreme work of one mighty person, Jesus Christ. After that, the apostles and the first Christians, through suffering and martyrdom, sowed the seeds of Christianity. Their giant work later gave faith to millions, and then hundreds of millions of human beings, in the road to salvation and justice, justice in Earth and Heaven. They improved and consolidated the position of Christianity so that it became dominant as the religion of many people all across the Earth. Even with a profound insight into the nature of things, the result of the work of a religious leadership may not be instantly obvious. All that long work when put together helped to raise man more and more above the level of earthly animal creatures.

That serves humanity's constant spiritual and material progress in our vigorous effort to attain higher levels of existence. In that way, Christianity, and in our present era, Russian Orthodox Christianity, help raise man higher and higher above the level of godless beasts and it definitely saved man from that primitive level. Everything we see in the present-day Russian Orthodox Church in the way of cultural enrichment is the result of the divine inspiration of individual persons. This started with the use of the first stone that was used to erect the first church and continued until the first Christian churches were erected. Then the Kievan Rus' came and brought Christian and Greek culture, and after that, the Russian Empire emerged, and it was followed by the military might and the admirable inventions of the Soviet Empire, and all of that originated from the mind of chosen individuals. We can realize that in these achievements higher spirituality, which provide the source of intellect and determination, was a component always present in the Russian People. In Russia is possible to see the spiritual and creative nature of man.

An old Russia ends only to be followed by other Russia supplementing the older achievements by new ones. Russians learn from mistakes. The path of Russia's evolution is marked by the suffering of millions and endured hundreds of years. In Russia and in other chosen peoples, spirituality is the absolute source for good decisions and conduct which all leaders require. In the same way, all effective military strategies originated in one particular spirit of determination and loyalty toward Russia and higher ideals. Man's first clever steps in the battle to control the planet must surely have been made by chosen members of humanity who were divinely gifted. This is easier to believe in the case of a Church. The example of an outstanding individual was necessary first, then that example repeated by early followers, then others repeated it at greater numbers until, at last, Christianity became an essential part of the culture of hundreds of millions. The first step man's behavior took that visibly differentiated him from animal behavior was the higher spirituality as expressed by symbolism and ritual. To comprehend this easily, we can look at the vestiges of human culture in ancient prehistoric remains.

Instead of occupying all of our activity wrapped in spectacles and only doing false appearances, we must give the People the spiritual preparation that they need to finally get rid of the spiritual weaknesses suffered by them in the present. Anyone who believes in more equal economics, but that is the sole core of his preoccupation, will not achieve any substantial results or any true change regarding the current situation. A People who becomes materialistic and is engaged in superficial economic and political changes would not have any chance of becoming victorious in the struggle for its future. A good economy offers no security and does not guarantee the People's permanent survival if we abandon the spiritual and cultural values which are the true source of greatness. Assuming that a Normative State would be only differentiated from other states by material gifts, like a better economic system, would be having no idea what Dasein really is. If we think the Dasein becomes the center of a political theory through only more economic equality and less material poverty, or broader participation in the economic process for the masses, we would have forgot the basis of material stability and prosperity is spiritual greatness, not materialistic decay.

The Fourth Political Theory does not rely on the idea of majority rule, that's to say manifested will, but rather on that of character, and therefore authentic will and the divine spirit responsible for it. A political theory that rejects the useless idea of blind rule by manifested will and gives the world's destiny to the principles of authentic will, and to the more capable and spiritual human beings, must make that the same divine principle it represents is also put forward by the smallest atom of the People's social organization, and we must make completely certain that the best souls become the spiritual and political leadership and the most important influence over the People. In order of doing so, separation according to spiritual ability and its mental capacity will be needed, and that cannot be achieved by the judgments of a materialistic age. The ultimate decision will be made after years of constant temptations and struggle through the daily aspects of spiritual and material life.

In that process, we have the way to recognize the most valuable personalities that have the spiritual and intellectual qualities needed by the People, to grant them the influence based on their ability to be useful to the People's destiny. The nature of the State's organization is of course associated with that of its geopolitical goals. In the case of Russia and also of India, their geopolitical goals are completely dependent on the intensity of the struggle between the US. and China, with the two empires weakening inasmuch as their greed and ambition make them collide against each other. A new Eurasian geopolitical space should emerge, one in which Russia is represented in a large Eurasian Union, a supranational entity with a single currency and which is in charge of directing the foreign policy of its members, doing away with the European Union. NATO must be replaced by a common Eurasian security and defense policy, therefore ending with North American influence in general. Above all, God's church will be united again, when the time of the Roman Catholic Church comes to an end and the Russian Orthodox Church fulfills its divine destiny. The Eurasian Union will have to entail close diplomatic relations with Russia's Church, as the Church and the Russian State will be one and the same.

But before that, Russia must solve one question of uttermost importance, that of reuniting the Russian cultural space and incorporating Ukraine, Belarus and the territories of the former Moldovan and Georgian Soviet Socialist Republics. That will not just safeguard Russia's geopolitical position as already stated in this book, but will fortify the spirit of the Russian People also. In the end, we can be sure it is Russia's destiny to assume once again its role as a full superpower, only that this time Russia's strength will be determined by its loyalty toward God above any other thing. We can not rely on a system that chooses its leaders by the ability to adapt themselves to the will of the majority together with the ability to gain support through demagogic ways and through the control of the media in the so-called "freedom of expression."

The central task for politicians should not be to gain the support of the majority as an end in itself; it should be the task of approaching God's will and therefore true human development of society with the appropriate policies and the task of raising People's awareness regarding central issues related to politics and the future of society. Unfortunately, most of the ones behind the current system falsely referred to as democratic, and who come through the popular vote and free competition between parties, are narrow-minded people who do not know or do not want to apply the solution to the problems of their society.

The fundamental principle for the functioning of Normativism is that the opportunists, the unscrupulous and the incompetent do not end up governing their peoples. Youngsters and adults alike must be educated in rejecting modern Western structures that allow liberalism, and all this can only be achieved with the perseverance of a movement and a religion with the right thinking and direction towards its goals. Mankind emerged from the lack of resources, chaos and ignorance based on the impulse of sages whose unusual personal characteristics allowed them to modify the reality that they had to face. These people have always been a small part of the population and fortunately not only have they used mere brute force to carry out their purposes, but they had the task of educating those under their command around a certain agenda and values so that they can also contribute in a better way to the transforming impulse of societies. Shared norms and values that organize the interaction of the parts of the social body must be established and protected, generating conditions for the cooperation between various actors and social agents. If the Russians are properly organized, including millions inside and outside the Russian Federation, and united under a proper religion and ideology, then there is nothing that can prevent Russia from being at the center of a true rebirth for the human spirit.

EDUCATION FOR LIVING INSTEAD OF EDUCATION FOR MISERY

EDUCATION IN THE THEOCRATIC STATE

We must choose to educate for living instead of educating for misery. The essential outcome of this realization is we must promote the spiritual qualities which are valuable within the People and encourage those qualities to grow in number and strength. The elements of the spirit and of the human mind and body are subject to hundreds and hundreds of spiritual and material conditions, even within the same spiritual race. The strength of a People ultimately depends on the spiritual races in it, and the value of the individual person also ultimately depends on the nature of his spirit. In the same way that peoples are different based on the balance of the spiritual races present in them, the individual person within his spiritual race is different according to his innate and individual qualities to other members of the People. A definite People is definite because its spiritual qualities are different, as expressed in the number and proportion of Righteous ones, and when that number is vaster, we must expect to found more Righteous of the higher hierarchies.

Once we are able to see how important the purity of the human spirit transmitted by our blood is, and the ability of a definite spiritual race and also of the definite ranks within that spiritual race, then the most important conclusion is that the education system must apply tests to the individual person, to show his spiritual nature and therefore the true importance of his intelligence and contribution. In addition to that, the education system must be a source for the enlightenment of Righteous souls through the necessary share of religious, psychological and ideological education besides the other subjects. It would be nonsense to achieve the judging of man's spiritual value rejecting the liberal claim that, "all men are created equal" if we don't have enough determination to achieve practical results in the People's education with a less materialistic and therefore more spiritual education. If the theocratic Normative State achieves its more important mission, that of the development and preservation of the spiritual strength within that State, then we must realize that is necessary to promote certain spiritual values when educating society and preparing individuals for their daily life, and we must make a room for wisdom in the People's mentality in what is related to their true purpose in life. Some things we have today exist thanks to the lust for money and material welfare, but there is also many creations emanating for materialistic feelings that mankind doesn't really need or which make little difference when achieving true happiness and a purpose in life.

It may be true money has become the supreme ruler of human life today, but time will come when man will kneel to God again. Material and thus economic creation frequently come from a rejection of the earthly pleasures and temptations of wealth. The most remarkable inventions and discoveries, including the most important knowledge of human civilizations, and also the most marvelous art, were not brought to our world by means of a desire for economic wealth. The desire for economic wealth is essential to make possible the proper functioning of an economy, but nothing more. If a purely materialistic mentality had been the sole one throughout history, mankind would have been without its greatest achievements. The most visible sign of decay is when higher achievements for the People are only driven by the immediate necessity to receive higher wages and income. Even when individuals receive better wages and income, that does not cause personal accomplishment to become fulfilled.

We must remember that the vocation which the individual follows is not the purpose of his life but only the way to gain his space in the People's economy. His job must be determined by his real and innate abilities, and by the education the People and their State were able to provide him. Therefore, individual contribution to the People must be determined by real capacity when being responsible for a task in which the individual has been made responsible for by the community. In that way, in the Normative State, it is not social position that forces specific jobs on the individual, but real ability which is spiritual and thus innate and not taught but safeguarded by the education system. Real abilities are a gift from God and for that reason, those abilities come from divine instead of human origin.

For that reason, higher human spirits must be trained to do their best for the People. In a Normative State individuals must be guided in their vocations so that each person is assigned to work, whether intellectual, physical or religious, that suits his real ability. The evaluation of the individual is judged by the importance of his contribution to the People as a whole and not on how much he earns, being meritocracy a mission for the People's organization, a mission which is only possible when realizing each individual is able to do his best only in the field that suits his ability. Of course, the material contribution of some jobs is greater than others, and the contribution of some ideas of born geniuses may be greater than that of someone working in the service sector, but the People depends as much on the service sector as it does on geniuses, because a genius sooner or later will need the service sector and the service sector will be in need from big intellects. The divine value does not depend on its importance by human standards, but on the importance of its primary and frequently ignored necessity: that which ultimately determines how fundamental work can be for the People as a whole.

Because of practical reasons, we cannot do away with the principle that a job's value in a human perspective should reflect how much someone earns from that job. But anyway, in contrast to this purely human perspective, is the divine one. People must be educated to bear in mind that the more the members of a People truly benefit from someone's work, the higher the divine value of that job. Within a merely human perspective, the value of a job lies in the observable material importance of a job for the People's economy. But the People must be educated to realize that the importance of all work is measured in a human perspective and also in a divine perspective which is not completely known by us but which must be taken into account, even if we humans aren't wholly aware of it. The result of a materialistic age is, of course, the disease of the human spirit, with consequent mental illnesses, lack of individual strength, and above all, lack of a People's strength.

This phenomenon is just the product of modernity, which carries within itself the incorrect evaluation of human work. Changing our evaluation of human work may seem difficult in modernity, when some mediocre product of society is considered more important than the most capable inventors, ideologists and of course religious figures, simply because people are accustomed to mere appearances. It must be the task of the Normative State to judge the individual man according to the real contribution, not by the appearance of his work, but by the genuine and therefore divine talent in his achievements. For that reason, the new theocratic State will have to teach a different attitude regarding labor, one which appreciates the value of individual work from the standpoint of the People as a whole in its destiny. In the case of the political leadership, if the new education system shows that the son of a high ranking State official is expected to become a worker in the service sector, just because the son of a common worker is most capable for the spiritual and intellectual requirements of a high ranking State official, then the same education system must teach someone should inherit his position thanks to his own merits, not to social position. In the capitalist world, this is, of course, impossible, but if civilizations with equivalent resources are competing, the civilization whose best talents constitute the intellectual, political and religious leadership will be in clear advantage over the ones whose judgment and values failed to put into the balance the natural ability of their members, feeding up certain parasitical groups and elites. The greatness of a civilization is determined by how well it trains its most capable spirits for the fields that they are suited most to, and how well the selection process places them to work for the betterment of the People's existence.

This is true for the intellectual, political and religious leadership of the People in every field, and for all those who take part in the vital cycle of a People's struggle for better living conditions and better moral qualities. Success can only be possible if the most capable and strong-willed human spirits are trained and correctly selected to lead in the different fields. It is the mission of the Normative State to provide the means and determination to search through the population and discover those personalities of innate talent and put them to work for the greatness of their civilization. State offices and cultural jobs should not provide places to someone just because he is of certain social class or family, but for individuals to accomplish their true tasks. It is not just the State's obligation to give education to the individual, but also to discover different talents and put them on the place where they belong. The talented human spirit provides his contribution by feeding up his talent with the correct knowledge.

Knowledge merely vomited into someone's mind is not enough to achieve human progress. First of all, talent must be discovered, and only then we can feed up that talent with the more suitable knowledge for it. Millions of untalented persons are thought worthy of higher education every year all over the world, while millions of others who are gifted in some way aren't educated in the right way, or go without any higher education at all. True talent and character, which are spiritual qualities, should be the means used to test people in their education, not just memorizing loads and loads of knowledge while creativity and the true potential of the human spirit are ignored.

As with dogs, modern education can be merely animal training instead of the so-called "scholastic" and "higher" education. It is full madness to apply animal training to some Homo Erectus until one believes they had been turned into worthless lawyers or pseudo-historians, while many in the Righteous spiritual kind must remain in a place totally unworthy of their innate quality. The human creative spirit can only flourish in achievement when talent and knowledge are joined, being knowledge just the necessary food which innate talent requires. Even the most complex knowledge and inventions are brought to existence by the ones with the appropriate qualities to do so, and of course, Russia is a country with plenty of people who demonstrate talents in every possible field. The result of just vomiting knowledge into the mind of someone is an individual who may have plenty of knowledge in various fields, but who is unable to put that into the practical situations of his life and the life of his People.

Modern education, instead of hammering the mind of individuals trying to place them above the average level, must transform the individuals into a hammer of their own, and lifeless and unproductive knowledge must be replaced by education for living through useful teachings, including religious, psychological and ideological ones, capable of feeding the talent and character of those who make possible the People's existence. Even someone who has no innate talent can learn a collection of scientific and artistic tricks, but all that is not different from teaching an animal some funny act. In the same way that in Normativism the bourgeois property ownership of the means of production is of organic instead of mechanical nature, so the education system must prepare people in an organic way, teaching and placing everyone according to their real abilities, and teaching certain religious, psychological and ideological values to forge a higher connection with the State. Doing so is the opposite of mechanical education, which consists of training a man for certain mechanical skills, just as it is done with some animals. The intellectual and spiritual life of the People will see its nourishment from an organic education system when even a small kid who grows up in a poor rural town later becomes a famous scientific, a famous artist or a famous leader. The use of innate ability is always subject to how wisely the education system and the People as a whole nourished that innate ability with knowledge and opportunities, but even if we look at elderly persons with innate talent, but who grow up without having the chance of a good education and of the good job opportunities, we can still appreciate a big spark in them.

Then, we should think about what would have been of that same elderly person if they had grown up from infancy with better education and opportunities: without a doubt their contribution to society and their personal achievements would have been truly important. In the same way, that spiritual, mental and physical training will be exercised in the education system, so too the correct classification and placement of people and their skills in order that the right persons are placed in the right positions, including of course the positions of the State and the Church. The State's education will be crowned with military service, which will be the completion stage of general education for the average Russian. All the efforts of the education system, all its spiritual, mental and physical training, all the money and time spent in that, will be to no avail if those efforts were given to someone who does not have the capacity and determination to protect and rescue the specific qualities of the Righteous spiritual race. To protect and rescue those qualities is the necessary path preserving Russia's spiritual foundations and assuring the fundamental conditions for future cultural and geopolitical achievements. Nobody should leave the education system without obtaining a complete understanding of the importance of being Righteous and of the existence of antagonistic spiritual races: the Righteous race and the Fallen race.

Young and old people must realize through learned concepts, instinct, and intuition, the importance of the Righteous spiritual race. The completion of the theocratic State's educational mission will require teaching a devotional appreciation of spiritual race into the ones which are the bearers of God's plan for mankind. When a People is able to follow that path, there is no earthly force capable of stopping that People from reaching its ultimate goals. By a new education for both the young and old, the theocratic State must shape persons which will be able to make the correct decisions regarding their own country, and then that same persons will decide the destiny of mankind. The only question is when destiny will completely benefit the Righteous instead of the wandering fallen ones, but the answer for that is only known by God. There is no doubt that this world is moving through increasing tribulations and that the Final Kingdom, that of Christ, is finally coming. That tremendous change is accomplished only when driven by the faith, wisdom, and determination of the Righteous humanity. No change at all will be made if we want to give equal concessions to God and the forces of evil, therefore being unable to take God's side when making the most important decision of our lives.

If we take the correct decision, when the Final Kingdom arrives a People of Righteous souls will be forged together by a common love for God and for each other, forever fulfilling ancient prophecies. For making correct decisions, the education system must support and increase the personal spirit of patriotism in the members of the People, and a sense of social justice as it was done in the Soviet Union, but free from the materialistic limitations of the defunct communist doctrine. Only when true social justice is understood as divine justice, and when the greatness of a People and its creed cause the highest joy, is when individuals are spiritually and physically healthy, feeling a rise in everyone's soul and mind, which leads also to physical health and common achievements. Compare that with modern states which are only rich economically but more than half of their people feel their existence as miserable and are incapable of loving and respecting themselves. Nobody will be proud of belonging to a State if the individual and the People as a whole do not found any reason for living more than materialistic goals and compulsion from money.

Being born in a specific country and pretending to love the history and culture of that country doesn't give someone the right to call himself a Patriot, unless the individual is capable of feeling caring passion for protecting and increasing the People's health related to their interrelated soul, body, and mind. Being born in a specific country does not prove anything. Maybe someone born in Russia will grow up only to be the greatest criminal and a new Yeltsin, or maybe someone born where God has destined him to be born could decisively turn the tide in this gigantic spiritual war. There is no such thing as patriotism if personal feelings are manipulated to benefit only certain social classes, as the U.S. government and its elites are doing with the American masses. There is no such thing as a patriotism whose only objective is to achieve the selfish interest of certain sectors of the population. People must be educated to realize the basic truth that he who truly loves his People is determined to fight not only for some flag and a piece of land but also for true social justice which is also divine justice, doing away with the poisonous liberal doctrine. Education must make sure the young person completes his mental formation as a complete Russian and not as a half-feminist, liberal, or something else.

School teachings, the curriculum in universities and messages brought by State media and forms of entertainment must be structured from that basic premise. From the numerous examples of great personalities in Russian history, the greatest must be selected and reminded to the youth and to the old ones, so that the great Russian past also serves for developing new faith in the People's destiny and constant patriotic pride. We must always bear in mind that when war, whether in the way of a foreign invasion or inner calamity and instability, came to any country, the lack of real patriotism was a crucial factor in the downfalls experienced all along with human history, including Russian history.

Educators, the State media and even forms of mass entertainment must be able to make important figures of both Russian history and

Christian Orthodox history to revive as the great chosen heroes they were, starting which Jesus Christ himself. This knowledge of the past provides a firm bond of common heritage and Patriotic and religious fervor which is necessary to hold the People together. Since an ideal State is complex and hard to put in simple words, it is very hard to make people see that specific form as the ideal one, and even more difficult to create the motivation necessary to let make persons feel the necessity of absolute commitment toward that kind of State. Superficial education is not enough, it is not enough to give some education aimed at just granting the individual some abilities used in the labor market and in basic social behavior.

As in Soviet times, ideas of self-sacrifice and solidarity must be promoted instead of individualistic selfishness, but this time Normativism and the Russian Orthodox Church will be replacing materialistic and flawed Communism and replacing the communist party of the old Soviet Regime. One truth must be made clear by the education system: any economical and technological achievement needs first of a healthy and therefore stable country, nourished which noble ideals. That general education must be present everywhere, even as obligatory subjects at the level of tertiary education, a level which is more important now than ever before. A civilization is fighting for its existence; a civilization whose history sparks since the origin of the Indo-European peoples and which encompasses not only the legacy of Russia but the entire legacy of the first civilizations of mankind and its Righteous race.

Ethnic, individualistic and temporal differences between individuals and peoples must not be allowed to put in danger the civilization that is the only hope for mankind's future. Building inner strength by teaching lofty ideals is as important as teaching the necessary technical abilities for the labor market. Of course, technology and natural sciences are absolutely necessary in this age of great scientific and technological advancement. Nevertheless, is dangerous for a People to aim its education exclusively at so-called pure sciences and materialistic knowledge. The People's theocratic State must structure the educational curriculum not only at some facts of history, mathematics, physics, biology, chemistry, etc. It is the task of the People's theocratic State to avoid this incomplete education. General education should be more than pouring certain technical knowledge and vague teaching of history and culture into the mind of the studentship.

General education must be integrated with the fundamental goal of preserving civilization through the theocratic State. The correct application of general and specific knowledge, nourishing spiritual and material life, together with selection by the State will avoid indecision and inner crisis in the studentship, that sort of inner crisis which cause some people attend three different universities because they are unable to choose the career most suitable for them. Instruction by the schools, universities, State media and forms of entertainment must prepare the People for their later life after they leave the schools and universities, and above all, those institutions and tools must strengthen personal character and spirit which constitute the basis for developing all kind of abilities in daily life.

The excessive specific knowledge poured into the mind of the studentship and which is often forgotten in later life must shortened by reducing the time of classes destined to that knowledge, giving space to the time required for the educational task of aiding spiritual qualities as character, perseverance, authentic will, and wise judgment, through the adequate educational curriculum which must include in it religious education, psychological training, and ideological knowledge. That general education should be imparted to everyone together with some specific education. More specific education should be left to the choice of the individual who now is able to take more correct decisions regarding his future and that of his community.

The individual will be taught carefully prepared general knowledge mixed with some specific knowledge, and then he will receive a more profound and specialized education in the field that he chooses as his occupation in later life. In that way, the State will provide the individual with the spiritual and psychological tools which are necessary for making a wise personal decision and arriving at the most suitable occupation in accordance with the specific abilities of the individual cases. Therefore, instead of wasting money and time, opportunities for more specialized and profound education will be offered to those who really are in need of it, in accordance to their authentic will. By doing so, the individual would be given the knowledge he really needs in accordance with their inner nature, instead of producing an overwhelming flood of knowledge often forgotten in later stages of life. No longer education for misery will be in place, that seeking to benefit an elite not by their true talent but only because of their social position or their capacity to retain useless knowledge, when talented individuals are forced into oblivion.

We must avoid that people spent years learning things which have no real meaning for them and which demonstrate no utility in their later life. Regarding the teaching of specific knowledge such as applied mathematics and engineering, that knowledge must be imparted with an emphasis on solving practical situations which are the ones being faced in real life. When an excessive mass of knowledge is unnecessarily poured into the mind of a person, regardless if that person is young or old, we create the danger of making them unable to remind not only unnecessary information, but also the useful knowledge. Our mind is divinely designed and therefore was made to absorb what it truly needs, so the human brain is not designed as a mere recipient for vomiting tonnes of unnecessary knowledge into it, that will just cause overloading of the human mind. Because of that, confusion and incapacity in daily life arise as unnecessary knowledge is retained and there is little space for essential knowledge.

APPROACHING AUTHENTIC WILL

In addition to the potential flaws of the modern education system, modern mass media, video games and other forms of entertainment is overloading the young brain with a flood of information, impressions and emotions that very few are able to control rarely. In that way, younger generations lost the ability to find and retain what is of greater importance for their present and future lives as individuals and as members of the People. If the State is smart enough, it will not limit its educational work to schools and universities; it will also put the necessary attention in structuring state media and forms of entertainment, including video games and social networks as a fundamental tool for education. When the young ones finally grow older, they will show to the State and to the World how much learning by the school, universities and State media remains, and also how much training in state-sponsored video games and social networks they went through.

The State's educational job with schools, universities, State media and forms of entertainment can be taken over by new generations, and the theocratic State will only need to make slight changes in the form of its education as time goes by. Only if the State's educational system is safeguarded to keep its basic form, and if there is awareness regarding the importance of that basic form, a theocratic State will endure liberal and materialistic weaknesses which are the infectious diseases of the modern age. The theocratic State of the future must be able to help train the authentic will and the decision making ability of the younger generations and the older ones. Since childhood, the State and its church must put into the minds and hearts of the Righteous ones that they must be prepared to accept responsibility and to make always the right thing, achieving the exact opposite of what is done with Fallen race behaviour. People must be prepared to have initiative and courage, instead of avoiding facing the problems and hiding themselves blaming others for their mistakes. The necessary training for that will begin at home and at the school, where a correct education will teach that being fearful and inactive when suffering daily problems is worse than at least trying to solve them and doing that incorrectly. A passive and inactive People is no different than sheep or fat pigs with no real purpose in life, so facing problems is always better than evading them with inaction or the self-destructive behaviour of liberal and feminist weepers.

Developing the necessary strength to come close to authentic will, which includes the determination to act bravely and assume responsibility, should be of the greatest importance when educating someone, no matter how old that individual is as long as he has a Righteous soul. That's the most important way of stopping widespread decay in the behaviour of political, economic and cultural elites, as well as widespread decay in the behaviour of the ordinary people. The theocratic State must put together teaching regarding character development along with religious teaching and gymnastic education.

Gymnastic discipline is not only good for the body, but also for the mind, so its combination with teaching for character development and religious teaching will act as a single structure. At school, at home and at other spaces for socialization, education must encourage the individual even since infancy to overcome eventual setbacks and pains with inner determination and wisdom. Everyone must know that surprises may arise at any moment, that all useful data must be obtained when overcoming situations, and that the individual must be able to train intuition because intuition is the way of overcoming the flaws of human reasoning. Doing away with the habit of complaining about anything must be taught as well, and that must be replaced by the virtue of facing the true source of problems, which only a Righteous soul with a healthy and educated mind is able to do. The Fallen ones will always be wicked parasitic criminals, that cannot be changed, but in addition to that, Righteous souls can be influenced by the Fallen ones and that is a danger which good education can avoid. The feeblest characters are the ones more vulnerable to Fallen race activity, but with good education, even someone who at the beginning appeared as feeble will show his inner strength when the time comes. The Fallen race individual will always remain as a Fallen race individual and the Righteous will always be a Righteous.

We can change the degree of someone's mental and physical abilities, but we cannot change the human soul, so the most important qualities of the individual come when they are born. In the case of women, and in times when Russia and other countries are experiencing low births, education must encourage them to have sons and prepare them for that. The Righteous woman must be trained to perceive and prefer the Righteous man instead of falling in a toxic relationship with someone of the Fallen race in an apparent heterosexual relation. In the same way, the Righteous man must be trained to perceive and prefer the Righteous woman instead of falling into the trap of the deceitful and toxic Fallen woman. If the innate detector in her brain is trained, the Righteous girl can detect the Fallen race degenerate because of his bisexual behavior and the tone of his voice. In the same way, the Righteous man can identify the Fallen woman by her masculine aspect and attitude which is caused by the masculine mask of her dark soul. In that way, we must influence the development of the relations between sexes transforming the mere sexual lust into genuine love into Righteous souls.

The current fashion trends are absolutely hijacked by the degeneracy of the Fallen race, so if real beauty was not completely hidden by the degenerate world of modern fashion, the seduction of millions of women by disgusting fallen bastards would not be the massive racial problem which it is today. A Righteous girl must find her appropriate Righteous companion, not some low life degenerate which will ruin her life. The modern perception of beauty must change, placing emphasis on the genuine beauty of a good spirit and an astounding mind, which allows also physical health and natural beauty, instead of the look of people who are obsessed with false artificial appearances in their bodies and their clothes.

It is a sign of the decay of modern generations to see how people are deceived by the fashion world of the Fallen race instead of discovering the natural beauty of the Righteous race. That current path in sexual relationships and preferences can lead to the ultimate psychological and spiritual destruction of our race. We must not allow ourselves to be deceived by all the tricks of the Fallen race. This is easier when the concepts of Righteous humanity flourish with the unity of millions of Russians and millions of individuals from other peoples. What once led the Russian and Soviet armies to victory was patriotic and spiritual unity that soldiers felt regarding their comrades and their common land. Unity and loyalty are the essential components to achieve the invincibility of an entire People. Confidence in the destiny of the People must be trained into the young and old members of Russia and her allies because they need that confidence to build inner strength. The theocratic State must direct its more substantial educational effort towards helping the individual in a way that encompasses all the necessary elements to build inner strength instead of just pouring excessive and unnecessary knowledge.

A healthy body is useless without a good spirit and a sound mind. Spiritual quality constitutes the basis for mental health, and mental health is necessary to maintain a healthy body. We must understand the human as an entity composed of the three inseparable components of the soul, bodily mind and body. The soul comprises the highest component, the bodily mind is in second place, and the body in third place, each component is crucial for the others. The liberal world can no longer hide the evil conditions making further development of the human race more and more difficult. They created a Western liberal civilization that is doomed to extinction. Modern generations, especially in the West, are ignoring visible threats which the ancient prophecies warned us about. Pushed by the madness of world elites and their servants they try to satisfy themselves hedonistically instead of facing both World and personal problems, believing that those problems can be solved by just patching up the current liberal system and avoiding responsibility in their personal lives.

Russia will either be the architect of a new theocratic State, or it will be facing the utter collapse of civilization not only for Russia but also for the entire World. Above all else, I am writing to those who do not see money as the purpose of their existence, but to those who remain faithful to God. I am not writing to you lowly Fallen race, because your only preoccupation is your selfish personal interests and your only God is your gigantic ego. The goal of true Christianity will only be achieved when the ancestral sin of mixing the Righteous spiritual race with earthly souls is repaired giving God Almighty only His original creation from heaven which is in His own image. This is possible as long as the world maintains many thousands of people who have the determination to take religious and political tasks under no other motivation or pressure than their faith towards religious commands and ideological duty. A Fourth Political

Theory can only have the Dasein as its object when there is the project of a civilization where People's first concern is not excessive consumption or the creation of androids and trans-human frankensteins, but decisive actions aimed at man himself together with his relationship with God.

People's spiritual development and economical achievements will fill the heart of the individual with confidence and joy. We must never forget this planet is the most important treasure for all of us because thanks to this treasure a strong mankind can gradually be shaped with those whose souls are of divine inspiration. Once a People and their State are in this path, they must direct their attention toward raising birth rates by encouraging fertility and giving the People plenty of reasons to live in this world and therefore a desire to give birth to children. If the fertility of the People's members is encouraged and birth rates are raised through a continuous and intensive campaign of education and economic stimulus, the result would be averting the death of the Russian People and its Righteous race because of spiritual, mental and physical decay caused by liberalism and the Fallen race behind it. The State and its Church must possess the will to defend their greatest resource which comes in the form of new children.

The birth rate is, of course, an essential factor that must be taken care of at all times. In the case of Russia and other European countries, they suffered a catastrophic decline in their birth rates, which were well below the levels needed for generational replacement. Fortunately, Russia has seen an unexpected recovery and births again exceeded the number of deaths in 2013, 2014, and 2015, but that was clearly not enough and it should not lead to becoming less guarded. A continuous effort, so that birth rates are always at satisfactory levels, should be made. The State and its Church must put an end to suicidal indifference that the government and its People show towards the economic and cultural elements required for having children. The theocratic State must assure that birth rates are not restricted by economical or individualistic considerations resulting from a bad economy and a bad education. As stated in a previous chapter, the new Normative economic system no longer experience the threat posed by the freedom of movement for business capital, so it is possible to collect taxes that no longer depend so much on the burdens of worker's consumption, and therefore the tax policy will acquire a much more favorable nature for common people, strengthening social policies and social protection networks of the State, including those aimed at raising fertility rates.

In this way, the People's theocratic State substitutes economic limitations and the selfishness of the individual with the economic and educational requirements for a decent living and therefore higher birth rates. With parents having children, we place the child as the People's most critical concern. We must make certain that the healthy existence of Russia and of the Righteous spiritual race is guaranteed for ages to come. The theocratic State must impart the command to be fruitful and multiply which was given by God to his Righteous race, by means of the same seriousness and persistence used to impart the other commands. The prevention of procreation among the Russian People and Righteous persons is not regarded as a bad thing in the morals of some persons, being thought as good in the disgusting world-view of liberals, feminists and other selfish or lazy people. In addition to abortions, contraceptives are offered everywhere, so a spiritual theocratic State will, therefore, have to raise the sacred institution of marriage from the present level of constant spiritual and psychological poisoning, in order that marriage is seen once again as a bless whose mission is to create children in the image of the Lord.

Marriage between the Righteous man and the Righteous woman should be promoted and helped by the religious, economic and ideological stimulus, and that will be correctly done only if people are trained by the education system to distinguish the Righteous individual in the way which I already stated. The mission of Righteous mankind could then be considered at an end with no more Fallen ones in our Planet, bringing back what was lost since the time of Adam. The final dream cannot be realized with the achievement of the luxuries of liberal and mourning feminist women, but with a strong People aware of the necessity for true spirituality and higher civilization. World history would have been radically different if the Russian People had possessed a stronger mentality necessary for unity inside the Russian cultural space and with other peoples. If that was the case, the Russian Empire today would be by Far the most powerful superpower of the globe. Regrettably, Russia no longer has a cultural space unified in a single country and the process of fusing the various original territories has not progressed enough to form the unified civilization which the Righteous race is desperately in need.

Before asking what is the ideal State that Russians and other peoples need and how we arrive at it, we must know what kind of people that State should include because the mission of the ideal State is to serve the ideal People. The Normative State only has to provide the context which allows the nourishment of the People's inner strength by exercising organizational power. If we speak of the true mission of the State, we must never forget the State is simply a tool for allowing the development of God's plan through his Righteous spiritual race. Authentic will when managing a State is only approached when the State is more useful to Righteous ones instead of being useful to individuals who are bringing the destruction of civilization. Even if the best form of government is put into place, it would never bring achievements without the innate abilities which are already present thanks to the spiritual composition of the People, which ultimately depends on the number and proportion of the race which is the sole bearer of civilization.

The liberal State is gradually killing the same abilities which make human civilization possible, and in doing so, they created lifeless inorganic states whose existence can be judged as failure in the task of addressing the true needs of the People, because of ignoring spiritual and cultural wealth and by destroying the very foundations of human achievements. Every State, regardless of how well structured it is, can only aspire to nourish a great civilization but not to produce the spark needed to create that same civilization. Civilization is not the creation of the State but of the divine skills of the Righteous souls. Once civilization is made possible with the spark of superior divine creativity and determination, the State only serves as the protector of that civilization by organizing its members toward unity and good leadership. The Liberal States will destroy civilization and even the planet as they allow the corruption of humanity, as it descends to the level of animals once more. But civilization and the planet would also be destroyed if the abilities only present in the Righteous race disappear with them, no matter how well organized the State is because it will be like the organization of a Zoo with the Fallen ones being trapped in the hell created by themselves.

So the ideal State can only exist with the ideal People, those whose abilities are innate. The mission of the State is training and protecting those abilities instead of trying to change the inner nature of human souls, which is impossible. Despite the fact that trying to transform the inner nature of human souls is impossible, the State is the most important tool to keep the Righteous spiritual race alive and strong. The true power of a State is conferred by the quality of its People, and the quality of the People is the expression of the spiritual make-up of the population, which gives higher forms of culture and civilization. The value of certain State, if enough, will not merely be expressed in the lives of the ones being governed by it, but also in other peoples all over the world which can be influenced and helped, this time not with materialistic and flawed communism, but with a much stronger ideology: the ideology for The Final Kingdom.

Liberalism, communism and nationalism are all the result of human error which nowadays brings the lessons needed to constitute The Fourth Political Theory as expressed in Normativism. Normativism is the only way to lead mankind to the highest freedom possible which is the freedom of approaching authentic will by the strengthening of spiritual, cultural and economic capacities. The State, instead of being a lifeless mechanical entity must be turned into a living organism made up of a dignified People. Only the Normative theocratic State is strong enough to protect the spiritual race which is the creator of civilization. Any State unable to achieve that is a failure in the presence of God and the souls of heaven. The State is a recipient. If the recipient is broken, it becomes worthless, but if its content is useless then the recipient does not have any purpose other than cultivating parasites which will eventually perish because of their inferior nature.

When acknowledging the State must be strong and the spiritual race which is its content must be of good quality, we sow the necessary seed to destroy the present system of global slavery, replacing it with a whole new reality. States that aid in preserving the present system of global slavery are just piles of rubbish whose only purpose is mankind's corruption and its eventual destruction. A whole new reality will emerge when states are able to allow the awakening of all the divine force sleeping in the Righteous race and therefore in peoples sharing its spiritual and cultural heritage. The ability of the Righteous ones is subject to the interaction with certain contexts. Those innate abilities may be dormant within them until a new context appears in their lives. If they had come to a planet with even more favorable conditions than the Earth, their previously dormant capabilities would have flourished just as what one sees in science-fiction films.

The harsh conditions of the cold regions, deserts, and oceans of most of our World forced conditions on them that prevented more development of their civilization-building power. The spiritually and creatively gifted Russia has much civilization building power which is partly dormant because unfavorable climatic conditions and foreign hostility currently do not allow the awakening of a more powerful Russian cultural space. All dormant forces will awake when the time comes. Current liberal states may exist in their inorganic way for some more time, but the corruption of spirit and culture allowed by liberalism has produced the most obvious cultural decline since the fall of the Western Roman Empire.

The current Western civilization and also the reborn Chinese empire may continue to rule most of the planet some more time, but as a result of the incapacity of their states to face the current spiritual, psychological, economic and climate problems, the general quality of life among both Western civilization and China will suffer a catastrophic destiny. In the same way that most of the species which once inhabited this world became extinct in prehistoric times, mankind will face the same fate if it lacks the spiritual and mental strength whose absence makes survival impossible. It is clearly visible how states that are fatally corrupted by the Fallen race cannot protect their populations from annihilation in the event of future global disasters. As we can consider the Fallen race as a failed and destructive creation, only the destruction of the Righteous spiritual race would condemn the destiny of our planet. If from a global catastrophe some men of the Righteous spiritual race had escaped, being capable of resurrecting civilization, even if it took thousands of years the Earth would once more show signs of human creative power all along its surface when peace is restored. There cannot be any disaster worse than the extinction of the ones who were made by God in accordance with His own image.

VOLUME II: GEOPOLITICS OF THE APOCALYPSE

INTRODUCTION

It will be the task of those sharing values as the ones uphold in the first volume, to push forward a fundamental change in the geopolitical relations that we have today. That change will come regardless if those who stand for a Fourth Political Theory are driving it or not because the life and death of countries and their civilizations are a process that does not need different concepts, it will happen, it will be apocalyptic, the question is: We have the strength to drive change? Or rather we will be not those changing things, but the ones being washed away with change? The fact that current political leaders pay little attention to this point of view is due in part to the nature of the so-called liberal "democracy", to which they owe their positions, but second to the fact that states had become lifeless inorganic entities, who seem like an objective in themselves rather than civilization, Dasein, and therefore spiritual and cultural strength, which do not coincide with the mere manifested will of a specific People, but always with the authentic will of those driving the real human development towards highest levels of existence.

Then, when authentic will becomes close to awakened persons, even the sudden conflict between civilizations which apparently were not enemies stops being a surprise, and are integrated into a truly evident natural system of basic and well-founded development for those peoples wanting to achieve higher forms of civilization, and also wanting to preserve the fundamental preconditions for that. Therefore, the preparation for cultural, economical, and military war is not only the task of great lawmakers and statesmen but also the unlimited preparation of a People so that their future could be assured by divine and thus natural law. That law is favorable when a civilization possesses both inner strength and the geopolitical importance to defend the cultural, economical, and military prerequisites of that same inner strength. If the political, cultural, and economic leadership of a People totally loses sight of this essential point of view or believes that it should arm itself only in terms of military weapons and techniques, it can achieve the momentary success which they want, but the future does not belong to that People since the relevance and continuity of their cultural and spiritual basis was not defended against those of other civilizations, capable of permeating the culture and spirituality of rival ones, either with better and stronger values or with the seed for liberal and materialistic decadence. Then all army establishments and technical capability either are vanished or end up just serving the interests of a stronger power.

"Euro-Siberia", a continental paradigm for revolution advocated by the recently deceased French journalist and writer Guillaume Faye, is the fundamental cultural and geographical space for the strengthening and preservation of Christian civilization with principles as those which I declared the previous year (2019) in "Horizons of the Fourth Political Theory." One thing that must be absolutely made clear: the heart of all the theoretical schedule of my work is Dugin's Fourth Political Theory, while Guillaume Faye's "Euro-Siberia" paradigm is like its lungs. This implies that Dugin's Fourth Political Theory cannot be really put into practice without Guillaume Faye's identitarian paradigm of "Euro-Siberia", and also vice-versa, the concept for an identitarian "Euro-Siberia" will be dead without a Fourth Political Theory capable of giving and preserving a true life for it. And that last statement, this necessary marriage between the two concepts, is one which in less than two decades from now should not even be discussed, anyone who will not believe in this is either not capable of accepting some terrible truths, or a traitor.

For the self-affirmation of peoples and civilizations, the lack of active foreign policy is an indication of a time when the natural forces for their self-preservation are paralyzed since a healthy natural instinct for self-preservation will drive an active and therefore ambitious foreign policy. Without a bold foreign policy aimed at the geopolitical relevance of not just mere states but that of cultures and spiritual values as a whole, one of the most powerful sources of inner and international strength is blocked. Due to the aforementioned, we always must look for ways in the construction of foreign policies that do not artificially restrict, in fact systematically, higher goals which come from higher spirituality and its authentic will, and the brains embarking in such an activity should not be restrained by a wall of stupidity against them, preventing them from achieving their real task: geopolitical relevance for higher forms of culture and civilization.

On the basis of their general spiritual value, conditioned by the phenomena of spiritual races, which unfortunately is completely forgotten by modern societies and modern "science", a People enjoy the certainty of having real, powerful strategic minds among them. The shortage of great strategic minds among all across Euro-Siberia finds its simplest explanation in the disintegration caused by the liberal doctrine in Europe, and the effect of both Marxist and liberal doctrines in Russia, as liberalism and Marxism ends up corroding all the vital elements in the life of civilizations. In the case of Russia, during the later stages of communist rule and the Yeltsin era, the decomposed internal leadership totally collapsed at the first moves of a few hundred rascals and defectors.

For five decades, the organization of the Soviet Army resisted the largest coalition of enemies of all time, from fascist regimes to the NATO alliance, but even an organization of men who were brave and competent in their tasks as the Soviet Army, had to obey the incompetent and cowardly elements who allowed a geopolitical cataclysm. One should realize the difference between the Soviet Army as an institution oriented towards centralization and patriotic responsibility, with the chaotic nature of the civilian institutions in both Marxist and liberal regimes, especially regarding the results of civic training for the leadership in both regimes. Regardless of how powerful an organization is, it can't survive when the most compelling reasons for the emergence of trustworthy leadership disappears, and those reasons are a good ideological basis and clear geopolitical goals. Who will be responsible for giving clear ideological and geopolitical objectives to an effective organization? This is a question even more important when we take into account that each decision being taken is the result of numerous ideological and geopolitical commitments, which will also have consequences in personal characters, including moral consequences. Flawed geopolitical projects adjust less to mighty organizations than those organizations can adjust to a clear and ambitious geopolitical goal.

Therefore, our task is not only producing an administrative apparatus but also having creative plans or ideas, to carry them out with the administrative apparatus tasked with executing defined geopolitical projects aimed towards authentic will. This is not possible with the irresponsibility that resides in the nature of current liberalism. In addition, through liberalism, individuals of inferior spirituality, almost as a law, become political and cultural leaders, so that in the long run this system not only is incapable of achieving great geopolitical goals, but it also prevents the emergence and, therefore, the work of those who are capable of destroying liberalism and putting great geopolitical goals forward. Spiritual races, as defined in the first volume of this work, and geopolitical goals seem to be related to each other because a People without healthy spiritual conditions cannot achieve important Geopolitical goals, as fewer strategic minds arose to produce the necessary transformation.

Across the pages of this book, the concept of "Geopolitical relevance" will be used extensively. When I mention the concept of "Geopolitical relevance", I refer to the relevance for specific cultural and spiritual elements of peoples and civilizations in relation to others, as those elements act as representatives of their spiritual life embodied in its cultural image. In fact, the set of spiritual and cultural values of peoples and civilizations, insofar as this values are generally visible to the rest of the World, speak of the true power of given countries over the rest of the planet, since without this power the cultural image of those countries and their civilizations would never have arisen over the others, and this implies the possibility of any external inference with the internal values of such countries and civilizations was not possible.

When one searches for the truly eternal factor which peoples possess, and realizes this eternal factor can only be expressed in the influence over culture and spirituality, then one becomes aware that such truly eternal factor in geopolitical relationships is the greatness and importance of a People as builders of its specific civilization. The less a country is capable of preserving and expanding the values behind its culture and spirituality, the less will achieve any real relevance in World affairs. Instead, other cultures and other civilizations, including the liberal civilization, will permeate and determine the entire life and will of a People until either it perishes under liberal decomposition, or until that People is elevated in higher levels because the rivaling countries became bearers of living Dasein, that is, the bearers of true civilization. The international liberal civilization must be seen as the mortal common enemy of all the values for preserving Dasein, therefore every existing organized strength of the Righteous understood as what they truly are, a spiritual race becomes ineffective as long as a People does not consciously remember the cultural basis for their self-preservation and take great care of it, building geopolitical relevance only for the preservation of that cultural basis which becomes a spiritual fortress against any eventual enemy. The result of not achieving the aforementioned is the loss of a decisive incidence over the World, and ultimately, decay and final destruction. Then the Fallen race can make its entrance in some of their many forms, and its cultural poisoning and spiritual corruption will not stop until their pestilence is completely eradicated.

The first signs of decay within a civilization are when those in charge of preserving it become unsure in their judgment regarding how to deal with their daily lives and with the rest of the World, becoming farther and farther from the authentic will, and instead sinks into a mix of manifested ideas and cultural bastardization which are incapable of giving real solutions. Once peoples and even entire civilizations no longer appreciate the cultural expression of their own spiritual heritage, directing their attention to the banal rather than the eternal, they renounce the force emerging from the cultural and spiritual life of mankind. The mixing of cultural elements and the descent of the Righteous spiritual race are then, at first, the consequence of a so-called predilection for foreign things which in reality is a covered invasion whose goal is to destroy a civilization.

People who do not longer recognize the highest values of their civilization are suffering from the final stage of that invasion, since the importance of a People's heritage as carried in culture and bloodlines only becomes fully effective when this value is recognized by the ones responsible for preserving it. Consequently, the greater the cultural and spiritual value of peoples and civilizations had become, the greater they must carry out the struggle for existence against other peoples and other civilizations. In parallel, the greater the internal powers of a People are put in this direction, the greater will be the possibilities for the affirmation of that internal power, and that internal power, in turn, increases the possibilities of victory in all the fields of a geopolitical struggle, conforming a necessary vicious circle. Thus, geopolitical power and geopolitical relevance ultimately reside in the cultural values of peoples and the inner strength of a civilization based on them. Each successful act for the preservation of those cultural values is a defeat for the other civilizations, including liberal civilization, and this is, even more, when each cultural creation is capable of rising mankind over its limitations, strengthening the position of peoples and nations not merely in a momentary, ephemeral way, but in an endurable and transcendental way.

The cultural value of civilizations and their peoples is also the expression of the general capacities of human life when we understand the real phenomena of spiritual races as shaping all the historical and cultural manifestations emanating from mankind. The expressions of this phenomenon can be of the most varied qualities, quantities, and types; but together they result in the only real standard for assessing civilizations and those who built them. Nothing is easier to replace than the loss of weapons and every organization can be shaped or renewed, this has been the case countless times in history. The individual European states and Russia had lost the potentiality of their economic and military forces in terms of the relative comparison against foreign superpowers, but even a greater problem emerges when we consider that incompetent liberal leaderships could not even achieve the most easier substitute for that: political unification for Euro-Siberia and inner strength for it.

The modern liberal statesmen and the peoples under their rule cannot understand the importance of Euro-Siberia as a political and cultural paradigm, in fact; they find it strange. This is a conception that seems to the liberal as strange as it is dangerous for him since it would mean an immunizing defense against any danger posed by liberalism and its bearer: the Fallen race. Precisely, our Euro-Siberian civilization, which in their fragmentation lacks the political unity which characterizes China, India, and the United States, has received a lot of attack from those who want to bury any future perspective for the perpetuation of mankind's higher forms. The most depressing thing about the surrender of real political and cultural unity for Euro-Siberia lies in the concomitant circumstances in which it takes place, as now, more than ever, the entire Euro-Siberian legacy is being torn apart and foreign superpowers are in more favorable positions. What is decisive for peoples in order to preserve their true existence as living entities is an authentic will for preserving living forces able to reach mankind's destiny: The Final Kingdom. The economic and military weapons are easily replaceable, but the spiritual and cultural weapons of the Righteous are not. Consequently, there is something that stands out above material strength, and that, in fact, is the true source of geopolitical power.

PART I:
BASIC CONSIDERATIONS

A REAL CONSPIRACY

THE US IS A COUNTRY SCHEDULED FOR DISSOLUTION

The United States, like any other country in the World, is home to many Righteous and hardworking persons. My only sorrow when writing this particular chapter of my work is that I know the truth revealed here will hurt all those people reading the English language version of this book, and they will become aware of a monstrous betrayal to them, a betrayal planned by their own elite. This betrayal will not be something new. A similar betrayal was made by the elite in charge of running the destiny of the Soviet People, destiny which was seeing their country divided into fifteen new countries and also total economic and social ruin. The truth is that some countries, especially superpowers, are scheduled for dissolution by their own elites because those elites have a total disregard towards the People who worked all their lives for their country, and who even died for it on the battlefield, the ones now death or maimed due to pointless fighting in Vietnam, or the absurd Soviet intervention in Afghanistan, and so on…

The elites currently running the US, the so-called "Deep State", do not have any real interest in the preservation of that country, on the contrary, they are (since decades ago) transforming the US in a country just as unworkable as the USSR was. The United States, as the Soviet Union in the past, is a country whose only purpose is to serve a temporary goal, and when that purpose is over, the idea of the US as a unified and prosperous country becomes totally irrelevant for the real elite, since they only want to continue with their power grip over the entire world. They will do so having their main headquarters in any country which is suited most for that, regardless of whether that country is in North America, Asia, or Europe. The ultimate result will be the same for them: the perpetuation of global slavery.

Liberalism and therefore capitalism, are systems whose continuity is tied to a cycle of permanent destruction and rebirth. In the same way that some economic downfall leads to a period of temporary growth, superpowers under liberal and capitalist guidelines follow that same logic. The British Empire had to fall so that the United States arose as the new superpower, and so the United States will have to fall in order that China becomes the new center for liberal and therefore capitalist domination in the future. The son ends up eating his mother: that's the only way in which Liberalism and Capitalism can perpetuate in the World. A superpower that gave rise to another superpower dies, but its economic and social system continues in another body because that economic and social system is like a wandering soul in need of a new host to carry new misdeeds, or as a parasite which needs a new body for World infection. The logic of liberal and capitalist perpetuation is, therefore, the same logic of what in the First Volume "Horizons of The Fourth Political Theory", I named as "the Fallen Race": a spiritual race of worthless parasites which are an ontological reality and not just a rhetoric tool.

The current elite in the US, those which are considered to be "The Deep State", use their symbolism everywhere, that symbolism is in the occult language and ritualistic practices inherited from ancient knowledge and therefore previous elites in other cultures. Already in the first Volume of this work, the basis of this occult language was described, a language that has as its origins a set of very ancient mathematics and astronomic knowledge. Therefore, the reader who comes to this second part of my work will be already acquainted with the numerical significance of numbers like "13" and "20", the dual relationship between those two, and also numbers "9", "11", "616", "144.000", among others.

Of all current symbolism used by the United States government, the most important is in the pyramid displayed by the dollar bill and forming part of the Great Seal of the United States, adopted in 1782. That symbolism (as I will explain further) is related to an ancient prophecy in the Bible, attested in the second chapter of the book of Daniel.

Daniel interpreted a dream of Nebuchadnezzar II, king of Babylon, about a gigantic statue made of four metals: a head of gold, a chest and arms of silver, a belly and thighs of bronze, and legs of iron, with feet made of iron mixed with clay. In Nebuchadnezzar's dream, a stone "not cut by human hands" destroyed the statue and became a mountain filling the whole World. Daniel explained to Nebuchadnezzar that the parts constituting the statue represented four successive kingdoms beginning with Babylon, followed by the fifth age of division and weakness, and the stone and the mountain (Kur-Gal) are God's Kingdom, The Final Kingdom, which, in Daniel's words it will never fall, nor given away to other people.

While prophecies in Daniel 7 and Daniel 8 were limited in their relevance to the times before and during the rule of Antiochus IV Epiphanes, it is the dream of Nebuchadnezzar II and its interpretation by Daniel which still are relevant to our time. In the present, we are aware that a large part of the prophecy in Daniel 2 already happened: the head represents the Babylonian Empire; the chest and arms of silver represent the Persian Empire; the belly and thighs of bronze represent Greece (during the Macedonian Empire and its successors), and the legs of Iron represent Rome, with one leg signifying the Western Roman Empire, and the other representing the Eastern Roman Empire. One leg gave rise to the Roman Catholic Church, while the other gave rise to our Orthodox Catholic Church.

The prophecy in Daniel 2 becomes, even more, easier to understand when we acknowledge that another famous prophecy in the Bible, that of Christ's thousand years rule is an indication of the thousand years in which the Eastern Roman Empire endured as the stronghold of Christian Orthodoxy. From the final East-west division of the Roman Empire in 395 to the fall of Constantinople in 1453, excluding 57 years in which Constantinople was occupied by the Latin Empire (between 1204 and 1261), and the months of union with Rome's Church from 12 December 1455 to 29 May 1453, the duration of the Eastern Roman Empire as the stronghold of Christian Orthodoxy was exactly a thousand years. The words are as follows: "And I saw an angel coming down out of heaven, having the key to the Abyss and holding in his hand a great chain. He seized the dragon, that ancient serpent, who is the devil, or Satan, and bound him for a thousand years. He threw him into the Abyss and locked and sealed it over him, to keep him from deceiving the nations anymore until the thousand years were ended. After that, he must be set free for a short time." (Revelation 20:1-3)

About the thousand years rule, the Book of Revelation mentions the following: "He who overcomes, and keeps my works to the end, to him I will give rule over the nations, And he will be ruling them with a rod of iron; as the vessels of the potter they will be broken, even as I have power from my Father: And I will give him the morning star." (Revelation 2: 26-28). Noteworthy, regarding the Fourth Kingdom (the Roman Empire) which precedes the fifth age, Daniel said the following prophecy: "Finally, there will be a fourth kingdom, strong as iron—for iron breaks and smashes everything—and as iron breaks things to pieces, so it will crush and break all the others." Therefore, the "rod of iron" crushing nations as the vessels of the potter, is a reference to one of the iron legs representing the Fourth Kingdom, namely the Eastern Roman Empire and its thousand years of existence. While one leg of the statue leads to the Final Kingdom of God (after leading to the First Kingdom of a thousand years), then the other leg leads to the very opposite of that.

To understand the relationship of the symbolism used by the US government with Daniel 2 prophecy, first of all, we must analyze the numbers being given to us in that symbolism. The numbers concerning us most are again "13" and "20", being those the basis of the ancient mathematical symbolism which was discovered and then used by the ones ruling humanity's world at the present. As already explained in "Horizons of the Fourth Political Theory", Number "13" represents the governments of darkness, Nimrod, and the rule of the Devil. The pyramid of a dollar bill has 13 steps, and the eagle has 13 leaves on the right foot and 13 arrows on the left. The shield on the eagle's chest with the US flag possesses 13 stripes, and on the eagle is the star of David composed of 13 smaller stars. Those who already read the first volume of this work will be aware of the great importance of an ancient mathematical system composed of "13" and "20", which forms the basis of a binary system used today by occult circles (in the same way it was used since ancient times).

Number "13" is just the side of this mathematical symbolism that people are aware the most, but not the only one, since this symbolism also has number "20" as the opposite of "13" forming together a binary system which when correctly understood, allows us to understand the language of the current elite. Together with the number "13", the number "20" also has a special relationship with the government of the United States, noteworthy is, for example, the curse of Tippecanoe", also known as Tecumseh's curse or simply as "the 20-year presidential curse", which is a pattern of deaths in office of US presidents elected or re-elected in years evenly divisible by 20, a pattern which took place between 1840 and 1960 (Redmond 2020). As a matter of fact, 13 plus 20 produce number 33, which is a number of key importance in occult circles including freemasonry. There are 33 degrees in Scottish Rite Freemasonry while the "House of the Temple" in Washington DC., USA has 33 outer columns, 33 feet high each. That number has various meanings, for example; it is Jesus' age when he was crucified and resurrected according to tradition, and also its the number of times the divine name Elohim appears in the story of creation in Genesis.

Nimrod, creator of the first empire after the Deluge and who tried to take the place of God (Genesis 10:6-10), was the thirteenth in the line of Ham, therefore the symbolism of those who founded the United States is inspired by the concept of familiar generation, representing a family of thirteen generations, each generation being twenty years each (in line with XVIII century standards). Besides knowing the pyramid has 13 steps, we must put our attention on the roman numerals at the basis of that pyramid: MDCCLXXVI, which is 1776 in roman numerals (the year of the United States Declaration of Independence). The Irish-born revolutionary leader in Philadelphia, and secretary of the continental congress, Charles Thomsom; explained this symbolism in the following way: "The date underneath is that of the Declaration of Independence and the words under it signify the beginning of the new American Æra, which commences from that date." (The Department of State Bulletin, 1980). Hence, the famous two mottoes at the reverse of the United States Great Seal which are read in Latin: "Annuit Coeptis", meaning "Providence has favored our undertakings", and "Novus Ordo Seclorum", which translates as "A new Order of the Ages."

But what almost everyone failed to realize is that the pyramid of the dollar bill does not only shows us the date in which the American Age began, but also a timeline that ends with the date for the scheduled demise of it, an event related to the prophecy in Daniel 2. When we are aware of that, we can easily decipher the meaning of those thirteen steps of the Pyramid as corresponding to 20 years each or what is the same: thirteen ages of twenty years each, for a grand total of 260 years (20 X 13). All that implies the famous pyramid of the dollar bill is showing us a timeline that starts in 1776, with the United States Declaration of Independence and ends 260 years later, in 2036. The first occurrence of the number 13 in the Bible is where it is written: "Twelve years they had served Chedorlaomer, but in the thirteen year they rebelled" (Genesis 14:4). The timeline from 1776 to 2036 is also a prophecy, which can be put as follows: "In the thirteen generation they will rebel".

According to the prophecy attested in the second chapter of the book of Daniel, four successive kingdoms beginning with Babylon would lead to a "fifth age", in which the legs of the giant statue in Nebuchadnezzar's dream are replaced by feet of "iron and clay". To further understand the scheduled self-fulfilling of Daniel 2 prophecy, we must be aware the United States is the successor of the Western Roman Empire, while Russia is the successor of the Eastern Roman Empire. They are the feet made of mixed iron and clay, and thus successors of the iron legs in Daniel's fourth age. What Daniel said about the fifth age is an accurate description of the current situation in the United States and the situation in the former Soviet Union when it tried to keep its fifteen republics together: "Just as you saw the feet and toes were partly of baked clay and partly of iron, so this will be a divided kingdom; yet it will have some of the strength of iron in it, even as you saw iron mixed with clay. As the toes were partly iron and partly clay, so this kingdom will be partly strong and partly brittle. And just as you saw the iron mixed with baked clay, so the people will be a mixture and will not remain united, any more than iron mixes with clay." (Daniel 2: 41-43).

The toes in each foot are symbolizing the dissolution of two empires, one in the East and the other in the West. Russia was already divided into fifteen states after the dissolution of the Soviet Union, and when the United States is also divided due to its own civil conflict, then the self-fulfilling of Daniel 2 prophecy will be complete, and another World Order will start, just as the Great Seal of the United States reveals, including the real date for the scheduled event: 2036.

Understanding symbolism is helpful to discover the scheduled path which current events are eventually leading to, a path in which global events as the COVID-19 pandemic and economic crises, or incidents of civil unrest in the United States, can be all placed together to form a hidden ladder which makes sense to the ones aware of the big picture. Of course, not all conspiracies are real (if not most), but we must recognize the fact that conspiracies do exist and are as relevant today as they were in the past or as they will be in the future, as governments and other relevant actors lack both transparency and goodwill in an age of massive wealth and power concentration, and the age when even the most fundamental pillars of civilization are being torn apart. In a scheme where the only important goal remains to keep a state of affairs which, if unchecked, can only bring us to total ruin and death, our most important weapon is knowledge and understanding.

One thing we should always bear in mind is that the global elite will do everything possible in order that a unipolar World is preserved, even dismantling the previous center of that unipolar World if necessary. That is in order to give rise as quickly as possible to a new center which by economic, social, demographic, and military characteristics becomes the most suitable pole for capitalists and therefore liberal domination over the World. It is becoming very clear that the country that is suited the most to become the guardian of the capitalist order and therefore the liberal order is China, due to its demographic size, its economic might, its ethnic and political unity, and its centralized and all-controlling elite, which have the economical and technological resources to exercise absolute control inside the borders of China and also control outside of it, by influencing the domestic policies of other countries which are becoming more and more economically and technologically dependent on the Asian giant.

The United States is no longer the country that is suitable the most for the task of preserving a unipolar World order, and this is first because of the demographic size of the United States in relation to China and also the economical size of the United States in relation to the potential size of the Chinese economy in the future. Secondly, because of the political, social, ethnic, racial, and even religious divisions which are becoming stronger every day and now can be exacerbated by the "Deep State" in the

US, to accelerate the demise of that country as a superpower. The process which we are seeing now in the United States is one which should be called "Latin Americanization." That which I call "Latin Americanization" is composed of three fundamental parts:

1) Gradual miscegenation of the biological "races" by interbreeding due to mass emigration and cultural change.

2) Growing political, social, and economical instability as that seen in Latin America.

3) A gradual process for establishing artificial frontiers between lands speaking the same language and sharing a common origin (as it happens with Spanish-speaking countries in Latin-America).

The demise of the United States as a superpower is necessary in the context of modern financial capitalism and its globalization since nowadays the United States is only an impediment to the overall strength of the capitalist World order. Such a World order is negatively affected if two superpowers are in the midst of an economic war whose consequences are the loss of profits for the elite and the creation of state barriers to globalization. Also, increasing possibilities of a direct military conflict between the United States and China which implies a thermonuclear war is, of course, contrary to the wishes of wealthy and powerful individuals who in the event of such a war are the ones who have the most to lose. Another reason why the demise of the United States is necessary for the elite is that only atheistic China can assure the final destruction of Christianity as a relevant actor in the world. Ironically, in the remains of Chinese Marxism, liberalism found the new fertile ground for its seeds, since the materialistic basis of Marxism and the elitism of the ruling classes in charge of the Chinese Communist party paved the way for capitalist and liberal rule.

For all the aforementioned, the global elite must at all costs avoid or at least shorten a second "Cold War", even with the dismantling of the United States since it becomes clear that such a second cold war between China and the United States entails a threat to the stability which the current system of global slavery needs to maximize the concentration of economic wealth and political power.

GEOPOLITICAL RELEVANCE: SHAPING ALL WORLD ORDERS

Internal politics is the art of preserving the vital force necessary for keeping a specific civilization alive through its own spirituality and all areas necessary for preservation. All the most crucial components for such a domestic policy were already pointed out in the first volume "Horizons of the Fourth Political Theory." But stating all those previous points would be completely in vain if an adequate foreign policy is absolutely lacking. In my own definition, foreign policy is the art of keeping the momentary and necessary geopolitical relevance of a given civilization to preserve it and expand it. If the task of politics must be the successful execution of a civilization's struggle (which requires knowing and pursuing what I call as "authentic will"), and if the struggle for the existence of any civilization ultimately consists in safeguarding the geopolitical relevance necessary to protect and expand a civilization, then this whole process requires, sooner or later, the use of force. The following final conclusions are derived: the acquisition of geopolitical relevance is always linked to the use of force, whether in a wise, non-destructive way or an unwise, totally destructive way. In both cases, however, a civilization needs weapons, including economic and cultural weapons, not just military weapons.

Furthermore, these factors should be examined from time to time and, in fact, new levels, both in quantity and quality, should be established in favor of the civilization being defended by those weapons, to the same degree that other civilizations become more powerful in the global stage. Destiny will teach them that, in the last analysis, all peoples are preserved only when their civilization and the geopolitical relevance of it are in a healthy and protected relationship with each other. When a People believes it can defend itself only with military weapons, giving up the use of adequate cultural and economic weapons, then it does not have the strength to break the enemy, neither an internal cultural and therefore spiritual value with which to carry their preservation with dignity. In some cases, the outcome we can observe is the overcrowding of countries, as in China and many other countries, which now, as a result of the loss of all real basic equilibrium between population and natural resources no longer have any chance of being able to develop in a sustainable way to feed their huge mass of people. That is, of course, unless at some point they go against other nations and other civilizations, to survive this economic and cultural world order in which natural resources are becoming scarcer and scarcer. If not, then the own weaknesses of those nations and civilizations will have brutal consequences for them.

As soon as a stronger civilization establishes the true strength of its power only to forget that superior cultural and economic tools have the same importance as military means, then that civilization will collapse. Weakened by vicious economic and cultural deregulation, the peoples being part of such a civilization no longer are ready to fight for the preservation and increase of its geopolitical relevance to face possible changes on the global stage. This is precisely the way open to decay in which first the internal strength of such a civilization fades away, as all spiritual, cultural, and military assets are destined for destruction. In such a context, ideals are weakened and, in the end, also the notion that a civilization urgently needs its own preservation through inner strength and therefore geopolitical relevance, which go hand in hand. Inner strength builds civilizations, that civilizations acquire geopolitical relevance, and they must protect and increase that geopolitical relevance in the struggle against other civilizations, a struggle which occurs both in the domestic and foreign lands. Above all, both the domestic and foreign lands are breeding grounds for spiritual and cultural bastardization, and for the decline of the Righteous spiritual race, resulting in infection centers where the spiritual parasites of the Fallen race thrive and eventually produce further destruction.

When a civilization is losing the battle for its own existence, then another civilization is able to put into motion a set of mechanisms which include even the elites of the first, acting as accomplices of stronger foreign powers because those foreign powers are in a position to bribe and subjugate the weak rivals. Only when a perfect balance can be established and perpetuated, the competition of great powers can continue with an actual war between them as the apocalyptic, yet rare result. The lack of geopolitical relevance faced by certain civilizations (not to be confused with the geopolitical relevance of mere states) leads first than any other thing to the concentration and mixing of completely different peoples in urban centers that become less and less cultural places, but rather gangrene of a dying civilization in which all the evils, vices and diseases seem to unite.

Those urban centers are finally considered as a necessary stage in the life of civilization and rob the People of those virtues that make it possible for nations and their common civilization to preserve their existence on this Earth. The danger to a People only concerned by their material welfare in a specific generation lies in the fact that easily succumbs to the belief that it can shape its destiny solely through materialistic goals. If a really strong People believes it cannot save itself and its civilization only through ephemeral material welfare, or if an economically weak People and their civilization do not want to be extinguished by an economically stronger one, then in both cases the curtain of economic phraseology will fade away, and war, in its cultural, military and economic forms always becomes a necessity. What is at stake is not merely economic sustenance, but the entire legacy of peoples as expressed through their cultural achievements and history. In this way, some civilizations receive the possibility of preservation, while others are deprived of it because this is the real result of the victory of one civilization using soft economic and cultural power over another who believes it can continue with its activities while much stronger powers are emerging just at the gates.

Since all the great powers of today are technological and military strong in some key area, the total cultural and economic conquest of the world carried out by a superpower like Great Britain in the past, the United States in the present, and China in the future is never a peaceful process as a ruling superpower believes it must hurry to use its advantages to triumph with them, killing other civilizations with a mix of economic and cultural might which is safeguarded by military power. That cultural and economic conquest of the world is the inevitable result of the unipolar World which global elites want to preserve in one way or another, as the constant concentration of wealth and global economic exchange are needing a sole ruling superpower capable of protecting (without undesirable competitors) the entire capitalist system with liberalism as its ideological weapon.

Although at first the primary actions of this struggle were military engagements, with former colonial powers waging their many wars of aggression, by now the ultimate weapons are cultural and economic might as a whole such as the one which the United States enjoyed at the middle of the Cold War with the Soviet Union, or as the one which China is developing in the present. The more the difficulties of the market increase, the more aggressive a ruling superpower will turn, and the more bitter will be the fight for the other countries. As this process advances further, nothing will remain of European and Christian civilization unless a bold plan is carried out, and ultimately, the whole Planet will mourn the consequences of this, not just Russia and Europe. As only capitalist interests begin to determine the fate of the World, the more liberal views and capital markets gain decisive influence, the more a unipolar system of global slavery will consolidate.

The unipolar system dies some time just to be reborn in a stronger way and therefore complete the liberal decomposition of mankind, which means no less than the triumph of the Fallen race and mankind's ultimate descent into darkness and total destruction. The initial result of this will be, of course, that a financial group earns trillions, but this amount will never be invested productively, amid the constant depredation of the World resources, the destruction of all human cultures, economic and social crises, and at the long run, also an uninhabitable planet. The peoples all across Europe and Russia have no interest in, say, a financial group or even a factory that opens a shipyard in Shanghai that builds ships for China with Chinese workers and foreign capital assets, even if corporations make their big amounts of profit. Because we must take into account the following: all those peoples, including Russians, have a keen interest in building ships for their domestic markets and in the shipyards across all the Euro-Siberian space, because in this way a certain number of men and women living there have the opportunity to benefit on what they can produce, as the already interconnected European market, and even more the European market plus all of Russia had more than enough capacity to absorb production through internal demand.

Already in 2010, the intra-European Union share of exports accounted 65.3% of the total exports in the European Union (eurostat 2012), and to this, we must add the consideration that total exports sales generated just $6.296 trillion out of a total GDP of $18.292 trillion for the European Union in 2019 (World Economic Outlook Database 2020). If to all of this, we add a complete integration between Europe and Russia, then the European problems regarding raw materials and energy will be made much easier to deal with, and Russia will have a much broader prospect for further economical, technological and cultural expansion. All of the above can be summarized in the following way: the Euro-Siberian space, if politically united, is capable of almost complete autarky (self-sufficiency) and prosperity.

While, on the one hand, for the reason already explained in the first volume (crisis of confidence by the private investors) the current capitalist system to stay healthy needs indefinite and exponential growth, the burden over the World's resources and ecosystems would become heavier and heavier until the process of modernization under the capitalist and therefore liberal guidelines becomes a grave for all civilizations. That will be our fate unless either mankind follows better guidelines, or unless a stronger power and therefore a stronger civilization destroys its rivals to rule supreme in the competence for the World's resources, which anyway will not grant it indefinite survival when better economic and cultural guidelines are absent. Thus, a fight for limited resources automatically becomes more intense, and that intensity becomes even more relentless the more industrialization and consumption advance, and, conversely, the more the World's resources shrink.

All European nations except Russia suffer from an inadequate and unsatisfactory relationship between the demand of their economies for raw materials and energy, and the raw materials and energy sources that can be found in the limited territory of those nations. By contrast, Russia suffers from an inadequate relationship between its large amount of territory and resources and its scarce internal demand, as Russia does not have in the present the population and industrial might of China, nor the combined population and industrial capacity of all other European nations when put as a whole. Therefore, we are facing the question of either European nations, including Russia take the logical path of political unification for the entire Euro-Siberian space, including its markets but also its cultural potential or the absolute fall of European and Christian civilization. The last implies World rule of a strong Chinese superpower in a new unipolar world, a succession of the one which the United States created in the 20th century, which in turn was a succession of the unipolar World created by Great Britain in the 19th century, while the World's resources become scarcer as time goes by.

When the Euro-Siberian space is politically unified, it wouldn't need selling the surplus outside its own cultural space, and it wouldn't need to obtain raw materials and energetic resources from outside. The meaning of such a unification lies in the fact that a perfect equilibrium will exist for the Euro-Siberian civilization, although such a perfect equilibrium is linked to a number of prerequisites in the form of better social and economic institutions as those presented in the first volume. The economy, which today is considered by many as the sole savior of distress among nations, under certain institutions and their good functioning can give a People possibility for a better existence. But that is only temporary if the relationship between a given civilization and its geopolitical relevance is forgotten, a geopolitical relevance which, as far as European and Christian civilization is concerned, is only possible through political unification of the different nations composing Euro-Siberia. The common citizens will believe they can find a decent daily income through solely the individual policies of their respective nations, rather than realizing that the strength of its People and that of brother Peoples must be unified and concentrated to defend their civilization which is the basis for granting new life for present and future generations.

Just as political unification will only provide a temporary improvement without better economic and social guidelines, also improvement in the sense of social and cultural reform will achieve only temporary relief without political and cultural unification, and what is even worse, without such a unification those social and political reforms will be not possible in face of the liberal behemoth and the competence of other civilizations. Social or political reform would never exempt peoples and their common civilization from the duty to unite that same civilization and thus adapt its geopolitical relevance in face of other peoples and their own civilizations. Distress is not the result of just an incorrect type of economic policy, but a consequence of the gradual death of those pillars which create and perpetuate the fruits of a given cultural space, generally available to a given civilization and the nations composing it. This would not be the case at all if confusion caused by the slogan of globalization had not grasped the hopes of individuals and, therefore, if they had not thought the products of liberalism and globalization were their way to eliminate individual and social anguish.

The entire Euro-Siberian space suffers from an unhealthy relationship between populations and raw resources, including energetic ones. In the case of the Russian Federation, a large land full of resources is lacking warm-water ports with direct access to the oceans while having low population density (only nine inhabitants per square kilometer). In the case of smaller European nations, they have their warm-water seaports and their bigger population density but the scale of those nations regarding both demographic size and natural resources is much smaller than those of current superpowers. The political separation between Europe and Russia, and among each of the individual European states is detrimental to the geopolitical relevance of a civilization which, if united under the correct guidelines, could easily be the stronger superpower for centuries and centuries to come.

The opinion that European and Christian civilization can survive without the political unification of the Euro-Siberian space is false, just as false as the opinion that both liberalism and Roman Catholicism are compatible with the survival of Christianity and European nations in the coming ages. The effects expected to be achieved through national divisions and classical European nationalism rest on a fallacy just as big as the ones that form the basis of liberalism and Roman Catholic institutions, which by the way serve as perpetrators for further division of the Euro-Siberian colossus. And when real unity in that colossus is finally no longer possible, then 21st century China will continue to expand its economic and military might in realms which the rest of the World never had to match before, just as when the United States was left as the World's single superpower immediately after the collapse of the Soviet Union. Also, from the military perspective, if a significant increase in military capacities for Russia and European nations is possible through more investment and investigations, then this would be possible in China but on a scale multiple times larger.

Regardless of how Russia, or let's say France, carry out the modernization and increase of their military might without political and economic unification for Euro-Siberia, sooner or later China will have a military capacity capable of easily destroying any adversary. This is relevant when we consider the World's resources are running out, and the nature of the current economic system demands the exponential increase of consumption, a consumption which is already colossal not only in the United States but also in countries with enormous populations as China. We must not forget that if the political unification of the Euro-Siberian space becomes a reality, a unified Euro-Siberia would enjoy a relationship between its Population and the resources in its large and infinitely more favorable soil than the conditions of China, India, and many Asian and African countries.

A WORLD OF CHANGE

International relations between peoples and nations have become so easy and close through modern technology and communications that the Chinese, the people in India, etc., regard North-American and European conditions as a standard for their own life. At present, the dreams of much of the World regarding a standard of living derive as much from the technological potentialities brought from Europe as from geographical conditions prevailing in Europe, North America, and Oceania. The standard of living of the peoples, in the long run, is not determined solely by the quantity of merchandise which a given country can put in the World market and its domestic market; rather, it is also subject to the availability of those raw and essential resources to sustain a modern economy. Also, the standard of living of a given country is subject to the judgment of the other countries and conditions within them, and that judgment can end up in rivalries, or in other cases, alliances and even political unification. The history of human economic development under capitalist guidelines is one of permanent and increasing consumption and therefore increasing yields over natural resources. If the goods and services produced within an economy cannot be consumed at the domestic market, the increase in production is destined to exports, but the overall burden over the World's resources always is increasing fast.

There is a way in which China tried to balance the disproportion between its large population and its fertile territory and resources. That way is Human birth control, with a one-child policy being established between 1979 and 2015, and then a second child policy since 2015. But even which such very harsh measures, the Chinese population stands at a staggering 1400 million human beings covering 9.6 million square kilometers, of which only 16.6 % can be cultivated (1.4 million square kilometers). Of those 1.4 million square kilometers, only 116,580 permanently support crops. To make matters worse, China is severely affected by a growing desertification process, caused by a combination of both human and environmental factors, including climate change (The World Bank, 2019).

First, a struggle between competing World Orders and rival civilizations begins, and only that World Order centered in a strong country and a strong civilization can survive. It is either the liberal World Order, with China becoming its great center for the 21st century, or the Christian World Order, with a real unification process for the Euro-Siberian space, which can only be possible under the guide of a stronger Russia and a stronger Church. Once a civilization, either as a result of spiritual weakness or poor leadership, can no longer preserve the preconditions for its geopolitical relevance in face of other civilizations with stronger peoples, then new World orders become inevitable because they are the way to adapt World conditions to the might of a given civilization. That is, in turn, the expression of the might which a living Dasein possesses in such civilization, at least temporarily until that living Dasein perish under liberalism and the Fallen Race.

All human freedom in this World is given by God and the pursuit of authentic will. The pursuing of that authentic will, divine in its origin, is the only way in which individuals, peoples, civilizations, and an entire spiritual race can earn their right to live and prosper in this World, as long as they possess the strength for this. The current distribution of World space turns out to be the competing ground in which civilizations can become victors, either through political unification, economic might, territorial conquest or a combination of the three. Anyone who ignores the permanent competition between civilizations and thereby competing World orders removes the greatest driving power for the development of his civilization. Regardless of what is the final result for that civilization, the wealth of a small group of men, and the greatness of certain commercial enterprises will always have new headquarters for their actions, taking advantage in the game of free forces and competition, a game in which the vast majority of mankind is just like pawns in a chessboard. The leadership for many nations has an interest in preserving the existing frontiers and political alliances just as long as those frontiers and alliances correspond to their interests, with elites undoing even the work of many generations when they face a situation which in a given moment is not favorable to them and that, therefore, must be changed using both human power and human weakness as fundamental tools.

Just as the Earth's surface seems to be subject to constant geological transformations, which causes previous organic and inorganic forms to disappear in a continuous change, civilizations and their geopolitical relevance are all exposed to endless change as God's Final Kingdom is not materialized in the way of all its crushing power, the same crushing power which is also present in nature when entire species and territories suddenly vanish. We should never consider a merely temporary solution as an eternal value that God will take under its protection to become a law of the future. The only permanent solution is the Final Kingdom, and the current political frontiers on Earth were not designed by a higher power, but by Man himself. Furthermore, no place on this Earth has been determined as the dwelling place of a People forever, nor even Israel for its Zionist fanatics, since the rule of God forced humanity to reshape new frontiers for thousands of years and he will do so until placing its enormous New Jerusalem, his Final Kingdom where it belongs to: a civilization of the Righteous for the Righteous alone.

The Final Kingdom will be bestowed by God on those who in their hearts have the courage to take possession of it, the strength to preserve it, and the spirituality to keep it pure. No one is assigned beforehand to the Final Kingdom, nor is it presented to anyone as a gift without having to work hard in the path towards authentic will. And if we want to talk about human rights, then, in this unique case, the Final Kingdom serves the highest right of all: it gives mankind the right to God, and therefore the right to true life, the civilization cultivated by authentic, divine will, in a balanced and honest way, so that the Righteous souls of mankind can receive their daily water of life. The water of life and freedom flowing to overcome the hardships of early existence. Since through those hardships the Righteous souls gain the civilization and cultural space necessary for their further well-being, they automatically find multiple compensations for those sacrifices necessary for the survival of Christian civilization.

This requires a determination to fight and assuming great risks, but after that, all early struggles and perils will be seen as the inescapable way in which Euro-Siberia adapted its human and material conditions, from time to time, to the arrival of eternal reward in this, a new Earth and a New Heaven, since the Earth and the Sky which Jesus saw two thousand years ago already had passed. Thus, the task of the leaders all across Euro-Siberian civilization should be conducting the struggle for its eternal existence, eliminating unbearable conditions in a fundamental way, implying the restoration of God's mankind and the increase of geopolitical relevance for the only civilization capable of achieving that task: Euro-Siberia as represented by its best elements.

In fact, we can fairly say that the struggle of a People's entire history, in truth, consists in safeguarding the elements of civilization that are required as a general prerequisite for sustaining the Righteous spiritual race, which is the living Dasein. However, the relationship between spiritual races and, on the other hand, the attainment of the economic and cultural resources favoring those of superior spirituality is conditioned by acts of special revolution, extraordinary processes, so that the human civilizations nourish from the difficulties faced at lower planes of evolution. Territory and political unity are of enormous importance in all of those extraordinary processes, an importance which nowadays is not completely evident as it was in the past or as it will be in the future, since the growth of a Civilization and the well being of its peoples is a process which became to many a natural thing, instead of what it truly is: something extraordinary.

The increase in geopolitical relevance of other civilizations, including of course those which in the long run will be the main bearers of liberal poison, can only be balanced by an extension in the geopolitical relevance of any civilization which considers its perpetuation as the most important thing. This especially applies to European nations. Since 1914, and especially since 1945, all peoples across Europe, including Russia, are seeing their geopolitical relevance to decrease more and more in relation to the growth of the United States in the 20th century and that of China in the 21st century. Both titans demonstrated that powerful superpowers could be built outside Europe, increasing their productivity and consumption, together with the might of their military power, while all European powers including Russia (also as the former Soviet Union) year after year became eroded in their power, and what is worst, they are seeing how their original European and Christian civilization cannot keep up with the growth of Liberalism as it is forcefully expanded by massive superpowers outside the Euro-Siberian space.

The nations composing all Euro-Siberia depend on factors that are partly beyond calculation and, also, beyond their power. World trade, the World economy, military alliances, etc., are all transitory means to ensure the existence of a given People, but if all those factors give rise to pathological and dangerous conditions, and the ensuing decline of geopolitical relevance, what are transitory means become permanent graves, even after making possible a better livelihood for a country during many decades. A healthy People will always seek to find the satisfaction of their needs inside the cultural space of their own civilization because the satisfaction of all those needs will be conditioned by the preservation of the civilization which made possible common grounds for human development and higher spirituality. Ideals that do not serve this purpose are evil to the core, although they may seem a thousand times more practical because they remove nations, peoples, and civilizations more and more from their shared authentic will towards eternal preservation. Therefore, ideals are good and healthy as long as they continue strengthening the internal and general forces of civilizations and therefore their Righteous elements, so that, ultimately, the Righteous spiritual race can be correctly guided and supported when waging the struggle for their existence as a living Dasein.

Sooner or later, spiritual collapse brings physical collapse, as the result of spiritual malnutrition caused when ideals and daily goals do not aim closer to any authentic will but rather to total ruin. Therefore, peoples and their civilizations can withstand a certain limitation of geopolitical objectives as long as they are given compensation in the form of worthy ideals, and since this is not the case in current Euro-Siberia, a greater geopolitical goal expressed by Russia will by the breeding ground for more worthy ideals when Euro-Siberia achieves political unification and cultural depuration. The more primitive the spiritual life of a civilization is, the more their geopolitical goals shrink until it finally considers consumption for a single generation or two as the sole goal of life. Ironically, the material well being will only increase in exact proportion as higher spiritual perspectives are in the process of becoming reality.

Whether a Civilization survives or falls is determined above all by the following fact: Regardless of how high the material well being of a People is, all that well being can only be perpetuated if the greatest ideals for a civilization enjoy big political and cultural relevance in the World scale, as they must be put at the forefront of all geopolitical considerations.

FOUNDATIONS FOR A FUTURE FOREIGN POLICY

AIMING TOWARDS COMPLETE SUCCESS

Peoples and entire continents want to adapt their standard of living to that of the most economically developed countries of the World. Those standards of living, as they increase over and over again holding the banner of larger and larger consumption, sooner or later end up colliding with the fact that general requirements demanded by a given People must adapt to the natural and human resources present in a certain territory, and eventually, all peoples and nations will have to adapt to scarcity in natural resources for the planet as a whole. In part, livelihood standards are determined by increasing technological development with which leading nations further develop new ways to satisfy new needs, within the boundaries of the same planet Earth. But also, standards of living are being pushed forward by the constant urge of the current capitalist system for indefinite and exponential consumption, since it is the only way in which an economic system based on the confidence of both investors and consumers can stay healthy. Consumption of goods and services produced in modern economies becomes so important that is more and more difficult for the individual human being to consider large families as a blessing rather than a burden over material aspirations.

The reason why I again emphasize the aforementioned is that all the military and political events in the centuries since the fall of the Western Roman Empire had not been able to give Euro-Siberia a political unity within which they can secure their cultural and economic life against those countries which now stand as economic and military giants, and those are, of course, the United States since the 20th century and China in the 21st century. Despite the fact that individual European states partially merged with others under larger associations like the European Union in the West or the Eurasian Union in the East, the hard truth is that those associations were only made for securing some specific economic interests while cultural and spiritual interests are not protected at all. In addition, a more decisive political unity, as that which gave birth to the United States was never an option, because when only economic interests are put in the balance, the result will be a lack of shared sense for unity, together with resentment and distrust towards the leading economic powers present in international associations as the European Union and the Eurasian Union, with Germany and Russia as the leading economic powers in those blocks, respectively.

Until economic and cultural unity is fostered together in a large Euro-Siberian space, encompassing that which remains of European and Christian civilization from Lisbon to Vladivostok, only then a true political unity among European nations will be much more than just daydreaming. Both the European Union and the Eurasian Union changed nothing regarding the primary need for political unity in an endangered civilization, and consequentially, they already began to crumble even as merely economic initiatives, with internal conflict and distrust as that which saw Britain leaving the European Union or the total failure of the current Eurasian Union as a tool to somehow approach the political unity which Russian influence enjoyed during the time of the Soviet Union. While the Flag of the European Union is perceived as an artificial construction unable of giving Europe any sense of real unity, the Russian tricolor flag fails to foster any desire for reunification in nations that formerly were part of the Russian Empire and the Soviet Union.

It is becoming more and more evident how real political unification both for individual European states and Russia's former territories will be impossible as long as the destinies of Europe and Russia are artificially separated by the evil forces of chauvinism, liberal interference, and religious separation. Almost a total end to fratricidal wars between European brothers was achieved after the wars of 1914-1918, and 1939-1945, but the major fruit of all that will remain the possibility of survival for European and Christian civilization when geopolitical fragmentation of the Euro-Siberian space is finally gone.

Ancient political and cultural unity in Roman times is Europe's most important lost tradition. On the one hand, that unity gave rise to a common European and Christian identity, on the other, it laid the foundations for Europe's spiritual and cultural influence far beyond its geographical borders: from central Europe to the Americas, from Greece to the easternmost parts of Siberia, and from England to the most ancient corners of mankind. From the cultural and spiritual importance of Euro-Siberia lies its fertility as a civilization, fertility which of course is under serious threat by the corroding nihilism of liberal and postmodern madness, and the growing influence of non-European civilizations which in the future could very well serve as headquarters for further liberal poisoning over mankind. As unsatisfactory as the current situation of Europe and Russia could be in the cultural, military, and economic senses, that situation is even more unsatisfactory when we try to look not just at the present situation but at any future situation in which Europe and Russia die out because of remaining mainly passive actors.

Everywhere are hostile cultures and states whose relative inaction until now is an attitude which will hold as long as the dramatic competence over natural resources and European and Russian decline do not put a more active plan at the bottom of their minds. And also, everywhere is the growing behemoth of liberal rot inside and outside the Euro-Siberian space. As for Russia, it has China in the east and NATO in the west grouped around her as large, powerful entities with a foreign policy which, in the case of NATO explicitly collides with Russia's existence as a sovereign State, and in the case of China, implicitly. Besides having to defend a 20,139-kilometer land frontier, Russia has boundaries with 14 countries, some of which are of decisive importance to the Russian economy. From a military point of view, after the fall of the communist bloc, these new Russian borders became even more unsatisfactory than those of the Warsaw Pact, since they ran directly through Russian-language areas and even the Baltic states are now NATO members, implying that a direct military threat is in place from countries bordering Russia's most populated western areas. The Russian people now face larger frontiers that are more difficult to defend, closer proximity for enemy states, and also political borders that do not encompass even the ethnolinguistic frontiers of Russia understood as a nation. It is clear that even as the new Russian Federation does not possess grand global objectives for its foreign policy as those which the Soviet Union had, it also does not have even the intention for further reunification of the Russian nation as its minimum objective in foreign policy.

Apart from the fact that the current Russian Federation does not cover even the entire Russian nation, but only the largest part of it, we must consider that since its founding, the Russian Federation had also assimilated toxins into the new state structure, the ill effect of that can be perceived as bourgeois inequality, with roots in former communist rule, and that bourgeois inequality, if unchecked, can give a liberal elite, and thus the Fallen race the possibility of destroying Russia and what is left of European and Christian civilization after that. If liberal rule finally consolidates in the entire world, its period in world history will be as short as it will be cataclysmic. But this planet cannot be conquered by ideology alone, nor any civilization can be built just by it: those who never had an idea of their own, but just arrogance and endless money cannot conquer that which was made by God for the Righteous. Because of this, the Final Kingdom will eventually come. The only question is: Which side will most people take? As for the side made of those choosing correctly, even if it is a minority of the Euro-Siberian population, they will not be short of the authentic will which is the builder of an inner force capable of carrying out everything necessary.

It is obvious that the current Euro-Siberian states with their liberal structures and their geographic and economic limitations will not be capable of such an act as building the Final Kingdom unless decisive action is taken by those of a higher spiritual nature so that Euro-Siberia will someday stand united politically and culturally, sealed off from liberalism and all alien ideological elements. Then, the spirit of Euro-Siberia and the individual souls within their peoples will never be corrupted again, and a sacred territory united in the highest political, cultural, and spiritual senses will shine as an eternal sun from the north, guiding the path of all mankind towards salvation.

Since the end of the Western and Eastern Roman empires, there have been weak attempts for the true political and cultural unification of European civilization; perhaps it was never seriously wanted, but in practice, a Patriotic State should under no circumstances promote division within a common civilization and common blood. On the contrary, a true Patriotic State will always strife for uniting and consolidating the civilization which saw its birth. That idea should be included in the education and life of all nations across the Euro-Siberian space, making them bearers of this ideal. The national state of bourgeois conception had become obsolete, firstly because the liberal elite now wants its dismissal and individual states cannot compete against the global elite, but also because in a World when some states already encompass entire civilizations, as it is the case of China or India, all other civilizations must at least ensure their political and cultural unity in order to survive. This does not correspond to the idea of a national state that the European bourgeoisie taught.

In past times, it was a matter of concern that nation-states ultimately included in its structures, for example, the millions of Poles in Poland, the French in France, the Russians in Russia, and so on. But as time passes, now the matter of concern is that separated peoples can unite to confront both the international liberal threat and also the threat from powerful foreign superpowers. This must be the founding principle of a grand foreign policy for Russia as it is the only state with the power to induce Euro-Siberian unification. The disproportionate balance between Russia's power and that of individual European states is a crucial factor whose aspects will be further analyzed in this book, in order to build a strategy for permanent unification not just only in the political aspect but also in the cultural and spiritual ones. This, of course, is conditioned by the internal strength of Russia, and therefore the task of its domestic policy will be to prepare the commitment of Russian power in such a way that the greatest possible success is assured, a success whose fruits will be not just for Russians, but for the entire European and thus Christian civilization.

Even when the goal of unification is achieved, preserving the power needed for this will require assembling all internal strength, but this time not just only from Russia's part, but from all the nations which were united to carry out the tasks of a higher form of civilization. The true unity for European civilization will become the definitive weapon with which a struggle for both spiritual and material goals can be successful over and over again until the ages of the ages.

THE FOLLY OF RESTORING THE RUSSIAN BORDERS AS A FINAL GOAL

All the folly of a policy aimed merely at border restoration is shown on the basis of the following considerations: first, if the current population of all former Soviet republics is used as a basis, a reborn "Russian" empire will have 290 million people. Of this number, about half possess Russian as their mother tongue, just 2% of the total World Population as of this year 2020. The entire region encompassing all nations which were part of the former Soviet Union produced in 2019 a GDP of about $5.811 trillion (PPP). By comparison, in 2019, the European Union enjoyed a GDP of $22.761 trillion (PPP), while China the same year produced a GDP of $27.331 trillion (also PPP), with perspectives for far more growth for this country (International Monetary Fund 2020). The current population of Europe is 747 million as of 2020 (based on the latest estimations by the United Nations), which is more than 2.5 times the population of a reunited post-Soviet space.

I must reject the idea that any other reason could be a standard for the ordering of foreign policy except the responsibility of truly guaranteeing the existence of a given civilization together with those who abide in it. What the liberal elites inflicted on Russia when dismembering it, as grave and humiliating as it was, at least gave an important lesson: to carry out a foreign policy in the name of ideology can be disastrous if an ideology (like Marxism Leninism) is unworkable and if both domestic and foreign policy is characterized by the most traitorous and cowardly elements in the history of any superpower. And what was the surest dishonor for any People? The enemy's occupation of areas that belonged to Russia in the past or the cowardice with which liberal elites, including former representatives of the Marxist delusion, turned the former Soviet sphere of influence into a criminal organization of deserters, pimps, black vendors and hackers?

Let's not be mistakes about the following position: the Belovezha Accords together with the subsequent Alma-Ata protocol which put an end to the Soviet Union were illegal, and the reasons for their illegality (already mentioned in the first volume of this work) also make illegal any change on the Constitution of the Russian Soviet Federative Socialist Republic (then part of the USSR) made during or after December 8th, 1991. All changes during and after that date were made by an illegal entity, and the Law of the RSFSR of November 1, 1991 "On amendments and additions to the Constitution (Basic Law) of the RSFSR" must be considered as the last legal change in the Constitution of Russia, which allowed the Russian flag to be a white-azure-scarlet, recognized the presidencies of the Republics forming the Russian SFSR, and made trial by jury a part of the Judiciary of Russia. I propose the total integration of the territories which composed the Ukrainian, Belarusian, Moldovan and Georgian Soviet republics into a newly formed Russian SFSR, after a referendum whose result will be determined by the voting of the five former Soviet republics as a whole.

But having just that or the total restoration of the borders of 1991 as the final goal of a Russian foreign policy will not solve any of the problems existing all across Russia and Europe. The result of bad foreign policies may be the fall of a given civilization and the loss of freedom for all of its peoples, and in fact, a foreign policy aimed merely at border restoration cannot resist real critical examination. As a theoretical possibility, it stands in the way of all practical possibilities aimed at the true preservation of Russian identity, which cannot be dissociated from the destiny of Europe and Christianity as a whole and vice-versa... This policy advocated by Marxists and "imperialist" sectors in nationalist circles will be as unsatisfactory in the long run as it is dangerous. There would not be any benefit in the future of the Russian People if merely a restoration of past borders is pursued as the final goal of the ones pretending to be restorers of the Russian honor. If the Russian People achieves the restoration of the borders of the year 1991, the sacrifices of the Great Patriotic War, the Cold War, and the '90s will be still in vain.

We must see all those historic events as momentary situations in the fight for the existence of the Russian People that has been going on for more than a thousand years, a fight whose outcome will also determine the survival of all the individual European states as bearers of a sovereign, genuine, European and Christian heritage. The 1991 borders were unsatisfactory in an economic, military, or geopolitical sense, and thus they did not protect Russia then, and even less they will achieve such a thing now. We can in the same way pursue the borders of the year 1721 or those of 1914, and so on, just as blindly as we can pursue the restoration of the Soviet Union's borders. It is nonsense to take the borders of any past year in the history of an empire and put that as the basis of a final geopolitical objective. The borders of any country are the momentary expression of economic, cultural, and military events that are not concluded developments but momentary steps, just as in a living organism whose structure must perform constant changes until the hour it dies.

The borders of 1991 were back then an expression of something incomplete, which is even more incomplete now in case restoration of those borders is achieved. When someone proclaims a foreign policy whose slogan is the preservation of a given People and its heritage but at the same time a slogan based only on the restoration of past borders and zones of influence, then he eliminates those more ambitious goals which are the ones necessary to guarantee the existence of a People as endangered as the Russian or as any European one at the present.

Once the restoration of the borders of the year 1991 is achieved, Russia will face again an encirclement made by the enemies of the former Soviet Union. Because if thirty years after the end of the Cold War, the former coalition of enemies (NATO) is still in place and growing with countries which were part of the communist block, then it is easy to realize the anti-Russian and anti-European character of NATO, whose ultimate objective is the destruction of Russia and also the destruction of European culture with its replacement by liberalism. The fact that Russia has to face a coalition of thirty states and still survives as a sovereign country serves as a testimony of the Russian strength, but also as a reminder of how bad foreign and domestic policies, in this case, those of the former Soviet Union can create a major disaster. All the current system of alliances, originally put in place in order to keep united even countries with divergent wishes and objectives but with strong antagonism towards the Communist block, now is being perpetuated with the goal of the final liquidation of Europe and Russia as bearers of civilization and their replacement by a liberal cadaver without any true incidence over the World's affairs, while the United States now and China in the future are able to command a global dictatorship.

There are no armies for peacekeeping, but only for achieving victorious wars, whether those wars are manifested in a purely economical and cultural way until enemies are subjugated, or if those wars are carried by means of the brutal violence of modern warfare. No coalition such as NATO would still be in place if the real aim for its existence is not warring against Russia's existence and against Europe's true sovereignty and cultural heritage: a war against civilization. NATO is now effectively acting as a police force for the peaceful subjugation of civilization, and a Russian policy aimed at merely border restoration will not change this situation. With the possession of enormous military and economic power, the United States created in the 20th century a situation which was unseen since the times the British Empire was at its height. In the 21st century, China is emerging as a new superpower of such dimensions that it threatens with creating a world order whose control and centralization will not have any parallel in history.

NATO will only serve the interests of those powers, because when the United States faces its demise as a superpower, NATO then will obey a different master: the Chinese giant. NATO, as the police force of liberalism, does not have any particular allegiance towards any particular country, but only towards a particular ideology: that of the liberal project. The situation created by North America now, and by China in the future, is (together with Russia's harassment through the European members of NATO) the most visible argument against a foolish policy that wants the restoration of former territories while it forgets safeguarding the Euro-Siberian space from its enemies. The destruction of NATO is the prerequisite for total Russian and European independence, and this will happen if Russia takes advantage of the short time span that will take place between the scheduled demise of the United States and China's emergence as master of the NATO puppet. How a preemptive action can be taken by Russia to destroy NATO will be discussed in another chapter, but for now, this point will be made clear: that preemptive action is absolutely necessary, and it is the only way in which mankind can be saved.

When Peter the Great received knowledge of Sweden's weakness as it was ruled by young Charles XII, he did not wait until Sweden regained its strength but immediately declared a war that ended in victory, marking the start of Russia as a new power in Europe. Now, Russia has to avoid every attempt of encirclement through NATO and China, and that needs a preemptive action for which a favorable opportunity will be present in some years from now. In Europe, Russia will have to counterbalance the superpower status of China which will become the future power of the seas (Thalassocracy), and the only way to do that is by forcing the political and spiritual unification of Euro-Siberia so that it becomes the future superpower of the land (Tellurocracy). Just as China, which is speedily growing and modernizing its naval forces knows its future depends on becoming a superpower of the seas as the United States is now and as the British empire was in the past, both Russia and the individual European nations must realize that their future, their existence, depends on becoming a unified land superpower. Regardless of what the momentary organization of the British Empire and the United States looked like at the beginning, they were constantly engaged in gradually becoming the biggest sea power of the World, until Britain overshadowed other former European powers and until the United States overshadowed Britain. The same goes for China, as it is constantly engaged in becoming a sea power until the demise of the United States is consummated and China's power over the seas becomes uncontested.

If the task of the old feudal and bourgeois national states had been primarily the political and cultural unification of Europe as it was in Roman times, then by now it would be evident how the unification of a civilization is also an indication of its internal strength, just as evident as it is now for millennial peoples as China and India. A new tellurocratic superpower must emerge, overcoming even the worst evil of our times: political and cultural division for which liberalism and Roman Catholicism are equally guilty. This is the true task of a Fourth Political Theory and of any traditionalist movement. The elimination of this general expression of decline for Euro-Siberian civilization (also known as European and Christian civilization) must not be reduced only to political rhetoric and worthless phraseology, but it needs a concrete plan with a scheduled execution in a not so distant future. The effects of this vice of humanity (inner division) appear in all the aspects of life in Euro-Siberian civilization, more than in any other civilization. Division, expressed in the ideological rubbish of modernity, in bourgeois nationalism, and in religious schism destroys the value of the most important civilization to ever have existed: European and Christian civilization, which must not be confused with what is often called "Western Civilization".

The concept of "Western Civilization" could only be inserted when the political and cultural divide of Europe was permanently planted due to the fall of the Western Roman Empire in the years between 395 and 476, while the Eastern Roman Empire remained until the fall of Constantinople in the year 1453. The idea of a "Latin west" and a "Greek East" is only an artificial construct that does not takes into account historical reality, as Latin and Greek heritages melted amid vast cultural exchange and political unification. This idea of an artificial separation in Europe between west and east only started to make sense when the Western Roman Empire completely fell, and this was the first symptom of future decay for the common European civilization which otherwise would have been politically and culturally united just as China and India are now.

"Western civilization" is the antithesis of European and Christian civilization. While "European and Christian civilization" refers to the true founding values of a united Europe as embodied by Christianity and the Roman Empire, "Western civilization" refers to the gradual death of a common European and Christian identity. This gradual death started through the separation and fall of the western portion of the Roman Empire, continuing with the separation and spiritual fall of the Roman Catholic Church centuries later, and finally through the three political ideologies of modernity: liberalism, Marxism, and nationalism. "Western civilization" represents the process of gradual demise for a genuine European and Christian civilization because of suffocating inner divisions and flawed ideological constructs, all poisoning Europe's mentality and causing the loss of much of its spiritual and cultural potential for self-preservation. With the fall of the Western Roman Empire, an individualistic and guilt-based mentality was able to replace the original collectivist and shame-based mentality which was in place until the central political and religious authorities collapsed, being replaced by a chaotic ambiance of competing kingdoms, clans and religious powers.

There is a truth that most historians and most people, in general, are unable to accept: the Roman Empire wasn't a part of Western Civilization. In fact, the fall of the Western Roman Empire was the event that created Western Civilization in the first place. Rome's Empire was full of intellectual, social, and spiritual concepts completely different from those which current Western Civilization possesses. The influence of post-schism Roman Catholicism, ancient barbarian kingdoms, the Protestant Reform, Liberalism, and so on shaped the world view which much of today's European and American peoples possess. Only with Western Civilization, the separation between Church and State originated, while during the times of Roman and Byzantine rule no such thing existed, with Church and State being one and the same. In the present, Christian Orthodoxy resembles that Roman tradition much more than its western counterparts.

The gradual collapse that the European powers including Russia suffer since 1914 lies not in events that began with the Great War but in much older inner divisions which can be traced as far back as Rome's political separation between west and east. While the full consequences of that catastrophic inner division were only evident from 1914 onward; today those same inner divisions push the following question: What is the current situation in Europe and the prospects for its future? Because unless there is a miracle, and I believe it will be, then our path will present itself as one of damnation and extinction. After all the cataclysms which Europe and Christianity had to endure, another question must be done: European nations had learned anything from all that? If the answer is Yes, then there is a possibility for educating European nations in order that they think not as separated entities doomed to extinction, but as a single living organism that is conscious of itself.

European armies, having won innumerable battles through the centuries, however, should be conscious of their greatest defeat: most of those battles were waged against themselves, against their common heritage and living. In the Great Patriotic War and the Cold War, the Soviet peoples had infinitely proved their courage and sacrifice, only to found themselves, just as all of Europe, weakened and beaten by the devastating poison of ideological and national divisions. Thus, the borders of 1991 only proved themselves as completely useless despite being obtained through the loss of 27 million lives first, and the incalculable economic and ideological losses of the Cold War after. The Soviet peoples didn't sacrifice their lives and their economic future for the Ukrainians to acquire their state, or in order that the Baltic countries could celebrate their participation in Hitler's army, and in the same way, the Germans, French, Poles, British, Italians, Hungarians, Romanians, Yugoslavians, etc. did not lose their lives so that Europe becomes a rotten liberal corpse devoid of any true culture and under the control of foreign superpowers. Truly if all the dead could rise from their graves now and see such a monstrous degeneration as the one currently in place, they would wish to not had kept up a single minute in their battlefields.

All of the current "imperialist" and Marxist proposals for restoring past borders and zones of influence had nothing to do with sound geopolitical ideas but rather with the lack of ideological and geopolitical objectives, whose outcome is delusional ideas of restoring past conditions which already lead to disaster in 1917, 1941 and 1991. During the times which preceded both world wars, as well as during the entire Cold War, the enormity of the Russian and Soviet territories served as part of the propaganda to eliminate the fear of defeat by foreign powers. Thanks to this propaganda, the Russian and Soviet peoples no longer believed in the necessity of conducting Euro-Siberian unification, either in a Marxist way as proposed by Trotsky or in a more ambitious foreign and domestic policy which the Czars could have pursued. The idea that something as big as the Russian Empire and the Soviet Union could be easily defeated was slowly erased through propaganda unleashed first within the Russian Empire, and also within its communist successor. Although in 1914 and 1941 the entire peoples of Russia and the Soviet Union became aware that the outcome of defeat would be catastrophic, once the year 1914 gave signs of imminent defeat for Imperial Russia, and once Nazi Germany was defeated by the Soviet Union in 1945, in both occasions Russia's patriotic enthusiasm eventually faded away, and the final outcome was a collapse in 1917 and 1991.

EUROPEAN UNITY IS IMPOSSIBLE WITHOUT RUSSIA

EUROPEAN UNION AS DISUNION

The idea of permanent unification for a large number of ethnic groups that share a common cultural background is far from being just Utopia. The Indian State is home to two thousand ethnic groups and 122 languages, while all major religions are being demographically represented, and Hindi is the primary language of only 43.6% of the Indian population according to the 2011 census. Yet all that diversity does not impede the Indian State from remaining a united entity for more than 1300 million inhabitants as of 2020, and therefore the World's second most populated country ready to surpass China by around 2024. Another paradigmatic example is that of the United States during the 19th and 20th centuries when through emigration, an international variety of different European nationalities were able to gradually merge and form a new North American identity. The cohesion of that identity lasted until the mid-'60s when the demographic, cultural, and political weight of ancestries whose nature is fundamentally different from that of Europe started to increase more and more.

India in the present and the former North American immigration policy are the confirmation that the successful political and cultural unification of nations is possible, and at the same time, India's experience with Pakistan, and North American experience since the mid 60's show that political and cultural unification is only possible as long as it involves ethnic groups who are not fundamentally different, sharing at least some defined foundations of a common civilization. Furthermore, even states which at their birth were weak in comparison to former world superpowers were able to remain united in the strong brotherhood of their ethnic groups as long as they did not try to assimilate groups of a nature incompatible with the Indian and North American cultural feelings and natural instincts. When cultural feelings and natural instincts are pointed towards the preservation of common traditions and a single patriotic feeling, then any process of permanent unification becomes not just theory but also enduring practice.

The intention of this chapter is not to criticize the idea that true European unity is possible as it is possible in other civilizations, but to criticize the absurd fallacy that such European unity is possible without the decisive participation of Russia. Just as in the previous chapter the attitude of Russian political circles only wanting border restoration was criticized, a parallel criticism should be made regarding European daydreamers, especially those in the current "European Union," who think that true unity for Europe can be achieved without taking Russia into account at all. The useless European Union, devoid of any relevance in the World's geopolitical affairs, devoid of any unity beyond just economic matters, and under the control of a liberal agenda imparted from outside Europe is a completely artificial construct, a bastard daughter of the current idea of Pan-European identity. In its current form, this sense of Pan-European identity is incomplete, as it does not realize a patriotically awakened and sovereign Russia is the only European actor who can reaffirm European sovereignty as a whole, not just Russian sovereignty. This will be possible through a Russian unifying impulse analogous to the one which the Roman Empire was able to create as its political and cultural expression against the menace of foreign powers and barbarism.

The nature of the emergence of the European Union induced the creation of a supranational entity that is incapable of displaying decisive actions in the geopolitical issues outside the European Union. Only when Russia's internal question is finally resolved through the reunification of the five orthodox states which constituted the Soviet Union, the installment of superior political institutions in Russia, and the use of Russia's power in bold and decisive action, then a compromise for uniting the Euro-Siberian giant can be forced over the individual European states, eradicating all divisional impulses aimed either among each of those individual states or between an anti-Russian Europe in the West and Russia's sovereignty in the East. The attempt to truly materialize the pan-European idea through a voluntary unification of small European nations, without having to be forced by the decisive impulse of Russia as a bigger European ruling power would lead only to a structure whose strength and energy would be absorbed by the rivalries and internal disputes that we already observe in the European Union, and because of that, any attempt of unification beyond merely economic interests would become just as impossible as it is now.

It is the task of the Fourth Political Theory to strengthen and prepare Russia to the maximum for the task of finally solving the European problem of fruitless division, whose origin is mutual competition in times when the geopolitical reality of the World was entirely different. In the future, only the civilization that has understood how to protect its internal strength through a workable super state and solid cultural guidelines will be able to compete with a mighty thalassocratic China and with liberal necrosis. In the way the Pan-European concept is being unleashed now, it would never be possible to create a structure that guarantees any chance of providing the material and spiritual cohesion of a future tellurocratic superpower because such a superpower to emerge and preserve itself requires a decisive centralization which only the authentic will of Russia's true mission can provide.

Russia, as the power that is capable of bringing Europe's unity after centuries of battles; will be giving its cultural and political mark to the entire European civilization forever. Just as, for example, the unification of Europe's tribes was previously a task of the Roman Empire which carried out a policy of Latinization over the centuries, all the outcome of Russia's struggles during past and future battles will decide how a united Europe will be in reality, which is in sharp contrast to current pan-European thoughts. Any real unification process is only carried out by a successful struggle of the strongest nation in a given civilization, and later that struggle turns into the successful struggle of the civilization as a whole because its existence is not guaranteed unless unification is constantly imparted by the nation which possesses the most power. We can see this in the way by which the Han People created a politically united and culturally homogeneous China; all of which required the constant political and cultural assimilation of other peoples and territories which became a united Asiatic giant. What the Han achieved in China is what the Latin culture would have achieved in Europe if it wasn't for the fatal illness of artificial division with the "Greek" east.

With the recent electronic technologies and digital communication, the difficulties which arose due to the lack of a unitary language in vast civilizations will not be the tremendous barrier existing in ancient times whose solution only came in a process of many centuries. Overcoming the differences of nations culturally divergent in some points but similar in the most important ones always have to materialize once the common grounds are pushed forward, crushing all divisions whose only basis is petty cultural and political points. Therefore, Russia's current dismemberment must be put to an end, and after that, a mature Europe can emerge, with its maturity being measured in how much it can protect its cultural and political interests in a united form of government and spirituality. This will be identical to the history of more ancient and therefore more mature civilizations as the Indian and the Chinese ones, and also to the story of the Roman Empire until its decay. Once Rome destroyed its archenemy (Cartage), and once it subjugated European tribes one after another, only then from European civilization could arise the strength enough to crystallize an enduring superpower.

When Alexander the Great tried to create his own enduring superpower, its preservation was made impossible after Alexander's death, because the Macedonian emperor failed to realize that his Utopian concept of a multicultural empire bounded by nothing more than some Macedonian generals and aristocrats could not endure the test of time, in any form comparable to a power actively engaged in the cultural and spiritual unification of its domains. Also, Alexander failed to realize a lasting unification of nations can only take place if those nations are similar in their basic cultural and biological heritage. If that is not present even a slow process of struggle for the cultural and political hegemony of a ruling nation becomes impossible, and a short-lived empire arises instead.

Let no one believe that such a form of thought as the one which created the current European Union, unable to find unity in even such basic issues as the COVID-19 pandemic, could mobilize any impulse towards Europe's self-preservation through unification and better domestic policies. The current European Union must be regarded as what it truly is: a project for the creation of a Fallen Race protectorate, controlled by foreign superpowers whose ambitions are in direct opposition to European hopes, and being driven by the instincts of an inferior spiritual race for which the entire scam was set in the first place. The idea of unification for the current European States, when forced by a foolish vision in which Russia is not the leading actor, is a fantastic and historically disproven infantilism. Even worst, when pursued as it was when the European Union emerged, it leads to material and spiritual chaos, to the bastardization of culture through liberalism and multiculturalism, and therefore to a decrease in the health and number of the Righteous spiritual race, while its nemesis, the Fallen ones, are quickly rising for achieving world domination.

At the end of the 20th century, it was already evident the current European Union is the ideal of all the liberal Fallen race bastards. These conceptions behind the European Union are in line with the madness of liberal democracies and with the cowardly and servile attitude of Europe's ruling class, as any past sense of national duty in them is gone and now are as dogs behind the bone of North American and Chinese masters. Thus, in the first place, the current Pan-European thought is based on the fundamental basic error that external strength trough unity can be based on internal weakness, which arises from an evident lack of values and the lack of a real center of power for holding Europe together, a task which could be achieved by Russia when taken into consideration. Otherwise, today the European Union would have become the greatest danger to both the United States and China, instead of being a lame political structure that is holding hundreds of millions as permanent hostages in the economic and cultural conflicts between relevant powers. As the total hegemony for superpowers outside Europe already became reality, that hegemony will not be eliminated until European numbers finally express their quality, because we must always bear in mind that unity is also an expression of quality, and in turn, quality is an expression of unity. Only internal strength pushes unity within a civilization, and unity builds more internal strength and so on.

Both NATO and the current European Union are never aimed in the sense of political, economic, and cultural preservation of Europe, but rather as a wave of disease which is currently attacking Russia to finish the killing of Europe once and for all. Given that today the military and economic destiny of Russia versus those of the United States and China is, in fact, also the destiny of all the other countries in Europe, there is, especially since the COVID-19 pandemic, a sector in the movement of Pan-European nationalists who not only want to oppose a united Europe against North American hegemony, but finally realize this task is only possible if Russia is taken into account, and therefore Guillaume Faye's Euro-Siberian paradigm. Only a new Pan-European movement, which establishes conscious knowledge against West vs East division in Europe and realizes that the decadence of this continent is rooted in this first division can still put mankind out of the abyss.

The fate of Europe will no longer be changed by stupid nationalist and Roman Catholic phraseology whose useless results had already been revealed by centuries of tragedy. If we do not put an end to that obsolete form of thinking, we will be facing the end of a civilization whose history has lasted two thousand years and which shaped all of World history forever. In the future World order, European nations, including Russia, will be as Austria and the Netherlands had been in Europe: once important empires that vanished in history. Spiritually, culturally, and finally in the economic sphere, they will atrophy further and further until finally sinking into a chaotic feast of worms, as food bags let to oblivion. All European nations, and even more important, all the remains of Christian civilization will have to give up their right to exist if only a few want to understand what this fate for Europe also means for Russia, and if only a few understand that if Russia sinks to such an abyss, such event would also condemn the whole of Europe…

After all, despite this danger already threatening the whole of Europe has already been perceived by some today, the question remains the same: we have the power to bring a new determination in the destiny of the World? As a Christian, I am convinced that the answer is "Yes". The ancient cultures which arose in Mesopotamia, Persia, Egypt, and Turkey, provide additional historic examples of how civilizations that once shaped the destiny of the World can vanish due to their vices and mindless inconsideration. The Righteous spiritual race, carried through its cultures and bloodlines, was slowly eliminated as the most valuable elements died out, and ancient civilizations were left without the original bearers of culture and State order. A cultural and biological mishmash of little importance saw geopolitical relevance being slowly taken from them to pass on younger and healthier World powers. If those conditions which also affected ancient civilizations are continued for only some decades more, all the enormity of Euro-Siberia will experience first its downfall as a cultural space, and after that, all mankind will soon or later see itself dragged out to hell and extinction because now we possess the technological means to easily destroy ourselves and the World's ecosystem.

We must regard the current European Union and NATO as a major move towards eradicating the Euro-Siberian natural space through an artificial system, which in everything is infinitely unable to bring the extraordinary achievements necessary to move towards greater stability. The extraordinary disparities that we can see everywhere in Euro-Siberia, ranging from the extremely positive to the extremely evil are only the effects of an artificial machine put in charge of something which was completely natural but too immature. Thus, Euro-Siberian civilization is like a child put under the control of terrible foster parents. When destroying the natural unification process which Russia and Christianity would otherwise impart in Europe, then all of NATO, the Vatican, and the European Union are in charge of artificially hindering European potentiality, because they are alien structures fighting a very natural instinct of European self-preservation.

All civilizations around the planet are impoverished in capacities and life span when their potent natural impulses are supplanted by artificial conditions, because those impulses only arise when a common consciousness is aware of its real necessities, and therefore of its authentic will. Since an authentic will is only revealed in the course of natural struggles all along historic paths, it never emerges from artificial impulses and their institutions, on the contrary, artificial institutions make possible the elimination of a country's authentic will and that of an entire cultural space. This is exactly as when fighting a child but in a way that seeks the elimination of natural impulses which God gave to him while supplanting them by stupid attitudes whose goals are creating a slave no longer able to discover authentic will because a slave is forever trapped in the manifested will being forced in his education.

To this education imposed all over the European nations, and all artificial impulses and institutions, we must also add the destruction of the original cultural and biological basis of Europe, which is carried out with forced multiculturalism as a consequence of mass migrations, and with massive birth control which arose from cultural and economic decline. This is something our whole so-called European intellectuals and all bourgeois politicians are pushing forward because of their political correctness, and because it's much cheaper to have slaves and foreign labor. The consequences of Euro-Siberia's gradual weakening will be even more serious in the coming decades because China rises as a new superpower that now has absorbed for almost a century the scientific knowledge and technical abilities of Europe and North America, and has perfected them with China's own knowledge and skills.

Only from the evil or naive attitude of the ones defending the liberal order arises the belief that a decrease in Euro-Siberian spiritual, cultural, and even genetic potential would not lead to a weakening of all technical and political strengths. Nations across Euro-Siberia, unlike the homogeneity of for example African nations are characterized by so many unequal constituent elements that liberal bastardization can remove from those nations the ones who have the greatest capacity for acquiring true knowledge, true courage, and therefore authentic will. Liberalization of culture, forced multiculturalism, and birth control are the recommended medicines for the salvation of European nations according to all representatives of a vision which falsely claims to be European integration, while in practice it is the vision for European disintegration, not only among national lines but also among cultural, genetic and spiritual lines. In fact, even Russia is already in the middle of this situation, despite the liberal process is not so advanced as in other European countries.

The economy, which is the only true motivation behind the current European Union is ultimately linked to the existence of a healthy cultural space. What the European Union represents is the notion that a given nation only needs some peaceful economic activity to prosper, while in truth this is the surrendering of Euro-Siberian cultural and spiritual weapons to the enemy. That the representatives of the European Union, NATO, and Rome today present themselves as adversaries of all the natural virtues is not a coincidence but a conscious manifested will be aimed towards surrendering a civilization. In this way, the final conclusion can be put as follows: we are witnesses of the struggle between two very different forces in Europe: the ungodly manifested will of NATO and the European Union, vs the divine authentic will of Euro-Siberian natural forces, including, of course, those of Russia's best elements.

EUROPEAN PUBLIC OPINION

It is necessary to understand that European division, especially the division between Russia and the rest of Europe, is fomented when public opinion is used as the enemy's greatest weapon. Therefore, from little disputes and incidents that arise from real conditions as the situation in Crimea, or from fabricated events as the Skripal incident or Douma's gas attack in Syria, NATO and the European Union set up a propaganda machine aimed at the division between countries that, by the nature of their vital interests are to become more and more dependent on each other. Thinking an ambitious foreign policy whose aim is Euro-Siberia's unification is important also because if that goal is not achieved, the representatives of liberal interests and of powers outside Europe will always find it possible to manipulate public opinion, and when doing so, they provoke small or fabricated incidents to become artificial justifications stirring the division between Europe and Russia and among all other European countries.

How public opinion becomes a weapon can be observed in the speed with which is set over small matters when remaining silent before the most serious events as Julian Assange's indictment and incarceration, or former French president Sarkozy being charged for corruption after alleged Libyan financial help in his presidential campaign. It is clear those behind the manipulation of public opinion do not waste any opportunity to increase and sustain their propaganda offensive against Russia, while simultaneously using this propaganda war to cover those events which are of real relevance. NATO's propaganda machine of the Cold War era far from being dismantled is still very much in place and serves as an extraordinary example of mass control. A disruption dating as back as the start of the Truman Doctrine and the Cold War is kept alive in the form of an artificial disruption over European vital relationships, and when the division between east and west is fomented again and again then it reaches dangerous proportions and it will do so until Europe and Russia completely overcome their artificial separations, which only can happen if Russia becomes aware of its ultimate objective in Europe.

Even the relations among longtime allies as the relationship between Russia and Belarus aren't completely rid of friction, as the events this year (2020) demonstrated when 33 people were detained in Belarus and accused of being Russian mercenaries with the task of meddling in Belarus elections. And then, public opinion is again manipulated to perpetuate the idea that real European unity is impossible and a chaotic disruption in vital political, economic, and cultural ties must be accepted as an inescapable destiny. The attitude of European representatives and the massive propaganda aimed at disruption serve as an indoctrination mechanism, because with them public opinion will never learn to pay attention to those details underlying every political event, and neither will they learn to ignore minor quarrels if necessary and realize the vital importance of Euro-Siberian unity in this time of World distress. Individual European states will never alone possess the force to do away with the political attitudes and propaganda aimed at confrontation with Russia and between themselves, and the reason for this partially lies in the indoctrination process being conducted since the start of the Cold War, whose aim is not only Russia's isolation but the European weakness and dependence arising of that same Russian isolation.

Public opinion is so susceptible to manipulation because European political representatives in both NATO and Russian sides, together with the ones under their leadership do not display any worthy objective in their execution of foreign policy. On the part of European countries which are part of NATO, they correctly believe that Russia still lacks the sufficient strength to protect European interests, but they are unable to realize that elites in charge of the United States are in a process of dismantling that country together with their foreign influence, and even now in 2020 the United States (in a deep economic and social crisis) retires thousands of its troops from Germany in a move echoing the USSR's social, economic and military disintegration when the Warsaw Pact ceased existing.

While those in charge of manipulating public opinion by constantly quoting human rights only talk about threatened small nations in Europe and the rest of the World, they really only take into account the interests of superpowers. They do not have any real interest in preserving the livelihood of nations and minorities as long as that does not serves as an excuse for favoring the countries ruling the World. As most of Europe is just a protectorate for foreign superpowers, not only countries as Russia are targeted as a whole but also individual persons and institutions, which is naturally essential for manipulating public opinion to such an extent that the totalitarian nature of liberalism becomes fully evident. A fundamental change in this current situation will only happen when Russia finally achieves a greater inner strength which will be reflected on a more ambitious Euro-Siberian foreign policy, and only when the conditions for that are suited the most in the short window of time between the total collapse of Atlantic thalassocracy and the complete transition to a global Chinese thalassocracy. Only when fundamental power relationships in the World are changed, it is possible to expect that current European states will be forced to abandon their Cold War hostility towards Russia, and vice-versa, once Atlantic thalassocracy implodes then Russia will realize how much important Euro-Siberian unification is as a weapon against a thalassocratic China.

It is necessary today more than ever that the average person in the European states and the Russian Federation change their opinion from an obsolete Cold War mentality to a common Euro-Siberian foreign policy that meets real internal needs since those internal needs are synonymous with achieving unconditional stability of a civilization fighting its last decisive battle. Only the Fallen race can have a keen interest in a European foreign policy which, because of its irrational nature, lacks any clear goal for giving Europe at least some kind of future. Public opinion when manipulated makes the execution of a coherent European foreign policy seem as a utopia or also as a dystopia, and to do the aforementioned, elites in charge not only are able to manipulate the perception of present events or future ones, because they are clearly manipulating history. When people are taught another nation's history in a distorted way or their own national history in a deceiving manner, then all we can expect is a false notion regarding the past becoming a false notion regarding the present and an even falser notion regarding the future. When monuments to Soviet soldiers are destroyed all along Eastern Europe, and common persons start thinking Nazi Germany was defeated not because they suffered 80% of their casualties against the Soviet Union but because of the D-Day landings, then those people will believe all of Europe and Russia are intrinsically evil and weak, thus in need of protection by a superpower beyond their frontiers.

In that way, all of the past, present, and future are subjected to a machine of lies whose objective is leading all individual European nations on the path of chaotic and aimless confusion, because every individual State has its own individual history, reflected in its own individual past, its present, and its own future, and that multiplicity of historical paths becomes one of the main weapons for Euro-Siberia's enemies, which put national memories against each other. In sharp contrast with China now and the United States, when it was in its golden age, all of the European memory, instead of being perceived as just shared history from a common source is more and more separated in order to create cultural schizophrenia. That cultural schizophrenia is induced in absolutely every field possible, because cultural division based on national separation needs also ideological division, spiritual division, economic stratification, linguistic chauvinism, religious schisms, worthless human art, etc. Public opinion reflects that the European bourgeoisie and Russia's inner bourgeois and Marxist circles had learned nothing from the past because all of European history teaches us that divisions inside Europe, including the division between Russia and the rest of Europe, only result in disgrace and foreign powers taking advantage of it. From outside powers and their puppet organizations, we can't expect any other intentions but those aimed at destroying Europe and Russia, because those outside powers know very well that only Euro-Siberia possess the strength capable of destroying the liberal World order of the Fallen race.

The Soviet Union, especially after Khrushchev's "Peaceful coexistence" policy no longer was capable of positively influencing public opinion in other parts of the World. Stalin, despite his brutality, was widely respected outside the Soviet Union after his policy of "socialism in a single country" was forcefully abandoned due to the Great Patriotic War, and both the victories over Nazi Germany and the creation of communist satellites in Europe and Asia sparked fear and admiration across the World. In sharp contrast, the weak "Peaceful coexistence" rhetoric from Khrushchev and his successors created the image of a selfish and weak state unable to expand its ideology and influence, because of a vision centered in the Soviet Union alone.

When a State is seen as a renegade because of its inward vision of things, ignoring the rest of the World and wanting merely to restore old borders and zones of influence, that is, of maintaining a given situation, that same State loses any admiration it can have from public opinion in other countries, as a renegade State is always considered to be devoid of any type of useful ideological content and stable character. The Soviet Union was able to positively influence public opinion across other countries as long as its ideology and influence were expanding under Stalin's last years, but after any ambitious foreign policy objective came to an end with Stalin's death, then all public opinion in both capitalist states and communist countries as China, Cuba, and Albania only saw in the Soviet Union a weak and selfish country. Meanwhile, the peoples of the Soviet Union were brainwashed into believing that the rest of the World held a good image of them when in reality the Soviet Union was regarded more and more as an "antisocial empire."

Since its foundation in 1949, NATO has always represented the same foreign policy objectives, regardless of who was entrusted with political power in Washington, London, Paris, and Brussels. During long periods of its millennial existence, China exhibited long-lasting and clear foreign policy goals aimed towards protecting Chinese interests. This stability in foreign policy gives a sense of security in the public opinion of both allies and enemy countries, while an ever-changing foreign policy is perceived as the first symptom of intrinsic weakness, selfishness, and madness. After a long-lasting and common foreign policy is established within Russia and the whole series of European nations, Euro-Siberia will have the possibility of regulating its internal relations permanently, and then its relationship with other civilizations. Self-interests can be achieved along a common Euro-Siberian path and not in the stupid selfish and inward vision of an isolated Russia or that of small "nationalistic" European countries. Gradually, the rest of mankind will also acquire a general understanding of a civilization's stable, definite, and confident foreign policy.

At the moment when the objectives of foreign policy no longer suppose a fight for the interests of a given civilization, but rather the preservation of a small or encircled zone of influence, then countries and civilizations start to lose their ability to survive, in part because public opinion inside and outside them perceives the weakness of a dying organism, which takes limited and incomprehensible decisions.

PART II:
EURO-SIBERIAN VS EURASIAN ORIENTATION

THE CHINESE JUGGERNAUT

PROBLEMS WITH THE EURASIAN ORIENTATION

A Eurasian orientation can be understood as an ideology centered on the belief that Russia does not belong either to the European or the Asian categories, while Eurasia as a geopolitical concept also forms the basis of a specific orientation in foreign policy in which the Eurasian continent as a whole remains the main axis. This Eurasian orientation is only partly correct. It is correct in the sense that such a Eurasian paradigm serves as a basis for foreign policy in the current times in which Atlantic thalassocracy is still not totally replaced by the future Chinese thalassocracy. It is incorrect in formulating that Russia does not belong to the European category while in fact, ironically, Russia is one of the last remaining strongholds of genuine European identity, while the current Western Civilization instead of truly belonging to that original European heritage, is just the expression of its gradual death and replacement by an artificial construct. Moreover, when a future Chinese gigantic thalassocracy is finally consolidated, then the Eurasian paradigm will crumble completely not just in its cultural aspect but also as a guiding paradigm in foreign policy because China will serve as a clear demonstration of how a thalassocracy can emerge from Asia just as easily as it emerged in the West.

The notion of Eurasia as a civilization is a mere artificial construction, as those behind it did not recognize the natural basis for creating a shared European identity because they perceived Roman-Catholicism and the three ideologies of modernity (Liberalism, Marxism, and Nationalism) as part of a new yet genuine European identity while in reality they only represent Europe's destruction. While the concept of Western Civilization forces an artificial separation within the same Euro-Siberian identity, the Eurasian concept supposes an artificial union with alien Asiatic civilizations with different historical, cultural, and spiritual paths. Recognizing this cultural and spiritual reality is essential because as soon as we understand how much the preservation of a common Euro-Siberian identity is needed, then this knowledge will impart its authentic will in the form of workable foreign and domestic policies.

Now, Eurasianists are those who swim with the current of a river while North American power blows as a fierce wind, but when the direction of the wind changes from North America's west to the Chinese east then Eurasianists, almost in a sudden, will see themselves trapped against the new direction going contrary to them. It is absolutely true that we must withstand the flow of public opinion in favor of North American interests with NATO and the current European Union as their puppets, but we, those who advocate a Fourth Political Theory, should never forget that stupid Cold War passions cannot become an obstacle in the way of materializing our inherent convictions. We should not consider that Euro-Siberian doctrine is Utopia because renouncing old alliances will be impossible for the West and for the East alike, even when renouncing those alliances will suppose the future freedom against the liberal enemy.

Today, all European countries which form part of NATO are the artificial enemies of Russia but at the same time its natural allies because of geographical and cultural reasons. The future objective of our foreign policy should not be to favor the east or the west, but rather a policy of Euro-Siberian strength against all potential ideological and cultural enemies. Future enemies, even if they are partners now become great rivals because a changing geopolitical landscape creates neither permanent enemies nor permanent partners, just permanent goals. A fact should not be overlooked: if Russia's political, cultural, and military unification with Europe is carried out, then for the first time Russia will have allies that are not leeches sucking on Russian technological skills as happened with the Warsaw Pact and as it is happening with China now. For the first time, Russia's alliance would create a technical accumulation that will greatly serve both Russian and European economies with the accumulation of technical skills and economic power.

China's dependence on Russian technological skills will not last forever. Today is a major factor of Chinese national security to have both their economy and their military to receive Russian knowledge and skills, but as China's potential is growing, those same Russian skills are creating the basis for China's technological independence in the near future. Even most importantly: just as China's technological skills are growing at an unprecedented level, so China is growing the size and power of its navy, confirming the suspicion that China's ultimate goal is to create the most powerful thalassocratic World order to have ever existed. Already as of 2020, western sources are reporting that China will have the World's largest navy by 2035, if not earlier (McDevitt 2020).

In addition, China Standards 2035 is an ambitious 15-year blueprint that Beijing possesses as its forthcoming objective. It will layout China's plans to set the global standards for the next-generation of technologies by the year 2035. Andrew Polk, a partner at Beijing-based research and consultancy firm Trivium China, told CNBC: "(China Standards 2035) is a combination of domestic exigencies and the need to improve their own economic performance and efficiency and their desire to set the standards, literally and figuratively, abroad." (Kharpal 2020). Therefore, China is expected to have the World's largest navy by 2035 and also set the global standards for new technologies by 2035. How convenient, right? Even more convenient is that all of this is scheduled to happen at least one year before the United States' scheduled dissolution.

The economic, military, and spiritual consequences of an alliance among Euro-Siberian nations, even a forced one, would be the opposite of an alliance between Russia and China. We must be sure that the strength of the Euro-Siberian space is maintained by those spiritual and material forces present in that space and not in any foreign superpower. Every attempt to divide Europe must be considered as an attack on Russia, and also, every attempt by a foreign superpower to put Europe against Russia must be considered by Europe as an attack over European interests. Such a foreign superpower, regardless of its nature, whether if it is the US now or China in the future will operate in such a way that its thalassocratic interests put divided Europe as a second-rank military power, serving as a giant military base close to Russian borders. With this, Russia will be subjugated sooner or later, and therefore Euro-Siberia's capacity to constitute itself as a single tellurocratic superpower will be gone forever. We must not allow this to continue happening in Europe! Russia's authentic will on its foreign policy will always contain that basic idea. And when Russia is able to push that idea over all the individual European nations, then, finally they will adopt this authentic will forming a geopolitical relevance comparable or superior to the one that China will have, and even to the one enjoyed by the United States during its golden years.

From the disaster caused by Cold War stupidity suffered in both western and eastern portions of a subjugated Europe, this continent, joining hands with a rejuvenated Russia, will need to change the direction of its foreign policy and save what it remains of its original civilization and heritage. In short, the catastrophe of the Cold War can be an infinite blessing for the future if experience teaches all European nations and all of Russia that no foreign superpower can be their savior. In the same way that the United States is no savior of Euro-Siberian interests, China at the long run will be no savior of any of Russia's interests because the Communist Party of China, characterized by a pragmatic vision serves only its own interests and they perceive all current alliances as a temporary solution. In pursuing the enormous tasks which God's civilization requires, all followers of the Fourth Political Theory must free themselves from current illusions and be guided by no other thing that desire for preserving the only civilization capable of bringing God's new era.

A giant Chinese superpower is becoming stronger and stronger, and this is our last warning signal to end all Cold War nonsense. Since 1991, the time has passed mercilessly, and a new hour for the World has struck, announcing the beginning of the end for human civilization as we know it. Now, with the COVID-19 pandemic, we have definitive signs of a gradual plan for destroying the United States from outside and from within. As Dugin likes to say: Nazi Germany and fascism ended with a violent death, killed while being still young, and in contrast, the USSR died as a senile, old organism. Now we must realize that the United States is in a path that only can lead that country into suicide. Its elite knows that a unipolar world, in order to survive, is as a patient in need of heart surgery once in a while. Just as the British Empire was removed as with an old, sickened heart, and replaced by the United States as the new center of the liberal thalassocratic order, then by the same logic the United States needs to be replaced by a younger, healthier center, capable of pumping massive quantities of blood required to keep a unipolar world alive and strong.

The conditions of global orders are similar to the conditions of living organisms with their vital necessities and structures. Today, of course, the conditions are changing and will be very different in the near future. To have a perspective of changing conditions knowledge of the past is of key importance. For example, we must analyze the conditions which lead to the Sino-Soviet split during the middle of the Cold War. In this historical moment, even when the United States and China were enemy states, China destroyed its ties with the Soviet Union not just due to some silly ideological and territorial disputes, but because China saw in the Soviet Union not a true ally but just a temporary partner, being necessary only as long as China's political unity and technological backwardness made impossible its survival without the Soviet Union.

After breaking its ties with the Soviet Union, China became closer to the United States, which replaced the role of the USSR in providing China with capital, knowledge, and technology from abroad. When the USSR ceased to exist, China developed a partnership with the new Russian Federation because the United States, as the sole superpower left in the World do not have to face any counterbalance in its quest for World domination, and Russian technological skills became for China a matter of national security again. But in the period when no partnership existed between China and the Soviet Union, all sorts of hateful attacks between those former Marxist-Leninist partners were carried out. The confrontation between China and the Soviet Union escalated to have its climax in the Sino-Soviet border war, when by 2 March 1969, border confrontations escalated into a conflict lasting until 11 September 1969. That conflict included fighting at the Ussuri River, the Zhenbao Island, and at Tielieketi (Lüthi 2008). The US decision of ending its involvement in the Vietnam War then became a pragmatic decision that allowed closer ties with China. After Richard Nixon's 1972 visit to China, then almost as an act of magic, the new alliance between China and the US changed the World's geopolitics forever.

In the context of this new alliance, China insolently dared to launch an invasion of Vietnam in 1979. The Socialist Republic of Vietnam (a close ally of the Soviet Union) invaded Pol Pot's Cambodia in 1978, and because Cambodia was a Chinese puppet State this was the pretext that China used to launch its offensive against Vietnam, which ended in a Chinese defeat despite their overwhelming forces. Noteworthy is that the US did not move a finger to stop Pol Pot's atrocities, on the contrary; the US transformed Thailand in a base for the Khmer Rouge to wage a war of insurrection against both the Vietnamese and the government that had been installed by Vietnam in Cambodia (CovertAction Quarterly 1990). The fact that the US was able to support one of history's most brutal assassins, putting its public image in risk and all that just in order to support its Chinese ally shows the reader how unexpected geopolitical relationships can emerge quickly.

The end of the Second Indochina War in 1975 must be seen as the point from which China was able to move from a weak, isolationist international policy to a foreign policy of gradual geopolitical success. From that moment China was no longer tied to absurd ideological slogans and started an expansionist policy that displayed its anti-Soviet and therefore anti-Russian character. Just as when the Chinese partnership mask fell during the Sino-Soviet split, we must not expect any different thing in the future, when the current mask of Chinese partnership with the Russian Federation finally is removed and China's commercial and naval fleet, together with its economic strength are able to control the waves, while forcing entire states to become Chinese satellites.

Among the many criticisms which can be made against the foreign policy of the former Soviet Union, one of them stands above any other: the USSR ruined its relations with the rest of the World because of its weak and senseless effort to preserve world peace by a passive attitude, instead of showing, as in Stalin's later years, a constant display of World influence which kept enemies, partners and allies alike with constant respect and fear towards the Soviet superpower. Suddenly, China became aware of the inherent weakness and selfishness of the Soviet Union, and with this, the Chinese intelligentsia realized that the USSR was not the better partner to rely on, but rather an entity doomed to collapse. The Chinese intelligentsia was smart enough to perceive that the Soviet Union's path towards collapse could drag China to its own collapse as happened with all satellite states in Eastern Europe. To avoid that fate,

China developed its own path, which supposed and implicit partnership with the United States. In the US World Trade and capitalist economy, the Chinese perceived a guiding light which they could make brighter by the merit of China's own characteristics.

But returning back to the current Eurasianists: has the liberal become their guiding light also? Are traditionalists and anti-capitalists going into battle with a weapon offered by international capitalism? Or do many recent Eurasianists think that something vital to the continuation of the capitalist and liberal World order will be beneficial to Euro-Siberian nations? If today's anti-capitalist and traditionalists circles are excited about the idea of an alliance with China, it is because they are not completely aware of China's current role in the World, and even less of China's future in the World's geopolitics. They only see in the US government their enemy, and rightfully so, but they do not look at all other current and future elements being used by Liberalism and its Fallen race. It is obvious: we cannot defeat Lucifer by invoking Moloch.

The fight against the initiative of the Fallen race to complete liberal rule over the world requires that traditionalists and therefore anti-capitalist circles acquire a realistic position towards China. We cannot put all the blame on common persons or even intellectuals for their warm feelings towards China when all individual European states and all of Russia are themselves in a fight to the death against their own inner liberal tendencies. Because current situations are so terrible that the entire Euro-Siberian region is turning into a liberal sewer, then we cannot expect the vast majority of anti-capitalist circles to condemn China, as both Europe and Russia are not able to completely condemn liberalism as a crime against humanity. As nations are unable to see in liberalism an evil plan in itself, even less they can see in Chinese growing hegemony a threat that could end any Euro-Siberian capacity for opposing the liberal order of material and spiritual slavery. If we pursue the goal of destroying this liberal order, it will be disastrous to rely on a superpower ruled by the same enemy, doing everything he can to destroy the remains of European and Christian civilization, including Russia.

Today, Russia is the next great target of liberalism because the Fallen race knows that if Russia's spiritual purity and authentic will disappear, so they can continue destroying the World without any military and economic power in a position to confront demonic forces and throw them into the endless pit of Hell. Chinese hegemony represents the 21st-century attempt of the Fallen race to achieve complete World domination as it tried before with other states and institutions whose strength pales in comparison to China's potentiality. That potentiality will allow China to infiltrate countries and even entire civilizations, undermining its internal structures as the US did with its rivals. Ironically, that same weapon is now being used against the US because the elites in charge are aware that China is the only modern country in a position to truly dominate the World, while the US is just an obstacle to the capitalist and unipolar system.

Liberalism will not disappear after the US scheduled demise as a Superpower, and this is because the liberal first seeds which once grew in the US are now sewed on China and the only thing necessary is the eternal factor of human selfishness and cowardice. We must not forget that the Fallen race, which dominates China today does not see Russia as an ally, but as a temporary and dangerous partner who must be subjugated and destroyed before it induces a Euro-Siberian political and cultural unification. Today, the Chinese political and cultural apparatus is conscious of its own power and therefore it is in the position to impose sophisticated repression over the hundreds of millions inside China, and this is just as a mere practice before trying to impose that repression over the whole world. We should not forget that the rulers of the Chinese Communist Party always were in possession of both a brilliant skill of deception and brutal cruelty.

As happened with the Communist Party which existed in the Soviet Union, of course, not all of those composing the Chinese variant should be considered evil and malignant by nature. But when we talk about ruling Marxist parties, we are dealing also with those who are the scum of humanity, always using the conditions of tragic hours in their respective nations to invade great cultures, while killing, torturing, and stealing millions of persons, including talented intellectuals, artists and men of faith, all suffering the Marxist thirst for blood. And in the present, seven decades after the Chinese People's Republic was founded, the cruel and totalitarian nature of Mao's regime continues with its newest successors, although in a much softer and sophisticated way.

We must not forget that like Marxism, liberalism is also a totalitarian ideology suppressing different opinions and values, and the rulers of today's China discovered that the totalitarian nature of Marxism could be morphed into liberalism's own totalitarian aspect.

ALLIANCES ARE NOT JUST PARTNERSHIPS

In the first volume, I briefly mentioned the difference between allies and partners. The word "partners" should be used to refer to those countries that only establish ties for some specific purposes but do not defend the other's ideological position. When one is not defending the other's ideological position, then all the important ties are of a short-lived nature, because they cease to exist as long as the conditions which made a partnership necessary aren't anymore. When two or more countries, if besides don't have clashes in their non-ideological interests also defend their mutual ideological position, then we can expect a much more enduring and friendly relationship. As history's greatest example of the difference between partners and allies, the case of the Soviet Union and the Western powers during World War II provides a classroom example. While the United States and Great Britain formed a close tie that implied ideological proximity, the friendly relationship with the Soviet Union vanished shortly after the war with Germany and Japan ended. Thus, the Western powers and the Soviet Union were not allies but just temporary partners in a temporary situation, and this became evident once the Cold War began.

When "nation A" which due to its ideological proximity to "nation B" is aware that war upon "nation B" is also a war on the ideology of "nation A", then a true alliance is born because any potential ideological threat becomes a matter of national security. Due to their ideological nature, all alliances, without exemption, are made to eventually start a war, whether a direct military conflict, proxy battles, or an economic and cultural war. We must never forget the objective of an alliance is war and no other thing, while the objective of partnerships is the very opposite since partnerships imply that nations, instead of war, are in need of some sort of peaceful coexistence. The current rulers of China are aware peaceful coexistence with Russia is needed in the present, but when the conditions which started that peaceful coexistence no longer are in place, then both sides will defend their respective ideological and therefore cultural positions, and this implies the immediate breaking of friendly economic and cultural relationships.

In addition, we should also realize it is naive to think that the elites in the US and NATO would have reacted passively by waiting decades if they saw in the Russian-Chinese partnership a true threat to globalist interests. As the elites running the US and NATO are much aware that China is necessary as the new heart of the globalist unipolar order, then western powers are giving China enough time to complete its technical preparations for economic and even military war. If this wasn't the case, and the western elites did saw in the Russian-Chinese partnership an existential threat to liberalism and globalism, a storm of missiles would have exploded over China at lightning speed. If the Russian-Chinese ties, instead of being a temporary partnership really supposed an alliance, and therefore a real ideological threat to globalist elites, then the actions by the West already in the time of the Third Taiwan Crisis (1995-1996) instead of supposing weak threats would have become a brutal military storm warning the rest of the World.

Although tensions between global powers are not always evident when a given alliance is formed, war is the fundamental motivation behind any alliance and the inevitable outcome. Close ties whose motivation is not ultimately to carry war but peace are therefore not alliances, but partnerships which if made in a foolish and futile way can have fatal strategic repercussions. Even if we imagine a fantastic scene in which mad US leaders launch a first nuclear strike against Russia just because they are angry, then the ensuing thermonuclear holocaust would take place on Russian and western territory in a matter of minutes, and Russia could not receive any effective support from China. From a purely military point of view, even in the present, a war against the US carried by an alliance between Russia and China would end in disaster, as it would force Russia and China to wage a thermonuclear war against the rest of the world. Nevertheless, this hypothetical situation of a direct military confrontation between Russia and the US is absurd as far as the rich want to become richer and not just corpses in some underground bunker.

What the Cold War between the United States and the Soviet Union has taught us is that the elites of global superpowers, although sometimes they are under great internal and external pressure always have the combination of some rationality and luck to avoid an ultimate thermonuclear Armageddon. Russia should have also learned the big difference between allies and partners. The Eastern European countries which sided with the Soviet Union, although they were just a small coalition of cripples, were forced to establish an alliance which on the basis of ideological guidelines and the sheer force of the Soviet power would have dragged all those states to a Third World War if it had occurred. In sharp contrast, Maoist China was just a temporary partner that saw the Soviet Union in the way a farmer sees rain to plant his crops. It is a problem for him if there is no rain, but after it is not needed then rain becomes a great problem also.

When we think about geopolitics, we must also realize the paradoxes of our deepest desires. Of course, we traditionalists and anti-capitalists have a deep desire for the total end of the current Atlanticist and liberal order, but our own strategy must not rely on those conceptions which we see wrongfully as the most easier ones, as is the case with the thought of a Russian-Chinese alliance. Reality will impose its harsh truth over those who thwarted the realization of genuinely great ideas, including, above all, the Euro-Siberian and Christian ideal. I do not doubt that many people currently believing in a Russian-Chinese alliance are very smart and skilled, but as soon as a small ray of hope can be seen, these persons immediately run after an elusive mirage that does not get them any close to their real objectives. Today's many circles of traditionalists and anti-capitalists (both inside and outside Russia) are putting all their hopes in the first drop of water they can see in the liberal desert, and in doing so, they are curtailed from doing the greatest task which Euro-Siberia and its Christianity need to survive this current desert of death and sorrow. To avoid being trapped in unproductive illusions and wishful thinking, we must realize the essential difference between a partnership and a true alliance, and in order to do so, we must show historical and current examples of those situations.

We can see in the Russian-Iran ties a classical type of partnership that can not develop into a true alliance. Iran's ideology, based on Shi'ite Islamic Universalism has nothing in common with Russia's current policy which moves along a path that seeks some secularism in Islamic regions as a deterrent for further radicalization. A radicalization in Sunni Islam could provoke a radicalization on the Shi'ite side and vice-versa, ending in a spiral of violence over entire regions, and that spiral of violence already forced Russia to intervene in the Syrian civil war to avoid the collapse of the Syrian government which is an important ally of Russia in the Mediterranean. But despite all that, Russia and Iran established a partnership because they faced the same enemy in the form of radical Sunni Islam aided by western powers and of course, Israel. Just as with the Chinese-Soviet relationships, the relationships which the Soviet Union had with Iran were tense as both states were contiguous ideological rivals. The Soviet Union even supplied Saddam Hussein with weapons during his genocidal war against Iran, and in the meanwhile, Supreme Leader Ayatollah Khomeini concluded that as Islam was incompatible with Soviet ideas, then all the support of the Soviet Union towards secular Saddam had an ideological basis.

Now Iran surely arrived at a similar conclusion, that Russia's involvement in the Syrian Civil War also has as its basis the promotion of Al-Assad's secularism in opposition to radical Islam, and therefore Russia and Iran, despite being forced to establish its current partnership, are very aware that ideological incompatibility is still alive in the shadows. Russia, with all certainty, will not go to war to save Iran, neither Iran will go to war in order to help Russia. But with China, the situation is entirely different. China will not hesitate to go to war if the existence of the current Islamic Republic of Iran is under serious threat from foreign military aggression. As of 2019, Iran has signed onto Xi Jinping's One Belt One Road plan, and the country is considered to be a key part of China's geopolitical expansion in Central Asia and the Middle East (Vatanka 2019). Therefore, what we see between Iran and China goes beyond a partnership; it is an alliance as far as Iran is too important in China's "Big Game" in Asia, and the consequences of massive military aggression over Iran will imply a Chinese military response.

While Russia's partnership with Iran, as with all partnerships is aimed towards peace, the Iran-China alliance is aimed towards war in the economical, cultural and military senses. One can reject my conclusion that Iran and China are true allies on the basis that their ideologies are not the same and their goals will collide sooner or later. But Iran and China have the most important ideological similarity possible: both are millennial civilizations with a proud nationalistic mindset. A millennial past forms the basis of a strongly nationalistic ideology in itself, regardless if that nationalism is mixed with elements of Islamic Universalism as in Iran, or with elements of liberalism (under the guise of Marxism) as it is happening in China. In the case of China, they will try to become the World's only thalassocratic superpower, and as for Iran, they will rely on Chinese support against Zionist fanatics in Israel and radicals from Sunni Islam which are supported by outside parties.

Because it is a theocratic Shi'ite State, Iran also serves as "cordon sanitaire" between China and Sunni Islam, since Iran, as a key component of Chinese geopolitical expansion in Asia is placing an unbreakable barrier that deters further expansion in the influence of Sunni Islam into World affairs, while China now already faces distress due to its own Muslim minority of Uyghur and Hui people, most of them being Sunnis. I mentioned this particular example of a true alliance (the Chinese-Iran alliance) because Russia is the state which needs to remember, more than any other state how bitter can be the consequences of a bad foreign policy when the difference between allies and partners is not clear. While during the Cold War the largest military and economic powers of the capitalist World formed the most powerful coalition in history, all that the Soviet Union could do was putting together some old and weak eastern European allies, attempting to confront NATO with this garbage that from the very beginning was doomed to collapse. The partnership established with China, incorrectly understood as an alliance, did not become a true alliance in part because the Soviet Union ceased showing its might, and relied instead on a "peaceful coexistence" policy which was the first sign of the Soviet Union's weakness and selfishness towards partners which otherwise could have become real allies.

With the Warsaw Pact, the Soviet Union achieved nothing more than a defensive society of small eastern European states, which long ago withdrew from relevant positions in the continental stage. However, what would have been useful to the Soviet Union then would be catastrophic to Russia today, since China during Mao's time is not the China of the present, even less the China of the future. The Asiatic colossus will not become the puppet of anyone, on the contrary; it started to become the puppet master.

INNER CHINESE CONDITIONS

Within the current inner situation with China faces, the end of the liberal element in Chinese ideology, which would imply the end of the domination of the Fallen race in China, would also be the end of the People's Republic of China. The current Chinese ideology, which is a mix of liberalism with nationalism, with the liberal component disguised as Marxism because the two ideologies are totalitarian, created a strong basis for domination inside and outside China. That ideological basis will prove itself even more useful to the Chinese than it is today, as the liberal ideology is characterized by its predatory nature over other peoples and the World's resources, and such a thing needs the nationalistic component because otherwise, the strong national State will collapse as no longer it would remain capable of exercising power over other states and over itself. Only with a strong national State, the plundering of natural and economic resources all over the world can be carried out.

To make it impossible for the Chinese to break free from the yoke of tyranny by using their own strength, China's original upper strata and original religious, intellectual, and artistic groups were all systematically exterminated. As those with the highest spirituality were gradually eliminated during landmark events in Chinese history as the Taiping rebellion (1850-1864), the Chinese civil war, the Japanese invasion, and the communist revolution, thereby the Righteous spiritual race was replaced by the Fallen race entering its place in China's ruling political and cultural apparatus. For millennia China has fed on its upper stratum composed of the World's finest intellectuals, monks, statesmen, and all sorts of great minds which created the basis for the Chinese civilization. Many ancient civilizations as the ones already mentioned in this book were created due to an upper stratum of people whose spiritual and therefore intellectual skills were much above the average. All those civilizations continued to exist as long as their original creators were there, who were born anew when their cultural legacy and their bloodlines were not facing Fallen race adulteration. After the demise of the original creators of a given civilization, that same civilization continues existing for some time because the inferior successors fed on the cultural and technical structures created by those before them until all finally collapses.

The Chinese civilization did not emerge from the political abilities of the Marxist and liberal rulers which took over in China, but instead, that civilization is an extraordinary example of the tremendous skills which superior strata can exercise within inferior elements. By surrendering its upper political and cultural stratum, China was deprived of that group capable not just of creating and maintaining their State during a century or two, but capable of creating a civilization and guaranteeing its existence for thousands and thousands of years. The fact that some peoples created a very successful and powerful civilization does not imply they will preserve it forever. Civilizations are made by men, strengthened by men, and also weakened by men himself, who is able to destroy and create just as God destroys and creates men. The ancient Chinese upper stratum was able to become a cultural fertilizer whose contributions benefited not only China but all of mankind, even in the everyday life of foreign nations in which most people ignore where such contributions originated.

Even with China's excessive bleeding during centuries of conflict, they were able again and again to reunite into a single state encompassing all of China's civilization and newly annexed territories, and this can only be explained by the great skill of Chinese statesmanship since ancient times, and the discipline established by the armies of the Chinese emperors reflected in today's Chinese army. The ancient skill of Chinese statesmanship and the discipline of China's military is what made possible an entire civilization is completely unified in the political and cultural sense, instead of being just a collection of separate Asiatic states with their own majoritarian ethnic groups or religions. China is today a strong unitary State not weakened by the need to establish a confederation or a federalist structure. The fact that now a giant unitary state is constructed in such a way that encompasses hundreds and hundreds of millions of inhabitants including the former territory for countless ethnic groups speak not of Marxist or liberal skill, but of the maturity of a very ancient civilization as represented by the best elements it once had.

Successive Chinese states, and their ancient ideas on how an effective State should be conducted removed the belief that China should be dismembered in small states according to unimportant ethnic and cultural guidelines, and when doing this, in contrast to Europe the political bodies governing Chinese civilization demanded the formation of a single State whose administration was conducted in a professional and serious way as long as elites in charge had the strength to impart its power. In China, a special idea of the State was carefully cultivated, that idea that sees in a single State the power for keeping a civilization united according to a spirit of self-preservation, a spirit which any civilization must possess to survive thousands of years. Another great success of ancient Chinese civilization was its ideas on how culture should be conducted, and that's how Confucianism and other schools of thought were developed because the maturity of China's civilization reached a degree in which its self-preservation instinct not only demanded an efficient and single State but also spiritual unity through philosophies providing harmony and coexistence.

The third success of Chinese civilization, also emerging from its ancient ideas is to understand that a civilization (which always has some inner differences between different ethnic groups) must be kept together by a ruling ethnicity. Therefore the successive Chinese states embarked on a policy of cultural and biological assimilation of the different ethnic groups into the Han majority, as cultural unity was correctly understood as a prerequisite for achieving political unity in an entire civilization, and both political unity and cultural unity only can be driven by a ruling ethnicity as the Han are in China or as the Latins were in the Roman Empire. Even when the Manchu dynasty was ruling in China, they were forced to accept the fact that those truly in charge of directing the destiny of China were the Han, and this was reflected in the way the Manchu adopted customs of the Han and relied on Han officials (Zhang 2016).

Meanwhile, in the much younger and therefore immature European civilization, all sorts of silly acts were glorified, including fratricidal wars among European brothers, the destruction of ancient knowledge, and the death or torture of great thinkers, together with the fomenting of Europe's division among national, religious and political lines. With all the ancient wisdom and discipline of Chinese civilization, not only the current strength of the People's Republic of China wouldn't have been possible, in fact not even something as a single Chinese State would be in place today. When in the late 18th century, China's strength started to decline, this was only due to China's own success. By that time, its population has tripled in a relatively short time, and ruling circles were reluctant to observe developments in the rest of the World, as their centuries-long success convinced them that China would remain the greatest superpower of the World. It was so for hundreds and hundreds of years and thus there wasn't any reason to believe it would lose that condition when faced by foreign powers. Nevertheless, any defeat that China suffered due to XIX century western intervention pale in comparison to the effect of inner revolts and the subsequent extermination of China's leading cultural, spiritual, and political stratum. While the Chinese economy only decreased slightly during the period of the Opium Wars with the West, the effect of the Taiping and Dungan rebellions was much larger (Maddison 2007).

During the Taiping rebellion (1850-1864), also known as the Taiping revolution, between 20 and 30 million people lost their lives, with 30 million more being displaced (Bickers and Jackson 2016). According to Stephen R. Platt in his book "Autumn in the Heavenly Kingdom", the real death toll could be as high as 70 million. The fact that during the mid-nineteen century China experienced a war that cost it even more lives than those losses suffered by the Soviet Union in the Great Patriotic War, together with the fact that this conflict is almost entirely forgotten now, are already mind-blowing. But what is even more incredible are the very cause and nature of this Taiping revolution: it was an attempt to Christianize China after Hong Xiuquan (the commander of that revolution) rebelled with his followers against the Qing dynasty and sought the formation of a Christian and theocratic government, thus forming an oppositional State known as "The Taiping Heavenly Kingdom".

This event, despite being one of the most crucial moments in mankind's history (and whose eventual repercussions are as large as those of both World Wars) should be thought in all history classes around the world but unfortunately, it is not. After a brutal war of extermination carried by the Qing dynasty, the Taiping revolution was crushed and China ended destroyed both in the material and spiritual aspects, as human and economic losses were unparalleled, and Christianity was thrown out from China. Thus, the crushing of the Taiping rebellion was the first and most important action of the Chinese Fallen race to exterminate the most valuable human and cultural elements possessed by China's Righteous spiritual race. The Taiping Revolution, sparking the second most bloody war in human history, and being far more destructive than the First World War, had as its outcome the destruction of Christian China, and serves as the perfect example of how a total war between spiritual races can destroy a given civilization from within, creating an inner weakness which foreign powers will always use in their favor. And in the case of China, the defeat of the Qing dynasty by the Japanese during the First Sino-Japanese War (1894-1895) made evident that China no longer was a World Power, and that condition of weakness explains the cataclysms it suffered in the following decades.

In 1912, the Qing dynasty was overthrown, and a Republic was established, which ended four thousand years of monarchic governments. Then it appeared that China was finally on the path of national sovereignty and modernization, but the new republican government proved weak and unable to put China back as a World Power. Between 1927 and 1937, the first phase of the Chinese Civil War started when communist insurgents struggled against the Republic of China. Both sides were forced to make a temporary truce when a massive Japanese invasion started in 1937, marking the beginning of the Second Sino-Japanese war, a conflict that claimed 20 million Chinese lives between 1937 and 1945. All of this killing and destruction created further extermination of China's best racial and cultural heritage. The Japanese, Communists, and the Nationalists all were naturally compelled to target political, intellectual, and cultural leaders when carrying their mass murders. To complete the annihilation of the upper elements of China's Righteous spiritual race the Communist Revolution was necessary, which proclaimed the People's Republic of China on October 1st, 1949 after the Chinese Civil War entered its final phase. There is no doubt that after communist ruler Mao Zedong seized power, his policies and executions directly or indirectly caused the deaths of tens of millions of people (Chang and Halliday 2005).

Mao's mass killings were all carried out under an absurd totalitarian doctrine which saw in terror and elimination of all independent thinking not only a means to an end but also an end in itself. When the ancient Chinese upper elements were finally liquidated, their cultural legacy, as it happens with all civilizations, was able to remain without its original creators. As already mentioned in this book, all current achievements of the People's Republic of China and its Communist Party would have not been possible without that ancient cultural legacy. But I must emphasize again that any cultural legacy cannot last long when its original creators aren't there. The Chinese Fallen Race will try all they can to keep a mummified Chinese civilization with the appearance of something alive, but for almost two thousand years China already was defending its unity and national interests not only to serve the interests of a political party based on foreign ideologies as it happens now but to ensure China's civilization endured the test of time.

To western observers, a century seems like a lot of time, but in the Chinese perspective it is really little, and they are right, it is. But as liberalism, which by its totalitarian nature can be disguised as Marxism is already shaping China's living, the current People's Republic of China will only be able to defend their future if they are the center of a globalist system that the US inherited to them. The destiny of the globalist system will be determined by China's ability to become the future master of the seas while creating the newest technologies, all of which will bring the resources of other parts of the World while China consumes and exports a flood of goods and services. Nevertheless, even all of this will not last forever, as liberalism and its Fallen race rather than strengthening civilizations only can bring their gradual demise.

In the historical sense, Chinese history is so vast and deep that no historian can encompass it completely, but one thing is certain: what happened in China during the 19th and 20th centuries supposed the death of the original upper elements of an entire civilization, and not just any civilization, but one lasting four thousand years and influencing the entire planet. The gargantuan consequences of this immense disaster are just as immeasurable as China's own history is. The total death toll of the Taiping Revolution, the Chinese Civil War, the Japanese invasion, and the Communist Revolution when put together is one hundred million human lives vanished over the course of a century. This is four times more than the Great Patriotic War cost to the Soviet Union, and all of this bloodshed was concentrated over China's best elements. In addition, we must consider that in the mid 19th century and in 1949 China had 400 million and 549 million inhabitants respectively, in sharp contrast to today's 1400 million.

When putting all these numbers into context then we come to the scary conclusion that even the World's most populous and enduring civilization couldn't avoid the liquidation of its leading Righteous elements, who were physically and culturally removed amid inhuman atrocity.

THE BATTLE OF CIVILIZATIONS

FUTURE DISTRIBUTIONS OF POWER

The objective of the Chinese Fallen Race has been achieved only in part, as the total success of this spiritual race depends on the suppression of the leading Righteous elements not only in China but all around the World. The additional objective of the current Chinese elite as carried both in their conscious mind and in their Nous, is to join hands with the rest of the Fallen Race in other countries and become their massive center. In this way, they plan to overthrow the remaining elements of God's race which yet are not subjected by Liberalism and its most important ally: Rome. There is what I call a "Chinese spell" which prevents the thinking of Russian foreign policy from arriving at the final point in which it must remain: Euro-Siberia's unity and the geopolitical relevance of its original civilization.

For the future, a Russian alliance with China makes no sense to Russia because the whole mentality of China's current and future ruling circles is one opposed to the mentality of any eventual tellurocratic rival. While some circles in Russia think that Russia's political and intellectual circles are exerting their influence in China, the reality is the exact opposite: it is China that is exerting its intellectual and organizational influence while Russia is kept in a fatal Cold War slumber. A false notion has been installed, that of a future multipolar world in which the United States, China, India, Europe, and Russia can all live peacefully together as in a fairy tale. But in reality, any multipolar world of such characteristics will be just only a very temporary phase which all the nations of the world will try to destroy as this enormous complex of rival States is unworkable as a lasting World Order. It is unworkable because first of all the World's most powerful countries will try to strengthen their own positions, as the result of not doing so implies their eventual collapse. In a capitalist system, which cannot just vanish automatically in an act of magic, such a multipolar world cannot last because it would inevitably lead to total economic conflict and to military conflagrations also. The reasons for this were already explained in this book while describing the nature of the liberal economic, cultural and spiritual system, all of that being incompatible with sustainable development as their nature is predatory and suicidal.

The other reason why a multipolar order composed of several states cannot last long is that the liberal elites had some degree of rational thinking, which is selfish rationality but rationality after all. If they didn't possess such a thing, they wouldn't have conquered the World, even less they would maintain the liberal order for as much as they did. In the selfish rationality of liberal elites, their economic and social order must survive at all costs, and any global power standing in the way towards a unipolar world (which a healthy capitalist system requires) must be destroyed in some way or another, with traditional weapons or conspiracy. As already mentioned in the first chapter of this Volume, the weapon they choose this time is a conspiracy to dismantle the United States just as easily as the Soviet Union was dismantled, because the unipolar World does not have an eternal center but rather that World system tries to become an everlasting center in itself, and in order to survive, it will move its temporary headquarters from power to power, from continent to continent. The British Empire in the past, the United States in the present, and China in the future all are part of a historical trend of capitalist accumulation and the eternal struggle between the powers of land and the powers of the sea.

This eternal struggle only can lead to two outcomes: either the multipolar world vanishes when a sole thalassocratic superpower triumphs becoming the ruler of the World or a new bipolar world is established when a powerful tellurocratic superpower is able to compete with a powerful thalassocratic rival. The bipolar condition of the World during the Cold War between the United States and the Soviet Union arose as a consequence of the irreconcilable difference between the United States being a power of the seas and the Soviet Union being a power of the land, and as already Aleksander Dugin pointed out in his works, a power based on land and a rival power based on the seas will both always build essentially different and antagonistic civilizations. The history of Rome vs Cartage is perhaps history's most iconic example.

Therefore, if Euro-Siberia is able to rise as a single tellurocratic superpower, it will be in constant competition with a thalassocratic China taking the role of the United States while the Euro-Siberian region is taking the role of the former Soviet Union. But it will be silly to think that future China will not have ideological and cultural differences in relation to the United States in the 20th century, but just as silly would be to think a united Euro-Siberia will not have major ideological and cultural differences with the former Soviet Union. A new bipolar World will be different from the old one, but one thing will be the same: two very different types of civilization will compete to survive. If the tellurocratic superpower loses that would imply the victory of Satan and his race, and if the thalassocratic power is the one who loses, then both the tellurocratic and thalassocratic orders will merge to create not just some unipolar World again, but a World beyond the World, that of mankind in the stars, exploring the unknown, reaching that which remains unexplored, and finally reaching God almighty in the lost paradise, the Garden of God.

In the next years, the whole World will be not aimed towards a multipolar order with stabilizing relations between States and Civilizations, but rather to a period of fast changes towards one of the possible outcomes mentioned here... Since China no longer has its original higher stratum, the current Chinese State can become the last resting place for liberalism, and that State will do everything it can to keep Euro-Siberia divided and in chains. If the individual European states, including Russia, do not change their current attitude what will remain will be a collection of states as insignificant in their political influence as in their contribution to human culture. China is consciously and unconsciously deeply rooted in its anti-christian and anti-European attitude, and the aforementioned includes an implicit anti-Russian attitude which was explicit during the Sino-Soviet split and sooner or later will be explicit again.

But our analysis must be one which is not standing in the incomplete notion of just a "Russia vs China", but rather realizes the complete notion is "Euro-Siberia vs China" because we must not think just of a struggle between two States, but a struggle between two civilizations, with Russia's destiny being also Europe's destiny and vice-versa. Both individual European states and China had summoned the dark spirits of liberalism, and they can't get rid of those spirits without the struggle of a tellurocratic Christian civilization against the idea of liberal thalassocratic rule by the Fallen race. The struggle of this tellurocratic civilization is in vital need of a Russia able to lead Euro-Siberian unification instead of being a culturally and politically isolated State waiting for the liberal hammer to finally crush its head.

But as important is to awake the consciousnesses of the other European states in the direction of their common survival, a survival which requires the destruction of the artificial western civilization, which exercises its influence through equally unnatural associations: NATO, the European Union, and the Vatican. All three are already the tools for thalassocratic and liberal rule over the World, and in the future, China will take the role of the United States as the keeper of those three demonic associations. They are like the dogs of prey waiting to get unleashed by their master and its gun. When the old master dies, it is only replaced by the new one. China's Communist Party received the Fallen race as its ruler and all of this required gradual extermination of China's ancient upper layer over the course of a century. Now the Communist Party of China must demonstrate its own ability to keep a civilization that was not created by it, despite receiving a bed already warmed by three immense giants: ancient Chinese civilization, the British Empire, and the United States.

While the ancient Chinese civilization created the cultural heritage from which the current Chinese state feeds upon, the British Empire created the first modern structures for liberalism and the unipolar world. North America provided with vital knowledge, technology, and economic power to help China emerge again as a World power, and simultaneously, the United States maintained the structures from liberalism and unipolarity which Britain once ruled, and when doing so they extended these structures until they reached control of almost all of Europe and other continents as well. Having all the aforementioned in mind, then we can arrive at the conclusion that the current Communist Party of China is enjoying structures and historical conditions which were not created by it and must prove its ability as the new caretaker of those huge structures.

But the difference between the founders and original keepers of Chinese civilization with the current Fallen race occupiers lies precisely in the fact that while the upper elements of the Righteous spiritual race can create and preserve their achievements not just for a century or two but for millennia, the selfish and incompetent Fallen race just acts as a temporal caretaker who can feed upon what he got only for a while. It is not capable of permanently keeping its host civilization healthy, as civilization is a legacy of the Righteous and the Righteous alone. Without the upper layers of this spiritual race, the organizational forms vital for keeping and expanding civilization would be unable to survive against those inferior organizational forms coming when civilization is dying. The Fallen race government is unable to survive to the Fallen race itself, and for that same reason, the People's Republic of China will not be able to survive to itself.

When any civilization is being created, the impulse for that is the encounter between individuals and cultures of a higher and lower spiritual nature, through which those of the highest spiritual nature, delivering the best intellectual and social skills are in the position to act for the common self-preservation of not only themselves but also the civilization created by them. Among other things, this requires overcoming the onslaught of inferior souls. Take away all the great elements that were inherited from China's ancient past, and the People's Republic of China would immediately face its total destruction in an instant. But even this is an incomplete picture because if we take away the liberal and unipolar structures created by the Western powers outside of China, the rule of the Communist Party would also collapse under economic and social turmoil. Despite the aforementioned, in the time span in which the government of the People's Republic of China will still remain strong, it can become a fatal dagger to complete the defeat of Christian civilization and Righteous humanity.

NATO AND CHINA ARE PART OF THE SAME PLAN

Already during the early Cold War, the anti-Russian orientation of China's rulers was so strong that even the shared Marxist-Leninist delusion of both powers could no longer control their distancing even when the Soviet Union's weakness wasn't as evident as later on. Therefore, it should come as no surprise when China becomes a NATO ally once the United States disintegrates from the inside such as the Soviet Union already did.

Exactly as the Chinese rulers from the Communist party found in Washington's thalassocratic World order the inspiration for their own long-term goals, the easy, liberal, effeminate lifestyle of most European NATO countries is more capable of fascinating China because that reality is closer to the materialistic goals of elites and the average Chinese people, rather than the harsher Russian mentality and lifestyle. And indeed, to an increasing degree, the Chinese bourgeois fascination with the artificial Western Civilization as embodied by London, Paris, etc instead of the genuine European civilization still represented by Russia is the sign of China's own liberal affliction. That liberal affliction represents the gradual demise of China's natural spiritual and cultural life inherited from ancient times, the same liberal affliction which caused the demise of much of Europe's own genuine spiritual and cultural life. And in the meanwhile, China's own liberalization will attract the liberal European more and more. In that way, China will be increasingly attracted to NATO and NATO to China.

As the liberalization of both China and European countries under NATO progresses, their cultural and spiritual dislike for Russia and traditionalism will increase and Euro-Siberia will perish under the waves of a new globalist alliance. Liberal and traditionalist mentalities have very little in common, even less when the traditionalist mentality is conscious of its existential war against the dark forces of mankind's lower elements.

China's communist revolution was not just a war against what remained of the old upper layer in China but in essence an inner war between two very different mentalities: a traditionalist and thus spiritual mentality against a materialistic mentality imposed by Western ideology. Marxism becomes the breeding ground of Liberalism as the materialistic nature of Marxist Communism is compatible with the materialistic nature of Liberalism. And to impose that materialism a totalitarian system is needed, and indeed both Marxism and Liberalism are totalitarian, so the transition from Marxism to Liberalism occurs because traditionalism and thus anti-materialistic ideas of civilization are oppressed by totalitarian means and replaced by the bourgeois conception of the World.

We could think that someday China, once again guided by traditionalism and righteousness, could get rid of its current chains and come forward as a true ally for Russia and the genuine European civilization. But that would require a major spiritual change in China, since a change in the inner character of the Fallen race is impossible, and unfortunately the spiritual war in China was already fought and lost by the Righteous spiritual element. The outcome of this spiritual war fundamentally explains the globalist character of China's economy and culture. But also, the outcome of China's spiritual war is not only causing repercussions inside China but also outside of it, as the Asiatic country possesses a geopolitical project in line with the globalist order of thalassocratic rule. If Russia becomes a true ally of China in the future, the result implies Russia's total liberalization and the final subjugation of Euro-Siberia. Liberalization and therefore subjugation of the World has always been the final goal for any ruling thalassocratic superpower. A true alliance between Russia and China will require the abandonment of Russia's own project for civilization, which in fact is Europe's original project of civilization. Russia's survival as a sovereign entity cannot be granted either by Muslim countries or by China. On the contrary, Russia would become even more isolated than it is today, as Euro-Siberian political and cultural unification is the only foreign policy capable of protecting Russia's future.

Both the European part of NATO and China possess direct borders on Russia and consequently, Russia will see itself militarily and economically surrounded by all sides and gradually suffocated by an immense ring of capitalist power. The national chauvinism of NATO's countries will be satisfied by Russia's estrangement, without noticing that all that chauvinism will be used as China's pawn in its own geopolitical game, in the same way, that currently, the United States uses the chauvinism of European countries to keep them basically as liberal protectorates, a condition which arises because national chauvinism engenders inner division among all European states, most importantly between European states and Russia. Thus, as easily replaceable pawns, Euro-Siberian countries are marching towards their destruction.

With China as a much more reliable basis for global thalassocratic rule than the United States is, then the liberal and unipolar world order will be much closer to achieving the final objective of complete world subjugation. There could be no better opportunity for NATO that the control of a new superpower much healthier than the North American one. A situation like that will enable NATO, the European Union, and of course Rome to successfully continue their battle of attrition against Russia and its Orthodox Church. Propaganda carried in mass media against Russia and its allies, and also against Europe's traditional values will continue in a future Chinese World Order in the same way that it is done now. In this age of fast communications and quick information, this propaganda can more than ever incite countries and peoples towards one another. Even with fake news and distorted facts, hatred and ignorance are easily pushed against Russia and against any nation which can be slandered.

During the Chinese Civil War, national republican China fought against the Chinese communists, and surprisingly the republican side received almost no support from western powers, which resulted in the communist takeover of China, an event known in North American historiography as "the loss of China". The man behind this event was Dean Acheson, the Unites States Deputy Secretary of State between August 1945 and June 1947, and United States Secretary of State between January 1949 and January 1953. Already during his service as Deputy Secretary of State, Acheson was Truman's most important advisor on foreign relationships, proposing a policy of containment towards the Soviet Union which became known as "The Truman Doctrine", and elaborating "the Marshal plan". During his term as Secretary of State, Acheson was the main responsible for NATO's creation in 1949, the same year the People's Republic of China was proclaimed by Mao Zedong. As incredible as it seems, both NATO and the Communist takeover of China are a part of a single plan pushed by the same person. While Acheson convinced the US government of not supporting national republican China, he simultaneously pushed for the creation of NATO as the twin brother of the People's Republic of China in a brilliantly conceived plan against Russia.

In his 1949 "White Paper" Acheson alleged that the lack of support towards national republican China was because it would be doomed to failure (Garson 1994). But it will be naive to believe such a thing, because if we do then we must also believe that the United States intervention in the Korean War happened by accident and all the resources used in that war couldn't be used to suppress Communist China when it was far less powerful. The truth is that Russia's defeat requires the simultaneous formation of a colossal alliance in the West and an equally colossal rival state in the East. In January 1950, in a Speech given at the US National Press Club, Acheson stated his real reasons for not supporting national republican China. In that speech, he argued that China and Russia were natural enemies of each other, and therefore the United States should stand aside and let that conflict develop. Acheson was aware that through a policy of direct intervention in China, the US could lose the possibility of forming a second front against Russia in the form of Communist China.

According to Acheson's own words: "I urge all who are thinking about these foolish adventures to remember that we must not seize the unenviable position which the Russians have carved out for themselves. We must not undertake to deflect from the Russians to ourselves the righteous anger, and the wrath, and the hatred of the Chinese people which must develop. It would be folly to deflect it to ourselves. We must take the position we have always taken—that anyone who violates the integrity of China is the enemy of China and is acting contrary to our own interest. That, I suggest to you this afternoon, is the first and the great rule in regard to the formulation of American policy toward Asia." (Acheson 1950). Thus, China's red revolution was indeed a revolution pushed by international capitalism and for saving that same international capitalism.

Having also in mind that NATO and the People's Republic of China are part of a single plan developed by the same person can help us even further to foresee complete harmony between NATO and China not just as crazy speculation, but a future reality unless Russia is able to change the European balance of power through a decisive action which I wish to describe further in this book. Russia entering an alliance with China against NATO would be in reality a Russia unsuspectingly entering an alliance with NATO, while becoming itself a pawn in NATO's plans for Russia's enslavement and the eventual subjugation and destruction of mankind. Why do people believe seriously that NATO would have waited all these years until China and Russia had built their economies and military forces? Such a thing only makes sense if it has been part of NATO's plan since the very beginning. In a realistic scenario, if the current Chinese-Russian partnership did suppose an existential threat to the globalist order, then China wouldn't have been allowed to grow the way it did without having to face western aggression even if it required blowing Chinese air bases and other strategic locations decades ago.

In the so-called Eurasian circles, desperation and wishful thinking pushed forward their current geopolitical thinking. With all of the aforementioned, people cannot see a very evident fact: what most of those Eurasian circles have in common with leaders of the United States Democratic Party and the US Deep State is that both are favoring permanent close ties with China, because, first of all, some little devils in Eurasian circles see themselves smarter than Satan. Obviously, if such an alliance between Russia and China becomes a reality in the future, its result will be the complete rule of the Fallen race in Russia exactly as in China and the West. It is impossible to save Euro-Siberian civilization by agreements with a State whose greatest interest is the destruction of this civilization, with Russia's total subjugation as the final step required for achieving that. The temporal Chinese-Russian partnership evolving towards a genuine alliance will only bring liberal poisoning to Russia while all of Europe is kept divided and under globalist control.

NATO'S THREAT

As the events since the fall of the Soviet Union had already shown, nothing will change NATO's attitude towards Russia, regardless of whether in Russia there is a political system based on free elections and a capitalist economy or if Marxist terror rules over Russia again. An association as NATO, always pursuing a clear and enduring foreign policy (Russia's destruction and liberal rule over the World) is aware that only a clear and enduring foreign policy can unite allies and subjugate states. As long a Russia remains a threat to the liberal world order, NATO will always seek its destruction since only Russia's isolation from the rest of Europe can prevent the emergence of Euro-Siberia as a single World superpower. Euro-Siberian tellurocratic rule is not compatible with thalassocratic domination inasmuch as thalassocratic superpowers will be always in need of control over vast amounts of land and its resources, while tellurocratic superpowers will always seek the acquisition of ports and sea lanes to survive.

The United States and China are in need of all the resources which their gigantic economic activities need, as capitalism will be always in need of constant and exponential growth to avoid its collapse. Meanwhile, Russia is in great need of control over sea lanes and the World's ports, to which Russia's massive natural resources and technical knowledge can be poured over the world, with Russia possessing an estimated 30% of all the natural resources of our planet (Korabik 1997) and also amazing technical skills developed during decades of scientific and military achievements. But to explain the clash between NATO and Russia just on the basis of economic realities is simplistic, as very different types of civilization are engaged in a struggle that will decide the fate of the World. European and Christian civilization, embodied on its traditional values natural to Euro-Siberian land is colliding with the values of a liberal world order imparted from the seas, and which has nothing to do with genuine European heritage but rather with its destruction. The impact of Russia's internal defeat with the fall of the Soviet Union did not put an end to NATO's anti-Russian attitude, but on the contrary, NATO membership expanded all across eastern Europe because that is the only way in which NATO's unilateral actions could achieve a final objective of such magnitude as killing an entire civilization. Russia's isolation requires more than just the United States' economic and military might, and in the same way, it will require more than the Chinese superpower to bring Russia to its knees in the future.

Despite being often portrayed as weak actors in comparison to the United States or China, we must have in mind that the European part of NATO, together with the European Union and Rome are all key elements whose combined power never should be underestimated. Despite the US still is responsible for most of NATO's military spending, the contribution of NATO Europe plus Canada accounted for 302 billion dollars as of 2019, much more than all of Russia's military spending, regardless if Russia's declared spending of 65 billion dollars in 2019 is not encompassing all real military spending. Also, NATO's expansion into Eastern Europe by the new memberships of former communist regions erased a buffer zone that existed between NATO and Russia, and naturally, this allows the further continuation of the anti-Russian Cold War mentality and the escalation of hostility and fear between the West and Russia.

Since its inception, NATO had not carried out any action in which Russian interests had been promoted to any degree, and in order to justify that attitude, NATO's leadership always has emphasized in their so-called safeguarding of Europe. This so-called safeguarding of Europe against Russia has always been the perfect excuse to keep Europe in chains. The only safeguarding which NATO effectively does is of the major geopolitical goals for superpowers outside Euro-Siberia. Thus, instead of safeguarding Europe, NATO actually is placing it in constant danger, by putting all of the European nations as basically human shields and sitting ducks in the event of any conflict with Russia or with Islamic organizations. For Russia, the policies of NATO all across the European continent are a matter of life and death, but it should be noted that the same goes for the individual European states composing NATO: the strategic and tactical considerations of this alliance are an internal deviation from the natural objectives of a rational and even intuitive common European defense. NATO's strategic and tactical considerations do not make any sense for European states as far as internal divisions between them are promoted rather than overcome, including the promotion of anti-Russian actions that are not beneficial to Europe in any of the economic, military, and cultural spheres.

The real nature of NATO's aggressive foreign policy became evident in 1999 when Poland, Hungary, and the Czech Republic entered the organization. It became even more evident when Bulgaria, Estonia, Latvia, Lithuania, Romania, Slovakia, and Slovenia all joined NATO in 2004. The years between 1999 and 2004 showed more clearly than the years of the Cold War what is NATO's real intention: Russia's subjugation and the total control over Europe. Even the fact that Estonia, Latvia, and Lithuania were part of the Soviet Union and the Russian Empire in no way stopped the aggressive tendencies of NATO, and this was demonstrated more strikingly by the Aegis Ballistic Missile Defense System, which is already starting its deployment in Eastern Europe. The dissolution of the Soviet Union represented only one of many steps in the direction of NATO's real objectives. By continuing its aggressive expansion against Russia, NATO made evident that its real objective wasn't just the containment of Communism, but also a clash of civilizations in which Europe and Russia must be totally subjugated to protect thalassocratic interests. Whatever impulses could emerge in Euro-Siberia to form a tellurocratic superpower, NATO will always try to inhibit them in a manner hostile to Russia.

From military, economic, and even spiritual points of view, allowing the existence of NATO will be catastrophic for Russia. This situation is not only dangerous in the European continent but also all around the World. Like during the Cold War, today we can also assume that in any part of the World in which Russian interests are at stake, and regardless of the reasons, NATO will always be Russia's adversary. Therefore, for Russia any moment of weakness, as it happened during the Yeltsin era will unfold its consequences in the form of rapid expansion of NATO's influence in Europe and in other regions, as Russia must be in the position to organize countermeasures against any aggression from outside and inside. The idea that Russia could be able in the long term to put up resistance by improvised means must be regarded as a false notion, with the new technological breakthroughs and keeping a few allies all being just temporary breathing until the harsh reality of economic and military numbers becomes fully manifested.

The desperate situation of a future Russian resistance against NATO and China can be put as follows: a system of alliances is in a position to threaten almost all of Russia without the necessity of a direct confrontation. The only thing required for Russia's subjugation is a gradual economic and cultural battle of attrition in which military means as missiles and aircraft only serve as the guarantors for it. Those military means for guaranteeing economic and cultural asphyxiation can prove themselves very effective with the current situation of the Russian borders, in which almost all vital Russian cities are all encompassed in a smaller western area neighboring NATO, and all that can be attacked by missiles and aircraft in a matter of few minutes, while in the meanwhile, all of Russia's Far East is exposed to China, including Vladivostok and the Russian pacific fleet stationed there.

The entire industrial and urban region in western Russia, including Saint Petersburg, Moscow, Nizhny Novgorod, Smolensk, Krasnodar, Rostov-on-Don, etc., are all within the almost instantaneous reach of hostile missiles and aircraft since the buffer zones which once protected the Soviet Union are no more. The distance between Moscow and Latvia (NATO member since 2004) is 802 km, half the distance between Moscow and Berlin, and the distance between Estonia and Saint Petersburg is 312 km. While western Russia is exposed to NATO, Vladivostok and the Russian Pacific Fleet are just 130 km from China. To make situations worse for Russia, the West extends its influence by aiding revolutions against pro-Russian governments, as it happened in Georgia, Ukraine, Armenia, and now even Belarus. Most of the financial aid money is channeled through Western NGOs and can be used to influence electoral and judicial systems through citizen mobilization. The European Union is still seducing peoples all across Europe with false hopes of economic prosperity and political stability, with propaganda exploiting frustration and ignorance by the ones being conducted through a skillful mix between misinformation and protest movements.

To all of the aforementioned, there are still more factors that should be also taken into account to realize how threatening NATO's position is, and one of the most important factors is that as already mentioned in this book, Russia lacks its own warm-water ports with direct access to the oceans. Each year, many of the country's ports freeze for several months, while Vladivostok is enclosed by the Sea of Japan, in which Japan was granted an exclusive economic zone. This situation of course halts trade into and out of Russia; and prevents the Russian navy from operating all across the World in the way NATO and Chinese fleets do. Another important factor for Russia's weakness can be found after making an historical analysis of its leaderships across history. Just as once in a while the Russian people enjoy leadership which puts them in a situation of unprecedented greatness, from time to time we find also very bad leaderships which place Russia back into total chaos, and this cycle was repeated more than once as the country was raised again and again by excellent leaders only to be put back into the hands of incompetent and selfish rulers, which created periods of total decay.

The most known examples were victorious Russia during the French invasion of 1812 in contrast to Russia during the First World War and the victorious Soviet Union in 1945 in contrast to the Soviet Union in 1991. But there are additional examples: the situation in the Tsardom of Russia in the later years of Ivan IV's reign and his successor Feodor I, which caused Russia's "Times of Troubles" (1598-1613) in contrast to the victorious Tsardom of Russia after the Great Northern War (1700-1721), or Russia's defeat during the Crimean War (1853-1856) in comparison to Russia's victory in the Russo-Turkish war of 1877-1878. By ruling above anyone else, a few people or sometimes even a single brain were capable of exercising tremendous influence in the course of Russia's history, either by creating great victories and achievements or by allowing major military and economic disasters. A new and strong spirit replaces the weakness of specific Russian leaderships until state structures become ossified and senile again.

In 1917 and 1991 the Russian Empire and the Soviet Union, respectively, were crushed as by then the main characteristic of their leadership was total incompetence, selfish attitudes and cowardly surrender, while in 1812 and 1945 the Russian Empire and the Soviet Union, despite suffering heavy losses, were characterized by the most memorable victories of their history, as a spirit of total hostility towards any foreign domination combined with a competent military leadership were able to turn seemingly total defeats into great victories. From 1812 to 1917, and from 1945 to 1991, it was not the Russian People as a whole who changed their internal essence, but their leadership when being passed to other individuals. Just as lions being lead by donkeys, the internal essence of the Russian People becomes fruitless if a miserable mentality and lack of vision take over the vulnerable State. When realizing that historical fact, we finally see that Russia under Nicholas II was the forerunner of Yeltsin's Russia. It is not a matter of whether Russia is under a monarchy, a Communist regime, or a system based on free elections, but whether Russia is ruled by capable people or not.

The Great Patriotic War is the most glorious evidence of an inner essence which enables the Russian People to devote themselves with courage, discipline, and intelligence against what seemed a vastly superior enemy. But regardless of this inner essence, the cycle of victories and decay will be put to an end in one way or another, either by Russia's successful unification of Euro-Siberia or by the final fall of the country into geopolitical oblivion. Today the World is changing much faster than at any time before, and it will not wait for Russia or the individual European states to regain their former positions of power. NATO, the European Union, and the Roman Catholic Church all combine their strengths to maintain the system of small European states without unified political and spiritual leadership. They want to maintain a certain balance of power between European states because this is vital to dominate them, and the only State in Europe which still wasn't forced into that balance of power is, of course, Russia.

As long as it exists, NATO will remain as the organization whose only purpose is to serve the interests of superpowers outside Europe, serving the United States now and China in the future by preventing the rise of Euro-Siberia. That remains as NATO's long-term goal since the Cold War with the Soviet Union, as the economic result of the Second World War was the surrender of Western Europe and its colonies to the military and economic power of the United States. The military result was the consolidation of the Soviet Union as the largest military power on land and the consolidation of the United States as the largest power over the seas. The battle against the Soviet Union's political control over the eastern half of Europe was the creation of the United States own political control over the western part of the continent, and thus two puppets emerged: the European part under NATO and the European part under the control of the Warsaw pact. With the presence of the United States military power, a naval war would have resulted in disastrous effects for the Soviet Union because of NATO's military bases, established all along the giant margins of the European and American Atlantic coasts and the equally long stretches of NATO's countries bordering the Mediterranean Sea in Europe and Turkey, together with those at strategic sites all around the World.

When the Warsaw Pact and the Soviet Union were dismantled, and NATO absorbed the eastern part of Europe under former Communist control, the European part of NATO rather than achieving some kind of independence only became an even larger puppet with parts of it bordering a weaker Russia. Despite Russia's current weakness, all of Europe continues being an easy target not only for Russia's missiles and long-range bombers but most European trade would be largely exposed to the danger posed by Russian naval power which still possesses a decent force of submarines and surface ships, capable of carrying nuclear weapons, hypersonic missiles and nuclear submarine drones (Status-6). All of the European parts of NATO can become trapped in its coastlines and sea lanes in a naval blockade if they are not protected against Russia by the United States.

That protection is made for the sake of Europe's enemies, as only its enemies would desire a divided and impotent Europe by eliminating Russian power in the continent. The Europeans achieved their Cold War goal when the Soviet Union's communist system was destroyed and the Warsaw Pact was dismantled, but anything beyond this is detrimental to Europe as a whole because a variety of factors (already explained in this book) make sure that without Russia there is no future for Europe, and in the same way, without Europe, there is no future for Russia.

A large amount of Cold War and post-Cold War propaganda enabled NATO to influence the European peoples against their own interests, and that is possible because NATO presents itself as an indispensable part of Europe, while in reality, NATO rather than being part of Europe is completely alien to it, as its creation and its goals all came from the same men who converted European countries to little more than client states.

During the era of Yeltsin's Russia, the idea of converting the country also into a permanent client State only failed because the collapse of the Soviet Union was so sudden and spectacular that entire generations of former Soviet specialists and military experts were still young and fresh, giving Russia a new basis for continuing as a sovereign State with President Putin, a former KGB agent, being in charge of handling the chaotic mess.

The conquest of the World by economic and cultural means gives NATO its true reason to exist, as an organized military resistance against economic and cultural conquest is made impossible through the combined power of the United States and its European allies, and in the future, it will be made impossible by the combined power of NATO and China unless something is done by Russia. We shouldn't see the competition between Russia and NATO as merely a competition based on economic and military factors. Besides those well-known factors, cultural and thus spiritual factors always should be regarded as the inner reason differentiating civilizations from one another: the artificial western civilization vs the genuine European and Christian civilization. When two civilizations are clearly differentiated from one another, they inevitably began competing with each other in all areas. Sometimes, when one of the competing civilizations proves itself as weaker than its rival, then a third party comes to its aid for keeping potential enemies divided and dominated. We can consider the United States and most of Europe as being swallowed by Western Civilization, and in the event of its partial collapse through internal conflict, especially inside the US, then the Chinese juggernaut will try to keep Western Civilization as a disease undermining all of Euro-Siberia.

Europe came viewing the Soviet Union first, and the Russian Federation now as a threat not only because of their military power and their influence on world trade but also because the very existence of Western Civilization is threatened even if in Russia a full consciousness of the country's mission isn't developed yet. Already in the times of the Soviet Union, even with Marxism controlling all of Russia and its satellites, a different project of civilization was being planned by Russia.

The failure of the Marxist project of civilization was because of ideological flaws which can be traced to its very origin, which lies not in Russia but in the Germanized Jewish mindsets of Karl Marx and Friedrich Engels, which saw in European and Christian civilization their natural enemy rather than an essential tool to fight capitalism. In short, the Marxist project of civilization was doomed to failure due to the inability of its ideologists to connect with European and Christian civilization, and because of this Russia lost a critical amount of time which allowed the historical trend of European politics towards anti-Russian alliances. The ideological aspect of the Cold War made Russia unable to take advantage of the fears caused in Europe by the growing strength of the United States in the global economy and the development of its massive military power. Even by 1945-47, a war-torn Western Europe had not taken yet its final decision of total alignment with the United States. For example, in 1946 the British Labour government under its Prime Minister Clement Attlee authorized Rolls-Royce to export 40 "Rolls-Royce RB.41 Nene" turbojet engines, which were reverse-engineered in the Soviet Union to create the Klimov VK-1, the first Soviet jet engine which saw significant production (Gunston 1989).

The United States did not totally break with its isolationist policy until European fears of communist expansion were triggered by Soviet influence in eastern Europe and the communist uprising in Greece, which proved as justifications for the Truman Doctrine in 1947. For two years (1945-47) the devastating effects of two wars against Germany generated feelings which proved stronger than anti-communist and anti-Russian rhetoric, and thus the Soviet Union did not pose an immediate threat to Europe in the eyes of many, but rather the economic and military power of the United States, by then the only country with atomic weapons while being by far the World's largest economy. The position of the European statesmen changed only because of Russia's ideological hostility, and that position became even worse when after Stalin's death the new Soviet "Peaceful coexistence" policy came to be regarded by enemies, partners, and allies alike as a clear act of weakness and selfish thought rather than a genuine desire for peace.

Finally, with the fall of the Soviet Union and its Warsaw Pact, the danger of communist domination in Europe dissipated forever, but not anti-Russian rhetoric and actions, because the path of NATO's diplomacy can be compared to Russia's use of the Imperial and Soviet armies: any present or future threat is fought to submission when a favorable situation presents itself. That mentality did not come from Europe, originally only worried by the ideological consequences of communism, but instead from the United States' thalassocratic interests, also present in China but in an implicit rather than explicit way. European politics and diplomacy were eventually absorbed by the United States over the course of many decades, and not without some frictions, most notably France's withdrawal from NATO in 1966, to which only fully returned in 2009. However, by now European politics were changed a lot by thalassocratic influence, and a rebellion of the European states in NATO against the liberal order is unrealistic for that reason and because of the traditional anti-Russian postures of Roman-Catholic countries in Europe, most notably Poland.

SPIRITUAL RACES AND GEOPOLITICS OF THE APOCALYPSE

A BASIC INSIGHT INTO GEOPOLITICS OF THE APOCALYPSE

May the holy duty that guides our actions give us strength and may our God remain our supreme guidance. May the righteous soul be our guide and our perseverance.

Speaking of such a thing as "spiritual races and geopolitics of the apocalypse", it is no easy at all for me, and I think it wouldn't be easy for any mortal. Our actions someday will show all of mankind, inside and outside Euro-Siberia, that the way to salvation for the struggling human species is the Righteous spiritual race. But before any other thing, the Fourth Political Theory and a Euro-Siberian movement must be aware of who their deadly threat is, and the struggle against it will be recognized, sooner or later, as the most important fight in mankind's history, with all other struggles being just fratricide among righteous brothers. All who currently endorse the Fourth Political Theory and all who are proposing the Euro-Siberian paradigm are with the great mission of awakening not only themselves and their own nation but all other nations who compose our World, our place in this universe which God created in his infinite wisdom.

The problem begins when the Righteous, blinded by false ideological paradigms and emotional fervor, instead of directing their struggle against the Fallen race enemy, they direct their wrath against the other Righteous, from whom they are separated due to a skillful work which the forces of darkness are carrying out since thousands of years ago. The righteous from all peoples and civilizations across the Earth must remember they are united by a common soul that came before the founding of any religion or any country. To preserve that soul and its divine cultures, it is necessary to denounce the Fallen race as an ontological reality that is the real cause of all drawbacks and all pain. Spiritual races do exist, and despite this fact is already known by many cultures, most importantly the ones in India, all of the Western Civilization ignores this essential element of reality, and in the genuine European and Christian civilization developing before Western Civilization, a true consciousness regarding spiritual race was not fully developed because of the immaturity of European civilization in comparison to a millennial civilization like the one in India.

While the real patriotic Russia is trying to build an alliance with India, the means of communication from all the representatives of the liberal world order and even some Russian media including platforms of Leonid Savin, "director of administration of the International Eurasian Movement", are already fighting against the Indian ally, all of which is part of a war of annihilation. They pretend to fly the flag of multipolarity but just serve the interests of China and its Pakistan ally and allow Muslim stooges to openly conduct their informational war against India and its current Prime Minister, Narendra Modi, the builder of a new nationalistic consciousness across India. In that consciousness, Hindu traditionalism is the main element against Chinese and Muslim aggression serving liberal globalism. The liberal circles in Euro-Siberia, including those in Russia, and of course those in America, are engaged in a campaign of lies in which the current Indian government is being presented as the reincarnation of Fascist Italy with Modi being the new Mussolini. We, the real traditionalists and men of faith, cannot stand aside and ignore this infamy, because if we ignore it, the fight against this global threat of liberalism which is now raging in India can defeat this Asian giant and destroy Russia in the short or long term, with all hopes for mankind being lost.

The Fallen race incites nations against India as it does against Russia. Its elites are so worried about having an Indian nationalistic state in their global financial empire that they desire to destroy it at the first moment they perceive elements of a traditionalist and nationalistic mindset. All the foolish criticism of Modi's government comes from the same liberal bashing used against Russia or against any government opposing the current liberal world order, including phraseology about human rights and threatened minorities. All this anti-Indian discourse is aimed to destroy India using other nations to get rid of this powerful State and its civilization, before it can make a hole in the globalist tyranny which is becoming as big as the one which Russia already made. Only powerful states with a traditionalist mindset are in the position to oppose the liberal tyranny over the defenseless civilizations which are their prey, and the reason for that can be summoned as follows: the traditions of powerful states like Russia and India only developed after many centuries of cultural knowledge and experience. From that experience, a cultural and spiritual barrier against destructive elements eventually arose, one which keeps key elements of liberalism and its spiritual race all under powerful check by cultural and psychological impulses that act as the civilization's own immune system. That is, of course, a reality in India, with a history sparking thousands and thousands of years.

Besides being founded over the basis of a very ancient civilization, the Indian State is also a natural creation emerging from the Indian people when struggling for their independence, and not just an artificial monster as liberal states across the Western World, or as the People's Republic of China. While the liberal world only can recall the obsolete thought of people like Locke, Voltaire, and Adam Smith as their "founding elements", India can trace its origins to such immortal thoughts as the ones present in the Vedas, the ancient political thought of Chanakya, the healing power of Budda's advice, and so on until reaching the great example of Gandhi, and all the current mathematicians, philosophers, statesmen, teachers and creators who the Asian country is providing to mankind.

But of course, nothing of this matters to globalist elites, neither to their Pakistani stooges, as we can see in the attitude displayed against Modi's government a mirror of the attitude displayed against the Russian Federation: it is the same gradual encirclement and the same war of cultural and economic attrition. That is the tactic of the Fallen race to subjugate the world when faced by powerful countries such as Russia or India. Today, liberal circles and the spiritual race they represent are the creators of artificial civilizations pretending to be European, Latin-American, Chinese, etc., but they cannot build so easily such artificial bridges in Russia and India. The Fallen race knows very well that their Western Civilization is already a bridge powerful enough to subjugate most of the European soul and much of America. They also know that the same project for building an artificial civilization of spiritual and material slavery has advanced in China thanks to an entire century of devastating genocides.

But they can hardly do the same with Russia or India, not without an intense battle between civilizations, one in which mankind's future will be decided forever. The master plan of liberal circles is turning all of the World's civilizations into faceless and artificial bastards, in which of course the Righteous spiritual race will found itself trapped with spiritual maggots in a World doomed to extinction. The Fallen race carried their misdeeds for thousands of years, and that has taught the righteous how to adapt in the competition against their enemy. This adaptation comes in the form of stronger cultural and psychological structures which are the basis of any healthy civilization. The same principle is the one behind the creation of nature's immune systems in living organisms: first, they must be exposed to the pathogen agents, only then they eventually develop a way to struggle against them. When struggling against them, pathogen agents become stronger over the years, but so immune systems. All that vicious circle is not stopped until the pathogen ceases to be endemic due to a final vaccine being found or when the pathogen no longer finds more hosts in order to survive.

The principle that works within individual organisms also works for civilizations: if the disease is stronger than the natural barriers against it, then civilizations perish. And in a global scale, if only one civilization or two retain their strength and possess enough geopolitical relevance, that can prove as an antibiotic whose effect expands to other regions, putting the international empire of the Fallen race under threat to succumb to the power of a healthy entity, like every disease in this world. However, if not a single healthy civilization remains within the vast collection of cultural cadavers and artificial entities that have been stripped of any spiritual qualities, then the liberal world order can finally proclaim their victory, but for a short time until a sick planet finally collapses and becomes uninhabitable as happens with the Earth's neighbors in our Solar System. The leading elements of the Fallen race are already approaching the time in which they can turn the Bible's apocalyptic prophecies a reality but in their own twisted version. Little they seem to know that their defeat is only a question of time, and if they know, they do not care anymore.

Before their defeat, they will try to completely devour all the states and civilizations which had proven easy prey to the forces of darkness. In order to achieve that, they will manipulate public opinion across all nations in a way in which it turns into a weapon of essential importance. Today, the destruction of India is not in NATO's explicit goals, but it is the desire of the Fallen race and it is a necessary goal for the liberal world empire. As for Russia, the rest of Europe did not seek its destruction; that was a North-American and Chinese interest. But as the nature of spiritual races is not confined to a single country or continent, the forces of darkness in North America and China eventually joined hands with those in Europe and even those in Russia who want its liberal subjugation.

As soon as the People's Republic of China was established, irritations between China and India reappeared during the same time that the Sino-Soviet split was taking place. In 1962 a war between India and China started, with some areas on the border with India being taken by Chinese troops. In 1967 further border clashes between India and China occurred, and now in 2020, skirmishes between the two countries are taking place due to China's aggressive policy of confrontation. India is facing what can be called a two-front war of attrition against Pakistan and China. As for Pakistan, it has fought a series of wars and standoffs against India since the independence of both states from British rule. Those were the Indo-Pakistani War of 1947, that of 1965, the War of 1971, the Indo-Pakistani War of 1999, together with the 2001-2002 standoff, and the more recent 2008 and 2019 standoffs. All of this puts into evidence a ring of alliances formed between liberal interests, China and Pakistan to suffocate India through an encirclement, and I must emphasize that all these tactics are the ones being used against Russia, which as a matter of fact, was India's most important ally during the time of the Soviet Union, and now closer ties between Russia and India still exist despite Russia no longer enjoys the influence of the former Soviet superpower.

While all of the aforementioned is taking place, western means of communication and some Russian media are all taking a position on the side of India's enemies, by criticizing Modi's policies and putting him as the Mussolini of our times. At the same time, hostile media in the West are trying to convince peoples that Putin is a wannabe Napoleon driven by megalomania. We can see by examples as these how is the nature of the Fallen race informational war against any element capable of threatening its financial empire. The attitudes of the Western media and of some of Russia's media is laughable considering that they put a blind eye to much of what is happening in China or Pakistan regarding human rights, but when Narendra Modi moves as much as a finger then it is presented as a tyrant and fascist emperor. Further in this book, we will return to the Indian question, as now I only mentioned this situation because it shows very clearly how spiritual wars are carried out in our XXI century.

The most important element in a geopolitical struggle between civilizations is that those who are Righteous and on the side of the Righteous are able to keep aside the divisions that are being fomented by the enemy. In order to foment divisions between countries, churches, and schools all sort of minor matters are used by the enemy as a pretext for aggression, always undermining the true resistance against the liberal plan. Sometimes, the division is necessary when a healthy institution or a healthy civilization wants to separate itself from a diseased entity in order to remain isolated. In some situations across history, there wasn't another option, as when the East-West schism of 1054 took place, or when Russia distanced itself from the Romanov Dynasty after 300 years, and from the Soviet Union after 70 years. But all those forced separations always occur under tragic circumstances, and those tragic situations arise because the Righteous elements do not have enough strength to avoid them in the first place. All that can be avoided by just remembering who the common enemy of civilization is, which are its ideological tools, and how its tactics can be carried out.

When people rant against the United States, they focus on it so much that they put all their intellectual and physical forces in a single front while leaving nothing to strike other headquarters of the evil globalist alliance. People with good intentions, including some harmless fools, end up serving the interests of the globalist enemy because they do not have the capacity to think beyond what their eyes perceive in the present. The difference between simple commentators and real political thinkers and strategists is that the first ones are not able to forecast any glimpse of the future, while the latter always have in mind not just present but also future threats and shortcomings. If we look at the situation from a logical and realistic point of view, we see that any call for a multipolar world in which several states can remain as a league of friends (as in those animated movies made for children) is in the most part just empty talk regarding an ephemeral situation that has no chance of lasting very much.

Purely fantastic ideas dreamed among people with good intentions and racketeers alike become the swamp in which truly great ideas sink. In the geopolitical fight among civilizations, which is the expression of the geopolitical fight between spiritual races, it is of essential importance to get rid of useless daydreaming and publicly denounce all liars and crooks destroying Euro-Siberian strategic thinking. That thinking can become a weapon of the enemy instead of being a patriotic weapon for the liberation of European and Christian civilization, a task which requires mutual understanding at Euro-Siberian circles and also at political and intellectual circles from all countries. Since, for political reasons, including the secrecy from the part of the most powerful entities running states, the reasons to endorse some necessary patriotic strategies could not be explained, so there will always be a majority of influential political strategists and political thinkers in general who will oppose completely new strategies and ideological constructs, which seem to them as delusional thought or schedules which imply too much risk for them.

When trying to build a totally new geopolitical approach, like the one based on acknowledging the reality of a World in which spiritual races and their conspiracies do exist, it is inevitable that key strategists and ideologists become suspicious because to them new thoughts do not seem clear, neither where those thoughts can lead peoples and their civilizations. They are accustomed to think only inside their closed mental box since very few individuals are true visionaries whose political philosophy in some cases, or their geopolitical strategies in others, are capable of giving an explanation to present events and also a plan for future action. To me, the ideological marriage between Dugin's Fourth Political Theory and Guillaume Faye's Euro-Siberian paradigm is the only way to develop a concise plan in the framework of a battle between civilizations, a battle in which spiritual races are the ones driving geopolitical change through ways which the common persons cannot understand. This is in part because the ultimate goals of certain political and religious associations cannot be disclosed so that the World's public opinion is aware of it.

Intuitively, political strategists should realize that it is foolish to pretend that they have the same degree of knowledge as let's say Vladimir Putin and Russia's external intelligence agency, or the US. Central Intelligence Agency. Neither they can pretend to have the same degree of knowledge as the Vatican's Intelligence Apparatus. All that we can do is trying to use all of the skills which intuition, which comes from the Nous, together with years of investigation and reflection can provide to those in search of the truth. We the political and philosophical thinkers have our own intellectual and spiritual weapons, but the major mistake we can commit comes when lack of humility and lust for ephemeral influence and material prosperity put our own intellectual and spiritual weapons against true lofty ideals, while putting even the most influential patriots away from the higher truths given by the Nous, and also from a Holy path towards God and mankind's salvation.

It is important to realize that the common people and most thinkers are not in the position to fully understand their government's intentions in the long run. Also, politicians, religious leaders, and billionaires, just as anyone else, are guided by their Nous (the eyes and mind of their souls), and not even they are capable of consciously acknowledging some of the consequences of their plans, but only unconsciously inasmuch as they have, as all of mankind, both a conscious mind and an unconscious Nous whose nature varies according to the nature of the different spiritual races and also the hierarchies among them. As I already emphasized several times since I wrote the first Volume, the nature of the Nous, just as the nature of the spiritual races cannot be changed, so they will not acquire a new attitude, even if those attitudes are leading mankind to the abyss.

Therefore, we must always impede spiritual enemies of European and Christian civilization, which from a broader point of view are the destroyers of any Righteous civilization, from using as their own tools the intellectual and institutional forces that patriots and traditionalists built over the course of years. The Fallen race is incapable of true original thinking, and they cannot build any civilization on their own, they only feed on previous civilizations and thereby steal previous knowledge and institutions.

SPIRITUAL RACE AS A MEANS TO EXPAND POLITICAL AND CULTURAL INFLUENCE

Just as the elites of different countries and civilizations are conscious and unconscionably guided by their inner spiritual nature, so the broader masses, which can be turned from mere unconscious masses into conscious People united by a common civilization. The general anti-Russian Cold War psychosis that propaganda has created in Europe and which sparked across other continents will continue until Russia is able to make use of the natural instinct coming from our Righteous spiritual race against the common enemy, and awake that natural instinct across Euro-Siberia through decisive actions sparking from the Russian authentic will, which is only part of a common Euro-Siberian authentic will towards spiritual and material self-preservation. In the last part of this book, I will enter into details regarding how those decisive actions must be carried out, but before that; all reasons for such bold planning must be totally explained for the reader to understand the gravity of the current situation and why bold planning is absolutely needed.

When a powerful government is conscious of its authentic will and therefore is able to awake the consciousness of the Righteous spiritual race both inside and outside its frontiers, then that government can win the support of both common persons and leaderships who are fighting a common spiritual enemy, even if the execution of that mission requires that a State engages into a fearless foreign policy sparking and supporting the spirit of rebellion across nations and civilizations infected by the Fallen race and its liberalism. When a State engages in a fearless but smart foreign policy, it gains the respect of the public opinion inside and outside its frontiers, because it shows to the rest of the World that a given leadership and its People are refusing to become a client state and are in possession of the inner force and authentic will necessary for protecting and expanding their civilization. In addition, all feelings of hopelessness in countries already surrounded start to be replaced by a restored sense of hope, just as when in ancient battlefields the King remained with his troops and was able to encourage them even when outnumbered or in a tactical disadvantage.

The globalist enemy will find more and more difficulties when trying to suppress the voice of the Righteous even when states are no more than the instrument for their control and suffering. A strong power that is able to stand up amid their enemies will serve as a demonstration that a superior strength is still among the Righteous and, the same superior strength will also be perceived in other states but in varying degrees, all depending on biological, cultural, and geographical factors. The limitations which arise from those factors all can be overcome when the careful work of a motivated state and a smart alliance policy is able to turn the balance in this spiritual war ravaging the whole World. Mankind's corruption is the greatest fact when explaining how strong powers and their cultures fall into oblivion, and the very first sign of corruption inside a State is when the attitudes of its leadership are guided by shortsightedness, selfish betrayal, and stupid servility. Both the public opinion in other states and of course foreign leadership instinctively perceive the corruption arising in a sick State, because nature has trained human beings to detect those behaviors which characterize a weak adversary or an unreliable partner.

This instinct is not confined to small social circles but reaches entire continents because mindsets are not separated by borders, but borders are separated by mindsets. In the same way that we observe weakness and obedience in a Dog that follows a master after being hit or deprived of something, we also observe weakness in states and political movements who act as pets of someone else. Just as people are able to perceive when a family or a circle of friends is unstable and doomed to fail, in the same way, public opinion and their leaders are able to perceive instability and lack of confidence in political partnerships, public structures, military and economic alliances, and of course in a religious institution. Despite basic animal instincts are the same regardless of spiritual race, it is the different nature of spiritual races that determine how and why those animal instincts are employed.

In the first volume, I extensively described what differentiates the attitudes of the Fallen spiritual race from the Righteous spiritual race, and now it is time to describe how that differences can be used in favor of the Righteous when trying to gain geopolitical relevance for their civilization, their states or their political movements. For this to happen, it is necessary to awake the self-consciousness of that spiritual race as a distinct and separate Dasein struggling for its survival. When that self-consciousness is advanced enough, and when it is able to take the structures of a given State, then everything from children's video games to the last TV show, every possible media, and social circle must work to awoke that self-consciousness even further, using perceptible and subliminal ways. The reader should not feel frightened by these last statements of mine, as the forces of darkness are already working using both perceptible and subliminal methods to poison the mind of millions and millions of people with cultural trash and propaganda, all inducing fear and degeneracy while curtailing the awakening of self-consciousness for the Righteous, until no longer is able to distinguish who the enemy is and how to struggle against it.

Gradually, implicit segregation will be needed to make the social and public circles of the Fallen race smaller and smaller. The segregation will be implicit rather than explicit because spiritual races, unlike biological races, are not differentiated by easily observable physical traits, but rather behavior. The reason why the segregation of biological races eventually failed as social projects as it happened with the Apartheid in South Africa or the Jim Crow laws in the United States is that segregating biological races implies explicit acts that public opinion inside and outside a country cannot watch just as passive spectators. But when implicit segregation is taking place, there is almost nothing that public opinion can watch, and that is a reality even with biological races as it happens now in the United States, and it will be a reality even more if spiritual races are the basis for implicit segregation rather than biological ones.

All of the above will be not just an act of domestic policy, but gradually it will turn more and more into an act of foreign policy, inasmuch as a state and its alliances increase their influence and are able to promote and expand their new ideology just as the Soviet Union did with a flawed ideology as Marxism-Leninism, or as the United States and Western Europe did with their liberal ideology. In the case of liberalism, the project of the Fallen race was promoted and expanded across all the World, and using similar tools the project of the Righteous can also be promoted and expanded across every country as long as cultural and political strength is displayed with a burning passion. In the present, we can observe how easily the emotions and actions of millions of people are manipulated by a system of propaganda that turns minor events into major points of disagreements, while important events are kept outside public opinion.

The impact of the combined use of propaganda and cultural influence is more powerful than ever because in our current age means of communication are able to carry information, disinformation, and cultural trends across all the planet with the speed of light. The way to fight against it is by turning upside down all this machine of cultural and informational warfare so that instead of serving those who are directing mankind towards darkness is directing the Righteous by arising a higher consciousness and promoting a devoted spirit. The oppression coming from foreign powers and inner enemies will be met by a hostile attitude and the uttermost dedication of God's mankind.

One reason for the failure of a State when trying to establish a successful policy of alliances and trying to expand its influence is when the ideology of that State is no longer able to raise positive feelings in potential allies and partners, and in the same way, it is no longer able to create respect and fear in the enemy. Eventually, it is unable to even raising positive feelings inside its own structures and therefore its collapse becomes imminent. The Soviet experiment proves as a very good example of how ideology affects geopolitical strategy and actions. Any State, even that of a superpower will face its downfall when the spiritual forces of mankind turn against it and finally break it to pieces or assimilate what its left of original political and cultural institutions.

Any foreign policy must take into account the immense power that cultural and ideological trends emanating from worldwide spiritual warfare are able to unleash when nothing strong can oppose it. That's why what it matters is the geopolitical relevance of a civilization as a whole and not just that of a given State, because no State can remain as a true sovereign entity when the very civilization which created it is under mortal threat by different civilizations which use cultural infiltration and political action as its weapons. In the geopolitical battlefield between spiritual races, the Fallen race will use liberalism to destroy civilizations and create artificial ones to supplant them, and in a unipolar world, regardless of which superpower is controlling it, that superpower will retain just the basic traits of liberalism in order that an elite is permanently in control, while other traits will be curtailed in order that the State is able to stay in control of the rest of the World.

The rest of the World will have to accept a variant of liberalism that retains even the most destructive characteristics so that states are not in a position to confront the superpower which keeps the liberal order centralized. When the United States was battling the Soviet Union, the traits of liberalism in the North American cultural and economic system were not allowed to the same degree as now and that was essential as an element for deterring the Soviet Union. Now, when the Soviet Union no longer exists and China is arising as a more promising center for liberal domination, the additional traits of liberalism are allowed to corrode the United States while causing distrust and revulsion outside and inside North America. The same process of growing distrust and revulsion which the Soviet Union caused in allies, partners, and enemies alike, is now being faced by the United States, despite its different ideology and geographical situation. Both the former Soviet and British empires, and the current North American superpower are sharing the same fate caused by the necessity of dismantling dangerous, problematic structures before they can continue disrupting the liberal world order because the spiritual battle keeping that system is way beyond the ephemeral existence of states which already fulfilled their historical purpose.

Only a State whose historical purpose is in line with God's plans for higher mankind will endure the test of time and overcome any attack from hostile cultural, economic, and political forces. The closer that State and its civilization are to authentic will, the farther they will be from the prospect of defeat and unnecessary sacrifices in the present and future generations because the problem is not only eventual defeat but even victories whose cost is much higher than it should. If the Russian People and its allies are in the position to finally overcome the conditions threatening to destroy European and Christian civilization, and the future of mankind with it, then they must remember the lessons of the Cold War because the alternatives are either defeat or a victory whose sacrifices are so terrible than human memory will be a cause of constant horror. If the lives of thousands have to be sacrificed together with their economic and psychological future, that would be a shame if all we can pass to future generations is continents in ruins, polluted wastelands, or mass confusion caused by a multicultural nightmare caused by the Western Civilization intending to destroy its Euro-Siberian predecessor.

Multiculturalism is not just the attempt to create some kind of Muslim and African state inside Europe but in fact the attempt to destroy the natural Euro-Siberian elements facing the artificial culture of Western civilization. The conflicts of Multiculturalism are just part of a broader war in the clash of civilizations, and the clash of civilizations is in turn just part of an even broader war between spiritual races whose origin and inner essence were not grasped by current science, which is not a reason to dismiss such a conception of the World which most of mankind forgot.

THE ELEMENTS OF WEAKNESS VERSUS THE BASIS FOR STRENGTH

All members of mankind share the same basic natural instincts, and the basic differences between spiritual races and their hierarchies cannot be changed, but still, there are differences that arise from particular conditions and therefore particular nations. Euro-Siberia is itself characterized by diverging points of view which emerged due to different mindsets evolving in the span of hundreds of years, and the same goes for all other civilizations. Differences in points of view are weapons that can be used either by the Fallen race or the Righteous. Therefore, each spiritual race will use a tactic that exploits every major weakness arising from a nation's particular point of view. In NATO, chauvinism from individual European states is used together with Roman Catholicism in order to spark division and destroy Euro-Siberian civilization, while in the meanwhile, Russia's own chauvinism is used to separate it from the rest of Europe. The Fallen race uses the weaknesses inherent to every nation to spread both division and confusion, while Western Civilization devours Euro-Siberia in its battle to destroy Christianity and true European identity.

The immaturity of Euro-Siberian civilization is a crucial weakness that the Fallen race exploits in their favor, as any young and therefore immature civilization, is characterized by inner division. The Fallen ones choose the way that appears to be the most devastating strategy to manipulate thinking in a given nation, pretending to separate it from the forces emanating from a common and natural civilization that is not bounded by political borders but only by spiritual struggle. While the authentic will of peoples being poisoned by cultural and political propaganda is kept away, a manifested will is imposed by the Fallen race in order that peoples do not act in a way in which their real needs are safeguarded. When economic, cultural, and military coalitions are formed, their only objective is to subjugate a given enemy even if that requires entire nations to be used as mere pawns and destroyed after the real objectives had been achieved.

The sentiments of entire peoples will be aimed towards the destruction of countries such as Russia or India after years and years of manipulation which are the result of historical processes whose duration goes much beyond a single life span. The offensive attitudes in public opinion against Russia or India were cultivated after many decades of propaganda, ideological and religious indoctrination, and acts of hostility being carefully prepared in order to incite hatred and ensuing confrontation. When we realize that all of the above is being conducted in the framework of a long-lasting spiritual war, then we finally understand why certain acts of hostility and confrontation can last many decades and even centuries. Two irreconcilable spiritual races are fighting for World domination and their projects could not be completed in a single life span, not even in a century, but required thousands and thousands of years of conscious and unconscious planning to build totally contrasting World orders. NATO could not have existed if a long-lasting historical process developing against Russia was not already there, a process that saw how the Roman Catholic Church and former European superpowers all tried to destroy Russia and its predominant religion but eventually failed.

Sooner or later the spiritual war taking place in the World will reach a final climax in Europe, and the Fallen race will not stop in his attempt to destroy Russia and what remains of Euro-Siberian civilization until a decisive hour of confrontation brings the destruction of the Liberal behemoth. To destroy it, the Russian state will have to overcome its main weakness, which is its tendency towards looking exclusively inwards and forgetting its roots in the rest of the European continent. Shared roots imply a shared destiny, and only with the destruction of those roots and the ties which they generate, it can be possible to finally break the spine of Russia and the soul of Europe together with it.

Two giant blows are aimed against Europe, the first being of course the trend towards economic and cultural liberalization, which requires the destruction of the genuine ethnic and spiritual elements. But we cannot ignore the other giant blow, which is the use of those same genuine ethnic and spiritual elements against themselves. That happens because those elements are kept in an immature condition in which they are unable to recognize Euro-Siberia as a single living entity and not just a collection of separated nations, ideologies and languages all destined to remain in permanent conflict and agitation. The entire process of globalization required each of the cultural and spiritual elements preceding it were acting as their own gravediggers. Global elites were able to exploit a gap between the slow pace at which the natural evolution of social systems occurs, and the great speed at which technological and geopolitical change takes place. Because cultures are not given enough time to develop their natural immune system against the destructive elements always existing in mankind, they cannot remain healthy because cultures and states always suffer from some major weakness which can only be amended after much time of social evolution.

The human psyche and institutions, just as a natural organism, always must adapt to a hostile environment, and if the environment changes in a drastic way without civilizations being able to adapt, then the inevitable result is what should be called "cultural fossilization", which is the gradual death of genuine cultures and their replacement with artificial entities as those of liberalism and also substitution by natural elements but of foreign origin.

In nature, when a plant or animal dies, their hard body parts also dissolve over time, while the sediment surrounding those parts hardens and leaves a mold of the original structures. That is how fossilization occurs, as fossils are not the original bones or other hard parts of organisms who died a long time ago, but only molds formed by the sediment surrounding them. When cultures and civilizations start to die, the same happens to them, as their original structures rot away and are replaced by cultural sediment whose spiritual pathogens were stronger than the fossilized victims. The pathogens in that sediments are, of course, what I call the Fallen race, while the Righteous spiritual race is in the vital task of becoming strong enough to avoid getting sickened by a combination of spiritual parasites and a lack of strong cultural and institutional elements.

Inner unity is a key element when building the required strength, and that unity is one of the elements which only the maturation of a given civilization can provide after decades of clashes based on national, religious, and political disagreements. It is impossible to condemn entire social classes and nations and thus spark conflict and distrust between them and suddenly put an end to that situation by an act of magic, but rather many years will be required before conflicts between essential social groups and nations finally are put aside and replaced by a common sense of unity towards a common enemy. But at least, the first step towards unity can be achieved in a sudden way, and that is destroying artificial structures tasked with preventing the natural process of cultural and political unification for Euro-Siberia. Those artificial structures, now consisting of NATO, the European Union, and the Vatican all are sediment full of pathogens ready to complete the killing and fossilization of their victims. As we cannot pretend to suddenly change the attitudes in each country, we must focus on a strategy to destroy that political, cultural, and spiritual sediment in which they are trapped.

The aforementioned does not imply that attempts toward awakening the consciousnesses in each of those countries should not be carried out, but rather is a recognition that those attempts only can be effective when the artificial structures governing Europe are destroyed before it is too late. Only then all European countries will move in a common path towards the survival and development of their common civilization, with all patriotic and cultural passions being aimed in the correct direction. The parasites that were dragged to the surface by the historical trends of liberalism and its allies are already exposed, and that is helpful in the struggle to defeat them, as their own criminal behavior is the best proof of their real intentions and their real identity. As the immune system of a civilization becomes able to recognize the pathogens and finally is able to fight them, historical trends are the basis for developing the required doses of resistance and self-awareness. Peoples become much more sensitive towards the attitudes of destructive agents and the time and conditions which favor their proliferation are quickly curtailed. Every battle for freedom leads to a stronger immune system, which in turn is able to overcome eventual struggles and thus always becomes stronger as long as its spirit remains pure.

During the Cold War, a general confusion in ideological ideas caused the leadership and public opinion east and west of the Iron Curtain to almost committing a complete suicide. While the inability to create a real European foreign policy not only continued after the Cold War but worsened, at least the consciousness of political and cultural circles inside

Russia and individual European nations is no longer trapped under the spell of Marxism and anti-Marxism and also started to become free of the false hopes of European unity without Russia and the equally false hopes of Russian unity without Europe. Despite the military, economic and cultural conquest of Europe by foreign superpowers and their agents has been almost completed, it is not safeguarded at all and therefore remains vulnerable to a counterattack. One of the reasons for this vulnerability is that the same artificial structures created to subjugate Europe are weak without the hand of their foreign protectors. The weakness of those structures lies in the very nature of their purpose as mere caretakers for foreign superpowers which want a weak and divided Europe, and as caretakers of the Fallen race, which is unable to build a civilization by itself but only can be a host in structures already established by others, and which start to decay as soon as the true founders are not in control anymore.

PART III:
EXECUTION OF
AN EURO-SIBERIAN DOCTRINE

NAVAL STRATEGY AND ITS CONSEQUENCES

RUSSIA'S NAVAL MUSCLE

As mentioned in previous chapters, Europe cannot overcome its chains without Russia, due to a combination of military, economic, and cultural structures engendered with the purpose of keeping Euro-Siberia subjugated. The old antagonism between Russia and the rest of Europe, as well as old rivalries between individual European states, will be always revived by artificial structures tasked with preventing Euro-Siberian unification. With such structures, liberal destructive tendencies will be in a position to give the final blow against Europe and Christianity, a final blow that requires Russia's isolation for its gradual economic and cultural asphyxiation.

But Russia possesses a weapon which is not much talked about: its naval forces. They are a crucial element in Russia's defense not only because of their present tactical potential as defenders of Russia's maritime zones and coasts, together with their role as deliverers of strategic nuclear weapons but also because of their strategic potential in a future in which the United States will be no longer the protector of NATO Europe, because (as already explained in this book) the United States is a country scheduled for dissolution due to its growing inability to maintain a unipolar World order. Globalist elites vitally need to put a thalassocratic China as the new center for the liberal system, and because of the inevitable alliance between NATO and a thalassocratic China as its new protector, Russia must act in the short time span between the US. demise as a superpower and the consummation of the alliance between China and

NATO, an alliance whose reasons were explained in great detail in this book and therefore do not need further explanation here.

Russia still possesses a decent force of submarines, in addition to surface fleets which despite the lack of a powerful group of aircraft carriers or warm ports with direct access to the oceans, still are able to conduct major regional operations. All of Russia's navy is now under a major project of modernization and expansion which now is being conducted by President Vladimir Putin. This project is crucial not only for Russia but also for mankind's future, and most people in patriotic circles, including Eurasian circles, are just unable to see that while quarrels over some chunks of Ukraine and Georgia are keeping public opinion distracted, Russia's naval muscle is on the rise because surely Putin and his team are already aware of why naval strengthening for the future is much more important than conducting a border restoration policy in the present. Currently, international conditions are not laid for that restoration policy as yet, with Russia's reunification requiring Euro-Siberian political and cultural unification as a whole.

Already in 2020, Putin revealed his plan to expand Russia's navy with 40 more vessels (RBC "Society" 2020) all of which is scheduled to happen alongside a major modernization process for Russia's navy, which will get hypersonic weapons to boost its combat capabilities, together with all sort of new technological capabilities as the Status-6 nuclear powered and nuclear-armed submarine drones. The crucial importance of these current developments in Russian military thought wasn't correctly asserted, because it is not just a technical process being underway, but also a major change from the traditional Russian military strategy which was focused almost entirely on its land army and nuclear dissuasion. First of all, this is because the policy of having large land forces eventually failed to protect both the Czarist Empire and the Soviet Union from collapse. During the Cold War, everyone could see how even immense land forces proved useless against the gradual economic and cultural asphyxiation that NATO exercised to break the will of the Soviet leadership and its people, which renounced to their own project of civilization in exchange for the western one.

European balance of power can be radically changed in Russia's favor if the Russian Navy hinders the development of world trade in a way in which all of the European parts of NATO will see themselves trapped by Russia's submarines and surface vessels in the sea, and by Russia's land forces in Europe's eastern flank, all supported by the always dissuasive threat of large stockpiles of tactical and strategic nuclear weapons, and the new hypersonic missiles and nuclear submarines drones. Besides the strategic factor consisting in those warheads being able to reach NATO's major urban and military centers, there is a tactical factor which lays in having a large stockpile of tactical nuclear weapons ready to wipe out European navies and their bases if they lack the current support of the United States. Dissuasion from nuclear, hypersonic, and unmanned weapons, combined with a naval blockade against NATO in Europe will necessarily force the civil and military leaderships in Europe to use whatever rationality remains with them and choose from two completely different outcomes. The first outcome implies Euro-Siberian political and cultural unification which not only Russia will enjoy but also all of the European nations as a whole. The second outcome is the nuclear destruction of human civilization. Making the correct decision will be rather easy considering the aforementioned.

However, if Russia does not have enough political strength to set this audacious plan into motion when the right time finally comes, then not just Russia, but all the planet will face the worst outcome possible: an eventual extinction of all civilizations and an uninhabitable Earth rendered as the impending consequences of a reckless cultural and economic system which is incompatible with mankind's survival. We have reached such a point that even in the unlikely case of NATO European leaderships being stupid enough to allow total thermonuclear destruction, that would be preferable to an outcome in which all of mankind starts to gradually starve and then boil as miserable rats, with a constant depredation of the Earth's resources and climate change being the wake-up call to all which still have at least half a brain working in their heads and do not seriously think that recent fires in the Amazon rain-forest, Australia and the US. West Coast were caused by satellites or just people running with matches.

Without the support of the United States, the European part of NATO would not enjoy the network of US. forces from all the long Atlantic and Mediterranean coasts, nor the support of the US. Forces stationed across other regions of the globe. The navies of European countries like Germany, France, and England will be confined to a smaller zone of water defending a much smaller area of land. The small territory of European countries as Germany, France or England and their closer proximity to Russia put them under enormous threat if they desire a direct military confrontation. The threat currently faced by the vast territories of the United States, Russia, or China is already great due to the development of nuclear and missile technology, but the threat faced by smaller countries is much greater regardless if they are small nuclear powers like France and the United Kingdom.

All of the aforementioned makes clear that in this age in which nuclear weapons, hypersonic missiles, and unmanned nuclear submarines are all available to Russia, a naval blockade against NATO in Europe (which includes Turkey's Istanbul) would have a totally different outcome in comparison to the submarine campaigns waged by Germany against Britain during both World Wars. The military hegemony of Russia in a Europe no longer under control from the United States would be in part a consequence of historical political dispositions which the thalassocratic influence of North America exercised in its European puppets, resulting in a divided and powerless Europe which depends on the United States as all protectorates do.

Just like the Soviet naval activities in the past, the current Russian presence in the seas does not require of a navy capable of conducting operations all across the globe, but only fleets capable of conducting regional operations which can isolate the European part of NATO without any necessity for large fleets of aircraft carriers and neither amphibious landings. Aircraft carriers and amphibious landings are only useful for countries that want to subjugate weaker powers from far away regions, but on a continental scale, which is completely different from the global scale all which is required is blockade and dissuasion. The tactical goals in such a situation have nothing to do with conducting immediate air attacks and landings, but with economic and psychological attrition from a blockade. If European countries belonging to NATO want to use their aircraft carriers against Russia, those aircraft carriers will be easy targets to a rain of the most modern missiles and unmanned weapons, thus the balance of power would not change at all just because Europe possesses some aircraft carriers of their own capable of delivering modern aircraft.

The reason why Russia's Navy still has the intention of maintaining at least a single aircraft carrier as with the Admiral Kuznetsov is not conducting operations against NATO or any major power, but just conducting air attacks against small military powers like terrorist associations and other opponents with low technology. Aircraft carriers and amphibious landings, like the trenches of France before 1940, became the basis of what Charles de Gaulle, if bring back to life, could regard as a new "Maginot Mentality", a term which refers to military plannings stuck in the strategies of past wars while creating a false notion of defensive security.

A clear continental policy must be achieved all across Europe if Russia and Euro-Siberian civilization are to survive. In the event of a Russian naval blockade, there are eight non-negotiable points that Russia should demand the rest of Europe.

1) Dissolution of NATO and its headquarters all across the European region and Turkey.

2) Dissolution of the European Union and confiscation of its currency, which will form the basis of a common currency for the entire Euro-Siberian region.

3) Surrendering to Russia of all strategic and tactical nuclear weapons in possession by other European countries and withdrawal of all nukes which third parties could still store in NATO Europe and Turkey.

4) Obligation to delegate all tasks of foreign policy to a supranational organization uniting all of Euro-Siberia under a common foreign policy, to regulate the relationships between its individual states and also with Euro-Siberia as a whole in relation to the rest of the World.

5) Obligation from each constituent State to contribute with a supranational fund having exclusive authority to finance businesses in Euro-Siberia. It will be composed of public capital obtained from sinking funds mandated on each business and that capital should not leave Euro-Siberian boundaries.

6) The activities of the Roman Catholic Church must be suspended under charges of being a criminal organization, and all its properties, including temples, must be requisitioned by the Russian Orthodox Church.

7) The Gregorian calendar imposed by the Roman Catholic Church must be dropped out and forbidden for usage in all public organizations and mass media, being replaced by a new calendar for all of Euro-Siberia.

8) The new Euro-Siberian supranational entity must be forced to establish separate diplomatic relationships with the Russian Orthodox Church.

Only by presenting and achieving demands which will change the nature of human civilization as a whole is that the work of centuries will be finally come to its completion, by asserting what should be done without delay or hastiness. If no one in Russia's leadership is capable of doing the aforementioned under any circumstances, then it must be considered that they joined the liberal side and are marching towards a bottomless pit. Additional objections to such a bold plan will also arise from Cold War mentality in Russia, which already proved itself unable of achieving victory, although this does not prevent the discrete circle of obsolete Marxists from howling toward their red moon.

The successful conduction of a continental policy aimed towards the rest of Europe is the only way in which Russia exercised a decisive influence over world history, and the same situation will be still there in the future. It is not as much a battle between Russia and the future, but a battle between Russia and its own past. As Russia must regain the spirit which was lost in the straits of Tsushima more than a century ago, it must battle against its own past in order to vindicate Peter the Great's founding of the modern Russian navy in 1696, which is also vindicating his founding of the Russian Empire only 25 years later. Russia saw how the Soviet army dissolved and its weapons slowly rusted in their storing sites, ending their existence in shameful abandonment because they proved unable to defend the Soviet Union from a war of economic and cultural attrition. If the Soviet Union had used all the enormous resources it wasted in its large land army to strengthen the Navy instead, the fateful repercussions of the Cold War defeat would at least be partially justified, as an independent Russian State would not have any fears regarding the future projection of its power over the waters surrounding Europe.

NAVAL AND DIPLOMATIC STRATEGY IN A FUTURE BIPOLAR WORLD

In the event of its successful political unification, Euro-Siberia must adopt a very careful naval and diplomatic strategy towards the People's Republic of China. In a future scenario in which a bipolar World as the one existing during the Cold War is once again a reality, all possible measures to avoid any potential danger must be undertaken and under no circumstances Euro-Siberia should underestimate the capabilities of a future China which would become the superpower ruling over the waves. In such a scenario, the new Euro-Siberian superpower must not fall into the same mistakes committed by Imperial Germany in the time of its rivalry with the British Empire prior to 1914, which eventually lead to Germany's gradual defeat in the First World War.

Imperial Germany serves as a perfect example of what a land superpower should not do if faced by a massive superpower ruling the seas and having control over world trade between continents. While Germany's strength was mostly based on its land army and in economic and technological influence over continental Europe, nevertheless Germany embarked on a naval arms race with the British Empire, an event with forced Britain to eventually intervene against Germany. What otherwise should have been a German victory was turned into a prolonged war that eventually put Germany to its knees by the severe impact of a prolonged naval blockade sparking hunger and mass rebellions. By provoking the British Empire with an attempt to build a powerful German navy, all which Germany did was diverting much-needed resources towards its navy and colonies instead of directing them towards the consolidation of its land army and its domestic economy, all of which would have prevented Britain's intervention in the first place, and even if the war with Britain had occurred anyway, the resources which Germany wasted in its naval arms race could have made a decisive difference if they were placed on the already powerful German land army and Germany's industrial domestic economy.

If Euro-Siberia embarks on a naval arms race against China, the possibility of a direct military conflict will escalate because China would feel its interests under a mortal threat by a superpower already strong in the land. The People's Republic of China, due to geographic and demographic reasons, will depend much more on resources and trade provided from overseas than an autarchic Euro-Siberia which is already full of resources in its own bast territory. While currently, Russia must focus itself in the strengthening of its Navy to force Euro-Siberian unification, the opposite path should be undertaken by Euro-Siberia once unification is achieved, as the focus should be strengthening its position as a power based on land instead of wasting resources in a naval arms race whose aggressive nature will force China to act in some way or another, increasing tensions and potentially resulting in mankind's downfall into nuclear Armageddon.

Instead of an aggressive policy based on a naval arms race as the one which Imperial Germany undertook against Britain, the new Euro-Siberian superpower must embark immediately on a containment policy against China, as the one which the United States and its allies successfully carried out against the Soviet Union. Such a future containment policy would imply a World divided into zones of influence in which each superpower will have almost exclusive authority, a scenario which already took place when the United States and the Soviet Union agreed their respective zones of influence and successfully avoided direct military confrontation. We can expect India, Central Asia, all of the Caucasus, Algeria, Syria, and Vietnam to remain inside Euro-Siberia's zone of influence, as the ties which those regions have with Russia will be even stronger with a unified Euro-Siberia, due to strategic reasons which place those states under direct threat by China and its allies, and in the case of Central Asia, the Caucasus and Algeria, a combination of geographical proximity to Euro-Siberia and their historical military and economic ties. Regarding Vietnam, it would serve as a key base in order to apply a successful policy of containment against China, as Vietnam is a long-term ally of Russia while remaining a historic enemy of China.

By contrast, we can expect the rest of Asia, together with Africa, North and South America, and also Oceania to fall into the Chinese zone of influence, as the economic and naval power of China will be able to successfully safeguard Chinese economic and military interests in those regions of the World. In that way, the entire planet will be divided once more between the zones of influence of a new tellurocratic superpower, and those of a thalassocratic superpower which will enjoy of enough time to build a potent navy and a strong economy but will remain dependent on resources and trade which can only be obtained from overseas in a situation mirroring that of Great Britain and its former Empire.

For China, the dominance of the seas will be just as important for its survival as the dominance of the land for Euro-Siberia. Both superpowers will be quickly aware of that and will protect their respective dominance of those different realms because doing the contrary would imply subjugation and destruction by the adversary. Also, just as stupid as it will be from Euro-Siberia's part to embark in an aggressive Naval arms race which will push the World into constant distress and potential nuclear war, it will be equally stupid from China's part to embark on a project aimed at threatening Euro-Siberia with a potent land army stationed both across China and its allies, because the intention of pursuing an arms race based on strengthening China's land armies rather than its Navy will also put the World under constant tension and danger of direct military confrontation between superpowers, and will also imply a waste of China's resources because that country only needs to rule over the waves and having nuclear and conventional forces only aimed at deterrence rather than aggression. As a historic example regarding a similar situation, the British Empire only desired to keep a small land force primarily tasked with keeping order and control in colonies, and initially, when the First World War started in 1914, all which Britain sent to Europe was a small expeditionary force of a hundred thousand men. Britain finally created a large army of its own only by the end of 1915 at the initiative of Horatio Herbert Kitchener, then Britain's Secretary of State for War (Simkins 2007).

While Euro-Siberia will need to develop a policy of contention towards its Chinese rival, in the same way, China will enforce a policy of contention against Euro-Siberia. In such an international situation, both superpowers will embark on an ideological, cultural, and economic war of attrition resembling that between the United States and the former

Soviet Union, and probably even a second space race to demonstrate technological and cultural abilities. The result of such a war of attrition will ultimately decide mankind's future and show who is on the correct side of history. If Euro-Siberia and China want to go into the future, supremacy over the land by one side and supremacy on the seas by the another can lead to a competence aimed at supremacy in outer space, and the aforementioned also must be regulated by both sides to avoid a militarization of outer space which will result equally dangerous for both sides. Such a competence in outer space will be instrumental to mankind's further development, including the creation of a future World order in which the Final Kingdom completed its elevation with complete victory over the forces of the Fallen race.

Instead of another unipolar World, the result of such a total victory will be a World order unprecedented in mankind's history, one which I call as "World beyond the World", in which God's mankind will reach the realms of a higher cosmic existence at the starry Garden of Eden provided by the Almighty. We will be not bounded by the limited experiences of our current Earthly prison, with authentic will finally bearing its greatest blessings.

But before such a condition for mankind is reached, the more China strengthens its dominance over the seas and its economic power in general, the more will harden its political and economic conditions over countries falling under China's zone of influence. This will be a continuation of the policy of gradual economic and cultural conquest of the World which the United States and the British Empire started before. This strategy for the gradual conquest of the World by the use of soft power (economic and cultural influence) works much better than the mere use of hard military power. Naturally, the aforementioned is because political and cultural institutions of states being conditioned by soft power will become unable of true sovereignty without the necessity by controlling powers for placing troops and civil administrators as Europe did with its colonies. The strategy of World conquest through soft power was already started by Britain but combined with the use of much military action and direct control in colonies. The United States perfected that strategy with its own soft power being exercised all over the Earth. Britain's strategy was perfected by its North American successor because unlike Britain the United States did not require keeping colonies under direct and permanent control.

The problem was that like Britain and France before, the United States required the almost constant use of its military might in a direct way. Despite it is not as essential as when keeping colonies under direct and permanent control, aligning states even under indirect control required the use of almost constant military aggression over key strategic points. Such actions need employing state of the art technology and expensive military training and maintenance. When Britain and France were trying to use their modern and well trained military forces to subjugate colonies, their engagements do not always prove successful, as always happens in War. In the same way, direct military engagements carried by the United States against smaller powers did not always prove successful or worthy of the cost... The Vietnam War and the Iraq War serve as the chief examples widely known to public opinion, but we can also mention the United States' 1982 intervention in Lebanon as one of the better examples of how direct military engagements carried against much smaller powers can have disastrous consequences. Because of the aforementioned, it can be said that the United States was unable to reach the final perfection of a strategy for gradual conquest by use of soft power, inasmuch as direct military engagements were required almost constantly.

We can expect the People's Republic of China to be the one superpower finally able to reach the final perfection of a soft power strategy, and even in the present, we can appreciate China's mastery on that strategy when analyzing the economic, cultural, and diplomatic ties between China and countries as far away as Australia. For the past decade, China has been Australia's largest trading partner and now accounts for 32.6% of its exports (BBC News 2020). As another example of Chinese soft power, there is the so-called "Bamboo Network": a connection between businesses operated by the Overseas Chinese community in Southeast Asia. That community already is controlling trillions in cash or liquid assets in the region and use that considerable amount of wealth to stimulate China's growing economy, with overseas Chinese also representing the biggest direct investors in Mainland China (Drucker 2006). We have countless examples of China being able to exercise its control towards the rest of the World only by using soft power, and in such a framework, the

Chinese Navy will act to protect economic and political interests overseas, with direct military aggression being almost entirely supplanted by Naval and Nuclear dissuasion only tasked with safekeeping a massive use of soft power. The only exceptions could be Taiwan and smaller insular conflicts, which wouldn't prove fatal to China's thalassocratic power.

In today's Africa, the People's Republic of China follows in the footsteps of former European empires. China has become the new central player in Africa's urbanization push, with a large percentage of its infrastructure initiatives being carried out by Chinese companies and/or backed by Chinese funding. If China directs and finances the construction of for example its gigantic dams all across the river Nile, that is certainly not an act of good willingness aimed towards improving the lives of poor Egyptian and Ethiopian communities, but rather to monopolize African resources. Since 2011, China has been the leading player in Africa's infrastructure boom, achieving by now a 40% share that has continued to rise while Europe shares declined from 44% to 34%, and US shares fell from 24% to just 6.7%, and those rapid drops will continue. Over a third of China's oil and 20% of its cotton comes from Africa, and in addition, the African continent has massive stocks of manganese, an essential ingredient for steel production, together with massive stocks of cobalt, coltan, and carbonatites, all basic raw material needed in modern technological equipment. (Shepard 2019).

If China is bringing to Africa the railroads and urbanization which the former European powers could not complete, that is not to make Africans happy and prosperous, but just in order that China can make better use of the continent and strengthen its economic and political domination over it. The same fate is being now underway for Latin America, and similar domination by soft power will be possible in North America once the elites running the United States finally dissolve their own country, as it is turning more and more into a massive problem for even themselves just as the Soviet Union became a massive problem for the ones in charge of it.

No cultural or civic associations will be established by China to improve the cultural and spiritual life of states under its zones of influence. When subjugating nations, the European empires of the past and now NATO discovered a long time ago that improving the cultural and spiritual life of subjugated regions only gives them weapons to strife for true sovereignty, and China is very aware of that. This will be in sharp contrast with the policies which a united Euro-Siberian superpower must carry out to preserve a future political and cultural unity which is vital for both sovereignty and the survival of its genuine civilization. While in such a scenario common policies for the spiritual, political, and cultural strengthening of Euro-Siberia will be determined by its own material resources, the domestic policies of the People's Republic of China will be determined by the material resources of others, and therefore the liberal mentality which is characterized by predatory lust will be able to grow even farther in China. Ideas such as preserving civilizations, even China's own genuine civilization are incompatible with ideas needed to plunder the World of its resources by cultural and economic warfare, as the United States and Rome's Church demonstrated.

In contrast, both Imperial Russia and the Soviet Union joined their territorial expansion in the east and west with a desire to spread Russian culture and Russian ethnicity to promote a basis for cultural and political unification and of course material and spiritual development. Russification during the time of the Czars, and also Russification as part of Sovietization were not just projects for cultural assimilation of non-Russian peoples, but also a widespread attempt at building and uniting a project of civilization with the Russian ethnicity as the drivers of that historical process. Russia's desire to expand its culture and ethnicity towards other regions is a result of its own nature as a tellurocratic power, as all powers based on land need the cultural and political unification of that land to prevent chaos and rebellion.

In contrast, thalassocratic powers as the former British Empire, the United States in the present and China in the future all do not need the cultural and political unification of subjugated regions overseas, on the contrary, their division and the eventual destruction of their original culture is essential to keep them controlled. The aforementioned is the most important difference between tellurocratic and thalassocratic powers as already explained by Dugin's colossal contribution in that aspect. Despite I am in disagree with Dugin's Eurasian approach and instead it is Euro-Siberia's approach which seems to me as the most promising doctrine for the future, the basic distinction between tellurocratic and thalassocratic civilizations must be regarded as a fundamental theoretical basis for explaining the World's geopolitics. But the Euro-Siberian paradigm and not the Eurasian one is the only way in which such a fundamental theoretical basis can be successfully applied in future practice, together with the successful practice of the Fourth Political Theory, and hopefully, in its final horizon which I decided to call as "Normativism."

As Russia's historical trend was always aimed at political and cultural unification whose basis is the inherent needs of a tellurocratic superpower, then there is yet another reason for believing there is no country more suitable than Russia for turning Euro-Siberian unification in a reality and not just a pipe dream. While other former European superpowers sought their expansion by acquiring overseas colonies, Imperial Russia and the Soviet Union sought their expansion by acquiring unity for themselves while trying to expand their respective projects of civilization rather than just trying to plunder regions beyond the seas. Just as ancient Rome once did in Europe and other regions, or as the ancient Han did in China, the authentic will of a given tellurocratic ethnicity uses its regional hegemony for uniting and maturing its own civilization by political and cultural expansion. In contrast, the manifested will which always characterizes thalassocratic powers will always put a given ethnicity to work not for strengthening its own civilization but to eventually destroy it together with the civilizations of other peoples, even if such ethnicity was previously a tellurocratic power, as the ancient Han people or medieval Englishmen once were before their mentality was pushed towards ruling the waves after a period of expansion whose demographic and geographical characteristics implied dependence towards overseas trade and the possibility of easy access to the waters covering 70% percent of our planet.

General political objectives will slowly shape the mentality of their respective countries as even common people would consciously and unconsciously recognize the basic line in which the foreign policy of their countries went along. Thus, the psychological consequences of different political objectives in divergent societies will widen the gap between thalassocratic and tellurocratic mentality, with two very different projects of civilization once again dividing the World, and once again not just in economic and military matters, but also in all cultural and ideological realms.

INDIA AND CENTRAL ASIA

INDIA AS AN ALLY

Russia now, and a united Euro-Siberia in the future, will infinitely gain if they keep India as a key ally due to a combination of strategic, cultural, and political reasons. As already mentioned in an earlier chapter, India is a State which still encompasses a genuine ancient civilization of its own making, whose thousands of years of existence developed an immune system against the pathogens currently destroying all of the World's cultures with their liberal project. But also, in India, there are many strategic reasons which make it a key ally for both Russia and Euro-Siberia to constitute a massive block opposed to thalassocratic interests and their liberal ideology, promoted by NATO and the People's Republic of China as both entities were created for the same goal and by the same strategist, with the intention of subjugating Russia and therefore allowing liberalism and the Fallen race to complete their conquest of the World.

Unfortunately, not everybody realizes the indispensability of India as the most important ally for a tellurocratic power like Russia or a future Euro-Siberian superpower. What is fortunate is that the time of these fools already came to an end in Russia's strategic thinking, as liberal elements in Russia and also certain director of the "International Eurasian Movement" are only consonant with the long-term goals of the globalist elites and their stooges, including so-called Russian patriots who are against the only World power that along with Russia still possess elements of traditionalism and nationalism in their domestic and foreign policies... While all authentic traditionalist minded patriots would instantly recognize the importance of strengthening an alliance with India, some people behind the idea of Multipolarity as an end in itself rather than a means to an end are in a conscious rather than unconscious alliance with globalism and its project of restructuring the unipolar world order, which China can keep in its tracks much more efficiently than the United States could.

Due to its position as a dagger close to China, its nationalistic orientation, and the nature of its civilization, India remains a golden opportunity in terms of opposing the thalassocratic project for unipolar subjugation. To India, such as with Russia now, its national interests are the ones driving India's fate, and not just an evil plan for subjugating the World under the liberal and globalist guidelines of the Fallen race parasite. That is even more important since the great moment when current Prime Minister Narendra Modi and his nationalist movement, the Bharatiya Janata Party won India's general elections in 2014. Even if the elements of liberal ideology and the spiritual pathogens behind it are desperately trying their adaptation to the current conditions in India, the statements of liberal circles outside of India already had shown which is the attitude of globalists towards the Bharatiya Janata Party and towards the policies of Narendra Modi.

With Narendra Modi and its movement, India's nationalism and traditionalism were given a solid configuration. Therefore, the Indian People have won a crucial victory against its internal menaces embodied in India's own liberal circles and the so-called threatened Muslim minority. We must always remember that the fight against the global hegemony of the forces from darkness will be not only decided by Russia but also by India. Being already as of 2020 the third-largest economy of the World with a GDP of eleven trillion dollars (PPP), and being in possession of its own arsenal of nuclear weapons together with modernized ground, air, and naval forces, the almost defenseless India which Gandhi saw seventy years ago is a lot different to today's India, and that difference will increase in the future once India's economic and military strength continues on the rise.

India is the sole World power whose strategic interests do not contradict with Russia's interests both in the short and long run, and that is kept as a constant reality since the times of the Soviet Union, with India's diplomatic ties with Russia being in part a legacy of the long-lasting alliance between India and the former Soviet colossus, both united in their common goal of keeping China and its Pakistani ally under check.

India even became ideologically influenced by the Soviet Union, to such an extent that the socialist policies of India's economy only could be partially dismantled after the Soviet Union collapsed (Mazumdar 2012). That is remarkable considering India's internal realm wasn't under direct military control from the Soviet Union but rather indirect control.

At the time when the Soviet Union still existed, China's anti-Russian attitude was explicit and also vice-versa. Now it is only an implicit attitude which will become explicit again, and when that happens, an alliance with India will become as strong as in the times of the Soviet Union because the goal of keeping China and its Pakistan puppet will once again become an explicit necessity not only from India's part but also from the part of Russia, and also for Euro-Siberia as a whole when NATO is finally destroyed. India's domestic and foreign policy was determined by India's own interests since the very day that the country became independent from the British Empire, and that is an important factor that explains why India's alliance with the Soviet Union was possible and why that alliance still exists with the Russia of today. Despite the current Indo-Russian ties are not as strong as during the Cold War, it is noteworthy how in 2017 India joined (as a full member) the Shanghai Cooperation Organization (Russia being one of its full members) even despite that organization is also integrated by India's arch-enemies, namely Pakistan and China. The fact that India incurred in such a risky move only to keep its alliance with Russia is a crystal clear demonstration of India's determination to remain on Russia's side as a matter of vital national security besides historic sympathy. Russia still is providing India with most of its military equipment, as between 2013 and 2018 Russia accounted for 62% of arms sales to India, and several major joint military programs link the two countries, as well as the selling of state of the art Russian technologies, including the lethal S-400 missile system to which western technology is unprepared as yet (Pandit 2019).

India is aware it will become easily surrounded by a powerful China with a future navy which will master the seas, and also by Pakistan's forces in close cooperation with China, and all of the above is worsened by the fact that Pakistan, China, and India are all nuclear states. Not only India is currently surrounded by the military and economic threat of Pakistan and China, but that threat will grow each year as both the People's Republic of China and Pakistan strengthen their economies and modernize their armies, including their navies. In addition, China is already in an initiative towards constructing overseas military bases, most notably its African base at Djibouti, and that tendency will continue in a strategy to gradually isolate India. Having all that in mind, India's fears towards the China-Pakistan alliance will grow more and more and so their necessity for close ties with Russia and of course with a united Euro-Siberia.

Despite a mutual sympathy between Russia and India exist as a legacy of the foreign policy of the Soviet Union, the present close ties, like those of the Cold War, also arise of clear strategic threats to India and to Russia as well, as the nature of such a threat will increase not only for India but also for Russia, which also will face a lot of danger in a future World in which China has become much stronger and menacing than today. In addition to economic and military threats, both India and Russia are resisting a cultural and ideological threat. India's vision of remaining as a sovereign state governed by ideas of traditionalism and nationalism cannot survive if India becomes like an island in the sea of decrepit liberal countries and hostile Muslim states, and neither Russia's own vision of keeping its own sovereignty and traditionalism will survive if remaining as an island in the World. Either the ideological ideas of India and Russia are able to form a block for political, economic, and cultural sovereignty, or both states will succumb sooner or later to the ideas of a World which is going in a direction contrary to theirs.

Both Russian and Indian governing ideologies will always remain in danger of being completely replaced by the liberal ideas of the Fallen race and also both states will face the growing threat of Islamic fanaticism as embodied by entire states as Pakistan or by terrorist groups, which already proved as cultural and military weapons at the service of liberal globalism as is happening all over the Middle East, and Libya now, and as it happened in southern Russia during the Chechen wars. Such a situation only can be prevented if Russia is in possession of the political will to finally give an eternal mark in the form of complete restoration for the genuine culture within itself and the rest of the Euro-Siberian cultural and geographical space. But even such a colossal cultural and political undertaking by Russia will be under much threat not only from the inside but also from outside, especially if a clear zone of influence is unprotected against Chinese expansion and also Muslim extremism, which will play in China's favor just as it is currently playing in NATO's favor.

In this future zone of influence, only an India permeated by traditionalist and nationalist values as the ones being implemented by Prime Minister Modi and his party will prove itself as a reliable ally on a permanent basis, as the danger of cultural infiltration by liberalism will be eliminated and thus the danger of India becoming another focus of infection for further expansion of the liberal disease. In the event that India acquires a weak government unable to protect its genuine civilization and its sovereignty, then Russia's enemies, which are the enemies of all Righteous mankind will take advantage and finally use India for their own benefit if that state becomes totally subjugated again as it was in the era of British colonialism, but this time with Chinese and Muslim masters. Just as the forces which determine the globalist agenda today do not just want Russia to remain isolated, but in addition do not want a Russia at all, the same mentality is applied against India, with their enemies longing for the destruction of that State and its civilization before it can become a problem too great for them.

As I already emphasized in earlier chapters of this work, a true alliance between countries, in contrast to a mere partnership always includes key ideological elements. An alliance between India and Russia will become impossible if Russia becomes swallowed by liberalism leaving India ideologically isolated, but it also would become impossible if India is the one being swallowed by liberalism. Partnerships have as their goal peace and thus only can be temporary while frequently leading to terrible mistakes by the ones engaging in them. Alliances always maintain war as their ultimate goal, either in its military form or in its cultural and economic forms, and wars do not leave space for mistakes. Therefore, alliances are only concreted after their states are consciously aware of the vital necessity for permanent ties due to the long-lasting nature of ideologies guiding their footsteps. With Russia and India understanding their shared global mission as both civilizations and sovereign states, any small quarreling which could exist due to the current partnerships of those powers will completely disappear and a long-lasting alliance will strengthen itself in a quite natural way.

As no strategic areas could arise enmity between India and Russia, the understanding of mutual friendship will be easy as long as both States remain as proud and truly sovereign entities with genuine civilizations still protected by their natural immune systems. The more such immune systems are still in place protecting Russia and India from the liberal gangrene, the more both states will also acquire more power on the world stage, and thus they will regard their mutual alliance as more important and reliable inasmuch as both States are able to provide more effective assistance towards the other. In Russia's case, such developments require the defeat of domestic and foreign menaces in order that Russia is in the position of finally uniting Euro-Siberia in the same way as Prussia was able to reunite the small states which became the German Empire in 1871, a former World power with much greater influence than Prussia's regional influence in the past.

In India's case, its own development as a civilization will continue a very ancient and solid trend towards further unification between its various constituting territories and ethnic groups, and in that process, India will become even more conscious of itself as a single entity under foreign threat. By such a process India will become stronger not just in the economic and military aspects but also in the cultural one, as any separatist wishes will be met by a crushing impulse towards unshakable unity, even if that requires putting India's Muslim minority under constant check, and in that India is not different from China for example, whose treatment towards its own Muslim minority is not precisely cheerful.

Destruction of the World's genuine civilizations progresses more and more, as reckless liberalism and financial tyranny subjugates states and turns them into additional headquarters from which a coalition of enemies can be placed to destroy everything standing in the way of the Fallen race. Globalist elites offer unsuspecting peoples false hopes of economic prosperity and political freedom only to reveal the real face of their projects, which is the ugly usage of entire peoples and even entire civilizations as hostages in a plan for World conquest, a plan whose result will be first the destruction of all the leading elites of the Righteous spiritual race and its replacement with rule by the Fallen ones and finally the madness of those new rulers themselves, with all of mankind's future being destroyed as a consequence. As such a particular type of chaotic madness arises from the inferior spiritual and cultural nature of the sons of Lucifer, we can expect that in the event of finally becoming rid of their last remaining shackles they will bring back with them all the Hell which are capable of inflicting.

Many of those states which now do not wish the complete subjugation and destruction of Russia and India will face themselves with no other choice than to align with China after the zone of influence of that country is expanded and solidified in such a way that small or weak local powers will have no chance of escaping once they are trapped in the spider's web. The same goes for Russia or India if they allow themselves to fall into weakness and cowardice. God is never on the side of weaklings and cowards, and as a matter of fact, he wasn't even on the side of the last Byzantine Emperor, Constantine XI Palaiologos, once he chose the Roman-Catholic Church and its servants instead of his original faith and his original servants, only to be betrayed by Rome and killed in the final defense of Constantinople against the Ottomans. The rest of the world has no reason to fight for the protection which Russia and India would not provide for themselves, and even if they acquire a more adequate protection in the future, alliances with smaller states will only come from those who already proved faithful to Russia due to historical and geographical factors already present during the Cold War, when those smaller states were not given time to fall into the spider's web of other powers.

Any power that is not capable of finding those strong alliances which can allow the continuation of its struggle against other civilizations will merely build a small network of weak states like the disastrous Warsaw Pact, whose only result was endangering both the satellite governments in Eastern Europe and the Soviet Union with the danger of war with NATO. As the Warsaw Pact dragged the Soviet Union with it once communist governments across Eastern Europe were wiped out, therefore, weak alliances besides placing its members into constant danger also are under constant threat by a domino effect unleashed once their weakest members do no longer desire to continue in such coalitions, as they will not risk themselves only for the sake of controlling powers which had already proven themselves as selfish and cornered entities. The fact that India is still wanting to be part of an alliance with the Russian successor of a former superpower that ultimately betrayed the interests of its allies and of its own Soviet People alike is an additional indicator of India's loyalty when conducting relationships with Russia.

As already mentioned in this book, that loyalty is not only the consequence of sympathy, but a common recognition from India's and Russia's part regarding the strategic threats which faced the two countries already in their past, and continue in their present and will continue in their future. The future of India will always be affected by its situation in relation to the Indian Ocean and the land-based threat of China and Pakistan, and the aforementioned implies that Russia's competition with China over hegemony in Central Asia is also important for India as it cannot withstand the ring formed by China and Pakistan without a strong land-based ally, who is in control of strategic points in Central Asia while also bordering China and being relatively close to Pakistan, which are conditions being met by Russia alone.

Also, when NATO is finally destroyed, then most tactical and strategic nuclear arsenals under Russia's possession, as well as conventional forces will be focused on forming an umbrella protecting India as a potent dissuasion against the event of aggression from China's and Pakistan's naval, land and air forces. In the meanwhile, India will continue strengthening its military, economic and cultural forces, and therefore China and its allies will have to face a formidable threat on two fronts, one from the north (Euro-Siberian and Central Asian regions) and another in the South (India). That is how a policy of contention against China can be successfully put into place rather than engaging China in a potentially suicidal naval arms race. India's lack of raw resources in relation to its large population can be supplemented by the vast resources present in Russia, which according to some estimates is the place for 30% of all the Earth's resources (Korabik 1997).

And in the event of Euro-Siberian unification, the entire economic might of Euro-Siberia will also come in aid of India's expanding economy, a much-needed help as China will try to monopolize human and material resources under the Chinese zone of influence. In exchange, India will provide Russia and Euro-Siberia as a whole with its strategic alliance to contain Chinese expansion outside established zones of influence, and in addition, the enormous Indian population will provide for a large market to sell the immense reserves of Euro-Siberian raw materials and energetic resources, as well as key technologies. Otherwise, all of that will have to be exported to China strengthening the position of that State even more.

NATO explicitly, and China implicitly (until being an explicit attitude again) do not want a Russia at all, regardless if it is a powerful state or not, and in parallel, Pakistan and China are displaying a similar desire towards India. Whoever is in charge of NATO, China, and Pakistan in the future, regardless if they are representatives elected by free elections, a military dictatorship, or a one-party state, they will always desire the subjugation and destruction of India and Russia as long as the thalassocratic world order is not finally exiled from all parts of the planet, and finally replaced by the World order of a higher mankind. No other country will face a greater threat than India in a future scenario in which Chinese military and economic powers increase until achieving the complete conquest of the World by means of soft power, which would be a reality if when the United States fades away Russia is unable to reshape the World's geopolitics in a direction favorable to Euro-Siberian and Indian interests.

Because those interests are not really acknowledged in most of Russia's public opinion when mass media and political analysts assume and openly declare the governments and peoples from Russia's current partners are under a permanent pro-Russian spell they forget that there is no such a thing, as all countries establish partnerships because of temporary goals, while true alliances will endure as long as there is not a fundamental change in the ideology of their members. In the same way, if India is currently establishing some partnerships with the United States and its NATO allies such a thing does not imply that India is under a pro-Western spell, but rather temporary developments which are not determined by the wand of a magician but by the temporary circumstances which arise in a World of rapid change. As the geopolitical situation of the World will move in the direction of China's thalassocratic domination and the United States demise because of the betrayal of the US elites against their own People, India will no longer look towards the West to search for protection from China and Pakistan, as only Russia and a united Euro-Siberia will be in a position to successfully provide that.

The fight to the death being now waged by a nationalist and traditionalist India against a shock front constituted by the combined cultural forces of liberalism and Islam, as well as the combined economic and military forces of China and Pakistan is the most remarkable proof of the value of an alliance with India because that country already demonstrated its strength rather than cowardly surrender and ineptitude. By using a combination of their unity as an ancient civilization and a political and cultural leadership placing the interests of their country above anything else, what India has demonstrated is the most impressive and unexpected struggle against the forces of Fallen race domination. While the Soviet Union died in cowardly capitulation, India endured four wars with Pakistan, another war with China, and several border clashes that continue up to the present. The survival of the alliance between Russia and India is also a consequence of India's demonstration of its capacity to survive in such hostile international conditions, and the strengthening of the India-Russia alliance is inevitable as those currently struggling against India will no longer receive military and economic weapons from Russia because of the temporary nature of their partnerships in comparison to a long-lasting alliance.

ASSESSMENT OF THE SITUATION IN CENTRAL ASIA

The situation in Central Asia must be assessed with a cold mind, free of miscalculations which uncontrolled passions from Russian nationalism could generate towards regions that once were part of the Russian Empire and the Soviet Union, and are home to Russian ethnic minorities to this day. Regarding all of the former Soviet Republics in Central Asia I am firmly convinced that regrettably for Russia, those lost territories cannot be returned back into full union with Russia again, and not because of a lack of will from Russia's part, but because as already three decades had passed since the collapse of the Soviet Union, ethnic and demographic balances in the former Soviet Republics of Central Asia had remarkably changed together with political and religious attitudes in those regions, now under the firm control of their original Asiatic ethnicities and under a revival of Islam all across countries in Central Asia.

According to the Soviet census of 1989, Kazakhs were only 39.7% of the total population in the former Soviet Republic of Kazakhstan, and half of the population was of European ethnic background. By sharp contrast, in 2014 Kazakhs were 65.5% of the population, with Russians decreasing from 37.8% to only 21.5%, and the overall Russian population in Kazakhstan decreasing from 6,227,549 to 3,685,009 people. The presence of other European minorities practically disappeared, most notably that of Ukrainians and Germans, which were respectively 5.4% and 5.8% of Kazakhstan's population in 1989 and by 2014 their presence decreased to only 1.8% and 1.1% (Statistics Committee of the Republic of Kazakhstan 2014). The situation in other former Soviet republics of Central Asia is much worse, as Russian minorities in Kyrgyzstan, Turkmenistan, Uzbekistan, and Tajikistan all had practically disappeared over the course of a few decades.

Unlike during the times of the Soviet Union and the former Russian Empire; the national identity of those regions has developed to such an extent that now are rightfully able to claim without shame the following: they also enjoy a history of their own comparable to that of European countries, and it will be a chauvinistic error to think otherwise. For example, the Kazakh Khanate (forerunner of modern-day Kazakhstan) was created in the years between 1456 and 1465, a century before Ivan IV "The Terrible" became the first Tsar of Russia. The city of Shahrisabz in modern-day Uzbekistan was the birthplace of Timur, a powerful Turco-Mongol conqueror with a vast Empire of his own in the 14th century (The Timurid Empire). We could cite many examples of the long and rich history of all those regions to understand, for example, why when in 2014 Russian President Vladimir Putin said that Kazakhs did not have any statehood before 1991 the only reaction he generated was anger in Kazakhstan and embarrassment from those who are aware that Central Asiatic regions enjoyed statehood much before the Tsardom of Russia was even created. Unfortunately, Russian statesmen and Russia's public opinion alike suffer from a tendency that consists of their inability to distinguish genuine ancient cultures and states like the ones in Central Asia from completely artificial creations as Ukraine, Belarus, and Moldova.

Besides the cultural factor, we must be aware of the military one, as countries in Central Asia will not be conquered back by Russia only with diplomatic babbling and propaganda, but only by wars so brutal that the return of Central Asia will be not worth of the cost, as hundreds of thousands in both sides will perish and also live under permanent fear and instability as happened during the disastrous Soviet-Afghan War (1979-1989) and the First Chechen War (1994-1996) only that unlike Afghanistan and Chechnya, such a battlefield will rage across a much vaster zone populated by millions and millions of people to which basically all of the Muslim World and Russia's enemies will come in their aid. The economic and moral cost of such wars will be immense, much beyond those which Russia can afford, and if Euro-Siberia as a whole is united as a single superpower not even the immense economic, military, and propaganda apparatus of that giant will be able to cope with the task of subjugating Central Asia, as it would be turned into a battlefield sparking destruction equivalent to at least six Afghanistan Wars.

The cultures and states of Central Asia instead of being mere artificial creations are proud peoples with a rich history and a determination of steel arising from both their Islamic background and harsh living conditions. Therefore, resistance against any invader will be met fiercely and indefinitely, until all of Central Asia's economic and social infrastructure is turn into smoking rubble while invading forces will be constantly facing snipers, ambushes by forces in possession of man-portable missiles, mortars, automatic weapons, and improvised explosives. All sorts of brutal terrorist actions will be carried out not merely inside the territory of Central Asia but all across Russian cities.

A third factor is the growth of Chinese influence in the former Soviet Republics from that region, which forces Russia to keep a strong bridge with Central Asia, whose countries should remain as key allies rather than enemy nations. China's economic influence in the region has incremented dramatically since 1991, and such trend sparked from both China's fast economic growth and its geographic proximity, but also from the disastrous economic, cultural, and military consequences which the collapse of the Soviet Union unleashed upon all of Russia and Central Asia. In fact, it is not solely China's economic influence that is on the rise in that region, but also Chinese military influence, with their military base being already built-in Tajikistan, a country which also has the Russian 201st Military Base.

As Kazakhstan, Kyrgyzstan and Tajikistan remain all members of the Russian lead Collective Security Treaty Organization, with all those countries maintaining a strong network of Russian military bases; China's military presence in the region is still much weaker in comparison, but regardless of this current fact, a great economic and military competition between the two powers is already shaping the reality of Central Asia. Russia must do all it can in order to make sure that the region is kept under its zone of influence as countries in Central Asia are all part of a big game in which China already set as its goal the gradual conquest of the World by means of soft power, with projects such as the massive Belt and Road Initiative, which is just one of many ambitious Chinese projects to gradually build a net extended across all the planet.

But outside strategic considerations, I wish to stress a crucially important historic consideration, one very easy to understand. Central Asia wasn't lost by Russia because of invasion by a foreign power, not even by local insurrection there. That alone could have provided a more or less firm basis to demands from ultranationalists regarding bringing Central Asia back to Russia. But as widely known to all, Central Asia was lost by Russia because it was betrayed by those who put their signatures in the accords and the protocol which criminally dismembered and destroyed the Soviet Union and Russia. Those responsible for the immense crime gave a definitive blow to any possibility of keeping Central Asia as an integral part of Russia because the cultural and political ties which were developed through the work of many generations were recklessly destroyed with the most pathetic display of political betrayal in all of Mankind's history.

The situation in Central Asia already started turning against Russia when the conflict with Afghanistan started. The events between 1989 and 1991 represented the final and irrevocable conclusion of what already was a situation of decline in Russia's power over the region by the time Soviet troops withdrew from Afghanistan in 1989. Anyway, the events from 1989 to 1991 in which not just Afghanistan but all of Central Asia was given away implied not only a betrayal towards Russian minorities in Central Asia but also to the Soviet Union as a whole, including the betrayal of all those who fought in Afghanistan unaware of the political movements which the ones sending them to their deaths eventually unleashed.

The return of a few million ethnic Russians still remaining in Central Asia and becoming assimilated by the Asiatic and Islamic elements is not worth the subsequent deaths of thousands and thousands of troops and civilians alike, together with the economic and social destruction unleashed by future wars which in fact were already fought and lost by the Soviet Union in the battlefields of Afghanistan and also in the political front formed by traitors who destroyed their own country. Another motivation to reincorporate Central Asia is so-called national honor, but anyone who seriously pretends the reincorporation of Central Asia into Russia must remember that national honor does not serve as protection from bullets and bombs, as all those territories only can be recovered by the use of force. Even the use of force will ultimately lead to nothing more than a major disaster, as invading forces will gradually crumble under military and economic attrition as happened in the war with Afghanistan, which, as mentioned above, sparked destruction which will be only a tiny fraction of the one which would be inflicted in a hypothetical attempt to reincorporate Central Asia in the future.

Regarding those Russians who are now separated due to the events of 1991, it must be said that despite their territorial reintegration is no longer possible, they can still be helped from a powerful Russia close to them, in the way of practical economic help allowing them to return if they want to, and also in the way of restoring Russia's true national honor which lies not in Central Asia but in the rest of Europe, which saw its birth as an Empire in a decisive defeat upon Sweden in 1721. Also, since the demographics of Central Asia are constituted almost in their entirety by the Muslim and Asiatic component, thus Russian and other European elements only will become increasingly assimilated until they finally lost most of their identity, becoming just another part of the Asiatic peoples now directing the cultural and political fate of their independent nations.

When realizing how much the demographic trend towards the disappearance of Russian minorities in Central Asia has advanced due to emigration, assimilation, and the increase in the population of native peoples, we are able to conclude that in a matter of a few generations Central Asia will be completely back to the hands of their original inhabitants, peoples who are characterized by a noble spirit and who met the two sides of Russia. Its former artificial side as a Stalinist machine for genocide, which heavily affected Central Asia with famine and nuclear testing, and also its side as a builder of cultural and infrastructure projects which still benefit Central Asia to this day. Russia has shown both its natural side as an engender of civilization and human achievements, and also its artificial side when Russia temporally lost part of its true identity and inflicted pain over its most noble neighbors. God's justice was on the side of those neighbors, and in a common brotherhood, they will march with Russia not by the ties of oppression, but by a common desire for the freedom and independence of natural civilizations.

TOWARDS THE FEDERATION

THE REALITY OF EUROPEAN NATIONALISM

An entire civilization conscious of itself must gain the means of political and cultural unity by absolute claims when it is finally understood that obsolete limits drawn by political forces of the past must be overcome to give Euro-Siberian peoples a renovated life. The Fourth Political Theory would never survive to the test of practice if it focused on an alliance with the nationalistic and chauvinistic elements which are keeping the Euro-Siberian space divided and subjugated by stronger forces. Instead of being paralyzed by the cultural and political considerations restricted in the national boundaries of individual European states, the Fourth Political Theory is only restricted by the spiritual link between righteous brothers, just as the Church of Christ. And in the practical execution of the Normative interpretation of Dugin's political theory, we must have an iron will to claim a God-given right to impose vital principles on the entire Euro-Siberian cultural and geographical space, regardless of the suicidal limitations of nationalistic and chauvinistic bourgeois considerations, which as far as Europe is concerned, they are just as bad as bourgeois liberal considerations.

When Guillaume Faye proposed the Euro-Siberian paradigm in no way it was just the pipe dream of the typical European traditionalist who does not possess the mental capacity to see beyond the obsolete bourgeois considerations imposed over him. Guillaume Faye saw how a truly successful traditionalist mentality must bypass the bourgeois restrictions which individual European nationalism imposes to paralyze the historical and natural processes necessary to save both individual European nations and Russia, which is vital to save mankind's civilization as a whole.

When formulating the Fourth Political Theory, Dugin also was able to see how nationalism as just another ideology of modernity is hindering the potentiality of a true struggle against liberalism, which is the reason for the incompatibility between nationalism and the Fourth Political Theory. However, when trying to overcome nationalism, we should avoid ignoring the distinction between genuine civilizations as the European and Christian one in relation to more recent artificial civilizations as for example Western civilization, to which the Roman Empire was never a part of (for reasons already mentioned in this book).

Thus, unification among nations under a common struggle of their civilization against liberalism will only work when such unification enjoys a firm basis which only their genuine common civilization can provide instead of the artificial binding of civilizations with totally different historical paths, as it is done in the theoretical frameworks of Eurasianism and their practical outcome. However, a unification of the nations sparking from a common European and Christian legacy is a path which we must always have in mind even if that requires the abandonment of some natural elements from individual nationalism to protect and restore the common civilization which created them in the first place. It would be far more reasonable to awake in Russians not only love and admiration towards their motherland, but also love and admiration towards the rest of Europe, still in possession of human and geographical marvels, while also awakening the love of the peoples in Western Europe, Poland, Hungary, etc. towards the cultural and geographical marvels of Russia, and also, of course, allowing all the nations in Europe to appreciate the fruits of their cultural and geographic might as a whole, regardless if we show, for example, the beauty of German cities to someone in Paris, the greatness of Prague to people in Madrid and Rome, and so on.

Instead of trapping the spiritual and political life of the French in France, the German in Germany, the Russian in Russia, etc., one of our fundamental goals is to set free that spiritual and political life to a much larger horizon of common brotherhood no matter how the trends of Western civilization affected a common horizon. That horizon will be immortal as long as the most powerful Euro-Siberian country, namely Russia is able to expand its own horizon as well, in the form of a natural impulse towards true European unification instead of restricting that horizon with mere border restoration. In the gradual expansion of a common spiritual and political horizon, all Euro-Siberian peoples will gradually get accustomed to looking beyond current bourgeois national limits, and instead, all of Euro-Siberia, one day, will be regarded as the true frontiers of a common motherland, whose defense will remain a task for all who share her breast. It should not be the goal of traditionalism to indoctrinate people on the basis of regional peculiarities whose relevance fades away in comparison to shared European and Christian elements teaching all Euro-Siberians to live not merely for petty regional considerations but rather for the task of elevating God's humanity.

Modern means of communication and transportation are changing more and more the way in which regions and political boundaries are reached, and this does not have only practical implications in those fields, but also psychological implications uniting mankind inasmuch as what once was perceived as enormous and insurmountable distances now is regarded as a much smaller space. A parallel process is taking place regarding cultural differences between European peoples, through communications accelerated by the new technologies of information closing the wall of cultural separation between nations, formerly established when ignorance of the other regions and their cultural values prevailed, preventing the various European nations from correctly assessing common bonds while overcoming mutual fears. The limited perception within past leaderships and common persons in individual European states, including Russia once were a determining factor which shaped all the political and cultural struggles of the past, whose result was a primitive bordering which survives in the present not because they possess some practical importance, but because the collapse of the Roman Empire thwarted the maturation of cultural and political frontiers in Europe just as for example the collapse of the Han in China would have thwarted the maturation of China's own political and cultural borders.

As for Russia, it was not rants aimed towards the rest of Europe which caused the Russian Empire to emerge and eventually become a major world power, but rather talented political, scientific, and military leaders as Czar Peter the Great, Russian polymath Mikhail Vasilyevich Lomonosov and Soviet military leader Mikhail Tukhachevsky, who seek in the rest of Europe Knowledge and technical tools which enabled Russia to completely change from its status as a second rate regional power. In contrast to the Tsardom of Russia, all across Europe history shows how other ancient regional powers who were unable to complete their evolution eventually ceased to exist or became completely irrelevant, as for example the Bohemian Kingdom, the Kingdom of Lithuania or the first and second Bulgarian empires. All who made the most to enable Russia's evolution were not blind chauvinists who did not care about the cultural and technical developments in the rest of the World, and the same is true regarding the men and women who elevated all other European states towards positions of greatness, as they were capable of realizing how disastrous cultural and political isolation is to advance the importance of any nation.

Even in the already small European states, secessionist efforts to provoke further division are nevertheless supported by many, as we can see in Catalonia as part of Spain or in Scotland as part of the UK. Every historical or cultural excuse is provided to put Europe against itself, with third parties always taking the real advantage because their major size and economic importance are larger than small regions whose pretensions of independence are ridiculous given the current circumstances. The right to unity is always superior to any right of secession within the borders of common cultural space, regardless of what the assessment of majorities is, because individuals in those majorities sooner or later will die and turn into ashes, but next generations will come after them and will find the task of their common survival more and more impeded by the mentality of previous generations.

An additional factor to take into consideration is that today public structures of the individual European states are under control by liberal elites and their Fallen race leeches. Since a true political and cultural centralization of Europe only can be carried out by Russia due to its condition as the major European power, and because a real European centralization goes directly against the wishes of globalist elites, the outcome of such a thing would imply the absolute destruction of liberalism and the uprooting of current political and cultural elites running most of Europe. Thus, there are two trends competing against each other, a contest between partial centralization as an artificial process being carried out in Europe by NATO, the European Union, and Rome and the total centralization which would be the result of a natural process driven by Russia. While the first one due to its weakness is not meant to favor Europe but rather to cause its eventual death, the second one due to its strong nature will represent a true Euro-Siberian response for protecting European interests instead of the interests of powers currently subjugating the World.

When the idea of the nation-states started to be used as churches use religion, then just like churches, nation-states created their own circles of followers, and the problem is that circles from devote followers inevitably will tend towards sectarianism, and sectarianism cannot be overcome by passive action but only by the use of force. Unlike the circles of followers from the Orthodox Church and the Roman Church, to which the idea of universality is key in their ideological conceptions, the circles of followers in national states have the very opposite as their key idea, as division rather than universality is at the front of any of their considerations. The universalist ideologies as Liberalism and Roman Catholicism take advantage because national sectarianism cannot compete as an ideological weapon with universalist projects, who although do not come without some sectarianism of their own in no way is a problem so great as when that sectarianism is based on ethnicity.

What is even worst is that many of those endorsing the chauvinistic positions sparking from their national feelings do not really have any workable project of their own, neither in the economic, cultural, or military aspects. All which they can do is summoning some ideological elements from fascism which already was defeated as an ideology first in the military battlefield, and also on the cultural battlefield after years of active cultural and informational war against the defeated ideology, which to make matters worse also engaged in all sort of atrocious and corrupt actions before being wiped out in a massive blood bath. The inability of nationalistic circles in Europe to create original thinking is a reality so patent that now some of them are resorting to paganism even despite they don't have the slightest idea of how pre-Christian beliefs were because most of the cultures they belonged to did not use writing systems and those which did employ them were the first ones to be conquered by Christianity, and that's why nobody in the present is praying to Jupiter or Zeus.

From a technological and cultural point of view, it would be easier today to govern all of Euro-Siberia than to rule the British Isles two hundred years ago. In the present, individual European states as France, England, Spain, and Poland seem small to us, but in the past, those same states were perceived as if they represented entire continents. The constant trend of technological and cultural change will continue in the future not towards the petty horizons of current European national states, but towards reducing geographical and cultural obstacles and the perception of size associated with them. The importance of those European national states diminishes not only in the economic and military aspects but also in the cultural and spiritual ones, as any cultural and spiritual aspect is intimately ligated to the notion of sovereignty, confined to small national states rather than an entire civilization, which should be united to provide geopolitical relevance to that civilization as a whole, which is the means to provide its sovereignty against any economic, military or cultural threat whatever their nature might be.

Ancient civilizations as those in China and India became aware that the entire body of their civilizations was in need of a centralized and powerful state even if that requires entering into conflict with the interests of constituting regions, minorities, and individuals as long as they pose a threat to the political and cultural unity of the civilization. Some individuals criticize the Fourth Political Theory because they are unable to see any difference with Fascism, but if they truly had read or listened to the complete exposition of Dugin's basic considerations regarding a Fourth Political Theory, then they would have realized he always stressed the necessity of mankind to achieve its maturity in the form of political unity against a common enemy, unlike fascism in which national divisions and chauvinism were promoted and only lead to its ideological downfall.

In that aspect, my contribution to Dugin's thinking is that in addition to not allowing nationalism and chauvinism to stand in the way of a true Fourth Political theory, also a given civilization as a whole must be able to correctly distinguish its genuine nature from artificial cultural constructions and place political and cultural borders accordingly. The current Russian Federation is only an intermediate towards the construction of a Euro-Siberian Federation, which will be the only true Eurasian Union. The Russian Federation of today is only a brief and very much incomplete step towards the idea of the Federation for Euro-Siberia as a whole. As Russia freed itself of the Marxist shackles and some vital improvements were conducted in Putin's era, now it became a large basis from which the remains of genuine Euro-Siberian civilization can be protected not only inside Russia but also in all European nations. If Russia renounces its mission as a suitable basis for that, then the true reason for Russia's existence will disappear together with any hope of rescuing European and Christian civilization from its current jailers.

Under current circumstances, every future mistake committed by Russia in its domestic and foreign policies will be just another nail in Russia's coffin as part of the common coffin for all Euro-Siberian nations. Current Russia is not in the position to allow itself another major historical mistake, since the next one would be the last one, without any possibility of starting once more from scratch as Russia did with its domestic and foreign policies during centuries.

A EURO-SIBERIAN FEDERATION WILL BE THE ONLY TRUE EURASIAN UNION

Despite all the decades which had passed since its creation, the European Union has been unable to obtain any place of its own in the hearts and minds of the European nations under it, and that should not be attributed to the loss of sovereignty of those nations, but rather to the disgusting and pathetic way in which the individual states belonging to the European Union behaved with their own peoples and with other nations in Europe. The most striking examples are immigration policies, the inability to put an end to the present condition of European nations as protectorates of the US, and the completely selfish way in which individual European nations behave in economic affairs and even a sanitary crisis as the COVID-19 pandemic. When Germany and France speak, the others must obey, without any concern towards the others as far as the interests of the major powers in the European Union and those of their North American and Chinese puppeteers are not being represented.

Even popular will in the United Kingdom, a country which was one of the leading powers constituting the European Union (until its final retreat in 2020) was able to denounce four years earlier (during the Brexit elections) that the European Union was not a representation of their interests, but rather those of an artificial bureaucratic machine which does not show any respect towards Europe but rather to international economic interests and of course to a cultural agenda designed to destroy what is left of European culture and sovereignty. The European Union is showing more and more its incompetence to achieve European unity but saying this will be hypocrisy if we ignore that in parallel, Russia's own project of integration, namely the Eurasian Union has miserably failed to reunite the former sphere of Russian and Soviet influence, with major economic and military projects being hindered because

Russia's own integration also depends on the fact of the integration of Europe as a whole, a process which only Russia can successfully drive.

Today, we can employ an appropriate historical analogy between the situation of Germany before its unification by Prussia during Bismarck's time and Europe at the present. In present-day Europe, just as in Germany before its unification by Prussia, a large number of small states are kept as skeletons without any practical reason for their existence. The current European Union can be compared to the former German Confederation, which was a weak association of 39 sovereign states speaking mostly German, an association created by the Congress of Vienna in 1815. Such association never was able to institute greater sovereignty for its constituent states but rather their subjugation by other powers after the Holy Roman Empire was destroyed in 1806. The current Russian Federation can be compared with the Kingdom of Prussia, whose economic and military power proved much greater than those of the small individual states constituting the German Confederation. When the Kingdom of Prussia was able to defeat foreign influence after achieving the crucial victories against Denmark in 1864, Austria in 1866, and France during the war of 1870-71, then Germany became a united Federal State replacing the previous Confederation.

In the same way, if Russia is able to defeat foreign influences keeping Europe divided, then a Federal system must be instituted all across Euro-Siberia, with Russia being the only possible driving force because of its military and economic power, and just as Prussian nationalism was the forerunner of German nationalism, Russian patriotism must be the forerunner of a Euro-Siberian patriotic sentiment. By then a Federation will be in place, with a common currency, a common foreign policy driving both the relations within European states and the relations of Euro-Siberia as a whole with the rest of the World, and also a common economic system, as there must be the obligation from each constituent State to contribute with a supranational Federal fund possessing exclusive authority to finance businesses in Euro-Siberia. It will be composed of public capital obtained from sinking funds mandated on each business and that capital should not leave Euro-Siberian Federal boundaries.

But to keep that Federation, the Russian Orthodox Church will bear a key responsibility which will be conducted in this way: Russia will be represented in such Federation in two ways, first by Russia's government headed by its Prime Minister, which will be an actual part of the Federation with rights equal to other constituting states. But also, it will be represented by the Russian Orthodox Church, with the new Euro-Siberian Federation being forced to establish separate diplomatic relationships with it. The leader of the Russian Orthodox Church will be in addition Russia's Head of State, as the figures of the Patriarch of Moscow and all Rus' and the President of Russia will be merged to create a single office once the last Patriarch dies, which implies Russia's transformation into a theocratic State. In this way, Russia's Primer Minister will represent Russia in his quality as head of government, and the leader of the Russian Orthodox Church will also represent Russia in his quality as head of State. While Russia's government and its Prime Minister will be an actual part of a Euro-Siberian Federation, Russia's Church and Russia's Head of State will remain separated from it.

The aforementioned is because in that way a powerful central authority will keep the Federation together as such central power must curtail the influence of individual European states constituting the Federation. And to maintain things in this way, the Russian Orthodox Church must have its own distinct military force conformed by a hardly trained and fanatic army formed not only by Russians but also by volunteers from all across Europe. That military force will be the only in Europe to be granted nuclear weapons, to deter any attempt of rebellion, while a common army for the Federation will be conformed by personnel from all across European nations and remain separated from the Church's army. Thereupon, the Russian Orthodox Church, Russia's head of State, and his military force will remain as the embodiment of the ideological, military, and cultural spirit which will allow the formation of a Euro-Siberian Federation and its preservation. The states constituting the Federation will exist for purely political reasons, but the Russian Orthodox Church, Russia's Head of State, and his separate military force will exist also for spiritual reasons, tasked with the mission to preserve The Final Kingdom, with shall never fall, neither given away to other peoples, thus contrasting with the fate of the former Byzantine Empire, whose thousand years of existence ultimately came to pass when the spiritual basis for it was neglected by its last Emperor, who died by the Ottoman sword shortly after being betrayed by those in Rome who still to this day pretend to represent the genuine Church of Jesus Christ while wishing to destroy the real one.

Individual European nations will only surrender those rights which will be essential to the formation of The Final Kingdom, while all other regional rights will be preserved and respected to keep a system in which individual wishes, mirrored by national desires, are balanced by the desires of the collective, mirrored by Euro-Siberia as a whole. The number of political representatives for the individual European States will be assigned to a Federal Parliament in accordance with the demographic size of those States, after elections in each of those states between their political groups. Each State will enjoy its own judiciary and political constitution who will have to respect the terms of the agreement which created the Federation. A common Constitution for the Federation will be also established, which will defend the aforementioned original agreement and give specifications regarding the institutions, rights, and obligations of the Federation.

The formation of the Federation will not be a result of the free will of all individual European states, such a scenario is just utopia. Instead, the Federation will be the initiative of one country, namely Russia, just as Federal Germany was achieved by Prussia's initiative by its condition as the largest economic and military power in all of Germany. That did not come by accident but by a gradual historical process which gradually established Prussia as a regional power after many wars and capable leaders as Frederick the Great, who even in the most adverse circumstances as those of the Seven Years War (1756-1763) were able to preserve Prussia's power. That condition of former Prussia is being now mirrored by Russia because of its own historical battles and its own capable leaders until Russia painstakingly achieved its position as the most powerful European country and preserved it. Those historical developments, having their root in Russia's long military and cultural history will not be easily repeated once more, and the aforementioned forces Russia to act in the right moment and the correct continent because otherwise, those historical processes would have been in vain.

The historical comparison between former Prussia and Russia is not far fetched at all, as Prussia also fought and won during a Global conflict to survive, with the Seven Years War being considered by historians as the World's first global conflict. Even Winston Churchill once described it as "The First World War" rather than assigning that label to the conflict of 1914-1918 (Bowen 1998). Just as Russia in the Great Patriotic War of 1812 and the Soviet Union in the Great Patriotic War of 1941-1945 had to fight for their existence, Prussia fought almost bleeding to death in a devastating global conflict to which it barely managed to survive, and those examples serve to demonstrate how historical processes in the formation of regional powers only came with circumstances which cannot be repeated as if they were a mere competence in a board game.

One can object that unlike in Europe as a whole, Germany was united by a common language which made unification easier, but the linguistic barrier in Europe and the World is slowly fading away because of new technologies enabling fast translation and faster speed when exchanging all sorts of information, with those modern technological tools improving as years go by. Therefore, not only past political and economic reasons which established individual European states already ceased to exist, but also a substantial part of the cultural reasons which divided European states and nations will also cease to exist because mankind is marching in a completely different direction. In the United States, which in its first twelve years of existence operated as a weak association of former colonies, the Federal system being put in place after the adoption of the US. Constitution did not only allowed the basis for the US. sovereignty in spite of the former British Empire, but also the extension of the US. power until achieving its status as a world superpower.

Euro-Siberia, like Great Britain and the Soviet Union in the past, the US now, and the People's Republic of China in the XXI century would also become a superpower, one based on land as the Soviet Union, but much stronger than the former Soviet superpower due to economic and ideological reasons provided by taking advantage of already existing Euro-Siberian conditions and a Fourth Political Theory capable of guaranteeing their preservation and strengthening in all possible aspects, even those beyond human power and thus within God's power. The dispute between current European nationalism and the Euro-Siberian paradigm is already forcing us to take a clear instance against so-called ethnic traditionalists wanting European division, and that dispute cannot be resolved by soft words and some fights in social media, but only by a victorious sword.

EURO-SIBERIA'S LAST RELIGIOUS BATTLE

While liberalism is destroying the basis for Euro-Siberia's cultural, political, and economic sovereignty, Roman-Catholicism and Atheism constitute the ideological basis for destroying the spiritual strength of all European peoples and the entire World. All of the aforementioned additionally come by the political and cultural division engendered by Roman-Catholicism and atheism because their disruption of Euro-Siberia's natural course is not limited to destroying spiritual life but it is also causing conflict in religious quarrels created by the Fallen race, which also are favoring national chauvinism, with Roman-Catholicism remaining a key part of it (as for example in Poland, Lithuania, and Italy). The current religious battle all across Euro-Siberia is a severe problem threatening the spiritual and material living of its peoples by the gradual erosion of a religious identity capable of truly uniting those peoples at the individual basis inside a single nation, while at the collective basis among different nations, and finally at an infinite basis between mankind and God.

While national chauvinism uses the rhetoric and legacy of Roman-Catholicism to create a false notion of separate identity and also hatred towards Russia and Orthodoxy, liberalism uses atheistic rhetoric and its legacy to create another false notion, that of Europe's traditional culture and values as artificial and worthless creations while ironically, atheism is an artificial and worthless creation in itself, pumped by the Fallen race mind which is unable of real spirituality and higher culture, and thus only resorts to applying flawed rationality by employing concepts which are incompatible with the natural essence of God's mankind. The combination of Roman-Catholicism and atheism in a common front against what remains of European culture is one of the most dangerous threats which a future Euro-Siberian Federation will have to face. Those dangerous threats need aggressive cultural and political warfare until they are completely exiled from the cultural and geographical space of European nations.

As for Roman-Catholicism and its Church, which I call "the Jewish-Roman Church" for not accepting the true creed imparted by Christ but rather the evil spirit of pagan Rome and Jewish Pharisees, one of its key advantages in relation to Orthodoxy was its centralized structure for conducting political operations to destroy both declared rivals and potential rivals. In the first volume, I wrote how Roman-Catholicism represents a major deviation from Christianity and how the Jewish-Roman Church was able to conduct Machiavellian political conspiracies against its Orthodox adversary while influencing modern western states in ways far beyond what is commonly acknowledged. Having the aforementioned in mind, one of the essential prerequisites for the creation of Euro-Siberia's Federation is the destruction of Roman-Catholicism and that includes also much of its post-schism legacy which only sowed additional seeds for further European division and chaos.

The Jewish-Roman Church remains a criminal organization such as it was hundreds of years ago, and all its criminal plots, including some of its economic activities and the covering of hundreds and hundreds of sexual abuses, are more than enough to demand the suspension of its activities and the requisition of all its properties, as it is done with any criminal organization being prosecuted by a public authority. That was the course of action of the allied powers in order to provide the legal basis for the dissolution of Nazi Germany, which was declared a criminal organization and dissolved accordingly. That same course of action will provide the legal and moral basis for dismantling the World's oldest criminal organization if Russia enjoys the political will to do so once it is in a position to destroy NATO and the European Union, which will be a possibility when the US finally goes down in history due to the same basic factors which caused the demise of the Soviet Union.

Not only post-schism doctrines of Roman-Catholicism must be destroyed, but also most of the other post-schism cultural legacies of their institution, namely national chauvinism based on them, general religious disbelief as a consequence of massive controversies in which Roman-Catholicism and its Church are involved, and finally the Gregorian Calendar which Rome imposed first over much of Europe and gradually over the entire World as one of its most important cultural marks. That calendar does not possess any superior practical value in comparison to the much more sophisticated calendars adopted by ancient cultures in Central America. As for general religious disbelief which Roman-Catholicism and its institutions engendered due to a major moral and doctrinal decline, the massive controversies widely known to the public which were sparked by the aforementioned are just the consequence of the Jewish-Roman Church being completely under the control of the Fallen race, and thus under its global scheme for satanic control over an enslaved mankind.

As for the Gregorian calendar, the practical benefits of replacing it with a much more sophisticated and useful Venusian calendar of 260 days already was explained in the first volume of this work. The Gregorian calendar does not have any doctrinal connection with Christianity whatsoever, as its origin does not lie in Christian theology at all, but rather in a primitive attempt of measuring time which proved unable to bring any spiritual and psychological benefits. Much in contrast, a sophisticated calendar as the 260-day calendar developed in Central America will have tremendous spiritual and psychological benefits as a consequence of the new calendar's capacity at synchronizing human feelings and spirituality with the cycles of God's creation.

I already explained in detail why such a calendar will bring those benefits and why it is totally in connection with Christian theology and thus it has nothing to do with pagan beliefs, in contrast to solar calendars as the Gregorian one, associated with ancient solar cults. But what I didn't mention is that in addition, the replacement of the Gregorian calendar by a completely new calendar will leave a tremendous cultural mark which would be much needed to provide the new Federation and Euro-Siberia with a stronger identity, as such a calendar will differentiate Euro-Siberia from the rest of the World and also from its past. The psychological implications of the aforementioned are immense because calendars are omnipresent in the lives of anyone, inasmuch as time dictates all of their existence and calendars are present in every house, every street, and in all institutions.

The new calendar will be a way of keeping the Euro-Siberian cultural flame always burning in every mind, with much more efficiency than by any propaganda efforts, and will ultimately establish an unshakable bridge between the material and spiritual world, a bridge which God's

Church cannot build without it. No building, not even the most splendid collection of artistic marvels will cause such an impact as a new calendar which by its intrinsic qualities will change the human psyche and spirituality forever, including the perception of their civilization and their common future in Earth and Heaven. With that, God's Final Kingdom will be manifested and ancient prophecies will be fulfilled, with the end of times ultimately coming not with the destruction of all which exists but with the destruction of human time itself, and its replacement by God's time in the form of a new counting of his ages. The promise of the Final Kingdom and the certainty of the end of times rather than being a frightful warning to mankind will be the fulfillment of God's love towards his Righteous humanity, and also the eternal consolidation of universal brotherhood among those in the Righteous path.

Regarding atheism, all of its rhetoric is based on foolish slogans and flaws in logical thinking. The last years have put the focus on the analysis of the root of every axiom, but sometimes through nonsense pruning the flourishing branches of our beliefs or the branches of our intellectual instruments, deceiving us to believe we can no longer assert a single proposition unless we safeguard ourselves by enumerating countless conditions that must be assumed. My unshakable faith is that these titans that we know as cosmic laws can be understood as long as one is not willing to close in on the conventions that humanity is often used to. The scientific method undoubtedly opens up new fields, stimulates the analysis of those already open, and takes up some known issues that have not been transmitted to the public as they should be. There is no greater faith than that of what is verifiable. Many close their eyes to history, science, and religion alike, chaining their emotions against decent human spirituality, cling to sordid ideals extolling pure greed or a childish humanism, and imagine a distorted universe of their own.

The debate between science and religion is a very old and well-known debate: faith and reason face each other in a battle between two completely different methods. However, it does not invariably have to be this way, some of the most important figures tried to reconcile science and religion in a single belief because the method of science should be the goal of religion. The scientific method can be employed to investigate spiritual matters, including those related to the material and spiritual liberation of individuals. Individualistic doctrines and practices, as well as collectivist practices, have tended to generate bad results by not being in the correct balance with the needs of a group of people conditioned by spiritual conjunctures which alongside the material ones are constituting the basis of all things.

In my work, I have decided to present a vision of worldly and otherworldly matters in a way that addresses various topics that one might not find a relationship between if we do not first realize that the fight for freedom is impossible without the fight for knowledge, since knowledge is power, and only power liberates. This book is a tribute to the figures of the past and the present whose bravery shapes the path of science and the path of religion.

My entire work, moreover, is a confession, a desire to express what I consider fundamental and sometimes disturbing truths, which condition what from our limited vision of the Universe we dare to call "reality." We still have a little time to choose, if daring to complete a journey through the deepest recesses of the Universe and also of our social systems, or perishing by our old limitations in knowledge. Because a common person should worry more about their daily affairs than learning these things, it does not mean they should be denied the opportunity to see reality from increased enlightening angles. Knowing the causes remains the key to the door of understanding, without knowing causes we are like puppets managed by implacable laws, which at times help, and at others hinder. The topics in this book should be further exposed in an understandable way for people who are not specially prepared, making an explanation as clear as possible, since the objective of this book is to strike readers in a deep way.

The mysteries that this book addressed will undoubtedly captivate many who want to enter them, but it will also create a moral profile because alternative approaches were presented that use the concept of freedom as the basis of the spiritual development of human beings. Just as Prometheus, who according to legend was a God who stole the divine fire to give it to men and was punished for that, knowledge did not come for free. Huge sacrifices were made and will be made so that the dream of achieving mankind's sovereignty gets closer and closer. Religion and science do not necessarily have to be two separate things, unable to unite in certain crucial places that have always made us wonder how far man's desire to know the unknown can bear real fruit. Perhaps, it will be the characteristic of a new age that religion and science, mind and intelligence, economics and morality are always united rather than separated, and such is the age of The Final Kingdom.

INDEX

Основы геополитики. Ду́гин, Алекса́ндр Ге́льевич. М., (1997).

Четвёртая политическая теория. Ду́гин, Алекса́ндр Ге́льевич. М.: Амфора, (2009).

Теория многополярного мира. Ду́гин, Алекса́ндр Ге́льевич. М., (2012).

Четвёртый путь. Ду́гин, Алекса́ндр Ге́льевич. М., (2014).

Русская война. Ду́гин, Алекса́ндр Ге́льевич. М.: Алгоритм, (2015).

Dugin, Alexander. The Rise of the Fourth Political Theory. Arktos. (2012).

РБК. "Путин анонсировал принятие 40 новых кораблей в состав ВМФ" https://www.rbc.ru/rbcfreenews/5f1d44899a7947349d758e18

Қазақстан Республикасы. Ұлттық экономика министрлігі. Статистика комитеті. "2014 жылғы мұрағат". https://stat.gov.kz/

Acheson., D. Speech on the Far East (January 12, 1950). https://www.cia.gov/library/readingroom/docs/1950-01-12.pdf.

Bickers, R; Jackson, I. Treaty Ports in Modern China: Law, Land and Power. Routledge. (2016).

Bowen, HV. War and British Society 1688–1815. Cambridge: Cambridge University Press. (1998)

Garson., R. The United States and China since 1949: A Troubled Affair. Fairleigh Dickinson University Press. (1994)

Gunston., B. World Encyclopedia of Aero Engines. Patrick Stephens Limited. (1989).

Silver., BJ. Labor movements and capital movility. The Johns Hopkins University. Cambridge University Press. (2003).

Costa Valles, M. Introducción a la economía laboral. Univ de Barcelona. (2005).

Drucker, PF. Innovation and Entrepreneurship. Harper Business. (2006).

Faes-Cannito, F. Gambini, G. Istatkov, R. Intra EU share of EU-27 trade in goods, services and foreign direct investments remains more than 50% in 2010. Eurostat (2012)

Fedorova SA, Bermisheva MA, Villems R, Maksimova NR, Khusnutdinova EK (2003) Analysis of mitochondrial DNA haplotypes in Yakut population. Mol Biol (Mosk) 37: 643–653. (2003)

Vatanka, A. "China's Great Game in Iran". Foreign policy. (2019)

Langdale, J. The Internationalisation of Australia's Service Industries Canberra: AGPS, for Department of Industry, Technology and Commerce (DITAC). (1991)

Chang, J; Halliday, J. Mao: The Unknown Story. Knopf. (2005).

Korabik, KM. Russia's Natural Resources and their Economic Effects. Penn State College of Earth and Mineral Sciences. (1997)

Maddison, A. Contours of the World Economy, 1-2030 AD (2007).

Malyarchuk B, Denisova, G, Derenko M, Kravtsova, OA. Mitogenomic Diversity in Tatars from the Volga-Ural Region of Russia.Molecular Biology and Evolution. 27(10): 2220-6. (2010)

Warf, B. Telecommunications and the changing geographies of knowledge transmission in the late 20th century. Urban Studies, 32(2), 361–378. (1995).

Warf, B. The Spatial Turn: Interdisciplinary Perspectives. Routledge Studies in Human Geography. (2008).

O'Donnell, G. Delegative Democracy?. University of Notre Dame: Kellogg Institute for International Studies. (1992)

O'Donnell, G. "Delegative Democracy". Journal of Democracy. 5 (1): 55–(1994)

O'Donnel, G. Notas sobre el estado y la democracia. CLAD. (2007).

Shepard, W. What China is Really Up To in China. Forbes. (October 3 2019).

Dahl, Robert A. Polyarchy: participation and opposition. New Haven: Yale University Press. (1971).

Dahl, Robert A. New Haven : Yale University Press. On Democracy. (1998).

Hall PA, Soskice D. Varieties of Capitalism: The Institutional Foundations of Comparative Advantage. Oxford University Press; (2001).

Schweickart, D. Against Capitalism. Cambridge: Cambridge University. Press, (1993).

Gramsci A. Quaderni del carcere. A cura di V. Gerratana . Torino (1975).

Manhattan, A. Vatican Imperialism in the Twentieth Century. Grand Rapids, Zondervan publishing house. (1965).

Gilbert. Scott F, Ziony Z. "Congenital human baculum deficiency: the generative bone of Genesis 2:21–23". Am J Med Genet. 101 (3): 284–5. (2001).

Mazumdar, S. Industrialization, Dirigisme and Capitalists: Indian Big Business from Independence to Liberalization. NMML Occasional paper history and society. New Series, Vol. NA, No. 7 (2012)

McClintock, E. A. The social context of sexual identity. Annual Meeting of the American Sociological Association. (2015).

McDevitt, M.A. "Chinese navy will be the World's largest in 2025". US naval institute. (February 2020)

Tucker A. W, Kuhn H. W. (eds.): Contributions to the theory of games, Annals of Mathematical Studies. (1950).

Lovelock, J. The Vanishing Face of Gaia. Basic Books. (2009).

Lüthi, L. M. The Sino–Soviet split: Cold War in the Communist World. Princeton: Princeton University Press (2008)

Redmond, Timothy J. "The Presidential Curse and the Election of 2020". Skeptical Inquirer. Vol.43 no. 6. (2019)

Sen, A. Markets and freedom: Achievements and limitations of the market mechanism in promoting individual freedoms. Oxford Economic Papers. (1993).

Sen, A. Development as Freedom. Oxford: Oxford University

Press; New York: Alfred Knopf. (1999).

Sen, A. Rationality and Freedom. Cambridge: Harvard University Press. (2002).

Przeworski, A. Sustainable Democracy. Cambridge University Press. (1995).

Graciarena, J. El Estado latinoamericano en perspectiva. Figuras, crisis, prospectiva. Editorial: Eudeba. (1995)

Hahnel, A., Robin, H. Looking Forward: Participatory Economics for the Twenty First Century. H. Princeton University Press. (1991)

Mao, F. How reliant is Australia on China?. BBC News, Sydney (June 17 2020)

Meier, G..M. Stiglitz, J. E. Frontiers of development economics: the future in perspective. World Bank Publications. (2001)

Simkins, P. Kitchener's Army: The Raising of the New Armies 1914 – 1916 (2007)

Stiglitz, J. E. Making Globalization Work. Penguin Books. (2006)

Harris, N. Currency Management: Issues and Strategies. In Investment V, Association for Investment Management and Research. (1994)

Kapur, D; Lewis, J. P.; Webb, R. C. The World Bank: its first half century: History. Brookings Institution Press. (1997)

Kharpal, A. "Power is 'up for grabs': Behind China's plan to shape the future of next-generation tech". CNBC. (April 26, 2020)

Krugman, P. Development, Geography & Economic Theory. MIT Press. (1997)

Dewey, J. The Public and its Problems. New York: Holt. (1927)

Gimbutas, M. The Prehistory of Eastern Europe. Part I: Mesolithic, Neolithic and Copper Age Cultures in Russia and the Baltic Area. American School of Prehistoric Research, Harvard University Bulletin No. 20. Cambridge, MA: Peabody Museum. (1956)

Gimbutas, M. The Civilization of the Goddess: The World of Old Europe. San Francisco: Harper. (1991)

Pandit, R. Speed up delivery of S-400 missiles, India to tell Russia. The Times of India. (November 6, 2019)

Platt, S.R. Autumn in the Heavenly Kingdom: China, the West and the epic story of the Taiping Civil War. Alfred A. Knopf. (2012)

Pope, M. H. El in the Ugaritic Texts, 2, Leiden, The Netherlands: E. J. Brill. (1955)

van der Toorn, K; Becking, B; van der Horst, P. W. Dictionary of Deities and Demons in the Bible DDD (2nd, revised edition). Wm. B. Eerdmans Publishing. (1999).

Zhang, J. "Manchu Sinicization: Doubts on the Ethnic Perspective of New Qing History." Contemporary Chinese Thought. 47 (1): 30–43. (2016)

CovertAction Quarterly, "On the Side of Pol Pot: U.S. Supports Khmer Rouge," Issue 34. (1990)

International Monetary Fund, World Economic Outlook Database. Accessed on June 29, 2020

The Official Monthly Record of United States Policy. Department of State. Vol. 80 (number 2043). (January 1980)

The World Bank. "Curbing desertification in China." (July 2019).

www.ingramcontent.com/pod-product-compliance
Lightning Source LLC
Chambersburg PA
CBHW020239030426
42336CB00010B/537